CALM BEFORE THE STORM

CALM BEFORE THE STORM

"The author of one of my favorite books, *Call the Briefing!*, is back with another memoir about life as the press secretary to two presidents. Marlin Fitzwater is a master storyteller. You can't believe all that he's witnessed, and we're blessed that he's willing to share his private writings and memories with us."
Dana Perino, FOX News, Co-host of The Five;
White House Press Secretary, President George W. Bush

"There was no one better at the job of working with the White House press corps than Marlin Fitzwater, a farm boy from Kansas who made it to the top as spokesman for two presidents. You'll find the stories Marlin tells fascinating (an inside look reporters didn't see) but also a welcome reminder of a time when presidents and their press secretary tried to do their jobs with integrity, honesty and civility."
Sam Donaldson, ABC News White House Correspondent

"My good friend Marlin tells his remarkable stories and includes his diary entries, offering firsthand accounts of some of the truly historic events he lived."
Andy Card, White House Chief of Staff, President George W. Bush;
Secretary of Transportation, President George H. W. Bush

"This book reads just like Marlin: It's keenly observed, brutally honest, clear-eyed, plain-spoken and sometimes really funny. It's also a valuable contribution to the history of the presidency, and of a challenging, dramatic moment in American foreign policy. It's proof of why he was appointed White House press secretary by two presidents—and was one of the very best."
Dee Dee Myers, White House Press Secretary,
President William. J. Clinton

MARLIN FITZWATER

CALM BEFORE THE STORM

DESERT STORM DIARIES & OTHER STORIES

SEA·HILL
PRESS

Excepts of presidential material, including speeches and press conferences, have been taken from two volumes: *Weekly Compilation of Presidential Documents*, Vol. 26, 1990. Office of the Federal Register, National Archives and Records Administration, Washington, DC, 1991; and *Weekly Compilation of Presidential Documents*, Vol. 27, 1991. Office of the Federal Register, National Archives and Records Administration, Washington, DC, 1991.

Photos: Melinda Andrews Fitzwater and White House photographers David Valdez, Susan Biddle, and Carol Powers.

Front cover image, top: *President's Kennebunkport Home* (from right to left) President Bush, Secretary of State James Baker, National Security Advisor Robert Gates, Press Secretary Marlin Fitzwater, 1990. Public Domain photo, available from the Bush Library.

Front cover image, bottom: *President Bush talks with the troops in Saudi Arabia,* 22 November 1990. Public Domain photo, available from the Bush Library.

Back cover image by David Valdez, photographer: *President Bush greets General H. Norman Schwarzkopf, who leads the Desert Storm Homecoming Parade in Washington, D.C.*

Portrait by Richard Whitney from the Marlin Fitzwater Center for Communication, Franklin Pierce University, Rindge, New Hampshire.

Photographs and images are protected by copyright law.

Resale or use of any images of this book is prohibited.

Marlin Fitzwater's personal papers available in Special Collections, Hale Library, Kansas State University, Manhattan, Kansas.

Presidential papers in George H.W. Bush Presidential Library, College Station, Texas.

Presidential papers in Ronald Reagan Presidential Library, Simi Valley, California.

Sea Hill Press Inc.

www.seahillpress.com

ISBN:978-1-937-72047-6

Library of Congress Control Number:2019943991

FIRST EDITION 2019

Printed in the United States of America

This book is dedicated to my family and friends,
and to the memory of George and Barbara Bush.

ALSO BY MARLIN FITZWATER

CONTENTS

FOREWORD

IN ADDITION TO HIS TALENTS as a spokesman for presidents, commentator, and novelist, Marlin Fitzwater is a brilliant diarist. He shows this in *Calm Before the Storm: Desert Storm Diaries and Other Stories,* in which he opens an important window into the presidency of George H.W. Bush, especially the pivotal decisions that surrounded the Persian Gulf War. As White House press secretary, Marlin was there and saw it all. In fact, he participated in many of the decisions he writes about. His chronicle is essential to understanding the dangerous conditions of the early 1990s and the people and events that shaped our world.

Take Fitzwater's diary entry of Feb. 1, 1991, not long after the Gulf War began. It shows President Bush constantly reaching out to advisers to gather information and help him make better decisions—an admirable trait in any president.

> Dr. Burton Lee, the President's physician, said the Pres. told him privately this week that the war would be over in days not weeks. Also the President said he had taken the decision about how to respond to chemical weapons used by Saddam, "out of the hands of the military. I will make the decision." As we start the ground war, that possibility draws closer. Traveling between Cherry Point and Seymour Johnson AFB, I mention the length of the war to the President, sitting at his desk aboard *Air Force One.* Brent Scowcroft and Governor Sununu and I are sitting on the couches.

> "All the Pentagon guys tell me it will be days, not weeks or months," the President said. "Isn't that what they tell you, Brent?"

> Brent nodded in agreement. He didn't say whether or not he believed it. I don't. It has now been three weeks and we haven't killed many Iraqis yet. I believe two or three months of fighting, at least. (I was wrong.)

Similarly, Fitzwater's diary entry of Aug. 7, 1990, is revealing on many levels. It shows not only President Bush's state of mind as his pre-war buildup of US forces was proceeding secretly in Saudi Arabia, but also reveals, quite poignantly, the pressure that surrounds all presidents as they deal with crisis and their intense desire to ease the tension. Bush asks Fitzwater to dinner, "Just the two of us." And that evening, after they take their seats in the Family Dining Room on the Second Floor of the White House Executive Residence, a grand setting featuring two ornate silver candelabras on the table, the president and the press secretary enjoy shrimp and scallops with white wine. There was much on Bush's mind this particular evening—he would announce the first US troop deployment to Saudi Arabia the next night at nine o'clock, thus drawing a line in the sand against Iraqi ruler Saddam Hussein's desire to dominate the Middle East. But Fitzwater sensed that Bush wanted a diversion, however brief, with a trusted adviser and friend.

> We finish dinner about 9:00 p.m. He walks me down to the medical office in the basement. He says he has a stiff neck. The nurses have taken some training on this neck thing. They're pretty good at working it out.
>
> I remember the quiet of the medical room, like my grandfather's living room on the farm. Grandpa Bob would play marbles or checkers with my younger brother, Gary, and me, then fall asleep about 9:00 p.m. I would watch him sleep, hearing only the gentle ticking of the grandfather clock. Stillness was in the walls. And so it is in the White House at night.
>
> I think the President invited me to dinner this night as a diversion, as a friend who would not spend the evening asking questions or talking about war. We had become very comfortable with each other, just being together, not saying much, but always supportive.

This passage, as with so many others in Fitzwater's work, blends the diarist's keen observations of historic moments with events from the author's own life, in this case, Marlin's upbringing in Kansas. At another point in the book, Fitzwater describes the farm community of his boyhood in the 1950s. A neighbor who was a Little League baseball coach had broken his arm the week before his hay was to be cut, and the men of the community automatically decided to do the job for him with their sons. It was simply the right thing to do. After a morning of hard work in the hot sun, the women of the community served lunch and the men began popping open bottles of beer. But not Max Malcolm Fitzwater, Marlin's father, who instead chose a Nehi orange soda. Marlin asked why his father didn't drink beer, and his dad said, "I just don't. I don't believe in it. It's OK if the others do. I'll stick to good old Nehi orange."

Marlin goes on to observe,

> That's all he needed to say, because that's how they teach values on the farm, or at least how my father did it. He didn't drink. He knew what he believed. He lived that way, and he let us know that you should live the way you believe.

Such stories provide many insights into Fitzwater's remarkable personal journey to the pinnacle of power at the White House and explain much about the American experience.

A personal diary can be an invaluable key to our past. If written well by people who were at the center of power or present during great events, as is the case with Marlin Fitzwater, such accounts provide much-needed perspective and add texture to history. They are vital to anyone who wants to understand what really happened in the past and how it relates to life today and in the future. This is the contribution of *Calm Before the Storm*.

Kenneth T. Walsh

US NEWS White House and political analyst;

Author of *Ultimate Insiders, Air Force One,*

and six other books on the American presidency

PREFACE

I believe Operation Desert Storm, often referred to as the First Gulf War or the War of Liberation, was a textbook case of historic presidential leadership. My diaries as press secretary during this period chronicled just one aspect of this remarkable conflict, a war to demonstrate that one nation does not have the right to invade another without provocation, and that America will stand up for its principles.

Desert Storm was historic for several reasons: moving over 500,000 troops halfway around the world in six months; an air war that lasted one month, followed by a ground war that lasted merely one hundred hours; a United Nations resolution authorizing the war; a thirty-five nation coalition that came together to fight and defend a principle; and when it was over, our troops immediately began coming home. We won. The so-called Vietnam Syndrome was put behind us, and the American public respected and admired our military. Our technology was demonstrated and impressive. Military leadership was inspiring. And when our president, who had directed every phase of the conflict, greeted American forces in a Victory Parade on Constitution Avenue in Washington, DC, it was with humility and national pride. My diaries describe the calm before the storm in the words of those who planned the conflict, and especially in the words of the President.

Serving two presidents was the grandest experience of my life. The 1980s were shining years with President Reagan and President Bush 41. President George Herbert Walker Bush kept a diary of some kind most of his life. So did President Ronald Reagan. I used to walk in on their chronicles—Reagan bent over his large red leather notebook and writing with a pen; Bush bent over his dictating machine and speaking in hushed tones. They were concentrating and careful about their words. By this date in 2019, we have seen the published diary of President Reagan, and we know President Bush's diary is coming. He told me nothing would be published until after his death.

So that became my working plan. As assistant to both presidents, and press secretary, I declined to write a diary because it threatened my integrity as a senior member of the president's staff. I seldom took notes in meetings because it always looked suspiciously like a "leak" in progress. Other staff, especially military, distrusted note taking. And fellow staff members were quick to recall leakers as "that fellow who took copious notes."

But I did save copies of memos and briefing sheets and notes that could serve as reminders, and I put a date in the upper corner. With a date, you can retrieve almost everything pertaining to a former president. But when Saddam Hussein invaded Kuwait in August 1990, it seemed like the kind of well-defined event that I should note, even if never published. So I sat in my hotel room at the Carriage House Inn in Kennebunkport, Maine, and started a diary.

After the opening days of President Bush's planning for war, and after he told America that the invasion "will not stand," the President went to his home in Kennebunkport to focus on the prelude to conflict. Several hundred members of the press went with him, and I gave daily briefings on presidential decisions and actions. That's when I went to a small bookstore on the second floor of the quaint wooden buildings that compose the town center and purchased four diary books that I could use for notes on the experience. Later, I purchased four more that accounted for the seven months of the conflict. In the eighth month, the President started bringing the troops home.

My White House diary starts with the invasion of Kuwait. My job as Press Secretary to the President was to record and present the official events of the presidency; but in my diary, I sought to record the private discussions and motivations.

President Bush saw himself as a servant of the people. Nowhere is that more evident than during Operation Desert Storm. The president spoke directly to the nation at least five times from August 5, 1990, to March 6, 1991—from "This will not stand" to "Kuwait is free." He also spoke to the nation through the press. When I took the job, he said, "Marlin, I want to come into the Briefing Room on a moment's notice and talk to the press." And he did that so often that one day, after five interactions with the press, Helen Thomas, the legendary UPI wire service reporter, came to me and said, "Marlin, stop him. We can't handle this many stories." But he never stopped.

In the presidency, there is no such thing as an idle thought. Other people give them meaning. Even as Press Secretary to the President, that was my most difficult realization: the real pressure of the job was knowing that every sentence had meaning. So I tried to record the key words, how I felt, and what the President said. By the time I left the White House in 1993, I had given 850 press briefings, all recorded today in transcripts at the George H.W. Bush Presidential Library Center. Many of them are also printed in the *Weekly Compilation of Presidential Documents*, massive books published by the Government Printing Office. But my diary entries in *Calm Before the Storm* represent my private views, written hurriedly and roughly, without editing, and tossed into a box in the late 1990s, unopened until 2014. They are the kinds of personal and human observations that every diarist records about their friends or family. Even today, many are painful—or too personal for even twenty-five years of privacy to soften the rough edges. Maybe in future years the archivists holding these documents will be able to release all of them.

But I am seventy-six now, and I want my friends and family to know some of these things today: how President George H.W. Bush approached the presidency, how he related to his staff and advisers, how his staff related to each other, about our fears and joys. I want my children, Brad and Courtney, to know what Dad's life in the 1980s and '90s was like. Lastly, I am proud of my White House years with Presidents Reagan and Bush, from 1983 to 1993, and I simply want to tell these stories before I forget them.

These diary entries are not journalism, and many of them reflect events that will need research for a full understanding. But most of them stand on their own as snapshots of life in the White House, although they were written in private. And finally, they are about me. Like all diary entries, whether they are written by a young girl on her bed at night or a President of the United States in the Oval Office, diaries are about the writer. Serving two presidents was the grandest experience of my life.

There are always division points in one's life, places where our minds change focus, and our ambitions achieve new dimensions.

Mine were on the farm, going to college, and working for the President of the United States—all reflected in some measure in this book. Over the last half-century, I've written stories about Holland Creek, some nonfiction and some fiction, that reflect my life at the time. My White House diary, of course, is nonfiction and has the sense of immediacy that goes with unvarnished truth, at least in my eyes.

This book came about at the suggestion of my publisher, Greg Sharp, CEO of Sea Hill Press in Leesburg, Florida. I met him at a book fair in The Villages. I told him I was hoping to put together a private book of my writings, about the White House, the Gulf War, growing up in Kansas, and stories of various kinds. He suggested a section featuring my Desert Storm diaries, and we collaborated to put together this book.

"I remember the war like it was yesterday," he said, "and people like to read about behind-the-scenes events, what really happened." Greg and his chief editor, Cynthia Sharp, suggested adding the statements by President Bush, start to finish during the war. I think it adds immensely to my diary entries. It also shows the wisdom and courage of President Bush as Commander-in-Chief. I am very grateful to Greg and Cindy for their direction and commitment to this project.

The handwritten diary books will be part of the Special Collections of personal papers in the Hale Library, Kansas State University, Manhattan, Kansas. I thank the Dean of Libraries, Lori Goetsch, for inviting me to leave my papers with the Hale Library, and for her generosity in creating a traveling exhibit of my life, and for her advice and counsel. Kansas State is my alma mater, and it is a great university.

I also thank Kristen Nevious, Director of the Marlin Fitzwater Center for Communication, Franklin Pierce University, Rindge, New Hampshire, who has supported so many aspects of my life. She has produced thousands of outstanding journalists and communicators over the last two decades, the true legacy of my White House years.

The cast of presidential advisers who guided the Liberation of Kuwait are legendary: Secretary of State James A. Baker III; Secretary of Defense Dick Cheney; Chairman of the Joint Chiefs of Staff Colin Powell; National Security Adviser Brent Scowcroft; Deputy National Security Adviser Robert Gates; Army General Norman Schwarzkopf; and Deputy Press Secretary and later Ambassador to Ukraine Roman Popadiuk. I am honored to have served with all of them.

Marlin Fitzwater
June 2019

PART I

—MY KANSAS YEARS—

FROM FARMHOUSE

TO WHITE HOUSE

Introduction to Part One

HOLLAND CREEK TWISTS and turns through the middle of Kansas like a childhood scar, jagged yet endearing, for twenty-three miles from the Smoky Hill River near Abilene to just south of Carlton. On the map, it is a thin piece of string. But in my life, it somehow ties together all the great adventures—from fishing with Grandma and plowing the wheat fields, to life on the Chesapeake Bay, to quiet dinners with the President of the United States.

Sometimes the creek runs dry, its bottom caked, and its fish lie dead on the banks. Other times it is reckless and destructive, tearing into the lives of farm families. My father rebuilt its bridge so often that he hated the creek. But I loved it. As I review a lifetime of stories, Holland Creek knots them together.

The Howie Place

THERE IS A place about ten miles south of Abilene, Kansas, where the earth, freshly plowed, is so dark and rich it looks like a blackboard freshly wiped with a wet rag. It is a place on a hill overlooking Holland Creek, just a half a mile away, with a set of farm buildings that bear my fingerprints on every stanchion, stall, and roost. It is the Howie place, laid out in a triangle with a small two-story frame house on the pinnacle of the rise, a red barn with stalls for a dozen milk cows, a shed for perhaps fifty pigs or sheep, and a hayloft even today full of bales of alfalfa that give the place an ageless aroma like the smell of a family lawn mower.

Fifty yards away in the remaining corner of the layout is the granary, with middle entry opening for the tractors and trucks to pull in and unload the wheat and corn in bins along each wall. They were money bins. For as the winter progressed, or new shoes and a baseball glove were needed, Dad would shovel a truckload of grain into an aging pickup truck and haul it to the elevator near town. Somehow, I never made that connection as a youth, the direct connection between a shovel of wheat and a dollar bill. It was just grain to me, to be played in or thrown at my brother in great handfuls or to be augered from a truck and endlessly scooped so it filled every corner of the bin and the maximum could be stored.

"Pick that up," my dad would say calmly when I dropped a scoop of wheat on the ground, "and don't get any dirt in it." I marvel today at his calm demeanor in this situation, and in all such misdemeanors of farm life, when I realize that it was dollars I dropped so carelessly to earth.

A lean-to shed was built on the side of our granary that was the family blacksmith shop. Dad spent long hours of mystery there, wearing a black spaceman's helmet and eye shield to protect him from the blue flame of the welder. He would touch it to plowshares and garden hoes and corn knives, and the big rough pieces of metal would stick together, with the line of weld forming a scar on the surface that seldom broke. Sometimes our old tractor would lose a metal attachment, and Dad would say the weld broke, a depressing admission of failure. And if it was another reason, he would proudly say, "At least the weld didn't break."

My brother, Gary, two years younger, and I watched the glow of the welder for hours, marveling at its mystical ability to glue metals together and listening for the sizzle when the weld was dipped in water to cool and harden. I always wanted to weld, even at age ten, to bring pieces of iron to a soft, red glow, and then hammer them into unnatural shapes on the huge anvil that stood in the middle of the shed. The sculptures formed in my mind, but Dad said no, it was too dangerous.

Between the house and the granary was a small chicken house, perhaps fifteen by thirty feet, that held the mainstay of our diet—a hundred chicks raised each year to cooking size—with a row of drawers with open backs that allowed the hens to roost and lay eggs. Each day, Mom would pull out the drawers and empty them for breakfast.

Many years later, on *Air Force One*, the press pool asked me about the farm. For me, it resulted in one of the most interesting pool reports ever to come off the plane, and certainly a surprise to the hundreds of city-hardened reporters who scoured the report for news of the president's activities. I explained to the press that of the farm's various treats for a youth, my favorite was "dressing" chickens. The first responsibility was the kill, a process of chasing the chicken around the yard, diving for its legs without getting a peck on the hand, and holding it upside down as protection against that aggressive beak. The site preparation had been done several years before when a large tree stump was cut flat across the top and two sixteen-penny nails driven about a third of the way into the center of the stump. Stuck in the edge, as if lodged there by Daniel Boone on some ancient hunt, was a two-foot-long machete whose wooden handle had gone white with the snows of time and whose metal blade was covered with the rust that signaled that this instrument of death was never to leave its post for other uses.

Once you have the chicken, its neck between the nails, hold its feet straight out behind it and prepare to sever the head with one sure-handed swing of the machete. Strangely, once the chicken's head is between the nails, it seldom moves, a sense of resignation setting in that can be disconcerting. It's best to hurry past that moment when the destruction seems more than a mechanical movement. The trick is in your command of the blade and the follow-through. The greatest nightmare is to effect a partial cut that might require a second swing, when the legs are kicking and blood is spurting. The other great fear is of mis-aiming the machete and hitting the nails. Never hit the nails. The impact reverberates up and down your arm in a most painful fashion.

Once the head is chopped, the most crucial moment comes: you must throw the chicken away from your body in one fluid motion, something like throwing a Frisbee, so that the death dance of the chicken can be played out, a desperate reflex by the muscles that causes it to flop all over the ground, headless and bleeding.

My grandmother eschewed this high-technology process and opted instead to simply grab the chicken by the head, swing the body in a wide circle, then suddenly reverse direction in midair so that the head twisted off in her hand while the body flew on to continue its dance of death. I tried it once, but couldn't stand the feel of the head in my hand. The machete was better.

Members of the press were appalled at this story, but as a boy of ten, I found it as routine as any other farm chore. Besides, the sooner we ate all the chickens, the sooner we could clean out the henhouse for roller skating. I had discovered with great celebration that the henhouse had a concrete floor. What a treat. No farm had concrete—not patios, nor sidewalks, nor porches, nor any other slab of artificial surface harder than wood. Dirt floors, hardened by the rains and tromping of people and animals, were quite sufficient for barns, granaries, sheds, and most chicken houses. So my brother and I asked Dad if we could clean it out for roller skating. He was disbelieving, partly at the thought of using the house for such a frivolous purpose, and partly at the prospect of two small boys actually shoveling about a ton of chicken shit. But we did it. When my brother would get tired, I would paint for him once again a picture of how we would be the envy of the neighborhood. And we were. The old steel-wheeled, lock-on skates would hold up longer than the soles of our shoes. Our acrobatic skating under three-foot-high chicken roosts and jumping over large cracks in the concrete made us the heroes I envisioned.

The Howie place was our third farm. "Sharecropper" has become a dirty word for its application to the poor, often immigrant, workers who pick fruits and vegetables and live in squalid little shacks on the dusty fringes of seasonal-crop farms, mostly in Florida, California, and Texas. But in Kansas in the 1940s and 1950s, a lot of farms were maintained by renters who paid with a share of the crop, usually one-third to the owner and two-thirds to the renter. The owners needed tenant workers, and the best way to provide housing was to build a new house to live in and rent the old one to the tenants. In any case, the result was a lot of tenant farmers living at subsistence levels, farming with used equipment held together with baling wire and spit, eating butchered cattle and hogs out of their own barns, and planting enough vegetables to put Irish potato farmers to shame. We always had potatoes in huge backyard plots, planted by the entire family. Best of all, the new potatoes came from the last year's crop. You simply cut up the old potatoes into sections with one eye per section, stuffed them into the ground in long furrows dug with a hand plow, then covered them over with a spade. In Kansas soil, it's impossible not to make potatoes grow. And it didn't cost a dime for new seed.

Wheat was another matter. It was the cash crop, but you had to borrow money to buy the seed to plant the crop. After the Depression, all farmers hated borrowing money because it so often meant losing the farm. Bankers were to be feared more than a plague of locusts or grasshoppers, although they too could wipe you out. Even today, with pesticides that can kill a giraffe in ten seconds, farmers still fear grasshoppers and certain other insects and speak of their hatred in passionate terms.

Wheat is always susceptible to everything destructive, but specifically to insects, rain, hail, tornadoes, and drought. God made them all, and He is a formidable adversary. Yet every year we put our lives in His hands, trusted in His benevolence, and excused Him when lightning would capriciously kill a cow or burn down the barn. When harvest did come, when the fields were full and the waves of yellow chaff floated and swayed in the hot summer sun, when the air was so dry that your nose burned, and the kernels of wheat were fat and hard, you knew that God was good. You were safe for another year. You could sit under a shade tree on an August afternoon and see a Thanksgiving table loaded with turkey and surrounded by a thankful family, Christmas with plenty of gifts, and money for the unexpected winter disaster, because the insurance policy for those amenities of life was in the bin. At those moments there could be no greater fulfillment.

Of course, there might not be enough in the bin for much improvement in your general condition, or fixing the roof, or installing running water or indoor plumbing. We never had running water, just the runoff from the roof after each rain that was guided down old spouts to the cistern. I often dreamed as a child about bugs getting in the water as it traveled down the roof, and I never trusted that cistern to keep the snakes out. So, when the hot months came every year and the water supply diminished, I secretly approved because it meant we would haul water in ten-gallon milk cans from the water plant at Sand Springs, about ten miles away. I knew it was safe.

The barn was still red, undoubtedly repainted at some point, but still carrying the marks in my mind of the most fascinating discoveries of growing up. On the front side, over the door to the pigpen, there are marks in the paint, surely not forty years old, and yet hauntingly similar to the scars of a thousand gentle basketball nudges as I arched another great shot off the wall and through the rim. The rim was a steel band removed from one of the wooden barrels that housed every kind of farm supply, from nails to apples. It was nailed exactly ten feet high, or at least as high as Dad could reach. The ground was slanted so that every shot was from a different level, and rocks in the soil meant that every bounce came up at a different angle. Quick hands and a quick eye, they said later. In one high school game against neighboring Junction City, we were five points behind with forty-seven seconds left. I stole the ball three times and scored on three successive shots. Quick hands and a quick eye, they said, borne of the imperfections in my private barn gym. Also born on those rocks, or at least discovered, was an intense competitive spirit. I virtually forced my younger brother to play, yet I never let him win.

I still hate to lose.

Also in that barn were the first sexual stirrings, and the ugly lessons of deceit. No child can play in a hayloft without feeling exhilaration. The hay is stacked in bales about three feet long, easily handled by an adult, and adequately managed by a ten-year-old. To have your own hayloft is to own Disneyland. I would stand in the middle of the hay and dream and plan of things to be built, houses and castles, forts and wagons, tunnels and hiding places so dark and so high that they could never be discovered, and if they were, the opening would be too small for Mom or Dad to ever follow. It was the kind of secret place every boy wants, or it could be shared with other children for a game of hide and seek, and it could be changed every day like Lego blocks. Every day we built a new playground.

One day, in the fifth or sixth grade, another boy pulled me aside at recess, looked over his shoulder for any teachers in the area, swore me to secrecy, and pulled a torn magazine page from his jeans pocket. It had been smudged and often handled. He unfolded it slowly, clearly indicating this was a forbidden treasure. It was a picture of a woman in a swimming suit, posed Greta Garbo style, but with a substantial bosom and cleavage showing. We just looked at it. Another boy rushed up. "Let me see," he said. We knew no other exclamations, hardly knew what we were looking at, and felt more excitement about the forbidden nature of the subject than any sexual arousal. But the spark was lit. There was something here. Some vague stirring that had to be pursued. A few weeks later the opportunity presented itself. Mom and Dad and Gary and I went to Salina, a slightly larger town twenty miles away, to shop. Salina was a treat. It had Nicener's: the biggest, most exciting dime store I had ever seen—with a candied-apple machine that gave the aisles a carnival smell, the first escalators in our part of Kansas (and the object of more attention than a Ferris wheel), and the first foot X-ray machine (where you could look at your toes right through your shoes). Science couldn't go much farther than that.

Right next door was a magazine store. I spotted it when we went into Nicener's, and a dark sense told me the pictures were there. While Mom and Dad were shopping, and Gary was looking at his toes, I slipped down a back aisle, out the door, and took those ten steps down the block to the forbidden fruit. The store was dark, musty, lined with magazines of every description, and tended by one old man behind a counter who eyed me very suspiciously. Fortunately, there was one magazine rack, just past the *Car and Driver* area and the *Popular Mechanics* display, where I could duck and be out of sight of the counter. I moved to it, looked about, frantically up and down the rack, and there it was. On the cover was a pinup, and one flip of the pages revealed several more. This was it. Now, how do I get it? I had to get back to Nicener's soon, so the decision was instant. I walked to the counter, laid down the magazine, and put a quarter on top of it. The old man looked at me warily, touched his scraggly beard, rubbed his bloodshot eyes, and asked, "Do you think you're old enough for this?" I instinctively knew that he had asked the right question, the one that allowed me to tell the truth, be confident, and still accomplish the task. He didn't ask if I was old enough, only if I thought I was. In later years I would often search frantically for the more narrow press question that I could seize upon to answer.

"Yes," I told him. He took the quarter. I took the magazine and walked quickly out the door. On the sidewalk, I tucked it in the front of my pants where it couldn't possibly be seen. I went straight to our car, a 1947 Dodge, and climbed into the backseat. I figured Mom and Dad had to be looking for me. They would know I wasn't in the store, so it would be logical that I had gone to the car.

It worked. They were angry, but they believed me. I sat in rigid silence all the way home, partly because I was scared and partly because the magazine was cutting into my leg just below my shorts. So when everyone got out of the car at home, I was slow, the last to exit. As the others went into the house, I went to the barn, to my secret place, to the hayloft, where I could sit for hours in warmth and comfort, staring at the pictures and wondering about the new sensations.

My dad would come home from the fields about seven or eight o'clock on a warm summer night, wash up, change into clean overalls and a fresh blue Sears and Roebuck cotton shirt, then come out and hit us baseballs for an hour before dark. It was the best time, to see Dad at play, laughing, hitting great looping flies to center field and telling us after each hit, "You have to run faster than that" or "Start as soon as I hit it." Then he would mock himself, this most humble of men, with a facetious brag, "This is the way we used to hit 'em at Westfall. Why, those fielders never saw them coming." The corner of his mouth rose ever so slightly, but the sparkle in his eyes lit up like diamonds. The good humor was full and on display. My dad, Max Malcolm Fitzwater, was liked. He smiled easily and often, yet because he didn't speak unless it was important, people took him seriously. I always remembered that.

In 1993, the Mississippi River went wild, breaking levees, destroying homes and towns, creating a thousand tragic stories that America watched on television for weeks on end. But largely hidden, some seven hundred miles away, rambled the little tributary known as Holland Creek, not officially so you could read it on any sign, but official enough that everybody said Holland Creek, and it must have been on some map someplace. It crossed the road just a half mile from the Howie place, and the receding waters from the Mississippi flood had left the hayfield dark and dirty, the wheat plastered to the earth like straw on a thatched roof, with huge gashes where combine tires had tried but failed to rescue a few bushels of wheat. It reminded me of 1951.

I remember the water coming up through the cornfield in '51. But we never thought it would come up the lane. Then it reached the hedge tree with the big green apples I used to throw at Gary while we waited for the bus. Then it came up toward the house, not really close, but we were the highest house around, and we knew that if it's that close to us, others were sweeping mud. I had grown animated just thinking about it. Afterward, Dad caught a fifty-pound catfish with his bare hands. Of course, it was just lying in the mud where the water had left it. He brought it back and hung it on the barn door and dressed it, and cut off the head and stuck it on the fence post. Slowly it deteriorated until nothing was left but the skull, and it was hanging on that post until the day we left, maybe even after that.

William Least Heat-Moon writes in *PrairyErth,* his wonderful epic about Kansas and its people, that the people don't speak of loving or hating the river. My own recollection of the '51 flood gives testament to that fact. I recalled the one year we lived in the little Howie place, another of old Hugh's places about three miles away. It was a small house, with coal heating and no indoor plumbing, located just across the road from old Hugh's home, and about five hundred yards from Holland Creek. It was two years before the '51 flood, and old Holland Creek warmed up by throwing her waters right up to our doorstep. I remember watching it edge up, like the huge boulder in *Raiders of the Lost Ark* that just kept rolling toward Indiana Jones. Surely it wouldn't reach the house—but it did. Surely it wouldn't come up the steps—but it did. Surely it wouldn't come into the house—but we watched it creep on up as Mom started putting everything on bricks or pickle jars to steal a few extra inches. It was like a bad movie, where the curl of the water oozes through the floor. The waters assumed a hard, fluorescent surface, as if some plastic coating were holding the water as it grew larger and would not break. And then it did. The crochet rugs became soaked. We put on our boots and lifted the furniture onto the pickle jars, and still the water came. It was dark and smelled like dirt, as if on the way into the house the creek had picked up the prairie and offered it a free ride, so the water still smelled dry and hot. Then it crested, about two inches above the floor, just under the lip of the jars, and we felt we had won. But the real work was just starting.

Even worse than getting water in is getting it out. As the river recedes, the water starts back. It is as if some unseen hand on a distant shore has lassoed the water and is pulling it away, sometimes fast and sometimes slow. It's crucial that you stay with it, with Mom in charge. When the water starts out, everyone grabs a broom and starts sweeping the water, because the water carries the mud, and if you don't sweep it out with the tide, it cakes in every corner and hardens in every thread of fabric. It seals the windows and leaves dirt in buttonholes so hard that the shirts must be thrown away. So you ride the water, and you cannot get off. "Keep sweeping," Mom will say, till she sees that your arms ache and your feet are swollen. You keep sweeping because although no eight-year-old understands the theory behind "riding" the water, you do understand that there is no alternative. There is no place to sit, and besides, you are working side by side with Mom and Dad. They are depending on you to help save the house, to get the mud out, to sweep continuously until the water is gone, and then the aches are filled with pride. You do not hate the river. You do not love it. It is there to be fought, and the winners are those who fight the longest and hardest, because in the end the river always wins. Pretty much like dealing with the press.

Tornadoes are far more ominous for a boy. They are unfathomable, yet the subject of endless stories of tragedy and Ripley phenomena that are no doubt based in fact, but fictionalized in their local application. I have no doubt that somewhere a tornado drove a piece of straw six inches into a tree, something about the pressure equalizing and creating a "straw of steel." But I doubt that it happened in our neighbor Tim Gruen's backyard, as the other kids said.

When we lived on the little Howie place, a cow was struck by lightning and killed, but I doubt that another neighbor's herd, Milton Nagely's, was picked up near the barn by a tornado and dropped in the pasture a quarter mile away with nary a scratch on them. At least I could never confirm it. And, according to schoolyard lore, several neighbors had their cars picked up and moved from road to field. Curiously, in these stories, the tornado seemed to have motherly qualities that picked things up violently but set them down gently and tenderly in some distant quarter. Such is the fiction of nature. Nevertheless, some credence had to be given these accounts because my father gave tornado drills and front-seat car lectures the minute the sky turned dark.

"If we're driving," Dad would say, "I'll stop the car. Get out and get in the ditch. It will pass right over you. Don't raise your head until it passes."

"How will we know when it passes?" I asked.

"What if there's water in the ditch? We'll get all muddy?"

Gary asked.

"You'll be fine," Dad said. "Just get below the surface of the land."

I used to have nightmares about jumping in that ditch and finding snakes, or trying to crawl up the ditch to a culvert, which was a tin flow-through pipe, usually big enough for a body to crawl into, that was used to let water flow under a driveway. That would be the safest place. But in my dream I never quite got to it before the wind picked me up and flung me into a tree, under equalized pressure that turned me into a "steel Marlin," and then I would wake up.

Several times, we saw the tornado coming over the far horizon. Dad would call us into the house: "Get in the basement, kids. Mom is already there."

We would go down the rickety stairs to the dirt-floor basement, cross the floor where Dad had once killed a black snake, and Mom would be under a large table in the southeast corner. Tornadoes always came from the southeast, some immutable law of God. He just never operated from the north. So, according to theory, the house, when it rose off its foundation, would move away from the southeast corner first, drop a few planks and foundation fragments on the table, and move on. Then we could get out using our ax, flashlight, hammer, jar of water, pickled beets, and assorted jams stored under the table.

Finally, Dad would shout, "Here she comes." He would come stumbling down the steps, race across the basement, and crawl in. A huge noise would be just behind him, like a train on the downhill side, picking up steam and running easy, a hundred boxcars pushing it to oblivion, and it was right outside our house. The house would shake, little flakes of dirt would drop from the walls, the jam jars would tumble on their shelves like Humpty's men, and Gary would start to cry. But then it passed. We would wait, holding our breath, and Dad would go upstairs, look out the door, and give the "all clear" sign. We always lost a lot of trees, but never any buildings. I never found a straw stuck in a tree, but I did think my dad was very brave.

Farm life in the 1950s was not guided by concern for pesticides or skin cancer or other scientific discoveries. It was basic, and it taught values. When Wilson Hoffman, my Pee Wee League baseball coach, broke his arm the week before his hay was due to be cut, it was automatically assumed that the team, and its fathers, would help put up his hay. On the given day, at least twenty families gathered on the Hoffman farm with at least five balers and a like number of hay wagons, and in a day's time did a week's work. It was hot and sweaty summer work, where by noon our overalls were a darker blue in giant splotches where the sweat had soaked through even the red country handkerchiefs that hung in our vest pockets. They wiped brow and neck alike with one fluid motion, starting on the forehead, moving down the face, under the ear, and around to the back of the neck. Also part of the uniform were Red Man boots, raw leather, in various states of wear, most rough and scratched with creases that had gone black with dirt while the toes had hardened from tromping through mud and manure. The men and boys worked together on hay wagons, pulling the bales out of the back of the machine. The tractor pulled the baler and the wagon, so the three contraptions formed a piece of field art with every angle showing, like some Calder exhibit being pulled across the skyline, with wheels and wire and exhaust pipes and levers, and Rube Goldberg's many moving pieces. When it was time for lunch, the whole caboodle of equipment was brought to a halt, grinding and screeching until no single part was left moving. The tractor was shut down and people piled off, clambering into a pickup truck and heading for the house.

On this day at Wilson Hoffman's, the women had prepared a whopper of a lunch, with crispy fried chicken piled high in glass bowls brought from home, potato salad as yellow as mustard and colored with green chunks of pickle and onion, and baked beans steaming hot in big blue metal bowls with lids that could be raised just enough to take a ladle full without letting the beans cool, as if they would in 95-degree heat. At the end of the long tables, usually plywood on sawhorses, sat three-gallon containers of iced tea, dripping with condensation, cold to the touch of hand and tongue, and available mostly to the kids. On the ground in washtubs were soda pop and beer. All the men took beer, pushed the caps off on the edge of the table, and launched into a big swig with some sort of exaggerated vocal expression of relief. My father walked over to where Gary and I were sitting, kicked another bale around with his foot, and sat down to open his orange soda pop.

"Why don't you drink beer, Dad?" I asked.

"I just don't," he said. "I don't believe in it. It's OK if the others do. I'll stick to good old Nehi orange." That's all he needed to say, because that's how they teach values on the farm, or at least how my father did it. He didn't drink. He knew what he believed. He lived that way, and he let us know that you should live the way you believe.

I went back to Abilene in 1988 to deliver the high school commencement address and I told this story to emphasize the importance of values, of knowing what you believe in. I spoke that day of Gorbachev, the end of the Cold War, and the Moscow summit that I would be attending the next week. But my best story was about Dad and his orange pop. As I was telling it, I looked for Dad in the audience, and he was looking at me with such pride and love that I thought my chest would burst, and he was crying.

My dad was amazingly secure with himself. His private code and good sense ruled his life, even in recreation. Once a year the farmers of Dickinson County declared a coyote hunt. Coyotes were the dread of all families, ugly mangy critters that lived in the fields and hedge lines and roamed the barnyards at night, killing chickens and lambs and calves, or anything small enough to be defenseless. Stories of coyotes killing small children abounded like tornado fiction, but I never actually knew a case. Even so, they spread fear. The county put a bounty on their heads, two dollars an ear, which gave them a Wild West outlaw mystique, and it was with a posse-like patriotism that farmers went to the annual coyote hunt.

We gathered at Rural Center School, a newly consolidated school near our farm that brought to an end the little red schoolhouses that had educated our parents. It was Saturday morning, the pickup trucks coming into the parking lot in a steady stream, with about every fourth vehicle being a one-ton wheat truck with large bed that could hold a hundred bushels, or about forty men on coyote hunt day. The men milled around the yard, polishing and fondling their shotguns, checking the shells to make sure they had enough, and talking about the coyote problems they had during the winter. Inside, the organizers from the Rotary and Lions Clubs were mapping out the sections to be covered. Flatbed trucks would fan out around four sections of land, each section being a mile long and, in Kansas, laid out as squarely and precisely as a checkered tablecloth. One man or boy would drop off the back of the truck as it slowed, every thirty to forty yards, and wait in a line along the road until a given time, prescribed to allow for the line to be formed the full sixteen miles around the four sections. Then a signal would be given and passed along, domino-like, to begin the hunt.

It was up to each family to use good judgment in determining the age limit for their children, usually thought to be about thirteen, because each man had to walk alone. There was one woman who walked the line that year, but she was gossiped about, known generally as "a strutter" and a show-off. Some of the men were reluctant to walk beside her. They said it was a "trust" thing. They said they wanted guns beside them that would fire without hesitation, and buddies who would not flinch from duty. Women weren't welcome, and kids weren't totally welcome either, but it was a source of great pride to walk beside my dad, even if he was thirty yards away. It was close enough, especially when there was a little dew on the ground, to carry voices, to talk with Dad in a low voice so as not to scare the animals. As we started across the fields, my first obscure feelings of power were manifested by adrenaline as I could see the line of men on both sides of me begin to move. It was like a machine, marching before an unseen hand, guided to a destiny of death and destruction.

Suddenly a rabbit broke out of the underbrush in front of me, darted about ten yards, then stopped to survey the approaching threat. He sat up, as jacks do, with ears straight and long, stretching for every murmur of threat, his eyes directly on me, questioning my intentions. My eyes locked on his and froze. I knew he would bolt in a second, with a movement so quick and swift I would never see it, and the white backs of his legs would show his course under a bobbing tail. I raised my single-shot .410-gauge shotgun, a Sears special, saw only the side of the jack as he turned to run, and pulled the trigger. Only a small kick in my shoulder, but I missed. Then on my left, from someone I didn't even know, came a volley of shots, three in a row, and the rabbit was down. The grass was high, but I could see the bottom of his foot, presumably not his lucky one, kicking in the air, then he lay still, waiting only to be picked up by the farmer and stuffed in the carrying pouch that was slung over his shoulder. "Sorry, Dad," I said quietly, and kept walking. "Don't worry. It took him three shots," Dad said after several steps.

As the sixteen-mile square began to get smaller, the rumble of gunshots was constant. The rabbits now could hear us coming and were jumping up more than a hundred yards ahead of us. Few men could shoot that distance, but then I realized the inevitability of it all. No matter which way the rabbits turned, they faced a line of men and certain death. What evil had rabbits perpetrated on our life to deserve this? Destroying gardens, I guessed. They ate the lettuce and cabbage.

We never saw any coyotes, but the word came down the line: "Charlie Sexton got one. That oldest Emig boy shot two. Don't seem to be as many this year."

After three or four hours, when our legs were beginning to cramp from the strain of climbing through weeds and vines and prickly underbrush, tiny specks began to appear on the horizon, first one, then another, until it looked like someone had drawn a dotted line across the bottom of the sky, and you could tell they were men with guns. Still out of sight were the rabbits, thousands of them running at full pace with whatever energy they had left, darting in every direction, some even panicking and turning back toward the lines, running full-face into a fury of gunshots, leaving only the strongest to make it to that deadly center of the hunt, when rabbits would actually run into each other, jump high into the air when shot, and dozens of men would shoot continuously until every sign of life was gone. It was the mad flurry of shots that made me turn away in horror. Dad drew me back with about a quarter mile to go.

"It gets dangerous here," he said. "Let's start to ease back. Just stay here with me." He shortened his step. I shortened mine. The men on both sides of us began moving ahead, but because the square was tightening, the men were getting closer together, and no one noticed that we were dropping out of the hunt.

When Dad and I fell back and came together, he said, "Here's where somebody gets killed. These guys are shooting right at each other. All they see are rabbits."

The flatbeds were waiting on the road near where the hunt came together. Everybody climbed in for the ride back to Rural Center. They started emptying rabbits onto the bed of the truck, until fur covered our feet and blood was running down the metal bands that bonded the bed of the truck. Then I heard a loud thud and looked over the cab of the truck onto the hood. It was a coyote, large gash in his shoulder, teeth bared and lips curled back so it looked like he was still eating, his eyes glazed, hair matted by water and blood and cock-leburs from the underbrush of many miles; spindly legs with pro-truding knee joints that had been scraped and healed, and scraped and healed, probably every month of its life. He didn't seem much of an adversary for our army, but he was ugly, dirty, and evocative of ridicule and fear. I was glad he was dead. We drove back to the school with the coyote draped across the hood, a sort of victory parade for the womenfolk, who were waiting with another covered-dish lunch in the school gym.

"I'm not too hungry," my dad said. "Let's go on home." We never went to another coyote hunt.

We moved off the Howie place in 1955. We were asked to leave, actually, so a new generation of Howies could move in. There were no hard feelings about it. If you're a renter, that's just the way it is. So, we moved to the Funk place, a much larger red brick house with barn and granary about five miles closer to Abilene. The farmland around the buildings was rented by someone else; we had only the house. We farmed other rented property on the two-thirds, one-third basis. After two years we moved to town, but Dad continued to farm rented property. I helped out whenever I could: weekends, summers, and certainly during the harvest.

The worst time for farming, in my limited view at age fifteen, was just after the harvest. The great euphoria of the harvest is over, the earth lies shorn like a lamb, marked by the stubble of the un-shaven, and alive in only two colors: black and brown. The wheat and oats, cut near the ground, and the corn, either cut or shocked or still standing, is all brown, toasted under a scorching 100-degree summer sun. There is no movement by natural things in Kansas in August. Humans and insects, dogs and locusts, all move with the gait of the aged as they bear the weight of the heat, anvil-like upon their shoulders. I have walked the sands of Somalia, Egypt, and Saudi Arabia, and I cannot say the Kansas heat has been bettered. For the sheer weight of it, the sun fits like a bulletproof vest, heavy and un-comfortable, driving the water from your pores and leaving cotton shirts feeling like T-shirts after a swim, hanging long and sticking to your arms and stomach.

The smell of dirt is always in the air. It rises from every activity, every footstep, the movement of tractors, trucks, plows, dogs, and fleas, going straight up in a plume that seldom meets a breeze to sway it, hanging in the air with stubborn stillness, as Coleridge wrote, like a painted ship upon a painted sea. The ultimate incongruity is that, traveling behind the greatest dust-raiser in the world, a tractor and plow, are seagulls. They hover and dive, flinging themselves at the black clods turned over by the plowshares, worn as smooth and shiny as polished silver, and cutting the earth in long strips behind the trac-tor. We had two tractors: a Minneapolis Moline with three-bottom plow that Dad drove, and a Ford Ferguson with two-bottom plow that I drove. Riding the tractor was knowing the eye of a hurricane, the drone of the engine that starts as a constant roar, then softens to a whine when your ears become accustomed. Toward evening, when the mind weakens with fatigue, the sound becomes a singsong dirge, rising and falling in time with the giant tractor tires, sometimes in perfect tune with a silent voice that sounds like Elvis but is really your own. You are alone at this point. The tractor bumps with every turn of the furrow. The front wheels have no support, and they wobble as if stumbling over rocks and dirt. And no matter how much you pad the seat, after a few hours your bottom hurts, your stomach aches from the jarring irregularity of the bouncing, and your mind numbs as you totally relax all muscles to help them absorb the shocks. You ride with one arm outstretched, reaching for the fender to help stabilize your body, and always over your shoulder float the seagulls. No farmer knows where the seagulls come from or why they are there. No one knows, least that I ever heard. For me, they were of another world, reminding me of another place, unknown and beautiful with sparkling blue water and no clouds of dirt.

I would dream of this place as the roar of the day settled in. Sometimes I would wake up just before the end of the row was reached, yanking the wheel hard to the left, stepping on the left brake to freeze it while the right wheel continued to turn, thus forcing the tractor to turn on a dime, much as a Boeing 747 turns at the end of a runway.

One day I was driving the Moline, pulling a three-rack spring-tooth, an ugly appurtenance comprised of thirty or forty curved ribbons of steel, welded to a single iron bar, that claw into the earth like a steel hand, breaking up the plowed earth in a further manicuring of the land. The rows were long that day, and several times I almost woke up too late to make the turns. At midafternoon, after the bologna sandwiches and potato chips were gone, and dirt was caked on my face, when all the discomforts of the tractor had blended into another world of clouds and dreams, I hit the wire. The end of the field was marked by weeds allowed to grow unmolested in the space it took to turn the tractor, and the weeds stopped at a barbed-wire fence. No longer useful for retaining cattle or sheep, the barbed wire draped and drooped itself along the edge of the wheat field, separating it from a crop of corn that now lay ruptured from the picker's jaws. As I woke up, I yanked the wheel from instinct, not even knowing my location, not knowing that the front wheels were in the wire and the barbs were locking themselves into the radiator fins in the front of the engine. I slammed my left foot onto the brake with the same motion, and as the huge machine started its spin, I realized I was too late, but I stayed with it. The wire started ripping and tearing, coming loose from the old wooden posts, spewing nails to a rusty grave in the dirt, and winding itself around the engine of the machine. Then just as the tractor came parallel with the remainder of the fence, the teeth of the spring-tooth caught another section of wire, which threaded itself into the matrix of machine and implement until they were bound like Gulliver by the Lilliputians. The pull on the engine was as if the tractor was tied to Mount Everest. It was overwhelmed, yet the front reared up like a horse making one desperate buck to free its unwanted rider, then died and settled to earth. I rode it to the moment of death, my hands glued to the steering wheel, my legs shaking with weakness, and then it was still. One moment the tractor was a roaring, tugging, bucking monster. Now, it was so still that the quiet of the sun could be felt on the backs of my hands. I climbed down off the tractor and started walking, aimlessly at first, then with purpose, then in a circle as I searched for an opening in the far-off trees that signaled the house and my car. It was a long walk, almost as long as those few yards from my West Wing White House office to the last motorcade on Inauguration Day 1993, yet I made it to the car and started the slow drive to town to tell my dad about his tractor.

I walked into the house, and he didn't say a word. Somehow, he knew that I was in trouble. "I'm sorry, Dad," I said, "my farming days are over." And they were. Dad gave up farming and sold every piece of equipment that we owned.

The wheat in Kansas grows so thick that you have to part it as you walk through. And if you kneel until the toes of your tennis shoes dig into the black earth, and if you push your arms through the mass of the wheat straw, you can lay the wheat down on the ground to form a perfect mat for dreaming. The wheat around you stands three or four feet high, and you can look up to see the clouds passing overhead. You have to wonder where they came from, and where they are going.

I used to do that with my dog, Mamie, named after Mamie Eisenhower, the First Lady of America in the late 1950s and always the First Lady of Abilene, Kansas, where I grew up in the living history of Ike's hometown.

There were plenty of dreams to be had in Abilene, where cattlemen drove their cattle in the 1800s along the Chisholm Trail for rail shipment to Kansas City; where Eisenhower lived and went to school, and later built his Library and Museum. But the best dreams, my dreams, were conjured up in splendid isolation in the wheat fields along Holland Creek.

The summer heat of Kansas weighs a ton, but if there is the slightest breeze, it waves the millions of wheat chaff in shimmering salutes to the sky, and the sound is cool, like the whirl of a fan. At midday, I used to make my bed in the wheat with Mamie's nose on my arm, lie still, and look straight up at the cotton clouds floating past. They moved so fast, entering my tunnel view of the sky and passing through in a matter of seconds. I must have been about ten, and that's when it first occurred to me that there must be a much larger world that these clouds were passing over.

The dreams began. They weren't about what I wanted to be, at least not in the sense of being a banker or journalist or presidential assistant. They were amorphous yearnings for a different place, where people were more plentiful than on the farm, and lived in different patterns. At that time, we didn't have television to show us the world, or even indoor plumbing. But radio and schoolbooks at least nurtured the idea that in some other place, perhaps Chicago or maybe along the Mississippi, people lived differently.

I dreamed of boys playing baseball in a distant pasture, looking up, and seeing the same clouds that had just passed over me. I wondered about the cloud's altitude and speed, and how big would the triangle be that tied me to those other boys, assuming of course that we both saw the same cloud at the same time. And if we could both see the same cloud, we must be able to find each other.

Then I would be gone, in our 1947 Dodge to another city, perhaps Salina, which was only twenty miles away. Perhaps to Kansas City, which was millions of miles away and had no form. Perhaps to war with Ike, if he was still leading a war. Those were my dreams, not to be something, but to search for something.

Ten years later, just graduated from college with a degree in journalism, I packed two cardboard suitcases and said goodbye to Mom and Dad in front of our little house in Abilene. I explained one more time why I wanted to drive to Washington, DC, and see what might be there. The clouds were passing overhead, and my only regret was not having Mamie for the trip.

In 1990, I attended my high school's thirtieth class reunion. Mom and Dad were retired and living in town. I left their home for the reunion dinner when the town siren went off signaling a tornado. The rain and wind were hard, so I circled the block and returned to the house. I ran up to the porch, jumped the three-step entrance, and banged on the door. No answer. I tried the knob, it turned, and I rushed in screaming for Dad. "Down here," a voice said, so I headed for the cellar, bounded down the steps, and moved for the southeast corner. Dad held the flashlight, leading me on hands and knees safely under the table with the ax, the jar of water, and the pickled beets. "Just think, Dad," I said, "how many people can say they've been on hands and knees, under a table in their basement, with the Press Secretary to the President of the United States?"

"That's better," Dad said, "than saying my son wasn't smart enough to get under the table during a tornado."

Thirty years later, my wife, Melinda, and I were visiting my brother in Abilene. We lived near Washington at the time, retired, and far removed from the threats of poverty and tornado. As we visited my brother's family in their small home in Abilene, the town sirens started screaming. "There it goes," my brother's wife, Lois, shouted. "C'mon everybody," she said, "To the basement." We went outside and the wind was blowing hard. Gary raised the wooden cellar door and motioned us into the cellar. It was dark and cold and the floors were dirt. But it was safe. And six of us sat on makeshift chairs for more than an hour until the city blew its "all clear" siren. Then we raised the cellar door and climbed the steps to survey the damage. And we thanked God we were safe. My mind whirled with memories of youth. It had been sixty years since I had joined my family in the cellar for protection.

Unfortunately, all those years ago, neither my father nor I were smart enough to get out of the sun, or at least to wear a hat during those endless hours of farm labor. Riding the tractor at age eleven was almost a treat. But the old Ford Ferguson with two-bottom plow soon became monotonous, as the engine droned for hours and I moved up one row and down the other, trying to stay awake to make the turns, burning my nose to a crisp in the Kansas sun. The ears and nose would burn first and peel first, but it was almost a badge of honor, a symbol of summer labor, and the only color that would tell my classmates of my summer pursuits. I simply could not tan. So we just got red, my dad and I, cutting sunflowers with machetes in the cornfield, or circling the harvest field with combine and truck, or pulling the hay out of the baler and throwing it onto the wagon. We worked together and burned together. Years later, we got skin cancer at about the same time. On television, during my press briefings, it showed red and blotchy on my face.

I took to hats, as the doctor ordered. It got so I would not go out without one. I loved those hats, with the big brims and long bills, warm in winter and cool in summer. They became a personal symbol, a part of my countenance at Camp David or Kennebunkport. Sometimes on television, they looked ostentatious or, as they say in Kansas, "show-off." But people came to understand. The word got out that I had skin cancer, and few people accused me of showing off. This pestilence, the sun, I could not beat. The water would recede. The tornadoes would pass. But the sun left its cancerous mark on my life forever in a 1971 nose operation to remove a basal cell carcinoma that left my nose with a graft from behind my right ear. It was a nine-hour operation by a plastic surgeon, who would remove a little nose, test it for cancer, and if any was left on the edge of the tissue, he would cut some more. He went back for more tissue and more Novocaine nine times. Twenty years later, when President Ronald Reagan had a similar skin cancer on his nose, removed with a "rhomboid flap" procedure, I explained the process to America with great confidence in my subject, and the memory of nine Novocaine shots still stinging in my mind.

Thirty years after packing my belongings and moving to Washington, DC, I retired from an urban life of apartments, townhouses, suburban homes, and world travel, and I bought a few acres of country property on the Chesapeake Bay. First thing I did was buy a tractor and a truck. I guess that's what farm boys do.

Mentors

MISS EDNA EDBERG was a legend before she was a person, at least in my mind. We were the first four-year class to graduate from the new Abilene High School, starting in 1956. And walking through the corridors was spectacular at the time, with windows rising two stories from the floor of the main lobby, the floors shiny clean and polished, the specialty rooms, like chorus, had built-in risers with the best acoustics, all in the most modern design. It seemed like a modern mansion to me, and like the best of new buildings, it also had a few of the best traditions of the past. One of them was the remarkable Miss Edberg, famous for decades of teaching Latin, and doing so with pride and passion for a language that had faded into oblivion, at least as far as I was concerned. Indeed, many of my classmates called Latin a dead language. And it was legendary that Miss Edberg abhorred the thought and took personal umbrage if anyone repeated the phrase.

I only saw it once, when a newcomer to Abilene High apparently hadn't heard the tale, and he asked why we had to study a dead language. It was a terrible sight. Miss Edberg grew stern in the face, her eyes narrowed, and a redness moved through her face as if someone had flushed strawberry Kool-Aid through her system. She didn't say a word. She just paced back and forth across the front of the classroom, as if searching for just the right words that would totally destroy the impudent question. I thought she might have a stroke. She didn't even look at us, as if we were unworthy, and I wished terribly that the new boy had not ventured this opinion. Miss Edberg was hurt deeply, and possibly with mortal consequences. It was one of those times when I was very aware of the consequences of thoughtlessness.

She stopped pacing, turned to face the class, staring each one of us directly in the face, and said in a very weak but steady voice, "Please don't ever say that again." Then she started to teach: about the derivative nature of the language, its history in the development of learning and culture, its role in the growth of Roman rule, and its application to the modern English language. It was as if twenty sentences were rolled into one. And when she stopped, we all stopped. Somehow we knew that a huge barrier had been crossed, and it didn't require us to understand all the elements of the language to know that the study of Latin was crucial to the essential fabric of this woman.

Finally, she looked at me and asked, "Latvius would you translate page sixty-four for us." There were sighs all around me as the class expressed relief that they had not been called upon, and there were a couple of giggles from those who knew I was dying inside, and totally incapable of translating the paragraphs. But there was no question in my mind about the seriousness of this situation. And I would be serious in my answer, even if I was wrong.

I remembered this exchange many times during my press briefings of later years, when reporters demanded answers to self-interested questions. I reminded myself that when an issue is of crucial importance to someone else, I should make it equally important to me. The questioner will never forgive anything less. And sometimes I would say to myself, "Treat this seriously, Latvius. Look them in the eye and answer directly."

Thirty years later, I received a call from Harold Edberg, Edna's brother and a fellow teacher at Abilene High, asking if they could visit the White House. I was ecstatic over the possibility of having Miss Edna Edberg in the Office of the Press Secretary to the President of the United States. First, I was a "C" Latin student at best, and I wanted to show the Edbergs that I had amounted to something; and second, I knew she would take the White House seriously, not as a political institution, but as the historical seat of government that had directed our democracy for nearly two hundred and fifty years.

When they arrived, we sat in my office and talked about old friends in Abilene, about Miss Edberg's current activities, and a little about how I got to Washington. Then I offered them a surprise visit to the Rose Garden, to attend a private meeting with the President. The roses were almost as red as the flush in Miss Edberg's face as I escorted her to a front row seat.

After the ceremony, we went back to my office to say goodbye. Then she said a remarkable thing, that I should have known would happen. She asked if I remembered my Latin name. For a nanosecond, my mind went blank, but I opened my mouth and out came the word: Latvius! "Latvius," I repeated. And she smiled, the widest smile I had ever seen her make.

GERALD (JERRY) LAUDERMILK, as new as the high school, was a recent college graduate from California who had been drafted into the army and sent to the most remote and desolate army base a California boy could imagine: Fort Riley, Kansas, home of the Big Red One, an infantry and tank operation that appeared to the nearby residents of Abilene as a maze of low yellow dormitories surrounded by thousands of acres of hills and prairies used primarily for firing bazookas. I never knew what bazookas were, but apparently, they were big guns. Jerry Laudermilk didn't see himself as a tank driver or a warrior, so he asked and received a discharge in order to become a teacher at Abilene High, a music teacher. And the first time I saw him, he was sitting at his piano in the front of the chorus room, looking like the captain of an empty ship, studying his keyboard and totally absorbed in his music. It was the way I would picture him for the rest of our lives.

Jerry's hair was smartly combed and groomed, as opposed to the crew cuts that the students wore. He almost always wore dress slacks and a plain white dress shirt with dark narrow tie, as if he wanted to be appropriate, but with no extraneous colors or patterns to distract from his basic purpose in life: to play music and direct singing. He looked young. And I suspected he knew it, because he smiled and laughed in class, but it was always within the confines of a proper student-teacher relationship. He built a wall of respect between us, and he knew how to be friends without ever fully inviting us to cross the line. I studied this quality for the four years of high school, and like so many qualities, I later emulated it in the White House.

I don't really know why I took music, except I actually thought I could sing. Plus, it just looked like fun to be in a room full of about forty coed classmates, and for a kibitzer, that's a delicious opportunity. It's also quite a test for a twenty-something teacher who girls swoon over and boys want to tease. Yet this young fellow had a very engaging way of managing his embarrassment by the girls and teasing by the boys. He sort of tolerated us by seeming to participate in the banter, then he simply shut it down, raised his baton, got a very absorbed look on his face, and ordered us to sing. I marveled at this technique because there were so many opportunities to lose control of the class, but he didn't. And furthermore, we all grew to love him. Once again, it was twenty years before I needed this kind of experience. But it was perfect for handling a nationally televised press briefing with fifty or so cantankerous, difficult, and boisterous reporters, including the obstructive Helen Thomas.

Another key lesson I learned from Jerry Laudermilk came just before our first public performance by his chorus. We had been practicing all sorts of ridiculous songs about "Pickin' up paw-paws down in the paw-paw patch," and it was some time before I learned that paw-paws were large fruit, edible and quite tasty, but seldom grown because they ripen too fast. But I did know instantly when it was time for the tenors to intervene in the song. And I particularly enjoyed that moment of entry when we tenors backed up the chorus with the phrase, "Way on down in the paw-paw patch." I hit the word "way" pretty hard. But Jerry kept the music flowing without disruption.

When the class bell ended, he asked if I would stick around a moment. When we were alone in the room, and I was suitably nervous, he said something to this effect: "Marlin, I know you enjoy singing, and I think we sound pretty good. But I have to ask a favor when we actually perform tomorrow."

"Sure," I said.

"I want you to just move your lips when we get to that part about the paw-paw patch."

I was stunned. It took a minute or so to realize what he was saying: my voice was so bad, and I was so far off key, that it would be better if I just didn't sing. He was watching me very closely to judge the reaction. After a moment, I said, "Fine. I can do that," and I left the room. Afterward, I was hurt, not because he asked me not to sing, but because I realized it was true. In fact, I realized that I couldn't sing at all. Then I became grateful that he even kept me in the chorus. I also realized that he was taking some risk in letting me sing any parts of the song.

The next day at choir practice was my first at learning not to sing. Remarkably it went fine. I sang all of the song with less intensity than ever before, and I simply dropped out for that one phrase. Nobody noticed. I didn't tell anyone I had been silenced. And Mr. Laudermilk never told anyone either. It was a marvelous lesson in the value of silence, and the value of trust, when two people can keep a secret because they don't want to hurt each other.

Years later, President George H.W. Bush called me into the Oval Office to say, "Marlin, I want to tell you a secret. I have arranged to meet Mikhail Gorbachev of the Soviet Union in six months, and I know members of the press are badgering you about why we haven't met. I don't want you to lie or say the wrong thing, even by accident. I leave it to you to decide what to say. But you cannot tell anyone about the meeting."

I walked out of the Oval Office, thinking, *This is just like Jerry Laudermilk and the paw-paw patch.* After that incident, I loved George Bush 41 forever because he trusted me. Although, I always wondered how many other members of the chorus were just mouthing the words.

After my freshman year in college at Kansas State, I ran out of money. I only spent seven hundred and fifty dollars that first year; three hundred dollars I got from Dad, three hundred dollars I borrowed from the bank, and the rest I earned on the student newspaper. So I was preparing to drop out of school for at least a year to pay back the loan and earn more money. But Dad had offered more money, and perhaps to take out another loan. I had a good job that summer and figured I could just make it another school year, at least if I got a better job at the college. But I had enormous guilt about taking money from Dad. So one Saturday I called Jerry Laudermilk and asked if I could meet with him.

Jerry was living in a small apartment over a wood frame building near downtown Abilene. I climbed the exterior steps at the end of the building and knocked on his door. I could hear the music playing, and he shouted for me to come in. I did, and I found him in the same situation where I had first met him, at his piano. The piano was at the end of one large room that amounted to living room, dining room, and kitchen. His head was down, and he was well into the piece. I wondered how he got the piano up those stairs that looked like a fire escape, and into the building. But I decided not to ask.

He motioned for me to sit on the couch, and I did while he finished the piece. Then he stopped and asked what he could do for me. And I told my story, essentially about taking my father's money versus dropping out of school for a while.

He came across the room to sit in an armchair beside the couch, and he became very serious. "Listen, Marlin," he said with no equivocation in his voice, "the most important thing in the world for your mom and dad is for you to graduate from college. You take every dime they can give you." I think he added some other things, maybe about my making something of myself. I don't really remember. All I do remember, and it rang in my ears for the rest of my life, was "You take every dime they can give you." He had set my course.

Years later, when my parents visited Washington and came to meet President Reagan and President Bush, my father reflected on my life by saying, "You know, Marlin, when I sit at home and see you on television, I often say, 'I can't believe that's my boy up there.'" Jerry Laudermilk probably couldn't believe it either, but I'm glad he had the wisdom to see the possibility.

DOROTHY ELLIOTT, the one person who could believe it, who never doubted for a moment that I would be anything less than the editor of a great newspaper, was one of the most basic and good people who ever taught a class. She was teaching journalism on the day that I walked in and asked, "Is it true that if I take journalism I get to go downtown during the day and visit merchants?"

"Yes," she said, sizing me up, no doubt as a lazy kid just trying to get out of school. "But it's not quite that easy. You have to sell ads for the *Booster*, the school newspaper."

"I can do that," I said, and bingo, I signed up for journalism. Not a particularly promising beginning. But after a few weeks of selling ads, which I rather enjoyed, Mrs. Elliott assigned me to write a brief story on the basketball team. It contained only a few simple paragraphs, but for some reason the editor put my byline on the story, by Marlin Fitzwater. And after the *Booster* was published, students approached me in the halls to comment on seeing my name in the paper, or to ask about the team as if I had some special knowledge. Wow. My ego had been tapped. Getting all this recognition was terrific. After a while, I discovered that journalism allowed me to write about most anything, and classmates asked for my views, and Mrs. Elliott even defended my right to report about anything. This journalism stuff was great. And so it began.

Mrs. Elliott wasn't profound, a great intellectual, nor filled with the insight that changes one's life, but she offered the one quality every young person needs to be successful: unqualified support. If she hadn't been there to tell me I could be somebody, my life would have been vastly different.

The final yardstick of this support came late in her life, when she also called to say that her family was coming to Washington and she would like to stop by for a chat. I was very pleased and told all of my staff that the teacher who made me US Press Secretary was coming to town.

When she arrived with her husband and two daughters, they were dressed to the nines, appropriate for the White House. And my staff treated them like royalty. My secretary noticed that Mrs. Elliott was carrying a shoebox and asked if she could hold it while they took the tour. "No," Mrs. Elliott said, "I brought it all the way from Kansas to give to Marlin."

When we got settled a short time later in my office, Mrs. Elliott began to tell me how proud she was of my prominence and success. She recalled a skinny, freckle-faced boy who just wanted to get out of class by selling ads. She told how proud she was when I went to college, when I started my own column in Kansas papers, when she saw my byline in the *Topeka Capital*, when I came to the White House, and when President Bush awarded me the Presidential Citizens Medal. Then she said she wanted to give me the only award she had, and she handed me the shoebox.

It was worn and yellow. I lifted the top off carefully, as if it might contain a jack-in-the-box. And then it was clear, she had collected thirty years of newspaper clippings about my life: about being Kansan of the Year, being selected by Reagan and Bush for the job, my announcement of Operation Desert Storm in Kuwait, and dozens of other articles going back to those college columns in the *Abilene Reflector-Chronicle* with the small picture of a crew-cut kid just below the byline. I didn't need to read the clippings to understand the meaning: she was proud of me. And she had followed every step of my life, undisclosed, all these years. It wasn't the only time I cried in the White House, but it was the best time.

PART II

—INSIDE THE WHITE HOUSE—

STORIES FOR FRIENDS

Introduction to Part Two

WORKING INSIDE THE White House is a personal treat, like the day Sophia Loren walked into my office unannounced, just to say hello. Or the day Ted Williams and Joe Dimaggio appeared in the lobby and Ted shouted, "There's Fitzwater." Or meeting the Pope four times. Or spending time with the Bush family. These are the stories I tell my friends. The ones you will never see in the papers.

Mrs. Bush and the New Team

EN ROUTE ISRAEL, JANUARY 1985. After Reagan's re-election in 1984, Vice President Bush began planning for his run for the Presidency. He hired an entirely new staff for that purpose, so in January 1985, I became Press Secretary to Vice President George H.W. Bush. Shortly after the hirings, the Vice President took a foreign trip to the Middle East to meet with leaders in several nations, including Israel, Jordan, Egypt, and the Gulf Coast countries. Most of us had spent little time with Mrs. Bush, and we looked forward to being with her on this trip.

But during the flight on *Air Force Two*, a troubling pattern of activity developed. Mrs. Bush had apparently made it a purpose of her trip to meet and "size up" the new team. She approached me as the plane approached full altitude over the ocean.

"Marlin," she said, "I have a question. You have a new employee, Michael Weintraub, who is a friend of our family. Do you know when he's getting married?"

"I think it's in June, sometime," I replied.

"You mean you don't know," she said sternly.

"No," I said. "But I can find out."

"Thank you, Marlin," she said.

I turned away to retrieve a telephone, thinking this to be a nice opportunity to be responsive to the Vice President's wife. I put a call through to my office, and Michael wasn't available, but my secretary said she would check and call me back. I told her the information was for Mrs. Bush, a bit of information that meant "urgent." She called me back with the date, time, location, and everything except the color of the bride's dress.

Mrs. Bush was standing in the aisle of the plane, talking to another staffer. I walked up and said, "Mrs. Bush, Michael will be married on . . . (such and such date)."

"Thank you, Marlin," she said. "And from now on, when I ask a question, I want you to tell me if you don't know. Don't guess. Don't make something up. I want just the correct information."

Perfectly reasonable, I thought. Then I discovered that all the senior staff had been similarly challenged. The ground rules had been made.

Years later, in casual conversation, Mrs. Bush asked, "Marlin, are you afraid of me?"

"Sometimes," I said honestly. In truth, I loved Mrs. Bush for many reasons. But I never forgot the rules.

Mrs. Bush and the Flyover

TEXAS, MARCH 1986. Vice President Bush campaigned across the country for legislators and state officials running for office. At one such event in Texas, we were attending an outdoor rally at which the Vice President and Mrs. Bush were seated with the guests of honor on a raised platform. When the chaplain finished his invocation, we were sitting quietly waiting for the formal introductions. Suddenly, with no warning in the program or from our advance team, three Air Force jets raised up from behind the stage, traveling about 200 miles per hour, at deafening speed. It was so loud, so low, and so frightening that all of us reflexively ducked and covered our faces. The only exceptions were the photographers, who apparently had been given an alert. Their flashbulbs went off at the exact moment when we all ducked for cover.

We were all shaken, and a little angry by the surprise. But we made it through the program. Afterward, however, the President's Photographer, Dave Valdez, alerted us to his discovery that some of the local photographers had terrible photos of Mrs. Bush ducking, screaming, and fearfully trying to hide from the roaring jets. These could have been photos of any of us. And I felt so sorry for Mrs. Bush.

The next morning, about five o'clock, I got up, dressed, and rushed downstairs in our hotel to check the local newspaper dispenser. The picture was horrible. The entire top half of the front page was a close-up picture of Mrs. Bush's face contorted in fear. I bought every paper in the machine. Then I ran around the block looking for any more places where newspapers were sold, and I bought all of them as well. I knew this would not work, of course, but I had to make the effort.

I returned to our hotel where our staff was having breakfast. I asked if anyone had seen the paper. Yes, they said, and a copy had been delivered to Mrs. Bush. My heart sank. But at least I had tried to do the gallant thing.

Thirty years later, I went to the movie *Florence Jenkins Foster,* starring Meryl Streep as an aging opera singer whose sad performance at Carnegie Hall had received terrible reviews. Her agent attempted to buy up all the newspapers in town, just as I had done. And he failed also. But I shed a few tears for his effort.

Dinner with the King

RIYADH, SAUDI ARABIA, APRIL 1986. Vice President Bush and his aides were invited to dinner in Riyadh with King Fahd. Typically, the dinner started near eleven at night and didn't end until middle of the night. There were hundreds of guests, and the huge room was beautiful in gold trim and chandeliers. As I arrived, our chief of protocol mentioned to me that I was seated at the head table just a few chairs from the King.

"No," I said. I shouldn't be there. There are many others here with higher rank.

"Wrong," the chief of protocol said. "You are Assistant to the President. And in the protocol book, you are a four-star general. There is no one higher."

"I don't care, I should not be there. Move me." So he gave the Saudi protocol chief some sort of crazy story about my having to take an important message coming from Washington and, therefore, I must sit near the communications exit.

And that's how I learned just how important I was.

Mubarak's Dinner

EGYPT, AUGUST 1986. Vice President Bush visited President Mubarak in Cairo. He had a beautiful dinner for Bush with hundreds of guests on the lawn of the presidential palace. Hundreds of candlelights surrounded the lawn, much like Christmas lights in paper bags at Christmastime. I was seated with the President's doctor, Burton Lee, and he got sick in the middle of dinner. Some kind of stomach irritation. I don't think he relished the prospect of going to an Egyptian hospital. So another American doctor helped him to an infirmary in the palace, where he recovered.

Later, in 2010, I went to Cairo with my wife, Melinda. We visited the Pyramids of Giza on the outskirts of Cairo. We negotiated with a camel driver for a ten-dollar ride on a camel. Once I got on my camel, another driver offered Melinda a ride at no cost. She accepted, and we both rode around in a small circle. Then the camels knelt down, and we were asked for more money.

There was no palace or friendly doctor around to help us this time, as we walked away from the screaming camel drivers. On the other hand, our pictures on the camels are still treasures, probably worth a lot more than we paid.

The Horse's Behind

THE WHITE HOUSE, MARCH 19, 1987. After several months of investigations and political challenges, the Tower Board released its investigation of the Iran-Contra Affair, February 27, 1987. They concluded that the President had not violated any laws, but he had exercised lax oversight of his national security staff. Ironically, so many people were fired over the matter that I was one of those hired to deal with the aftermath. I started as President Reagan's last presidential press secretary in February of 1987.

When the Tower Board report came out a couple months later, I was assigned to set up a press conference for the President to accept the report publicly, and to say he had made a mistake.

The press had blown this press conference up to such a degree that some people thought the President would wilt under the pressure. But all the President really had to do was live through it. It was my first formal press conference with the President, and I was scared to death.

It was to be prime time, from the East Room of the White House, with every reporter in America either in the room or watching. Everything seemed to be in order. The President had a prepared statement. He would be on camera for twenty-two minutes. That meant about thirteen questions. And I knew the President was ready with what he wanted to say. What could possibly go wrong?

I was supposed to meet the President at the elevator bringing him down from the living quarters. But about fifteen minutes before the designated time, the usher called to say the President would like me to come up to the living quarters for a few minutes before the press conference. *Oh no,* I thought, *now what?*

I took the elevator up and was met by the usher, who guided me into the living room. I was so nervous, I don't even remember who all was there. I looked for the President. Our eyes met, and he said, "Marlin, come over here. I want to show you something."

I got within a few inches of his face, and he pointed down to his tie. The room went silent. Then I noticed this bright gold blob of a tie tack right in the middle of the tie. The President just stood there. So I looked closer, then realized what it was.

My heart jumped. It was the ass end of a horse.

All I could say, was, "Oh, Mr. President."

All I could think was, *Oh my goodness. He's calling them a horse's ass.*

Finally, I collected my breath enough to say, "I don't think I would wear this, Mr. President."

No one said a word. Then I looked at my watch and said, "Mr. President, I have to go down and give the networks a two-minute warning. I'll see you at the bottom of the stairs."

The President was laughing when I left.

When he came down the stairs for the press conference, he was still wearing the tiepin. I said nothing. He walked up to the podium, answered the thirteen questions, said thank you, and walked out. The press said he had done just fine. The public said he did even better.

And no one, not one person in the press or the living rooms of America, even noticed the horse's ass tiepin. The President wore it several times after that, and it was never mentioned by anyone.

Sotheby's is selling off some of his private possessions. I asked about the tiepin, but it's not for sale. I don't know where it is today. But I do have two photos: one of the President wearing the pin; and one of just the horse's ass, excuse me, the tie tack.

Reagan at Brandenburg Gate

BERLIN, JUNE 12, 1987. Speaking on a platform in front of Brandenburg Gate, President Reagan implores: "Mr. Gorbachev, tear down this Wall." I am crouching directly below the President, under the platform, and listening to him, and to thousands of East Germans who have gathered on the other side of the Berlin Wall. They move away like a rustling herd of cattle in a thunderstorm. They want to hear the American President, but they are afraid of the big guns on the Wall, and they are afraid to applaud. The crowd on the Western side is cheering wildly; on the Eastern side you can only hear their feet. Very moving speech.

I had been reluctant about the "Tear down this Wall" comment by the President. Our staff had raised the issue again with the President on *Air Force One* as we arrived in Berlin. He said simply, "I want to do it."

As I crouched under the speaker's stand that day, I still doubted that the Wall would come down any time soon. But I loved the President for saying it. And on November 9, 1989, the Wall came down. He was right again.

In the Meetings

WASHINGTON, DC, DECEMBER 8, 1987. President Reagan met with President Gorbachev in the White House Cabinet Room. It was their first meeting in Washington, and my first joint press briefing with Gorbachev's press spokesman at the time, Gennadi Gerasimov.

We had two briefings together before the first formal meeting between the Presidents. And it seemed to work well. We both understood that we were not there to disrupt or disagree or cause any problem. We wanted to help the press understand what was happening.

As both delegations gathered outside the Cabinet Room, I mentioned to Gennadi that he could sit with me in the back row by the windows, where we could directly see and hear our principals. He looked at me quizzically, then said, "I'm not allowed in the meeting."

"Then how do you know what happened, for briefing the press?" I asked.

"They tell me," he said.

"Think about this," I said. "After this meeting, we break for lunch. Why don't you go to your foreign minister after this meeting and tell him the American press secretary always attends the bilateral meetings."

Sure enough, in the first meeting after lunch, Gennadi and I sat together. He leaned over and said quietly, "It worked."

From then on, we sat together in meetings around the world.

My Friend Mr. Gorbachev

WASHINGTON, DC, DECEMBER 8–10, 1987. I never dreamed I would meet a head of state. Certainly not of a Superpower. But I never dreamed I would meet a US President either. Yet here I stood in the Diplomatic Reception Room of the White House in 1987, waiting for the arrival of the General Secretary of the Soviet Union, Mikhail Gorbachev. Must have been twenty-five of the high and mighty, including President and Mrs. Reagan, waiting to greet the new leader of the USSR, who had never been to America before. His reputation preceded him.

He was rumored to be a "new kind of leader," who smiled, had a sense of humor, and most importantly to me, had a sense of intellectual curiosity. Before becoming Assistant to the President, I had been a journalist. And I wanted to know things. As Press Secretary to President Reagan, I wanted to know everything about Mikhail Gorbachev—his handshake and his eyes especially. That's how quarterbacks and press secretaries judge people.

I watched as Nancy Reagan gave the President his good luck kiss and sent him out to greet the most important man who would ever visit his Administration. And she never left his side. They escorted the Gorbachevs into the White House and helped them with their coats on this cold December day. I was still ten feet away, but I always tried to stay within hearing range.

I looked down at Mrs. Raisa Gorbachev, and horror of horrors, her hose were down and gathered around her ankles. Oh no, I thought, she can't walk. Everyone will notice. At that very instant, Mrs. Reagan glided past my shoulder, enveloped Mrs. Gorbachev around her shoulders, and whispered, "Come with me." In the midst of the coat confusion, Mrs. Reagan guided her guest about four steps, around the corner to a vacant room. In just seconds, they returned to the reception, situation repaired.

I looked around to see if anyone else had noticed this diplomatic move, and no one appeared to share my amazement. The two principals were cool as cucumbers. Later, during an art gallery visit, Mrs. Gorbachev was reported to be lecturing Mrs. Reagan on the intrinsic values of communism. But my guess was that Mrs. G. had developed a high degree of gratitude for Mrs. R., regardless of her feelings about democracy.

There was one more incident of note. A few days before the official visit, the White House press corps was writing their "set up" stories, and looked to me for help in setting the tone for this dramatic meeting. More than seven thousand correspondents from around the world had been credentialed to attend, and we had moved the White

House Briefing Room, which holds about fifty reporters comfortably, to the grand ballroom of the nearby Marriott Hotel. Every country in the world suspected peace in our time, and they sent correspondents to Washington. Our press corps had the same expectations, and they pressed me for specifics about the President's proposals for peace.

I felt expectations were getting out of hand and a dose of reality might be useful. So I commented during my regular daily briefing that the press should keep in mind that we, the US and USSR, are old enemies, not old friends, and we would have difficult issues to discuss. The press took this as a declaration of unnecessary pessimism and led almost every newscast with the "old enemies, not old friends" quote. The President and our national security officials thought this a reasonable quote because they wanted to dampen expectations a bit as well. But I knew I would not hear the last of this language for some time.

I met Chairman Gorbachev and his press secretary, Gennadi Gerasimov, before the first official meeting, and all was going smoothly until the Chairman's official reception for President Reagan at the Soviet Embassy. My invitation had been delivered just days before. Social enthusiasm in Washington was running high. Everyone wanted to attend.

I walked into the lobby of the Embassy that evening and became part of a sizable crowd moving toward the grand staircase, excited about meeting Mr. Gorbachev in the receiving line on the second floor. I was moving up the first steps to a bend in the stairs, when two burly bodyguards moved down the stairs. One on each side of me, they took me by the arms, lifted me, and moved down the steps. When it became clear that this was not an ancient Siberian greeting, I looked up and saw a Soviet Embassy press attache watching the whole performance. "Boris," I shouted, "Help me!" When it was clear that I was about to make a scene, he motioned to the two guards to release me. They did, on the bottom step. But the scene was not over.

I was shaken, but not stirred, as James Bond might say. I headed back up the stairs, joined in the receiving line, and acted as if nothing happened. When I reached Mr. Gorbachev, he smiled and shook my hand. Then his interpreter, Pavel Palazhchenko suddenly stepped forward and exclaimed, "This is the man who said we are old enemies, not old friends."

Gorbachev's smile dissolved instantly. He yanked his hand away from his greeting. Then he raised his arm again with a clenched fist. It stopped about a half-inch from my nose. "If you were in my country," he said, "I would scold you." His face was red. He lowered his arm, and I quickly moved away from the line. My knees were shaking and my legs felt like rubber. I went to the nearest chair to collect myself and see if anyone noticed. I didn't see any evidence. So I stood and went to my designated table.

But one person saw it all: our Presidential Photographer. He later gave me the best, and most unbelievable, picture imaginable. Pavel is looking over Gorbachev's shoulder, and the leader of the Soviet Union's fist is clenched right in front of my nose. Nobody, American or Soviet, ever said a word to me about it. But it was the beginning of a new friendship.

In 1989, Vice President George H.W. Bush became the forty-first President of the United States and, remarkably, he invited me to be his press secretary, making me the only press secretary in history to be appointed by two presidents. Robert Early, FDR's press secretary, volunteered to help President Truman after his president's death. He served for two weeks. And Pierre Salinger joined three other JFK staff in staying on with LBJ after Kennedy's assassination, primarily for transition purposes. He served for two months. But neither Early nor Salinger were ever appointed to jobs with succeeding presidents.

President Bush had been a part of the Summit Meetings between Gorbachev and Reagan in the 1980s. But the first move he made as president was to order a full review of US foreign policy to identify new initiatives for his Administration. I had attended the Summit Meetings in Washington, Moscow, and New York. President Bush had made it clear that he intended to continue the quest for an end to the Cold War.

The press is an impatient group. They were still in a daily business (pre-Internet) in 1989. And almost every day they came to my briefings to ask: when will the foreign policy review be finished? In the meantime, Chairman Gorbachev was pursuing an aggressive program to focus his country on arms-reduction efforts, including public proposals to reduce weapons in Europe. But he never actually presented a specific program for negotiation. Yet his proposals were getting plenty of publicity and putting pressure on the US to respond. The press were saying: Gorbachev makes proposals, where are ours?

One day I became exasperated and blurted out, "Gorbachev throws out arms-control proposals like a drugstore cowboy." It was a mistake. The press immediately headlined the story as FITZWATER CALLS GORBACHEV A DRUGSTORE COWBOY. This is an old Kansas term that farmboys used to call classmates who made promises they couldn't keep, usually about girls or sports. I guess arms control was a reach too far.

Oh no, I thought, *here we go again.* I immediately went to President Bush and told him I had made a mistake and would resign that day if he wanted. He said, "Let's wait and see what happens." It turned out that nothing happened. We didn't hear from the Soviets. But I am sure Gorbachev read this quote and tucked it away in his mind that Fitzwater had given him a zinger again.

Although President Bush talked with Gorbachev by telephone in the months ahead, we didn't see him again until the Malta Summit on December 2, 1989. Coincidentally, the Berlin Wall came down just a month earlier, on November 9, 1989. That added even more drama to the Malta meeting. President Bush prepared a seventeen-point proposal for Gorbachev that defined a new US–Soviet relationship, based on the idea that America would support the Soviet Union in becoming a part of the world community.

When we arrived on the Soviet cruise ship *Gorky* for the first meeting, the two leaders lined up their staffs for introductions. The new Bush team was about to meet the Soviet delegation for the first time. When Gorbachev started down the line, he approached me with a smile and shook my hand. He looked me in the eye and said in a voice loud enough for the US team to hear, "You they kept!" He turned to President Bush with a full-throated laugh, and I joined in the humor.

It was indeed a new beginning. The world had changed, and the two leaders sat down to consider the future. Bush laid out his plan for Gorbachev to attend the G-7 meetings of industrialized nations, participate in World Trade and economic meetings, and increase trade with the United States. After Gorbachev said the German people should have the right to determine their own destiny, work began on the reunification of Germany. The Cold War had truly ended, and the hard work of change had begun.

In my view, Mr. Gorbachev was one of the most courageous and dynamic leaders of the twentieth century. The next decade is now known as "The Special Years." Bush and Gorbachev became close friends, and I eventually wrote a play, *Empires Fall,* about their personal diplomacy and how it changed the world. Its production on the stage of Ford's Theatre in Washington was another highlight of my life.

Reagan to the Rescue

CONNECTICUT, MAY 18, 1988. President Reagan is speaking at his last military academy commencement as President, the US Coast Guard Academy in New London. The Academy is near my home on the Chesapeake Bay, and I wanted to go. We flew to the Academy from Washington on *Marine One*, the President's helicopter. Flying on the chopper is one of the great treats of the presidency. There is no airport, no baggage, no schedule, and the view from a couple hundred feet is the best.

But the helicopter flight for the commencement was pure fun and celebration. On the ground, we had to go to a stadium holding room for a few minutes until everyone was in place. I learned never to pass up a restroom when you travel with a President, because you never know where they are going or for how long. And when they leave a room, everybody leaves.

So I was in the men's room, when suddenly I heard the most

frightening thing: complete silence. That means the President is on the move. I reached for the lock on my stall, and it wouldn't respond. I started shouting, "Help, help, let me out."

At that point, apparently one of the Secret Service agents heard my plea, just as the President and his admiral escorts were about to get into the limousine for a trip of one hundred yards to the speaker's platform. "Mr. President," he said, "I think Marlin is locked in the men's room."

It was reported later that the President got that unmistakable twinkle in his eye. The one we all recognized when he was about to pull a practical joke, or at least tell a joke.

And instead of getting in the open door of the limo, he just turned and walked back into the locker room. The admirals had no idea what was happening. They just followed along, as the President strode up to the men's room doors and shouted, "Marlin, come on, you're holding up the President." Then he turned and walked out.

At that moment, a Secret Service agent applied a screwdriver to the door hinge; in two nanoseconds it was crashing to the floor. I ran out the door, just as the President plunged into his seat in the limo. And two admirals applauded me as I ran for the second limo. That, my friends, is humiliation. And, it was Ronald Reagan's great sense of humor.

KGB in the Square

MOSCOW, MAY 29 – JUNE 3, 1988. President Reagan's first visit to Moscow in the summer of 1988 was not going as smoothly as hoped. Reagan wanted a preliminary day or two of symbolic activities that would dramatically demonstrate American principles to the Soviet people. The President was staying at Spaso House, the home in Moscow where the US Ambassador to the Soviet Union lives. But the fear of Soviet listening devices planted in the walls of the home were so great that a soundproof meeting room was constructed in the lobby. It was small, with no windows, one conference table with eight chairs, and loud jungle music playing outside. The President sat with his advisers, knee to knee. That's where we started each day.

Then President and Mrs. Reagan took a walk in the Arbat, an open shopping area near the residence, and the crowd grew so large and so fast that the KGB lost control and the secret services rushed the Reagans back to the residence. (I told this story on February 6, 2015, at the Reagan Library to honor the President's birthday at his grave site.)

Then the President had dinner with Soviet dissidents at the US Embassy, which drove the Soviets crazy. The President also visited a monastery to emphasize freedom of religion. He spoke at Moscow University to discuss freedom of speech and assembly. And all of this was before he had ever mentioned a word about arms control, which was to be the focus of the first meeting.

The arms control meeting, most of which had been predetermined by our official negotiators, went well. But there was a hang-up when Gorbachev demanded a simple sentence in the communiqué that said both countries favored peace. But it turned out that the Soviet and US sides had argued about this language all night because it has special meaning in the world of diplomacy. It meant détente. By the old Kissinger definition, this meant no disagreements. Gorbachev wanted it in. The American side did not. And finally, Gorbachev grew angry. He shouted at Reagan, "Why won't you let this in?"

Reagan said no, we had negotiated this language, and it would remain unchanged. Gorbachev challenged him, shouting, "Mr. President, don't listen to George (Shultz); don't listen to Frank (Carlucci). You don't have to listen to them. Speak for yourself."

At this point, I am sitting directly behind General Colin Powell, National Security Advisor. I see Colin tear off a corner of a page of notepaper and scribble a brief message to the President. He is sitting beside the President and hands him the note. The President glances down, then looks up and says again, "The answer is no."

At that point, Gorbachev asks for a private moment with the President. Reagan and Gorbachev rise and move to the end of the table. The rest of the staff rise and move to the other end of the table. Then Gorbachev, who is several inches shorter than Reagan, crowds close to Reagan and starts shaking his finger. Reagan never moves. He just says no, again. Suddenly Gorbi realizes he is beaten. His shoulders slump. He drops his head. He says, OK, let's go to the press conference. He puts his arm around Reagan, with his hand on his shoulder, looks up, and smiles broadly. As they walk out, the staff exits behind them. I notice that Colin's note is still on the table. I grab it and hand it to Colin. It said, "This means you agree to never criticize them again. " Reagan understood this meant détente. And he never budged from his response, "No."

Then, just as we rose from the table, a member of my staff entered the room and said, "The Soviets won't let American cameras film the walk in Red Square."

"Get me Gerasimov," Gorbachev's press secretary, I said. That only took about two seconds. Gennadi came in the room as Reagan and Gorbachev left.

"Gennadi, " I said, "Reagan wants to praise Gorbachev and say good things about the Soviet Union. Don't you want the American people to hear and see that message? Put at least one of our cameras in the pool with the leaders."

"I'll take care of it," he said. And he did.

So at last, after all this turmoil, we begin the walk in Red Square, for me the most important part of the trip. Reagan, the archenemy of communism, the architect of the Evil Empire, was about to turn the corner. He was a master at turning the tide of history, at catching the crest of change, whether it be in Red Square or at the Brandenburg Gate in Berlin.

As the two leaders emerged from the Kremlin and entered the square, several small groups of people in the square moved to collect themselves. They were all dressed in common clothes, women in floral print dresses, work shoes, some wearing babushkas; men in open collar shirts or casual jackets. All were ready to tell the President a different story.

The first small group included a young mother who handed her child to Gorbachev. He held the baby in his arms and presented it to Reagan to admire. The next group started asking the leaders questions. And a little short peasant woman in the third group asked Reagan why America wouldn't share our space telemetry data with the Soviets. When I heard this, something was flagged in my brain. Something was wrong with this picture. A peasant woman asking about space telemetry. And then a closer look at these groups suggested I had seen them before. Of course, they were our drivers from the hotel, our maids who cleaned the rooms, the hotel concierge, and the elevator operators. These folks were all KGB. Probably everyone they could find who spoke English.

I edged over to Howard Baker, Chief of Staff to the President, and asked if I should tell the President. He said, "Go ahead."

I sidled up to the President and asked if he could step away from the group for a moment. I told him the groups were KGB.

He returned to conversation with the Soviets and never said a word about the groups.

Then I noticed that Reagan was letting Gorbachev do all the talking. The President would say only a sentence or two to each group. I worried that Gorbachev was getting all the TV time. Later I went to the television networks' editing rooms in our hotel. Bill Plante of CBS pulled me aside and said, "Look at this, Marlin." The news reports were full of those single sentences from Ronald Reagan, each one on an important principle of democracy. The Great Communicator was scoring again. President Reagan wanted this opportunity to show a different relationship between the US and the Soviet Union. Reagan said he no longer thought the Soviet Union was the Evil Empire. History was changing.

And there was one other remarkable event that day. It turned out that Vladimir Putin, a young KGB officer, was apparently among the crowd, or at least there is a photo of a very young, blond man who appears to be Putin. Putin denies the photo is of him. But I saw the picture, and I believe he was there.

Mrs. Mao at Home

BEIJING, CHINA, FEBRUARY 1989. I visited China several times with President Bush. We stayed at the official guesthouse in Beijing. I took a walk among the houses, beautifully landscaped with pools and gardens. Suddenly, Chinese police were around me. They told me to return to the US delegation house, and I did. Later I was told I had stumbled into the gardens around the official guesthouse of Mrs. Mao, who had been under house arrest by the Chinese Government since Mao's death. This was where she lived. We were neighbors for a couple of days.

The Cabinet at Camp David

CAMP DAVID, JULY 22, 1989. The Cabinet is invited to Camp David for recreation and meeting, a classic President Bush social event, of the kind held regularly at the Walker's Point compound in Kennebunkport—tennis, swimming, hiking, whatever anyone wanted.

A dinner for the Cabinet and wives is at Laurel Lodge, the same location where the President meets and entertains Gorbachev, Yeltsin, Major, and other world leaders. The after-dinner entertainment is Doug Jackman, a friend from Philadelphia who gives motivational speeches. He asks, "Do you like who you are? Do you like what you do? Do you like what you're doing?" Very funny. And his last line was always, "President Bush is the greatest guy in the world." I tried to write down his stories so I could use them myself, but he spoke too fast.

Senator Dole was a special guest, and the President celebrated his birthday. Dole told some stories, and he was good at it. He said, "I was last here seventeen years ago. Nixon asked if I liked being Republican National Committee Chairman. I said yes. He said, 'This is your last day.'"

Dole was getting a new job. He also pointed out that this was the first time the Cabinet had gathered at Camp David since Jimmy Carter had invited his Cabinet to the Camp, and then fired them. Replaced the whole Cabinet, but it didn't help.

Carol Powers, Mrs. Bush's photographer, who I was dating at the time, played tennis against Susan Baker and Joanne Kemp. Jack Kemp and Bill Bennett played against Vice President and Marilyn Quayle. It was great fun, and several other guests gathered to watch. But Jack Kemp, apparently in response to the sun, took off his shirt to play. Mrs. Bush, watching from the sidelines, waited not one minute to shake her head and then leave, without saying a word. But she didn't need to. It was no coincidence. All who had visited Walker's Point knew the house rule: keep your shirts on.

Lt. Col. Higgins

RETURN TO WASHINGTON, DC, JULY 31, 1989. At home, I'm sleeping in, staying at home, while the President travels to Chicago. Natalie Wozniak, in the National Security Council (NSC) office, calls me to say the President is returning to Washington due to the reported hanging of Marine Lt. Colonel William R. Higgins, who had been kidnapped by Hezbollah terrorists in Lebanon. Higgins was head of the UN Peacekeeping Force in Southern Lebanon.

I rush to the White House and meet the President as he arrives on *Marine One* from Andrews AFB. He walks over to the waiting press pool to discuss the murder of Col. Higgins. He says he still doesn't have final confirmation of what happened, but he had called Col. Higgins' wife to comfort her and bring her up to date.

The President told the press, "There is no way that I can properly express the outrage that I feel . . . It is a most troubling and disturbing matter that has shocked the American people."

I go to the Oval Office with the President, [Deputy National Security Adviser] Gates, and [Chief of Staff] Sununu. The President is frustrated and angry. "If I could, I'd knock the shit out of them," he exclaims. He calls Bill Webster at CIA, "We're just sitting here wringing our hands; what have you got?"

"Nothing," says the Judge. "We can't confirm. We believe he's dead, but can't confirm."

President Bush turns quickly to the CIA in these kinds of situations, because he knows from experience what kind of resources they have.

At 5:30 p.m., the President convenes a meeting of the NSC in the Cabinet Room to consider the crisis. Webster says Hezbollah is afraid of Israel. [National Security Advisor] Scowcroft disagrees, says Hezbollah has taken US hostages because the publicity mileage is better. Scowcroft and Bush are angry at Israel for not telling us about Higgins. Everyone asks, "What the hell were they thinking?" Meaning, why was Higgins exposed? Eagleburger, munching peanuts and cleaning his teeth with his tongue, mumbles, "It had to be a trade."

Issuing a Statement

WASHINGTON, DC, JULY 31, 1989, 10:30 A.M. Sununu calls me from Scowcroft's office to ask what I think of the statement on hostages: "Bush calls for release of all hostages." I think it's too obvious that we're asking Israel to release its hostage (a trade). They rewrite the statement.

The Governor calls with a new statement: "Bush calls on all parties to release all hostages as a humanitarian gesture."

The official statement said: "Tonight I wish to go beyond that statement with an urgent call to all, all parties, who hold hostages in the Middle East to release them forthwith, as a humanitarian gesture, to begin to reverse the cycle of violence in that region."

It's still obvious what we want, but it gives us some cover against criticism from the Jewish lobby. I call it out to the wire services.

Reuters immediately asks: Does this mean Israel too? I don't answer directly, but I repeat the original statement. The message to Israel has been sent: let Obeid go.

Note: Sheik Abdul Karim Obeid, senior cleric in southern Lebanon with the Iranian-supported Hezbollah, and two aides were kidnapped on July 28 from the cleric's home in Jibchit by Israeli commandos.

NSC Meeting

CABINET ROOM, THE WHITE HOUSE, AUGUST 1, 1989. National Security Council meeting in the Cabinet Room on hostages. Admiral Crowe, chairman of the Joint Chiefs of Staff, has been asked for a plan to attack the terrorists. He lays out maps and charts in front of the President and describes targets, aerial photos, buildings, compounds in the Beqaa Valley of Lebanon.

The Admiral asks, "Our guys find it important to know whether you want to prioritize the mission, on getting our men back. Obviously, if we don't worry about the personnel, we have better odds on the mission—lower bomb runs, that sort of thing."

I thought this was strange, but consistent with the Admiral I knew from the Reagan years. He didn't like risks. And I couldn't imagine any President, ever, deciding to increase the risk to personnel. Those decisions are what admirals are for.

President Bush said, "Tell your men I stand behind them, whatever happens."

"Thanks, Mr. President, that's what they want to hear." I wasn't surprised that Crowe was not reappointed months later. (The Admiral sent a secret back channel note to the President saying he would like to be reappointed as Chairman of the Joint Chiefs. He wasn't.) Then he opposed Operation Desert Storm and testified against the Administration before Congress. He also became a politician, endorsed Bill Clinton for President at a time when Clinton was under fire for avoiding the draft. In return, President Clinton made him ambassador to Great Britain.)

Later in the meeting, the President decides, "If one more dies, we strike Lebanon and Iran."

I recalled privately the President's words, "If I could, I'd like to knock the shit out of them."

That's what he planned: bomb runs and guided missiles, then follow up with submarine-launched cruise missiles.

Secret Meetings

AUGUST 11, 1989. I suspect the President is working with the Russians to help with some kind of attack against Hezbollah, or perhaps send some kind of secret message to Hezbollah.

As often happens in the White House, I got a confidential call in the afternoon that the President appeared to be having a secret meeting in the residence, with the VP, Baker, Cheney, and Scowcroft. This group was scheduled to meet in the Oval at 3:00 p.m. to discuss chemical weapons ban negotiations. Instead, they went to the residence, I suspected to meet a secret guest.

We had another meeting at 7:00 p.m. in the Oval, with Scowcroft, Gates, and a CIA representative. In a side conversation before going in, I mentioned, "Most everyone in the Oval meeting today fell asleep."

Scowcroft said, "Not me."

Gates said, "They were sleeping through you."

But that may have been a clever CIA comment to put me off the secret meeting in the residence. My source saw the special guest and said he looked dark, which could have been Yaqui Kahn, the Pakistan Foreign Minister. But the source saw Kahn on TV the day before and said it wasn't him.

I knew we were skeptical of Kahn as an intermediary. He is thought to tell both sides of the story what they want to hear. Later, at home, I am reading *Russia House*. It hits me: The mystery guest could have been Soviet Deputy Foreign Minister Alexander Bessmertnykh. Margaret Tutwiler [Assistant Secretary of State for Public Affairs] told me earlier in the day that he had a secret meeting with Secretary Baker. It could have been a deal on chemical weapons, or it could have been Iran and the hostages. Bush and Scowcroft are preoccupied with the hostages.

In the 7:00 p.m. meeting, I comment to Scowcroft that the 3:00 p.m. meeting with Iran specialists seems to say: solve Iran first, then the hostages. Scowcroft says, "We have to do the hostages now; Iran is a long way off."

Message to Israel

KENNEBUNKPORT, MAINE, AUGUST 17, 1989. A *New York Times* article by Tom Friedman says the White House is upset with Israel over the kidnapping of Sheikh Obeid. Bob Hall of USIA and I studied the story. It looked like exactly what we were saying in the formal statement. We didn't believe Scowcroft or Gates would put the issue on the record so bluntly—that's why we asked for "all hostages from all countries" to be freed. Somebody just wanted to get their name in the papers. Our guess is Richard Haass, NSC Mideast expert. Hall calls him. He admits being the source. He says he had breakfast Friday with the Israeli Embassy staff. They said they "got the message" and transmitted it to Jerusalem. There was no anger.

Gates calls me at the Shawmut Inn press office and says Scowcroft is upset. He wants to know the source. I don't tell him. I figure Gates, former CIA deputy director under Bill Casey, may be testing me. But the next day, Gates tells me Haass admits being the source of the story. Scowcroft says he will talk with Haass and Dennis Ross, at State, to stop this talk.

It often happens that presidents get upset by leaks of stories that aren't leaks at all. This is a good example: This was an official story, released by the White House, written by Scowcroft, decided by the

President, and directed at Israel. Everybody in America knew what we were saying. But seeing it on the record was inconvenient.

(I was part of three FBI leak investigations, and in every case, the culprit was found to be a presidential assistant or agency head. Ambassadors are often sources as well. Chasing leaks is a waste of time.)

Extradition Order

KENNEBUNKPORT, MAINE, AUGUST 19, 1989. At 2:30 p.m., we release a statement on Columbia extradition orders by President Barco. Brit Hume, ABC-TV correspondent, writes a spot in five minutes for the evening news, then rushes out to Kennebunkport tennis courts for the Fitzwater Invitational Tennis Tournament. He wins the tournament, rushes back to the Shawmut Inn press center at 6:00 p.m., does a stand-up in his tennis shorts and a suit jacket. His story is fine. That's life at the summer White House.

Yeltsin's Unscheduled Meeting

THE WHITE HOUSE, SEPTEMBER 11, 1989. Boris Yeltsin, member of the Russian parliament at the time, visits the White House to establish his credentials on foreign policy. He doesn't have an appointment with the President. Worse, he has been drinking. He gets out of his limousine and enters the basement of the White House, where he asks a passing secretary to see the President. Word is sent to General Scowcroft, who asks Condi Rice, our Russian expert who speaks the language, to meet him and bring him to General Scowcroft's office.

Yeltsin tells her, "If I can't see the President, I will see no one."

When his two traveling companions were asked to wait in the

basement, Yeltsin stopped, folded his arms, and exclaimed in a loud voice, "If they can't go, I won't go."

Finally, he goes to see Scowcroft and offers ten ways we could help perestroika. He suggests we could go to Mars with Russians, adopt Russia as a sister state, and urge American investors to build ten million apartment units in Russia.

(Scowcroft had alerted the President to Yeltsin's presence. But Gorbachev had already asked the President not to meet with Yeltsin in the Oval Office.) President Bush came down the hall to Scowcroft's office, shook hands with Yeltsin and welcomed him to America, then left. Yeltsin went out to the waiting press corps in the driveway, and said, "I have just had a long and productive meeting with the President."

He got what he wanted.

Mexican President Salinas

THE WHITE HOUSE, OCTOBER 3, 1989, 1:00 A.M. The President is meeting with Mexican President Salinas. In the Oval's outer office, I am waiting with Scowcroft, Sununu, and Bernard Aronson of State. Brent gets a call from the Pentagon about a coup attempt in Panama by the Panama Defense Forces against Manuel Noriega.

Brent asks: "How about the bridge? CNN says the bridge is open." We are watching on the TV in the President's outer office.

Brent: "Can we signal the Panama Defense Forces that we're on their side—that there is no doubt where we stand?"

Brent: "Have we secured the causeway?"

Aronson to Brent: "Can we go on radio?"

Sununu: "Noriega may bring troops in by air. Can he?"

Brent: "We don't really know where he (Noriega) is, do we? The US has helos and A-37s in the air—surveillance."

Sununu, standing feet together, hands in front of his face like guillotine blades. He gestures, chopping the air downward, and says:

"Send the signal."

Brent: "It is blocked."

Sununu: "No it's not. It's on CNN."

Brent: "Their troops are there to block if necessary."

Sununu: "I mean, get the troops and tanks up on the bridge where the PDF can see them."

Brent: "They can see them."

After Salinas leaves, we go into the Oval and brief the President on Panama. He orders a briefing from the Pentagon before his upcoming meeting with Soviet General Yazov, who is here to discuss arms-control issues at the Pentagon.

I'm wondering, how many days will there be when a coup in one country breaks out between meetings with the leaders of two other countries? And presumably, neither Salinas nor Yazov has anything to do with Panama.

"We Have Noriega"

OVAL OFFICE, OCTOBER 3, 1989, 1:45 P.M. The President has a previously scheduled lunch with elected officials, then returns to the Oval to meet with Cheney, Sununu, Gates, Scowcroft, and myself for an update on Panama. A rebel coup is apparently underway in Panama to capture Gen. Noriega.

Cheney says Cisneros (US General) has met with rebel leaders. They claim they have Noriega in custody. He is safely in their hands. They will not give him up. They want to retire him to some retirement home in the mountains.

The President: "How did Cisneros see these guys?"

Cheney: "I guess he (the rebel leader) just walked into the Commondancia. He's a ballsy guy."

The President: "If he just walked in, where are his troops? Wasn't he stopped? Isn't there any fighting around the compound?"

Cheney: "I guess not."

The President: "Here's what's needed. The rebels have to say: 'We have Noriega. We have the government. We need support for democracy. We need US help to preserve order in the city.' Then we say: 'Yes, we'll help.'"

Cheney: "OK. I'll ask for five things: (1) Cisneros should re-establish contact with the rebels; (2) Find out rebel intentions about Noriega; (3) Will rebels accept extradition or expulsion of Noriega? (4) The Rebels should ask for our help; (5) Tell US General Maxwell Thurman to prepare to use military force."

The President: "I've reached the point I'm ready to consider military force."

Sununu: "We should take in five trucks, give the rebels sanctuary, take Noriega out."

Scowcroft: "Reaction in Latin America will be bad."

The President: "I think we should go in and get him out. We'll have a bad time of it for a while. But then it's over."

As the meeting ends, the President asks: "At this photo op with Yazov, can I say that the rebels have Noriega? That they seem to be in control?"

Cheney stands up to leave, starts to say something, but doesn't. He leaves.

I respond to the President's question about the press.

"No," I say. "Cheney's report leaves all kinds of holes. We don't know where Noriega is. We know hardly anything. I recommend you say we're monitoring events, on top of activities, but there is still much confusion in the area."

"It's only 2:30," I add. "We have three or four hours to comment and still get on the news. We need more information."

2:30 p.m., Yazov walks in. The photo op goes as I had indicated.

The President greets Yazov, praises Gorbachev and his reforms.

He says: "Nobody today is talking about an arms race. We're talking reductions. It's time to go ahead. You have to crawl before you walk, but we're moving."

Yazov: "We are very close on ALCMs, bomber counting rules, and verifications have been moved to the forefront. Goodwill on both sides means verifications can very easily be achieved. You have

American inspectors everywhere today, base visits, bomber inspections, open skies."

The President: "Let's keep pushing."

Yazov leaves by Oval Office door. (Yazov later was part of the coup plotters in Moscow who tried to kidnap and overthrow Gorbachev.)

The President, Baker, Scowcroft, Gates, and I start for the outer office, ready to enter the Cabinet Room for an NSC meeting on Polish aid program. As I reach for the Cabinet Room door, it opens and Aronson walks in.

"Mr. President," Aronson says. "It's over. Noriega's troops have taken the compound. Noriega is free, and the rebels are being rounded up."

The President: "That sure doesn't square with what we just heard. Are you sure?"

Aronson: "Yes, sir."

The President: "OK." He led us into the Cabinet Room. The Panama coup was over.

Note: For a brief time in October 1989, Noriega fell into the hands of rebels under the command of Major Giroldi. This attempted coup against the Panamanian dictator was quickly suppressed. The failure of the coup prompted the US military's invasion of Panama two months later, in December 1989, to remove Noriega from power.

Old Ebbitt Grill

WASHINGTON, DC, WEDNESDAY OCTOBER 11, 1989, 9:00 P.M. We're in the Old Ebbitt Grill basement party room for an Ed Rogers bachelor party. I get a page asking me to call the White House switchboard. I did, and Speaker of the House of Representatives Tom Foley was on the line.

"Mr. Fitzwater," he says, "I want to tell you about a remark that will be in tomorrow's *Washington Times*, by the White House correspondent Frank Murray. I did a background breakfast this morning with several reporters. Murray will say I said that about capital gains, 'the President is like a mad dog after a bone.' I just wanted you to know I never said that. I have denied it. But despite my denial, they are going to use it. I've never had this happen before, where a quote was completely made up."

"Thank you for calling, Mr. Speaker," I said. He wanted me to tell the President. I'm sure he figured better me than him.

Leak on Malta Meeting

OCTOBER 30, 1989. The President calls at 7:30 a.m. asking me to come to the Oval. Scowcroft, Sununu, and Gates are there. The President says he will announce Tuesday at 10:00 a.m. a meeting with Gorbachev on Malta, or an aircraft carrier nearby. The President has told me privately a month ago that this was coming. Sununu didn't know I had been told. He said this had been in the works for some time and they couldn't tell me. I just nodded.

The President said, "I don't want this to leak. Someone will think they owe someone, or want to do someone a favor and tell that reporter." I nodded and said I would be ready.

At 6:30 p.m., at home, Margaret Tutwiler called me in high dudgeon.

"Do you know what our principals are doing tomorrow?" she asked.

"Yes," I replied.

"Have you seen the plan for this—the floating part?"

"No," I said.

"The press will go crazy," she said. "They will be all over us." Her voice rising, "I have to brief on this. They don't want to take the press on the floats."

"Calm down, Margaret," I advised. "There's plenty of time to deal with details. I'll call you tomorrow, and we'll talk about it."

"This is going to get out," she said. "Five or six people have called me about it."

"You mean press?" I asked.

"Not press, but five or six of our people."

"Margaret, you better not talk to anyone. I'll call you after the press conference tomorrow."

At 8:00 p.m., "The *Post* has it that Bush is meeting with Gorbachev the first week in December."

"Roman," I said, "Just say no comment, and hope they quote you."

At 9:30 p.m., the President calls, "I hear the *Post* has the story."

I relate the Tutwiler phone call to the President. "Five or six people at State are like telling the world," he says.

"I'm just sick about this," the President says. "I'm going to call Jim [Baker]."

Hostage Story

THE WHITE HOUSE, TUESDAY NOVEMBER 7, 1989. My Deputy for Foreign Affairs, Roman Popadiuk, called to say, "Don't talk to anyone about hostages. Something's up." That's the kind of heads up that has saved my life and reputation many times.

Ten minutes later, Roman arrives at my office, "The *LA Times* called about a story that the United States sent a team of people to Frankfort over the weekend to receive hostages. Randy Beers of the NSC [NSC staffer for terrorism] told me. Neither Gates nor Scowcroft knows."

"Does the President know?" I asked. Knowing his famous compartmentalization of information, one couldn't be sure the President knows even if Scowcroft and Gates don't.

I went to the Oval and asked the President. He didn't know and was quite surprised. He reached for the phone and called Brent. Brent said he didn't know either. "If somebody did this without telling us, their job is over," he said as I left the Oval.

I hurried to Brent's office to cover myself. Maybe the President and Brent were both feigning ignorance just to throw me off the track. Also, I didn't want Brent mad that I went to the President first—especially if he really didn't know about the hostages.

I met Randy Beers outside Brent's door. I asked Randy, who was just going into Brent's office, to tell Brent that I had asked the President because of the *LA Times* story. Randy said that he hadn't told Brent about the possible hostage release because Brent was so busy.

I went back to my office to meet with Roman. Roman had called Horace Busby, State's Terrorism Director, who told him the story was true. State sent a plane to Germany loaded with medical people, etc., to receive a hostage. They did it partly because it was the tenth anniversary of the Iranian embassy hostage taking, partly because there had been telephone intercepts that a hostage might be released, and partly (maybe 5 or 10 percent) because of the settlement of $567 million in Iranian assets claims at the Hague Tribunal. (Later, Roman Popadiuk was appointed our first Ambassador to the newly independent Ukraine. After our Administration ended, Roman served as Executive Director of the Bush Presidential Library Foundation for more than thirteen years.)

Earlier in the day, Gates had assured me of no connection between the claims settlement and a hostage release. No quid pro quo. And there wasn't. But State had considered it in their equation. Brit Hume, ABC News, had suggested a link after getting a call from Roone Arledge, President of ABC News. I assured Brit of no link.

I went back to the Oval as Brent was emerging. He said to tell the press, "Nothing to it. Nothing at all."

I went into the Oval, alone. The President said, "Brent says nothing to it." I looked skeptical. "Don't you believe it?" he asked.

"Well," I stammered, "Brent means nothing happened. Nothing planned (but we had sent a special hostage release plane to Germany). But I'm dealing with perceptions. And the *LA Times* will certainly make it look like we linked the claims release to an expected hostage release."

Later, at home, about 8:30, Roman called. "State has talked to the *LA Times* and told them everything. They have the whole story, which was the right thing to do."

The next morning, it was all in the *LA Times* of November 8.

Once again, did Brent really not know? Was it all an innocent mistake by Beers in not telling Brent about the State plane? Or was it Brent, the President, and Gates all knowing but wanting to say nothing that might stop the hostage release, or foster accusations about linking money to hostages? I don't know, and never will. No hostage was released.

Lech Walesa

NOVEMBER 14, 1989. After a private dinner with Lech Walesa, leader of Solidarity in Poland, President and Mrs. Bush took Mr. Walesa on a private stroll around the White House grounds. By accident, Richard Kramer, author of *What It Takes*, and I also were taking a stroll. We all met in the Diplomatic Reception Room about 9:00 p.m.

Lech said they had "a real home-cooked meal," laughing at his own comparison between a Gdansk shipbuilders' lunch and a presidential spread.

It was a warm, beautiful night, and the Bushes invited Kramer and me to join them for a walk around the South Grounds. The talk was casual, but the President thanked Walesa for his remarks at dinner, where he said, "I support what you are doing in Eastern Europe, and I will say whatever you want about it."

At one point the President told a story about visiting an Alzheimer center in Florida during the campaign. "As I was starting my speech, one old man leaned over to another and said in a loud voice, 'This is bullshit.' The other man replied, 'When is Ike coming?'"

For Kramer and me, it was a special evening.

Memo on Malta

MALTA SUMMIT, DECEMBER 1989. The first formal meeting between President Bush and Mikhail Sergeyevich Gorbachev, General Secretary of the Communist Party, and in 1990 President of the Soviet Union, occurred in December 1989. Prior to that, Bush had met Gorbachev briefly during a funeral in Moscow, during the Gorbachev–Reagan Summit in 1987, when Vice President Bush accompanied Gorbachev on his walk down Connecticut Avenue in Washington, and in New York City during a goodbye visit between Gorbachev and President Reagan. All were brief encounters. This first Summit Meeting with President Bush was held in Malta, at the new President's suggestion.

Coincidentally, and historically remarkable, the Berlin Wall fell on November 9, 1989, just a month before the two Superpower leaders were scheduled to meet.

They only had one month to plan their discussion around these new circumstances. Gorbachev was moving the USSR toward democratization, and Bush was moving toward a new East–West relationship following seventy years of the Cold War.

As Press Secretary to President Reagan, I had attended summit meetings with President Reagan in Washington, Moscow, and New York, sitting in the bilateral meetings and watching the Soviet leader closely. He was a mesmerizing figure.

And it seemed to me as President Bush's new Press Secretary, that the new President might benefit from a study of Gorbachev's style, techniques of debate, and emotional qualities that he exhibited in the Reagan summits. So I wrote the President a memo on my observations, a copy of which is attached. It has been declassified [Declassified Per E.O. 13526 ISOO 2017-03, SCS 7/12/17].

This memo marks the beginning of Bush-Gorbi relationship that led to Madrid Conference/US resolution support from USSR. As a result of this memo, President Bush said, "I want to go first. Set the agenda."

THE WHITE HOUSE
Washington
November 20, 1989
Memorandum for the President
From: Marlin Fitzwater
Subject: Reflections on Gorbachev's Personal
Summit Style

In three summit meetings with President Reagan
(Washington, Moscow, and New York), President
Gorbachev tried three distinctly different
personal tactics for dominating the meetings. But
the common thread in all three was that he did
try to dominate. In addition, while each meeting
showed a progression in his sophistication and
mastery of diplomatic skills, there always came
a point where the basic, feisty, street fighter,
Georgian emerged.

Washington. In the Washington summit, Gorbachev
quickly established his objective of stopping
SDI, in return for a START agreement. With his
Ministers negotiating the issue in side meetings
with Shultz, Nitze, Ridgway, and others, Gorbachev
set out to intimidate President Reagan through
his mastery of arms control issues and his
knowledge of the history of previous agreements.
Speaking rapidly and excitedly through two two-
hour sessions the first day, Gorbachev read from
handwritten notes in a small spiral notebook.
His gestures were fast and flamboyant, moving
his arms in wide circles, slicing the air with
an open palm, and pointing his finger at the US
delegation. It was an impressive performance,
as he recalled the substance of a 1925 treaty
and tried to tell the President exactly how many

ships were in the US Fleet, and their locations.

President Reagan raised all of our concerns about the various arms control issues, and Gorbachev would respond to each one of them in great detail, challenging the validity of every US argument. At the end of the day, President Reagan was drained. He told Howard Baker that he needed to go home and brush up on his facts if he wanted to compete with Gorbachev. Wisely, Senator Baker told him not to do that, but instead to simply remember who he was and the ideas he represented.

The next day, Gorbachev began the opening session with the same techniques. President Reagan did not try to engage the arguments. He simply held firm to the US positions, repeating our commitment to SDI. On the second day, the situations reversed, with Gorbachev growing ever more frustrated that his arguments were not making any headway. Indeed, they were not even being engaged. In the end, we were able to negotiate an agreement in the side groups that the START process would continue, with an understanding that SDI would be set aside.

Moscow. On Gorbachev's home turf, and at the prime of his rise in power, Gorbachev undertook to challenge the President in the most personal way. Again, the issue for discussion was progress on the START treaty and compliance with the ABM treaty in terms of SDI testing. But clearly, Gorbachev's primary goal was to get a final communique that committed the US to "detente." He wanted to be able to tell the Soviet people that the problems with the US were solved.

As at the Washington summit, the language of this debate was being negotiated in side meetings at the ministerial level. Shevardnadze was obviously reporting to Gorbachev that those talks were not going well. Shultz and Ridgway were not willing to budge on language the Soviets wanted, which amounted to a detente situation.

As we entered the final session, Gorbachev focused on the specific language of the communique and demanded answers from the President as to why the Soviet language was unacceptable. President Reagan knew it was unacceptable and would not budge.

The Gorbachev tactic in his situation was to accuse President Reagan of taking orders from his subordinates. At several points he said, "Don't listen to George on this," or "You aren't going to let Frank tell you how to do this, are you?" The President remained passive and calm. He simply overlooked the challenge and said he believed strongly that the language of the US side was the only language he could accept.

Gorbachev asked for a caucus. The two sides stepped back from the table and huddled. Shultz and Powell emphasized again that the United States relationship was based on our continuing ability to raise issues such as regional conflicts, human rights, and military posture. They explained that the Soviet language would gloss these issues over, indicating that we no longer had major disagreements in these areas.

The President and Gorbachev walked around to the end of the table for a final discussion. They stood toe-to-toe, with Gorbachev, a much shorter man, gesturing wildly, demanding that President Reagan explained why he would not accept their proposal. President Reagan said calmly that he could not accept it and only the US language would do. Gorbachev's shoulders sank. He started to turn away, but abruptly the old smile and laugh came back. He shook hands with President Reagan and accepted the US language.

New York. In this meeting, which you attended, the highlight of the session was his impassioned plea for understanding and support in America of *perestroika.* But you will recall that he started the conversation with the challenge, "I know there are many in America who don't want *perestroika* to succeed." Even though this exchange was more gentle than at the other two summits, it demonstrated once again that he is combative by nature, and he likes to make his points from a challenging position—by putting the other fellow on the defensive.

In summary, you may want to consider how you will respond to this kind of testing. Do you want to engage him point-by-point, or lay back and hear him out? You may want to consider an opening set of remarks that establishes not only what you want out of the meeting, but remarks which demonstrate the kind of man he is dealing with.

Gorbachev reads the popular press and will no doubt drop references to articles or quotations he has read about you. This also means that he has heard the criticism about caution and timidity, etc. My guess is that he will test your style and personality early in the meetings.

Two pre-Malta meeting statements seem to be right out of the Gorbachev mold for past summits. The first is his warning that Western nations should not try to export capitalism. This puts us on the defensive right away. It also sets a benchmark by which the public will judge whether or not we are being differential to Gorbachev, and he knows that our natural proclivity is to not challenge him in public anyway.

The second maneuver is Gennady Gerasimov's statement that the Malta Meeting will dump the Cold War to the bottom of the Mediterranean. This is their typical "raise expectations" maneuver.

In each of the other summits, the Soviets spoke publicly of great achievements, and then tried to hold the US responsible for not reaching those levels. In Moscow, when Gerasimov and I were briefing after one of the sessions, Gerasimov claimed that we had reached agreement of bomber accounting rules and at least an understanding on sea-launched cruise missiles. Neither of these was true. I challenged him immediately. And later in the evening, we had to hold a special briefing to knock down the false euphoria of these statements.

In Malta, the nature of the meeting is much different than past summits, but the techniques may be the same. I remember the lessons I learned as President Reagan walked through Red Square. Gorbachev and Reagan walked around the Square moving from one set of "private citizens" to another. I began to recognize that many of the citizens were actually our drivers from the hotel motorpool, no doubt KGB.

It also became apparent that each cluster of people was coached to ask a set of questions on a specific issue that had been discussed in the meetings only moments before. One group asked about the joint space mission to Mars, which we had declined; another protested SDI; etc. The lesson here is that every move the Soviets make at these affairs, no matter how pleasurable or informal, are pre-planned and staged. Already, the Soviets are moving a group of "celebrity briefers," no doubt such people as Georgi Arbatov and Vladimir Posner, to hold further briefings in the International Press Center in Malta.

Situation in Panama

THE WHITE HOUSE, SUNDAY DECEMBER 17, 1989. I go to the White House to pick up a ring I had purchased for my son, Brad, for Christmas, which I had left in my desk. While there, Roman calls about a Marine killed in Panama. He says the President is holding a meeting in the Situation Room at 2:20 p.m. to discuss it. I leave the White House to attend a Nancy Reynolds Christmas party. I meet Cheney coming out, and I'm going it. So I soon head back to the White House.

First I go to the bathroom, and as I'm coming out, I meet Scowcroft, Gates, Cheney, Powell, and the Joint Chiefs of Staff operations officer, General Kelly, going to the residence. I fall in line.

In the basement, Hugh Sidey, *Time* magazine, sees us and calls out, "Hello, working on Sunday, huh?" I worry that we're exposed. On the other hand, Sidey was a close friend of the President and had obviously been in the residence for a visit. I figured that meeting had to have been arranged by the President, and he must not have worried about one meeting the other.

The President greets our group at the elevator and invites us to his office. General Kelly sets up his charts that describe the situation in Panama, where the Marine was killed.

General Powell lays out a plan for invading Panama and capturing General Manuel Noriega, President of the country. He covers all of several possible locations where Noriega could be. Neutralize the Panamanian Defense Forces. Get the new government of Endara and Ford to step in. "For a few days, you're going to own Panama. We have to keep it running till the new guys take over."

"Can't we take Noriega out surgically, without neutralizing the PDF?"

"We could, but our chances of success go down. The PDF could aid Noriega. They could kill Americans. The right way is to do it all," General Powell says.

The President is worried, but obviously amenable.

Secretary Baker emphasizes Endara/Ford rule. He describes cables to the Allies saying that Noriega's public declaration of war against the United States is unacceptable.

I summarize the President's press conference statement of December 16, when he says, "He (Noriega) is an indicted narcotics dealer, and he ought to get out . . . He single-handedly aborted the free will of the Panamanian people, the will being expressed in open and free elections."

"When could you go?" the President asked.

"We need forty-eight hours," Powell says. "During the night. 1:00 or 2:00 a.m. Wednesday morning."

"Well, let's do it," the President says. "Looking a bit embarrassed, thinking of the historic significance, he sits up slightly and says more formally, "I believe we do it. What are the steps to be taken?"

Baker: "I'll send cables tonight. Can you write up guidance and get it to Margaret Tutwiler (State) and Pete Williams (Defense)?"

"Yes," I say.

I go back to my office and call my neighbor to let Brad and Courtney into my home for a 4:00 p.m. Christmas party. It's 4:00 p.m. now. I take another thirty minutes to write the guidance on Panama, and call Roman and Pete Williams. At 5:00 p.m. I'm home for Christmas with my son and daughter. We have dinner at Bilbo Baggins, and the kids think their leather jackets are awesome.

The Panama Invasion

WASHINGTON, DC, TUESDAY DECEMBER 19, 1989. The invasion is set for 1:00 a.m. At 3:00 in the afternoon, I am smoking a cigar in the Briefing Room with reporters and photo dogs. Natalie, my secretary, appears in the doorway, asks if I could get out. In the hall, she says the President wants me.

I enter the Oval to find the Panama group, plus Bill Webster of CIA, and Thornburg, the Attorney General.

The Panama Group is meeting after a Bush/Cheney meeting on the role of the military in the drug war, which was set up as a cover for the real 3:00 meeting on Panama.

President Bush called me to the Oval Office on Monday to ask about bringing General Maxwell Thurman, commander of our base in Panama, to Washington on Wednesday as cover for the Tuesday night operation in Panama.

I advise against it. "Not necessary," I say. "Probably just arouse suspicion and start reporters to digging." The President agrees and abandons the idea.

The President is going through the Scowcroft time line for invasion: H hour is 1:00 a.m.; H-7 is 6:00 p.m. the evening before. The first item is for the President to call Congressional leadership.

All assignments made, the President wished Colin Powell good luck. Colin says all plans are going well, except for twenty airplanes from Ft. Bragg. Some of them are iced up. De-icing is underway.

At 7:00 p.m. Brit Hume, ABC; Jim Miklaszewski, NBC; and Wyatt Andrews, CBS come to my office. They say that NBC reports C-130s landing every ten minutes in Panama. Scowcroft says impossible.

The reporters ask me directly about an invasion. "I won't

comment on operations," I say. "I'm denying nothing. I won't rule anything in or out."

Wyatt Andrews quips, "It's not preposterous." We all laugh, remembering that the night before President Reagan invaded Grenada, Acting Press Secretary Larry Speakes asked the NSC Advisor John Poindexter if it was true, and he said, "Preposterous." Larry tells the press, "Preposterous." Within a few hours, we had invaded and US students were kissing American soil.

"I deny nothing," I say. "I'll call you if anything happens." They are suspicious, but they know I'm involved, and I won't be left out of the loop. The big fear with Speakes was that he wouldn't know. He didn't know about Grenada.

(The press all know that national security advisors prevaricate about everything. First, they have all the secrets; second, they trust no one; and third, they don't know how to tell the press nothing.)

The Network correspondents indicate they might not leave the White House that evening. I say fine. None of them have had enough to report. I pull the curtains in my office so the press can't see in, I turn off the lights to make the casual observer think I've gone home, and then go to Scowcroft's office. The General, Sununu, and Gates are there, discussing the situation. Everyone was quiet, just waiting. Scowcroft says the plan is going well. The NBC report must be simulated. I check with the Situation Room. They've had no wire service reports.

The President spends the rest of the day making phone calls. He goes to a Christmas party at 6:30. I'd asked the President where he would be tonight. "I'll be in the Oval by 12:30," he said.

I go to my office, lay down on the couch, with severe pains in my stomach from eating solid food. (I had lost fifty-five pounds on an all liquid diet, but had stopped it just days before. Now I wished I had some of those fifty-five pounds back.)

At 8:00 p.m. it's dark. I see Maureen Dowd and Andy Rosenthal of the *New York Times* walk up the driveway. They stop to peer in my window, then go to the Briefing Room, then come back past me to peer in General Scowcroft's window. Finally, they leave. I try to sleep but can't. The cleaning lady bangs on my door at 9:00 p.m.; it's locked, and she goes to get a guard. I stick my head out.

"Sorry," she says.

At 10:30, I get up. I call Roman and Natalie at home, to come in. They have standing orders to come in if I call, without asking any questions. I promise to never do it without great reason.

Our plan is for a 12:00 midnight call out to the press corps and a 1:00 briefing. I want to brief as soon as shots start flying in Panama. I know that television cameras are in Panama, waiting at key locations like the airport and the presidential palace.

At 7:00 I had gone to the Roosevelt Room, just two steps across the hall from my office, to write a brief statement for announcing the invasion at 1:00 a.m. I like the Roosevelt Room because it is quiet, and in the middle of key offices, like Oval, Chief of Staff, VP, NSC Advisor, and Press Secretary. Also, Teddy Roosevelt's Nobel Peace Prize sits on the mantle over the fireplace. I think it's good to plan a war with the peace prize looking over your shoulder.

The Deputies group, which generally consists of the Deputy Secretaries of Defense, State, Treasury, CIA, NSC, etc., monitors all crisis situations and makes sure information is being circulated from all foreign points to the right decision makers in the government. These are the people who actually know what's happening.

The Deputies group is writing the official press statement, but I wanted my own in case theirs was too bureaucratic.

At 11:00 p.m. Bernard Aronson, Assistant Secretary of State for Latin America, has also written a statement for the President at 1:00 a.m. It looks good, but I argue with the President going out at 1:00 to make a statement. Aronson thinks the only image people should see is Bush.

"This is the biggest military operation since Vietnam," he said. "People should wake up to an image of the President telling them what's happening." I agree with his theory, but not his technique.

I go to Scowcroft's office, to tell them of Bernard's plan. They agree with me, however. Bernie comes in, argues for the President.

"I don't believe the President should appear at 1:00 a.m. That puts him in an operational role. If something goes wrong, then he has to go out and explain. All we'll have done is wrap the President in a disaster," I said. Gates, Scowcroft, and Sununu agreed. The Deputies group started to draft a new statement for me.

Later, I found out that Aronson and the NSC staff had worked the entire weekend of December 17 on a plan of action for Panama. They were kept in the dark about the President's plan. On Tuesday they found they had been totally out of the planning. Aronson was being rejected everywhere, and was not a happy camper. But he was acting in a vacuum.

At 12:00 a.m. Sununu is getting nervous. I tell him that a 1:00 press announcement might give Noriega advance notice of the invasion. "What if Noriega is propped up in bed with his mistress and sees me come on CNN to announce an invasion," I say. "Let's wait till there's no question but that he knows. (At about 12:45, telephone intercepts showed that Noriega already knew the invasion was set for 1:00 a.m. He was ready. I would note that, indeed, he was at his mistress's house that evening, but not when the first bombs began to fall at 1:00 a.m.)

At 12:00 the President comes in, dressed in suit pants, shirt and tie, dark sweater, hair messed up like he just woke up. I go to the Oval Study, and he is making calls. He is angry about the Foley call. Foley said a woman *NY Times* reporter called him at 6:00 to say the Pentagon pool had been taken to Panama. The President is furious. I don't know anything about their pool. Nothing has appeared on the wire services. No reporters have called me.

The Vice President comes in. "This is just what I was afraid of," he says. "We can't trust this pool arrangement. Why couldn't they take reporters from Panama—why from the US? I say nothing. Sununu asks how this could happen. I know better than to argue with this media lynch crowd.

"Everything is fine," I say. Nothing has been said publicly. However, CNN reported that the White House press corps had been summoned to the White House for a briefing.

"How did that happen?" Sununu asked.

"We had to call them at home ahead of time in order to get them here by 1:00 a.m. Remember, they've been asleep in Rockville or some such place," I say. "Don't worry, everything is fine."

I go to the Situation Room and go over the press statement with the Deputies group at midnight. Gates leaves to visit the President in his study. I make marginal notes on the statement. CIA reports radio intercepts that Noriega knew of the 1:00 a.m. invasion time. Defense Department believes he is in Cologne, trying to get back to Panama City. Four fake motorcades are spotted. Fake helicopter movements are spotted. I race up to the study at 1:30 a.m.

"Mr. President, I think it's time to make the announcement."

"OK," he says. "Do you have to take questions?"

"Just a few," I say. "Don't worry, I won't give out any bad information."

"Go ahead," he says. "We'll be watching." He gave me a small grin. It was the first and last for days.

The President was in a deadly serious mood. No chatter. No teasing. But at least he was sitting up in his chair. At 12:30, he had been slumped in his pissed-off position, as Richard Cramer so well describes in his book, *What It Takes*. I go to my office. My staff is gathered.

"We're ready to unlock the doors," I say. "Remember, everything you say will be noted, and used. Don't comment on staff movements or any reports from Panama. Call the briefing, meaning a member of my staff picks up the intercom microphone and announces to the Briefing Room that Mr. Fitzwater's briefing will begin in two minutes."

I walked out nervous, a good sign, afraid I would stumble over the words. Statements always scared me. The Q and A was better. My head was up, I was in charge, I knew what I wanted to say and not say.

The last question was Helen's [Helen Thomas, UPI]. I was angry at her insistence at the time, but later I would be glad she asked the question. "So," she said, "your objective is to get Noriega?"

"That's an objective," I said, and walked out, never looking back.

Days later, with Noriega still not captured, I would remind the press of that comment. "Only an objective," I would say.

After the briefing, I went back to the Study. The President was on the phone. Scowcroft and Sununu said "good job." I felt good and went to the Situation Room to join the Deputies meeting. All the military reports were good—but Noriega had not been located. I remembered Colin Powell's final words to the President on December 17, "Things can get messy. We have a lot of twenty-year-olds with guns. But the military will do well. It's the law-and-order phase that will be difficult. And we may be chasing Noriega for days or weeks. But we'll get him." Colin's scenario was almost perfect. We did get him.

The President went to bed at 4:00 a.m., got up two hours later, and gave a speech to the nation from the Oval Office at 7:00 a.m. He began by saying: "Fellow citizens, last night I ordered US military forces to Panama. No President takes such action lightly. This morning, I want to tell you what I did and why I did it." George H.W. Bush knew how to govern.

I followed up with another tick-tock briefing late in the morning, and laid out for the press corps all the President's activities in the days preceding the invasion.

Author's Note: Bush's Address on his decision to use force in Panama, as well as my briefing, are available in the Presidential Papers for December 21, 1989, which may be found at many libraries, or by searching online.

The Rafsanjani Call

WASHINGTON, DC, FEBRUARY 1990. I was sound asleep when the President called, I think about 9:00 p.m. I answered groggily. The moment I heard the President's voice, I sat up and squinted, trying to see the clock, shake the sleep from my eyes, and concentrate on his words. He said something about a situation that requires we issue a press release related to Iran. Can I issue it?

"Yes," I replied.

"Can you come in?" he asked.

"Yes," I replied.

Then he must have detected that I was a little fuzzy. "Well, maybe you can handle it from home," he said.

The word "Iran" tripped my alert wire. "No," I said, "I'll be there."

We hung up. I changed clothes, putting on a tie and my Harris Tweed jacket in case I had to go on camera. I had long since learned that every emergency in my business could end with a press briefing or an on-camera statement.

I raced to the White House through the empty streets of Alexandria. Nine o'clock was a little late for a cigar, but I lit one anyway.

Richard Haass of the NSC staff met me in the basement, just outside the Situation Room. "Go on up to the residence. Scowcroft is there. I'll be in the Situation Room." (That meant to me that there was a national security problem, probably in the Middle East because that was Haass' specialty. Most likely some military problem, like a terrorist attack on Americans, an Iranian attack on a US ship, or something like that requiring a statement by the US.)

"OK." I went to my office, shed my jacket, grabbed a note pad, and headed for the residence.

I walked into the President's study, and it was dark. Only a desk lamp was on. The President was slouched at his desk, wearing a red sweater, black pin-striped suit pants, wing tips, and an open collar white shirt. He looked like he had been at a social function, probably called to the phone, got involved in the conversation while shedding his coat and tie. He also had on a white windbreaker with Ivan Lendl's logo on the back (one of many gifts from sports figures).

General Scowcroft was standing in front of the desk, wearing a dark business suit, but saying nothing. I thought it very strange to be standing in a darkened room, but clearly they had brought the problem into the room and didn't want to disturb the first lady.

The President looked up, no greeting, and said, "Marlin, I had a call from Rafsanjani" (Iranian President Akbar Hashemi Rafsanjani). He shoved a yellow legal pad across the desk for me to look at, then took off the top page and handed it to me. A handwritten statement in blue ink and his distinctive left-handed script was in the center of the page. It amounted to six or seven lines, written large enough to take up the full legal-sized page. Interesting to me because that's the way Helen Thomas takes notes during interviews: just a few lines, sometimes just a few words, per page. Later in the evening, the President types the sentences on plain paper for me to take with me.

The first sentence says we welcome something. I remark as I read that "welcome" may be too much.

It appeared to me that Rafsanjani, President of Iran, had called the President to say he was going to release some US hostages at 10:15 that night, and he wanted a statement by the President welcoming the release at exactly the same time. He had even dictated the statement.

I suggested "welcome" is too much. "Are you going to mention hostages?" I added.

"No," he said.

"Did you talk about hostages?" I asked.

"Yes."

"I recommend you take out 'welcome.' This looks a little too eager, especially if we can't repeat our request for a hostage release."

The President: "Go ahead, edit. This isn't cast in stone."

I edit out "welcome." Later, at his typewriter, he puts it back.

I decided to listen only. This was not an editing session. Scowcroft was trying to confirm the 9:15 phone call.

"The suspicious thing is, the translation didn't leave any time to get new language from Rafsanjani," the President said. "I talked. He translated. Then immediately says, 'Rafsanjani said . . .' But he didn't give him time to say it."

Then I realized the President and Scowcroft thought the call was probably a hoax, but they didn't want to dismiss it if it were real. Hostages were at stake. And we didn't have many ways to check authenticity.

At 10:30, after the scheduled release and joint statements, the President says, "Does Rafsanjani speak or understand English? That might explain it."

Scowcroft checked with the Situation Room. The "Sit" Room called back after checking with their Iran expert, "Rafsanjani speaks not a word of English."

The President looked crestfallen. He repeated for Scowcroft and me, "Not a word."

There were long pauses after every sentence, as the President and Scowcroft considered their options, or searched their minds for possible ways to check out this call.

Scowcroft said, "We called back the number left by the caller. Someone answered and asked for an interpreter. Then he hung up." Scowcroft added, "We called back. The person who answered asked when you had called. We said 'just minutes ago.' He left the phone and never came back. Very strange."

The President wondered aloud, "Who could get through to Rafsanjani?"

It was quiet. No one talked. There's sort of antiquated silence, like walking into a museum at night, where nothing has moved in a hundred years. A grandfather clock ticked in the study, one that I had never noticed before. It sounded like my grandfather's upright clock in his farmhouse in Kansas, a warm and reassuring feeling. As a boy, I would play marbles with Grandpa Bob until he fell asleep. Then I would listen to the clock and not make a sound that would wake him up.

The President: "How about de Cuellar at the UN?" (UN Secretary-General Javier Perez de Cuellar, of Peru)

The President picked up the phone, called de Cuellar.

"Hello, Javier, I need your help," the President said. "I had a call from Rafsanjani earlier tonight. He said he wanted better relations, and a possible hostage release Wednesday or Thursday. But we can't confirm the call.

"He said he wanted a public statement released in one hour, not tomorrow. It had to be tonight.

"He said Foreign Minister Velayati (Ali Akbar Velayati) was coming to the UN soon and could meet with me. Is that true?"

"Yes," de Cuellar said.

"Could you help us out on this?"

[Secretary-General] de Cuellar offers to have his experts make inquiries, and he will call Velayati.

The President feels a little better. At least Velayati is coming to the UN. Javier de Cuellar is someone he trusts.

More silence.

Scowcroft: "This doesn't fit. Too many questions."

The President: "Yes. First, the interpreter problem. Second, the hang up on our call back. Third, this demand for an immediate public statement."

More silence. *Tick Tock, Tick Tock.*

"Damn," the President said, "I just hate to miss an opportunity . . . to get the hostages out. I'd hate to have them say tomorrow, 'We gave Bush a chance and he wouldn't put out a statement.'"

More silence.

I sat without moving, thinking of my last time in this room, Sunday December 17, planning the Panama invasion. Big decisions are made in this room. Tonight, Millie, the Bush spaniel slept curled on the couch beside me, oblivious.

Scowcroft: "The National Security Agency says it will get a real-time report if Iran radio broadcasts their statement."

"It's now thirty minutes past the deadline," I volunteer. Both sides were to issue a statement at 10:15 p.m.

The President: "Let's ask Webster (Bill Webster, Director of CIA) if he has any ideas."

The President places the call. "Bill . . . (President repeats story). Can you check any of this?"

Webster calls back in a few minutes, reports that Rafsanjani neither speaks nor understands English. The phone numbers our caller gave for call back are not official numbers."

The President asks: "Where do you get these call back numbers?"

Scowcroft: "From State." But he checks and discovers the numbers were given by the caller. Another suspicious item.

It's 11:15 p.m., two hours after the original call; one hour after the mutually agreed time to release statements.

"Well," the President says, "let's shut her down." A phrase from his oil drilling days, when he had started to drill with such enthusiasm and optimism, and then realizing there was no oil, and they might as well "shut her down."

We speculated that it could be that someone in Iran was trying to set Rafsanjani up for a fall, or just trying to make it look like Rafsanjani was dealing with the US.

The President: "We should alert Rafsanjani if that's true."

Scowcroft: "de Cuellar's inquiry of Velayati will do that. If it's real, Velayati will know. If not, he'll know it was a set up."

The President: "That has to do it. Hell, we can't get through to Rafsanjani anyway. Marlin, take this statement."

The President typed it on blue five-by-seven notebook paper. "I'll call you to release it."

"OK," I said. "Good night, Mr. President."

Note: This story centers around the Americans held hostage in Lebanon by clandestine elements of Hezbollah. Rafsanjani was elected President of Iran on July 28, 1989.

Peggy Say

THE WHITE HOUSE, MARCH 16, 1990. It's the five-year anniversary of Terry Anderson, Associated Press reporter, being taken hostage by Hezbollah in Lebanon. His sister, Peggy Say, is holding a rally in Lafayette Square, across from the White House at 12:00. The President is not going.

At 9:30 a.m., the President decides to go see the cherry blossoms. I can't believe it. I can hear Helen [Thomas, UPI] screaming: "How can you go to the tidal basin but not to the hostage rally?"

I go into the Oval. Sununu joins me. He says to the President, "Some are concerned that you should not go to the tidal basin."

The President grows stern. Frowns. Sets his hands on his desk. Turns to me, says, "I will not change my plan. There is no relation between the two. The rally is not till 12:00. I've already delayed going to Camp David, and lunch with Quayle. I won't change."

"OK," I say, somewhat sheepishly, and leave.

The President accepts the St. Patrick's Day shamrock in the Rose Garden, then returns to the Oval.

"OK," the President says to me, "Let it never be said I won't reconsider my position. Maybe I should meet with Peggy. I wanted to anyway. It's right."

The President then goes to the tidal basin as planned, but he gives a quote to all the networks filming the cherry blossoms, "I will never stop trying to get hostages out."

He meets with Peggy Say in the residence. She is very supportive. He does the right thing once again. Shows that you can talk President Bush into doing something, but it's hard to talk him out of something when his mind is made up.

Note: American journalist Terry A. Anderson, Middle East bureau chief for the Associated Press, was taken hostage by Shiite Hezbollah militants and held for six years and nine months. He was the last American hostage to be released from Lebanon, on December 4, 1991.

Dinner with Dennis

BERMUDA, GOOD FRIDAY SUMMIT, APRIL 13–14, 1990. President Bush and [UK] Prime Minister Thatcher agreed to meet in Bermuda because it is a British territory, and Mrs. Thatcher could stay on the British ship Britannia. Her husband, Dennis, didn't accompany Mrs. Thatcher on all trips, but he did on this one. Dennis had a reputation for liking a good drink and for being a down-to-earth businessman who didn't always observe all the protocols.

After the meetings, the two leaders had a departing dinner with their delegations, where both leaders gave an informal toast summarizing the achievements of the meetings.

It was a small dinner, with both delegations and several Bermuda guests and spouses, including the prime minister and his wife. I happened to be seated five chairs down from Mrs. Thatcher and President Bush, who were across the table from each other. Next to me was the wife of the Bermuda parliament's speaker of the house, a black woman of distinguished appearance and a terrific dinner companion. We had animated discussions about politics and local culture. I noticed that she seemed somewhat reserved about her dinner companion on the other side, Dennis Thatcher.

As President Bush finished his toast, and Mrs. Thatcher was about to begin hers, the speaker's wife turned to me and asked, "Do you hear that?"

"No, what?" I said.

"Dennis just told an unacceptable story; I won't stand for it."

She was raising her voice, and I was fearful that she might lose control.

"Well, we're about through," I said. "We just have the toast. Let's wait and discuss it then."

"I've never heard such a thing," she said.

"Yes, but we'll be done in a minute."

"I'm leaving," she said.

"No, please don't," I said. "Take my hand and look at me."

She took my hand, and it was a sturdy but shaking grasp.

At this point, I was afraid the President or Prime Minister could hear us. I could hear the toast ending.

I clasped her hand, with both my hands, and I held her strong enough for her to know that I would not let go, and she was not leaving. And our eyes were locked, even as tears started down her face.

"Thank you," I said, as the last words of the toast ended. And just as President Bush began to rise from his chair, so did my new friend. She stood up, said thank you to me, and walked out.

I don't know if anyone else at the table noticed, but no one ever said a word.

No New Taxes

THE WHITE HOUSE, MAY 7, 1990. The President asks about my briefing.

"All about taxes," I say.

"We're getting ready for this," he says, and pauses, swallowing hard. He can't say the words, "tax increases." But he continues, "It's going to happen."

"It will be tough," I say. "Nobody (the press) really cares about the deficit. Nobody sees the problem we're trying to solve."

"Think about it," he says. "We need to be ready."

I read his lips. They say no new taxes. I predict a poll drop of 20 points—on taxes and credibility.

Bourguiba's Brother

TUNISIA, MAY 14–17, 1990. I joined President Bush for lunch in Tunis with President Habib Bourguiba, who was president of Tunisia from 1956 to 1987. Bourguiba was known as "Father of the Country," and he claimed to be a friend of the West. As we entered his office, I noticed a credenza that was covered with pictures of President Reagan and President Bush. But our foreign affairs briefers in Washington said Bourguiba was suffering dementia and some irrational behavior. We were a little nervous. But the lunch went well, and as we walked out of the dining room, President Bush whispered to me that our host seemed fine. Then we walked across a ballroom to a special meeting room where the President was going to meet with the foreign minister.

In the middle of the big room, President Bourguiba walked up to me, grabbed my arm with some force, and began screaming at me. I froze. Both delegations froze. Then the foreign minister rushed to my side and whispered, "Don't move."

I had no intention of moving. Then the minister began talking quietly to his president, and he released my arm. As two others from the Tunisian group gently guided Mr. Bourguiba away, the minister whispered to me. "He thinks you are his estranged brother, returning to kill him."

I walked quietly away. President Bush walked on to his meeting. I returned to our staff meeting room to calm my nerves and shaking knees.

An Old Editor

ABILENE, KANSAS, JULY 25, 1990. I introduce Ronald Reagan on the front steps of Eisenhower's boyhood home in Abilene, Kansas, my hometown. Great day for me. It was Eisenhower's birthday. (President Reagan said I was his Great Communicator. We walked together through the crowd with all my relatives and boyhood friends shouting and screaming.)

I heard a familiar voice shout: "Fitzwater. Fitzwater." I look toward the rope line, and there is Bill Colvin, retired editor of the *Manhattan Mercury.* I worked my way through college on the advertising staff of the *Mercury* in Manhattan, Kansas, where Kansas State University is located. I once had a huge argument with Colvin because I had not alerted him to a campus story, even though I did not write for the *Mercury.* He called me every name in the book, and I left Manhattan after graduation without speaking to the editor.

Now, here he was twenty-five years later shouting my name. I asked President Reagan if we could stop walking for a minute. I took two steps to the rope line. Bill Colvin shook my hand and said, "You are the greatest Press Secretary in history."

I said, "Thanks, Bill," and rushed back to the President's side. Reagan loved the story.

PART III

—LIBERATION OF KUWAIT—
THE PRESIDENT AND MY DIARY

Introduction to Part Three

AT THE END of July 1990, I left Washington, DC, for my annual trip home to see my family in Abilene, Kansas. When the call came to tell me that Saddam Hussein of Iraq had invaded Kuwait and the President wanted me to return to Washington, I asked the President's location at that moment. He was holding a National Security Council meeting and afterward would be flying to Aspen, Colorado—primarily to meet with British Prime Minister Margaret Thatcher, who was speaking at the Aspen Institute. I said I would meet the President in Aspen.

I immediately booked an airplane from the closest airport in Kansas. That's the day I started keeping a diary. It was pretty basic, with abbreviations and fragments; I wanted to remember what the President said.

The Persian Gulf Crisis encompassed the operations leading to the buildup of troops, code-named "Operation Desert Shield," as well as the combat phase, "Operation Desert Storm." It all began when Iraq invaded Kuwait at two o'clock in the morning Iraqi time on August 2, 1990, (which equates to August 1 at six o'clock p.m. in Washington, DC). The President was informed of the initial signs of the Iraqi action on the evening of August 1 at approximately nine o'clock p.m. by National Security Advisor Scowcroft.

For several months, tensions had been mounting between Iraq and Kuwait. President Saddam Hussein viewed Kuwaiti and United Arab Emirates oil production as "economic warfare." Iraq accused Kuwait of stealing oil from the Rumaila oil field, located on the Iraq-Kuwait border. Saddam Hussein threatened military action. Then, after failed negotiations, it began on August 2, 1990, when Saddam Hussein launched an invasion of its neighbor Kuwait, sending 100,000 troops into the country.

President George H.W. Bush reacted immediately to freeze Iraqi assets in the US, met with his National Security Council, and left for consultations with Prime Minister Thatcher in Aspen. I began my diary of the Persian Gulf Crisis. During this phase of the crisis, known as Operation Desert Shield, President Bush formed a coalition of thirty-five nations contributing to an ultimate invasion force of over 500,000 troops, for the defense of Saudi Arabia and against Saddam's "million-man army."

On January 16, 1991, Operation Desert Storm was launched with US air strikes on military targets in Iraq and Baghdad. The ground war started with troop movements on February 24, 1991, as the US-led coalition of ground forces invaded Iraq and Kuwait.

The war ended approximately one hundred hours after the launch of the ground forces—in the White House, on the night of February 27, 1991. And one day after that, on February 28, 1991, President Bush announced a cease-fire. Kuwait had been liberated. The President began bringing troops home within days.

Part III contains excerpts from eight diary books written by me while press secretary during the Persian Gulf War. I continued writing following the war, sometimes in the form of diary entries and sometimes as recollections. There are sometimes gaps in the sequence because I couldn't write every day. And sometimes there are non-war events, but they are all a part of the White House panorama during the Gulf War. In addition to a select number of my diary entries, we've interspersed presidential speeches and statements that highlight the significance of the fast-developing events, and show the tenacity of President Bush in presenting the war to the American people.

Phase I:

—The Invasion of Kuwait —

Operation Desert Shield

Wednesday August 1, 1990
The White House
The White House issues its first official statement, the evening of August 1:

The United States strongly condemns the Iraqi military invasion of Kuwait and calls for the immediate and unconditional withdrawal of all Iraqi forces. We have conveyed this message to the Iraqi Ambassador in Washington and to the Iraqi Government through our Embassy in Baghdad. We deplore this blatant use of military aggression and violation of the United Nations (UN) Charter. Together with Kuwait, we are calling for an emergency session of the UN Security Council.

Thursday August 2, 1990

The United Nations Security Council (UNSC) Resolution 660, condemning the invasion, passes by a vote of fourteen in favor.

August 2, 1990
The President
At 8:05 a.m. on the morning of August 2, 1990, in the Cabinet Room at the White House, the 41st US President, George H.W. Bush, delivered to the American people his first comments on the Iraqi invasion of Kuwait:

The President: Let me make a brief statement here about recent events. The United States strongly condemns the Iraqi military invasion of Kuwait. We call for the immediate and unconditional withdrawal of all the Iraqi forces. There is no place for this sort of naked aggression in today's world, and I've taken a number of steps to indicate the deep concern that I feel over the events that have taken place.

Last night I instructed our Ambassador of the United Nations, Tom Pickering, to work with Kuwait in convening an emergency meeting of the Security Council. It was convened, and I am grateful for that quick, overwhelming vote condemning the Iraqi action and calling for immediate and unconditional withdrawal. Tom Pickering will be here in a bit, and we are contemplating with him further United Nations action.

Second, consistent with my authority under the International Emergency Economic Powers Act, I've signed an Executive order [EO 12723] early this morning freezing Iraqi assets. That's to ensure that those assets are not interfered with by the legitimate authority that is now occupying Kuwait. We call upon other governments to take similar action.

Third, the Department of State has been in touch with governments around the world urging that they, too, condemn the Iraqi aggression and consult to determine what measures should be taken to bring an end to this totally unjustified act. It is important that the international community act together to ensure that Iraqi forces depart Kuwait immediately.

Needless to say, we view the situation with the utmost gravity. We remain committed to take whatever steps are necessary to defend our long-standing, vital interests in the Gulf, and I'm meeting this morning with my senior advisers here to consider all possible options available to us. I've talked to Secretary [of State] Baker just now; General Scowcroft [Assistant to the President for National Security Affairs] and I were on the phone with him. And after this meeting, I will proceed to deliver a long-standing speech. I will have consultations—short ones—there in Aspen with [UK] Prime Minister Thatcher, and I will be returning home this evening, and I'll be here in Washington tomorrow.

AUGUST 2, 1990
MY DIARY

I joined the President at the Aspen, Colorado, airport at noon on Thursday August 2, 1990. He looked good stepping off the G-20 aircraft, preoccupied, but smiling and walking tall, and knowing from a thousand plane trips before that well-wishers, friends, and press were ready to record that first glimpse of the President of the United

States, George Herbert Walker Bush. I walked toward him, as if for instructions.

He put his hands on my shoulders. "What's new?" he asked.

"Everything's fine," I said.

His gesture of recognition signaled to the press that I had a special relationship. He did it on purpose, knowing instinctively how those things count. My comment was a signal too—to let him know that I was a friend who would be at his side no matter what happened in the days ahead.

We went by limo to the Catto Ranch, (Chalet of Henry Catto, Ambassador to Great Britain) secluded in the Rocky Mountains near Aspen, past the Sorry Creek Town that had T-shirts that said, "George Bush and Margaret Thatcher slept near here." (They didn't of course.) The President got on his limo public address system and greeted the roadside crowd, some of whom were giving us the finger. For those who emerged from the trailer park next to the tavern, this was probably a very warm and traditional greeting, like "How the f__ are you, George?" We laughed.

At Catto, the President immediately went to his bedroom, in the back of the house, and asked about his phone call to King Fahd of Saudi Arabia. Brent Scowcroft, National Security Advisor, who was traveling with the President, had placed the call and said, "It's coming." The President paced the small room, picking up objects, replacing them, and practicing in his mind the conversation to come. He was already starting to build an alliance. Calling on his friends: King Fahd, [Egyptian President] Hosni Mubarak, King Hussein [of Jordan], the Amir of Kuwait, and others. He referenced a last meeting with all of them—in the Palace in Riyadh, on the Sultan's yacht in the Bay of Oman, applying suntan lotion to King Hussein's forehead before boating in the Gulf of Aqaba, getting Hosni a hot dog at the Orioles game, watching Prince Bandar crawl into the cockpit of a US built F-16 in the desert of Saudi Arabia. He knew these men. And he was about to offer help.

In offering, he was also asking. In his mind, he knew he would have to stop Saddam Hussein, and he would build the greatest alliance since World War II in just five days' time. Today was the first.

(The coalition building actually lasted nearly six months.)

Margaret Thatcher arrived at the Catto ranch just as the President was hanging up with King Fahd. He rushed out to the driveway as she emerged from her limo. She was there to give a previously scheduled speech at the Aspen Institute.

AUGUST 2, 1990
THE PRESIDENT
Excerpt from remarks following a meeting with UK Pime Minister Margaret Thatcher in Aspen, Colorado:

The President: Let me first welcome Prime Minister Thatcher back to the United States. It's a very timely visit, and as you can well imagine, we have been exchanging views on the Iraq-Kuwait situation. Not surprisingly, I find myself very much in accord with the view of the Prime Minister. I reported to her on contacts that I've had since I left Washington: personal contacts with King Hussein; Mr. Mubarak of Egypt, President Mubarak; President Saleh of Yemen—a long conversation just now. I can tell you that Jim Baker has been in close touch with the Soviet leadership, and indeed, the last plan was for him to stop in Moscow on his way back here.

We are concerned about the situation, but I find that Prime Minister Thatcher and I are looking at it on exactly the same wavelength: concerned about this naked aggression, condemning it and hoping that a peaceful solution will be found that will result in the restoration of the Kuwaiti leaders to their rightful place and, prior to that, a withdrawal of Iraqi forces.

AUGUST 2, 1991
MY DIARY

Aspen, Colorado. The President meets with Prime Minister Thatcher in the living room of the Catto chalet. "No small country will ever be safe if we allow him to succeed," she said. "And Hussein will never stop with Kuwait. We must act together—all of us."

The President said this aggression could not stand. One country should not be allowed to invade another without provocation.

AUGUST 2, 1990
THE WHITE HOUSE
Statement by Press Secretary Fitzwater:

President Bush and King Fahd of Saudi Arabia discussed the Iraq attack on Kuwait in a telephone call at approximately 4:45 p.m. MDT. The two leaders spoke for nearly one-half hour. They agreed that the attack on Kuwait was absolutely unacceptable, and they discussed possible options for dealing with the situation. President Bush described the conversations he had earlier in the day with the other Arab leaders and with Prime Minister Thatcher. The President emphasized the United States demand for the immediate and unconditional withdrawal of Iraqi forces.

FRIDAY AUGUST 3, 1990
MY DIARY

Washington, DC. The President convenes a National Security Council meeting in the Cabinet Room. General Scowcroft says, "We must not allow this to succeed."

The President says the invasion "is absolutely unacceptable."

Judge William Webster, CIA Director, says Iraq forces are within eight miles of Saudi Arabia.

General Powell says, "We need some US forces in Saudi Arabia as a signal that an invasion of Saudi Arabia means a conflict with the United States."

Richard Darman, Director of the Office of Management and Budget, and always worried about costs, asks, "Are we prepared to fight to back that up?"

The President responds, "I haven't heard the military options that would allow such a decision." The President was careful not to declare a course of action at this first meeting. He wanted to hear independent views. In my view, however, the President had decided to liberate Kuwait at his meeting the first day with Margaret Thatcher. "This will not stand" was on the tip of his tongue. I later asked him if, indeed, he was convinced on that first day that we would have to invade Kuwait, and he said, "Yes."

Author's Note: In Colorado, Mrs. Thatcher commented to the

President, after he had surveyed world leaders to consider whether or not they would be supportive of an Allied response, "We must not go wobbly, George."

The President said, "I like that phrase." The President repeated it in his press conference after the meeting, and some reporters wrongly interpreted it as Thatcher telling Bush not to go wobbly. In fact, she said "we." And the President used the phrase often.

A military briefing on options was set for Sunday at Camp David.

AUGUST 3, 1990
THE PRESIDENT
President George H. W. Bush announces the deployment of US Navy ships to the Persian Gulf. In his address to Congress, the President declares a national emergency and prohibitions against Iraq:

To the Congress of the United States,

Pursuant to section 204(b) of the International Emergency Economic Powers Act, 50 USC. section 1703(b), and section 201 of the National Emergencies Act USC. section 1621, I hereby report that I have exercised my statutory authority to declare a national emergency and to issue two Executive orders that:

— prohibit exports and imports of goods and services between the United States and Iraq and the purchase of Iraqi goods by US persons for sale in third countries;

— prohibit transactions related to travel to or from Iraq, except for transactions necessary for journalistic travel or prompt departure from Iraq;

— prohibit transactions related to transportation

to or from Iraq, or the use of vessels or air-craft registered in Iraq by US persons;

— prohibit the performance of any contract in support of Government of Iraq projects;

— ban all extensions of credit and loans by US persons to the Government of Iraq;

— block all property of the Government of Iraq now or hereafter located in the United States or in the possession or control of US persons, including their foreign branches, and

— prohibit all transfers or other transactions involving assets belonging to the Government of Kuwait now or hereafter located in the United States or in the possession or control of US persons, including their foreign branches.

The Secretary of the Treasury is authorized to issue regulations implementing these prohibi-tions. These two orders were effective 5:00 a.m. EDT, August 2, 1990.

I am enclosing a copy of each Executive order that I have issued making these declarations and exercising these authorities.

I have authorized these measures in response to the Iraqi invasion of Kuwait, which clearly constitutes an act of aggression and a flagrant violation of international law. This action is in clear violation of the national sovereign-ty and independence of Kuwait and the Charter of the United Nations. It threatens the entire structure of peaceful relations among nations in this critical region. It constitutes an unusual and extraordinary threat to the national security, foreign policy, and economy of the United States.

The measures we are taking to block Iraqi assets will have the effect of expressing our outrage at Iraq's actions, and will prevent that government from drawing on monies and properties within US control to support its campaign of military aggression against a neighboring state. Our ban on exports to Iraq will prevent the Iraqi government from profiting from the receipt of US goods and technology. Our ban on imports, while not preventing sales or Iraqi oil to third countries, denies Iraq access to the lucrative US market for its most important product.

At the same time, in order to protect the property of the legitimate Government of Kuwait from possible seizure, diversion, or misuse by Iraq, and with the approval of the Kuwaiti government, we are blocking Kuwaiti assets within the jurisdiction of the United States or in the possession or control of US persons.

We are calling upon our friends and allies, and all members of the world community who share our interest in the peaceful resolution of international disputes, to join us in similar actions against Iraq and for the protection of Kuwait.

George Bush
The White House
August 3, 1990

AUGUST 3, 1990
THE PRESIDENT

Excerpt from remarks on the Iraqi invasion of Kuwait, made from the South Lawn of the White House:

The President: I listened to Marlin's briefing, and I know most of your questions have been handled. And I don't intend to have a major question and answer period here; but I wanted you to know that first off, we view this situation with gravity. We view it as a matter of grave concern to this country, and internationally as well. What Iraq has done violates every norm of international law.

I have been meeting this morning with my top security experts from the defense side, the economic side; and I'll have another such meeting tomorrow at Camp David. I've been talking to some of the world leaders, and one of the reasons for the delay is I've just hung up from talking again to Margaret Thatcher, informing me of steps that the United Kingdom has taken. We are moving with them and many other countries in terms of how we view these international sanctions—tightening that up along the way.

I talked also to another staunch friend of the United States just a few minutes ago: President Özal of Turkey. Turkey, as you know, is in a very strategic location of geographical importance—importance as a steadfast member of NATO. I think it's fair to say that President Özal and I look at this matter with the same sense of urgency and concern.

So, we're following it closely. We've got many diplomatic channels open. I will be making several other calls to world leaders before I go to bed tonight, and I expect over the weekend. But before I left here, I wanted to make very clear to everybody how strongly I feel about the nature of this uncalled for invasion and our determination to see the matter resolved.

SATURDAY AUGUST 4, 1990
MY DIARY

The NSC meets in the Laurel conference room [Laurel Lodge, Camp David] on military options. The President wants to intervene with Saudi support. But there is no invitation from them yet. His Friday phone call to King Fahd was reassuring, but he didn't ask for help. He wants a few days for the Arab world to absorb their situation. Prince Bandar, the Saudi Ambassador to the US, called the White House and the Pentagon for a briefing as soon as possible. He wants US ground forces, but Saudi ground forces may not be forthcoming. This tends to reinforce the idea that under the Arab gowns there is no fight.

General Schwarzkopf lays out a ground attack from Saudi Arabian soil involving 100,000 troops, 500 tanks, many divisions, a reserve call up, AWAC planes, bombs, tactical aircraft—all capable of driving Iraq out of Kuwait. He suggested it would take seven to twelve months minimum.

General Powell says we must put enough US force, men and planes, on the ground in Iraq to let Saddam know that an attack on Saudi is an attack on the US.

Defense Secretary Dick Cheney said yes, but we must be prepared for total war, lasting months, costing billions of dollars. All agree. Cheney says our objective is to drive Iraq out of Kuwait, and overthrow Saddam Hussein. If no overthrow, he still will have scared Kuwait into submission, effectively controlling OPEC and the Persian Gulf.

The President says, "These guys aren't twenty-five feet tall. They have never been attacked from the air before."

Sununu wonders about Mecca, whether Iraq might want control of religious shrines.

Cheney says, "We aren't going to bomb Mecca."

All agree we can't act without the Saudis. We need their bases, support, and their checkbook to pay for it.

Webster leaves the room at 9:45 a.m., makes a call to CIA, returns; reports Bandar says Turkey foreign minister will say Turkey won't shut off the oil. Turkish Prime Minister Özal told the President he would. Bandar says they are playing good cop/bad cop. The President is concerned about all this uncertainty and possible deception. He considers another call to King Fahd, but instead sends Secretary of Defense Cheney on a personal mission to Saudi Arabia to meet with King Fahd, to find out exactly where they stand.

Another meeting is set for Sunday night in the White House at 7:00 p.m. to review a CIA covert plan.

SUNDAY AUGUST 5, 1990
THE PRESIDENT
In this exchange with reporters on the South Lawn of the White House, President Bush said, "This will not stand," This was his declaration of war, and he repeated it many times.

"THIS WILL NOT STAND"

Hello, everybody. I just wanted to fill you all in on the diplomatic activity that is taking place—extensive diplomatic activity around the world. I've got to go in now. I'm getting another call from President Özal of Turkey, with whom I have been in previous conversation. Yesterday I talked to him.

I talked this morning to Prime Minister Kaifu, and I applaud Japan's stance: cracking down on the imports from Iraq. I just hung up, up there in Camp David, talking with Prime Minister Mulroney. We're all in the same accord— he and President Mitterrand, with whom I've spoken, Chancellor Kohl, Margaret Thatcher. I think the alliance, the NATO alliance, is thinking exactly the same way on this. I also talked yesterday to Kuwait's Amir and gave him certain assurances.

What's emerging is nobody seems to be showing up as willing to accept anything less than total withdrawal from Kuwait of the Iraqi forces, and no puppet regime. We've been down that road, and there will be no puppet regime that will be accepted by any countries that I'm familiar with. And there seems to be a united front out there that says Iraq, having committed brutal, naked aggression, ought to get out, and that this concept of their installing some puppet—leaving behind—will not be acceptable.

So, we're pushing forward on diplomacy. Tomorrow I'll meet

here in Washington with the Secretary General of NATO. And Margaret Thatcher will be coming in here tomorrow, and I will be continuing this diplomatic effort. And I'm sure you know of the meeting I had in Camp David with some of our top military people, and I will continue that kind of consultation as well. . . .

I'm not going to discuss what we're doing in terms of moving of forces, anything of that nature. But I view it very seriously, not just that but any threat to any other countries, as well as I view very seriously our determination to reverse out this aggression. And please believe me, there are an awful lot of countries that are in total accord with what I've just said, and I salute them. They are staunch friends and allies, and we will be working with them all for collective action. This will not stand. This will not stand, this aggression against Kuwait.

AUGUST 5, 1990

Following Saddam Hussein's takeover, Iraqi foreign official Walid Saud Abdullah threatens "interests and nationals" of countries that level sanctions or take other "punitive measures" against Iraq and its new proxy government in Kuwait, stating, "These countries should not expect us to act honorably . . ."

MONDAY AUGUST 6, 1990

THE WHITE HOUSE

Statement by British Prime Minister Margaret Thatcher on UN Resolution 661 imposing mandatory sanctions against Iraq:

May I support the President of the United States in saying that the news from the United States and the strength of the vote—thirteen votes in favor of mandatory, comprehensive sanctions and no votes against—is very good. That means that it becomes law in all the countries of the world. That is extremely good. It also follows the strong support that has been given by the European countries in their condemnation of the action of Saddam Hussein in invading Kuwait. Japan also condemned strongly, and so did the Soviet Union. So, really, the world is condemning the action, and the United Nations resolution will become mandatory and mean that those sanctions must be enforceable.

I cannot remember a time when we had the world so strongly together against an action as now, and I hope that those sanctions will be properly and effectively enforced as a positive action against what we all totally and utterly condemn.

TUESDAY AUGUST 7, 1990

United States military forces arrive in Saudi Arabia. The first wave includes American and British ground forces and paratroopers, fighters, helicopters, and destroyers.

AUGUST 7, 1990
MY DIARY

President calls to ask if I could join him for dinner. "Just the two of us," he says. The first US deployment of troops to Saudi Arabia is secretly underway. Tomorrow the President will address the nation at 9:00 p.m. to announce the move [speech follows]. We are drawing a line in the sand, as General Powell had suggested.

I arrive in the residence at 6:30 p.m. for cocktails. Brent, John Sununu, Richard Haass, NSC staff, and Don Rhoads (a friend of the Bush family) are there.

The President asks my order. "I take a scotch on the rocks."

"I'll join him," the President says, "only with Vodka."

They are watching the news at 7:00 p.m. Brent excuses himself from the group. It's not clear whether I'm to stay for dinner or leave. I'm thinking maybe I confused the invitation. I edge toward the door when the President says, "Come on, Marlin, let's go eat."

We are going to the private dining room, the Family Dining Room, just across the hall from the living room on the second floor. Everything in the White House has a title. The President calls the Oval Office bathroom, Room 500.

As we cross the hall, I notice the dining table and chairs are

Chippendale, seating for ten, but set for two. One place setting is on the end of the table, and one on the side, wine and water glasses, two silver candelabras, ornately carved as if given to some past President by a foreign potentate. The crowning image of this picture is two tall waiters, standing at attention, one behind each chair. I thought I was walking on the set of TV's *Downton Abbey.*

The room is dark due to the four wall murals of colonial settlers landing at Baltimore Harbor, trading and engaging in the commercial activities of the day.

Fear struck me. How will I keep a conversation going? Somehow the historical significance of dining alone with the President, the night before the military deployment that could change post–Cold War history, didn't weigh on me. The President was a little tense, preoccupied, but still in good humor.

"This chef is great," he said, "from Maison Blanche. What are we having guys?" he said to the waiters.

"Shrimp and scallops," one said as he poured the wine.

"This wine is good, Marlin, 1989. Reminds me of the wine Don Rhoads got for Doro's wedding. God, we love that guy. But I told him, none of that champagne stuff. Go over to the White Barn and get some white wine."

Don brings back this stuff with grape leaves still floating in the bottle. Ghastly stuff.

"We can't drink this," I tell him.

"The liquor man says they sell a lot of it," Don says.

I say, "I don't care. Take it back and get something better." Don brings back Soave Bolla. Doro still talks about the cheap Soave Bollo. She should have seen the first stuff.

The President mentions the war only briefly. "I hope everything goes well tonight," he said. The first planes and troops are due into Saudi Arabia about three in the morning.

We finish dinner about 9:00 p.m. He walks me down to the medical office in the basement. He says he has a stiff neck. The nurses have taken some training on this neck thing. They're pretty good at working it out.

I remember the quiet of the medical room, like my grandfather's living room on the farm. Grandpa Bob would play marbles or checkers with my younger brother, Gary, and me, then fall asleep about 9:00 p.m. I would watch him sleep, hearing only the gentle ticking of the grandfather clock. Stillness was in the walls. And so it is in the White House at night.

I think the President invited me to dinner this night as a diversion, as a friend who would not spend the evening asking questions or talking about war. We had become very comfortable with each other, just being together, not saying much, but always supportive.

WEDNESDAY AUGUST 8, 1990
The United States launches Operation Desert Shield.

AUGUST 8, 1990
PRESIDENT BUSH
President Bush speaks to the Nation, live on nationwide radio and television, at 9:00 a.m. from the Oval Office.

"WE MUST RESIST AGGRESSION"

In the life of a nation, we're called upon to define who we are and what we believe. Sometimes these choices are not easy. But today as President, I ask for your support in a decision I've made to stand up for what's right and condemn what's wrong, all in the cause of peace.

At my direction, elements of the 82nd Airborne Division as well as key units of the United States Air Force are arriving today to take up defensive positions in Saudi Arabia. I took this action to assist the Saudi Arabian Government in the defense of its homeland. No one commits America's Armed Forces to a dangerous mission lightly, but after perhaps unparalleled international consultation and exhausting every alternative, it became necessary to take this action. Let me tell you why.

Less than a week ago, in the early morning hours of August 2d, Iraqi Armed Forces, without provocation or warning, invaded a peaceful Kuwait. Facing negligible resistance from its much smaller neighbor, Iraq's tanks stormed in blitzkrieg fashion through Kuwait in a few short hours. With more than 100,000 troops, along with tanks, artillery, and surface-to-surface missiles, Iraq now occupies Kuwait. This aggression came just hours after Saddam Hussein specifically assured numerous countries in the area that there would be no invasion. There is no justification whatsoever for this outrageous and brutal act of aggression.

A puppet regime imposed from the outside is unacceptable. The acquisition of territory by force is unacceptable. No one, friend or foe, should doubt our desire for peace; and no one should underestimate our determination to confront aggression.

Four simple principles guide our policy. First, we seek the immediate, unconditional, and complete withdrawal of all Iraqi forces from Kuwait. Second, Kuwait's legitimate government must be restored to replace the puppet regime. And third, my administration, as has been the case with every President from President Roosevelt to President Reagan, is committed to the security and stability of the Persian Gulf. And fourth, I am determined to protect the lives of American citizens abroad.

Immediately after the Iraqi invasion, I ordered an embargo of all trade with Iraq and, together with many other nations, announced sanctions that both freeze all Iraqi assets in this country and protected Kuwait's assets. The stakes are high. Iraq is already a rich and powerful country that possesses the world's second largest reserves of oil and over a million men under arms. It's the fourth largest military in the world. Our country now imports nearly half the oil it consumes and could face a major threat to its economic independence. Much of the world is even more dependent upon imported oil and is even more vulnerable to Iraqi threats.

We succeeded in the struggle for freedom in Europe because we and our allies remain stalwart. Keeping the peace in the Middle East will require no less. We're beginning a new era. This new era can be full of promise, an age of freedom, a time of peace for all peoples. But if history teaches us anything, it is that we must resist aggression or it will destroy our freedoms. Appeasement does not work. As was the case in the 1930's, we see in Saddam Hussein an aggressive dictator threatening his neighbors. Only fourteen days ago, Saddam Hussein promised his friends he would not invade Kuwait. And four days ago, he promised the world he would withdraw. And twice we have seen what his promises mean: His promises mean nothing.

In the last few days, I've spoken with political leaders from the Middle East, Europe, Asia, and the Americas; and I've met with Prime Minister Thatcher, Prime Minister Mulroney, and NATO Secretary General Woerner. And all agree that Iraq cannot be allowed to benefit from its invasion of Kuwait.

We agree that this is not an American problem or a European problem or a Middle East problem: It is the world's problem. And that's why, soon after the Iraqi invasion, the United Nations Security Council, without dissent, condemned Iraq, calling for the immediate and unconditional withdrawal of its troops from Kuwait. The Arab world, through both the Arab League and the Gulf Cooperation Council, courageously announced its opposition to Iraqi aggression. Japan, the United Kingdom, and France, and other governments around the world have imposed severe sanctions. The Soviet Union and China ended all arms sales to Iraq.

And this past Monday, the United Nations Security Council approved for the first time in twenty-three years mandatory sanctions under chapter VII of the United Nations Charter. These sanctions, now enshrined in international law, have the potential to deny Iraq the fruits of aggression while sharply limiting its ability to either import or export anything of value, especially oil.

I pledge here today that the United States will do its part to see that these sanctions are effective and to induce Iraq to withdraw without delay from Kuwait.

But we must recognize that Iraq may not stop using force to advance its ambitions. Iraq has massed an enormous war machine on the Saudi border capable of initiating hostilities with little or no additional preparation. Given the Iraqi government's history of aggression against its own citizens as well as its neighbors, to assume Iraq will not attack again would be unwise and unrealistic.

And therefore, after consulting with King Fahd, I sent Secretary of Defense Dick Cheney to discuss cooperative measures we could take. Following those meetings, the Saudi Government requested our help, and I responded to that request by ordering US air and ground forces to deploy to the Kingdom of Saudi Arabia.

Let me be clear: The sovereign independence of Saudi Arabia is of vital interest to the United States. This decision, which I shared with the congressional leadership, grows out of the long-standing friendship and security relationship between the United States and Saudi Arabia. US forces will work together with those of Saudi Arabia and other nations to preserve the integrity of Saudi Arabia and to deter further Iraqi aggression. Through their presence, as well as through training and exercises, these multinational forces will enhance the overall capability of Saudi Armed Forces to defend the Kingdom.

I want to be clear about what we are doing and why. America does not seek conflict, nor do we seek to chart the destiny of other nations. But America will stand by her friends. The mission of our troops is wholly defensive. Hopefully, they will not be needed long. They will not initiate hostilities, but they will defend themselves, the Kingdom of Saudi Arabia, and other friends in the Persian Gulf.

We are working around the clock to deter Iraqi aggression and to enforce UN sanctions. I'm continuing my conversations with world leaders. Secretary of Defense Cheney has just returned from valuable consultations with President Mubarak of Egypt and King Hassan of Morocco. Secretary of State Baker has consulted with his counterparts in many nations, including the Soviet Union, and today he heads for Europe to consult with President Özal of Turkey, a staunch friend of the United States. And he'll then consult with the NATO Foreign Ministers.

I will ask oil-producing nations to do what they can to increase production in order to minimize any impact that oil flow reductions will have on the world economy. And I will explore whether we and our allies should draw down our strategic petroleum reserves. Conservation measures can also help; Americans everywhere must do their part. And one more thing: I'm asking the oil companies to do their fair share. They should show restraint and not abuse today's uncertainties to raise prices.

Standing up for our principles will not come easy. It may take time and possibly cost a great deal. But we are asking no more of anyone than of the brave young men and women of our Armed Forces and their families. And I ask that in the churches around the country prayers be said for those who are committed to protect and defend America's interests.

Standing up for our principle is an American tradition. As it has so many times before, it may take time and tremendous effort, but most of all, it will take unity of purpose. As I've witnessed throughout my life in both war and peace, America has never wavered when her purpose is driven by principle. And on this August day, at home and abroad, I know she will do no less.

Thank you, and God bless the United States of America.

THURSDAY AUGUST 9, 1990

UNSC Resolution 662, stating Iraq's annexation of Kuwait "has no legal validity," and is "null and void," passes by a unanimous vote.

AUGUST 9, 1990

Iraq closes all of its land borders and announces that foreigners in Iraq will not be allowed to leave. The estimate of foreigners in Iraq is 1.3 million, including about 3,100 Americans. All embassies in Kuwait are told to close by August 24.

AUGUST 9, 1990
The President officially informs the Congress of deployment of US Armed Forces to Saudi Arabia and the Middle East:

```
Dear Mr. Speaker / Mr. President:

On August 2, 1990, Iraq invaded and occupied
the sovereign state of Kuwait in flagrant vio-
lation of the Charter of the United Nations.
In the period since August 2, Iraq has massed
an enormous and sophisticated war machine on
the Kuwaiti-Saudi Arabian border and in southern
```

Iraq, capable of initiating further hostilities with little or no additional preparation. Iraq's actions pose a direct threat to neighboring countries and to vital US interests in the Persian Gulf region.

In response to this threat and after receiving the request of the Government of Saudi Arabia, I ordered the forward deployment of substantial elements of the United States Armed Forces into the region. I am providing this report on the deployment and mission of our Armed Forces in accordance with my desire that Congress be fully informed and consistent with the War Powers Resolution.

Two squadrons of F-15 aircraft, one brigade of the 82nd Airborne Division, and other elements of the Armed Forces began arriving in Saudi Arabia at approximately 9:00 a.m. (EDT) on August 8, 1990. Additional US air, naval, and ground Forces also will be deployed. The Forces are equipped for combat, and their mission is defensive. They are prepared to take action in concert with Saudi forces, friendly regional forces, and others to deter Iraqi aggression and to preserve the integrity of Saudi Arabia.

I do not believe involvement in hostilities to imminent; to the contrary, it is my belief that this deployment will facilitate a peaceful resolution of the crisis. If necessary, however, the Forces are fully prepared to defend themselves. Although it is not possible to predict the precise scope and duration of this deployment, our Armed Forces will remain so long as their presence is required to contribute to the security of the region and desired by the Saudi government to enhance the capability of Saudi armed forces to defend the Kingdom.

I have taken these actions pursuant to my constitutional authority to conduct our foreign relations and as Commander in Chief. These actions are in exercise of our inherent right of individual and collective self-defense. I look forward to cooperation with the Congress in helping to restore peace and stability to the Persian Gulf region.

Sincerely,
George Bush

Note: Identical letters were sent to Thomas S. Foley, Speaker of the House of Representatives, and Robert C. Byrd, President pro tempore of the Senate. The letter was released by the Office of the Press Secretary on August 10.

FRIDAY AUGUST 10, 1990

In Cairo, Egypt, the Arab League Emergency summit takes place. Except for the Palestine Liberation Organization and Libya, the Arab countries condemn the Iraqi invasion of Kuwait and call for Iraq to withdraw its troops. By a narrow margin, the summit votes to send Egyptian, Syrian, and Moroccan troops to support Kuwait in the Gulf.

Schwarzkopf meets Col. John Warden III at Central Command (CENTCOM) headquarters in Tampa, where planning begins on the US air strategy for Desert Storm.

The President announces the appointment of Dr. Condoleezza Rice as a Special Assistant to the President for National Security Affairs.

AUGUST 10, 1990
MY DIARY

6:30 p.m. I arrived at Walker's Point for dinner with President and Mrs. Bush, Columba (Jeb's wife), Lovie Towns and his family, Daphne Murray, "Greasy" Bell (George deBenneville Bell) and his family. Greasy was an old school chum, hair slicked back, wearing yellow pants, a purple sweater, knit shirt with collar up, yellow socks with a spider-like pattern. Prep all the way. He summered at Prouts Neck near Portland. "Known him (the President) and his family for thirty-seven years," said Greasy's wife, Bertie Bell, at dinner. Friends of the President know exactly how many years and days they have known him.

Bertie was in white slacks, pink knit blouse, and those forever preppie freckles that go with beach houses. One can imagine George boating or clubbing with "Greasy" as skinny college kids.

The President strides into the room, obviously energized by the work of international doings. "An update, Marlin. I just talked to Hussein, twice, and Prime Minister Kaifu."

"Kaifu has been strong," I say.

Bush squints his eyes, shakes his head for emphasis, and says: "Strong. That little guy has come through. I'm giving him some gentle nudges toward military help." He pushes his hands out in front of him. "Not too strong, though," showing the delicate nature of the approach.

The guests start arriving and war is gone. He greets all the guests joking, kidding them about old experiences. Sophia is still arguing with her father, Greasy. James plays to a two handicap. The President pulls out *Golf Digest* with himself on the cover. Article by Dan Jenkins. Greasy and Jamie kid about his form. The President challenges them to a match at Prout's Neck. All mythical, of course.

At dinner, Greasy laughs loud and openly. It's a trait common to Bush friends, the ability to kid, tease, and laugh. "Are you still calling me Grease Ball?" Greasy says. "No, it was Greasy. What was it, George?"

"What do you put on that hair anyway?" the President asked.

"Water," Bertie says. Everybody knows it has stronger properties than water, probably Wildroot.

The President pulls me aside, "Hussein's coming to Washington tomorrow. Maybe Walker's Point. Brent's worried it will look like a reward."

"I don't think so," I said. "The press thinks he's a loser, a wimp. They will think he's going to get chewed out."

The President turns back to his dinner guests. After dinner, we adjourn to the living room. Bertie passes around some butter chocolate candy from Prouts Neck. Daphne asks me to come over for a day of tennis or golf. I agree.

"When," she says.

"Name it," the President says, "I dare you."

"Next Tuesday," I respond.

"Daff," the President says, "Who have we got over there for Marlin? Forty and attractive."

"How about twenty-one?" Greasy says.

"Maybe Margaret," Daff says. "She's forty and six-four."

"What?" I appeal. "Enough."

It was the President's way of initiating me into the greater Maine family.

Mrs. Bush interrupted, "George, don't you have to get ready?" It was the signal to end the evening. It was a system the two had worked out from years of entertaining.

SATURDAY AUGUST 11, 1990
THE WHITE HOUSE
Statement by Press Secretary Marlin Fitzwater:
President Bush called President Mubarak of Egypt at 5:45 this morning to congratulate him on the successful outcome of the Arab League meeting. President Bush praised President Mubarak's constructive role in securing passage of the resolution to send Arab troops to participate in a multinational force. The President said the Arab League action was very favorable and gives a significant optimism for the future of the mission.

President Bush this morning also telephoned Amir Isa bin Salman Al Khalifa of Bahrain to thank him for his efforts on behalf of the resolution and to discuss the situation generally. President Bush plans to call Amir Khalifa bin Hamad Al Thani of Qatar.

The United States welcomes the participation of forces from so many countries in our joint efforts to fight the aggression of Saddam Hussein. Military participation by Canada, Australia, West Germany, France, Belgium, and the United Kingdom signal a high degree of unity. We expect others to join this group as well. The NATO pledge of support was also important with so many individual countries bringing their resources to bear on the situation.

We are pleased to confirm that eleven Americans, including Penelope Nabokov, have been able to leave Iraq and cross the border into Jordan. We do not have details on their departure, but it is encouraging that this group has been able to join other Americans in leaving Iraq and Kuwait. Our Embassy is in contact almost hourly with Iraqi officials concerning the safety of US citizens.

There are news reports this morning in three different publications showing three different levels of eventual troop strength in Saudi Arabia. We will not comment on these stories nor provide any numbers on troop strength for obvious national security reasons. Similarly, we will have no comment on the stories today about a possible blockade. We have said in the past that planning for a blockade is underway, should it be necessary.

Right now the United Nations sanctions are being widely implemented, and there is no Iraqi oil leaving Turkey or Saudi Arabia. The embargo appears to be having a considerable effect. We are pleased that Venezuela, Iran, and other countries have indicated ability to make up for oil shortfalls. Fortunately, oil stocks in the United States are quite high, and the surge capacity around the world is also high. America is in a very positive situation in terms of its ability to withstand existing oil disruptions.

Note: The statement referred to Penelope Nabokov, a ten-year-old girl from Albany, California, who was taken into custody by Iraqi troops on August 2, when her commercial air flight was grounded in Kuwait City during the Iraqi invasion of Kuwait.

WEDNESDAY AUGUST 15, 1990
MY DIARY

We have a briefing on the war planning in the Joint Chiefs of Staff conference room in the Pentagon. A Naval captain gives the intelligence briefing on Iraq's capabilities and positions. Very strong and threatening. He gives five indicators of a possible invasion of Saudi Arabia by Iraq. Two had already happened.

"What's your judgment?" the President asks. "Are they coming?" General Powell, chairman of the JCS, says not now. General Schwarzkopf says, "The first two indicators involving locations and formations, could also be defensive postures. And our attack route into Kuwait is the same as their attack route into Saudi Arabia. They may or could be just planning to defend against us."

Schwarzkopf doesn't like all this talk about "Iraq's window of opportunity" closing. "That could spur them to action," he says. "I would rather we talked about a wide-open window, so they think they have time."That, of course, goes against our original theory of putting troops in Saudi Arabia quickly to keep Iraq from attacking.

After the briefing, the President, General Powell, DoD Secretary Cheney, Secretary Baker, and Brent meet privately in Cheney's office for twenty minutes to talk about a reserve call up. They agree to call up "Specialists." Like doctors, troop transport people, etc.

The President's speech that night is great. Includes my suggestions about WW II, post–Cold War takeovers. I gave the ideas to (Deputy National Security Adviser) Gates earlier, and he called Richard Haass with the ideas.

THURSDAY AUGUST 16, 1990
MY DIARY

KBP (Kennebunkport); Day of Signals. King Hussein of Jordan had called a couple of days earlier to say he wanted to meet privately with the President. President Bush wanted to meet him in Washington on August 15 when we were there. Jordan was the only Mideast country not to join the coalition against Iraq. Speculation was that King Hussein, a close personal friend, wanted to explain his decision to the President, or perhaps he wanted to deliver a personal message from Saddam Hussein.

King Hussein wanted to come to Walker's Point instead of Washington, on August 16. I advised the President that Walker's Point would be a satisfactory site if we didn't have any social pictures or recreation activities during the visit. General Scowcroft wanted no pictures, but then he relented to allow pictures at the helicopter on arrival and departure. This was Signal #1 for King Hussein: it will not be business as usual.

Ten minutes before King Hussein's arrival, I walked from the main house down to the helicopter landing pad to check the arrangements. There stands my good friend Sig Rogich, who is our television and staging guru. He is getting ready to bring the full press pool out of their waiting area, "to get a beautiful picture of the King and the President walking together."

"We don't want beautiful pictures. We want crummy pictures. We want no opportunity for a press conference and shouted questions. Above all, we don't want the pool where you just put them."

Sig gave a signal and the Secret Service immediately tore down the ropes for the press and moved them away just as the chopper's roar could be heard in the distance. Minutes later President and Mrs. Bush came walking down the driveway. He is wearing a blue blazer, dress slacks, and tie, perhaps the most business-like I had ever seen for a meeting at Kennebunkport. It was Signal #2 for the leader of an enemy country: he was in hostile territory, and it would be strictly business. No fun and games today. Mrs. Bush was dressed in white slacks and a Sanpan straw hat.

As the group walked up the drive toward the main house, the President invited his guest into his mother's house next door for a private meeting. Mother Bush, ninety-two, soon emerged by wheelchair and went to the main house with Mrs. Bush, leaving the two leaders alone.

Brent Scowcroft and one Jordanian note taker stayed with the President and the King. This was Signal #3: King Hussein would not be seated in the spacious family living room for this discussion. The Bush living room is a symbol of warmth and friendship. Secretary Baker and other staff waited in this room for the private meeting to end.

After nearly an hour in private discussion, the President and the King moved to the main house for lunch with the rest of the group. At lunch, King Hussein said he was not carrying a message from Saddam, but said he wanted to explain why he had not joined the US-led coalition. He explained the long history with Iraq, their mutual trade relationship, the transportation routes through both countries, and why he could not ignore these factors. But the reality for us was: he picked the wrong side.

At 2:00 p.m. the President asked me to explain the press arrangements to King Hussein and the attending group of staff. I told the King that our press pool was waiting by the chopper. "Talking to them is entirely your option," I said. The President stood up to leave, saying, "Someday this will be over, and I hope we will be strong friends again."

The two shook hands, and the President guided the King out the door. A short way down the driveway, the President said he wanted to stop in to see his mother.

"I need to stop in here to see Mother," he said, "She lost her brother this morning. Jim Baker will see you to the plane. Goodbye." Then he turned and went into the house alone.

This was Signal #4. The President would not see King Hussein off. The King proceeded on down the driveway, walking alone at the head of our group, looking straight ahead. The President had not lightened his burden. The forces of history had him in a death grip. At one point he said, "We have to prevent an explosion."

King Hussein walked directly to the press, with the chopper engines running, and began to tell his story. Secretary Baker gave a signal for the engines to stop. The King said he had a good meeting with the President in which differences had been narrowed. He said no shipments had gone through the blockade of Acaba and he would abide by the UN sanctions. Strangely, the press was hostile. That was Signal #5.

AUGUST 16, 1990
MY DIARY
Kennebunkport. The Saudi leadership has asked to see the

President, and by coincidence, the President was scheduled to follow King Hussein. They arrived about 3:05 p.m. and were ushered into the main house at Walker's Point. Prince Saud al-Faisal, the Foreign Minister, and Prince Bandar, the US Ambassador, were greeted warmly.

The President welcomed this opportunity to reassure our Saudi allies. "We're very pleased with the progress," he said. "We're determined to see this through. Our troops are doing well under the joint command. I want to express our resolve, although I don't see an out at this time."

"Our military planners feel that today (emphasized today), it's unlikely that Iraq will attack Saudi Arabia. (He meant at this point in our deployment.)

"How would hostages be viewed in your part of the world?" the President asked. "Would that be a basis for military action?"

The President has said repeatedly that we will not have a repeat of the Iranian hostage crisis in the late 1970s. I personally believe the President will act if any of our hostages are killed.

After a more detailed review of our troop deployment status, the group moved back down the driveway toward their helicopter. Prince Bandar led the two delegations, looking resplendent in his snow-white summer gown.

Ellie LeBlond, Doro's four-year-old daughter from her first marriage, joined the group from out of nowhere and walked close to Prince Bandar, looking up at his gold embroidered gown. Ellie is a cute, energetic, and angelic-looking little girl, with thick glasses that enhance her charm. At one point, Ellie stepped on the Prince's gown, but he steadied himself and touched her shoulder warmly.

Then he reached down and gave Ellie his "worry beads," which he has been carrying, usually to express a wide range of emotions from impatience to meditation. She begins twirling the beads around her finger and pulling them as if to break the thread. I panic, thinking of all those beads rolling down the driveway in violation of who knows what taboo. Then she ran to the Prince's side to give them back, but instead drops them on the driveway. The Prince picks them up and hands them back to her. She motions as if preparing to throw the beads into the Rubyrogosia bushes along the driveway, and she does. The Prince stumbles into the bushes, finds the beads, and emerges to say, "I think I better keep them."

He dangles them at his side where I can get a good look. They are ebony, mixed with diamonds.

AUGUST 16, 1990
MY DIARY
Kennebunkport. The President is told that his Uncle John Walker has had a heart attack and has been taken to the Biddeford, MA, hospital. But Mr. Walker dies at 6:37 p.m. The President arrives at 7:02.

FRIDAY AUGUST 17, 1990
MY DIARY
Kennebunkport. Later that morning Bob Gates arrives at the house and starts his morning intelligence briefing of the President, "I hear you had to rush to the hospital to see your uncle. How is he?"

"Dead," the President said without ever looking up.

A small example of how difficult it is to keep track of everything that happens to a President in a day. Gates knew the status of the world, but missed the death. And the President couldn't spend much time in mourning, because the war was waiting. So they both deal with the issue as best they can, and move on.

AUGUST 17, 1990
An Araqi official announces forced placement of men at strategic sites, "We're relocating the foreign men all over the country at airports, air bases, military bases, industrial plants, communications centers, power centers and oil refineries—wherever Iraq considers it has a vital installation, one exposed to the American threat in Saudi Arabia."

SATURDAY AUGUST 18, 1990
MY DIARY
Kennebunkport. Bob Gates calls me at the Nonantum Hotel at 7:40 a.m. to say we have a statement on AMCITS in Iraq/Kuwait.

American citizens were taken hostage in both countries.

I go to the press office in another hotel, the Shawmut Inn, to read the statement and release it to the press. It's benign, expressing our great concern. Privately, the President was upset, even angry, about the hostages. I suspect that if an American is killed, the President will order an immediate response. The war will be on. Indeed, I suspect that if one of our embargo warships, no matter from what country, is attacked, the war is on. Fortunately, neither case happened.

I went out to Walker's Point to clear the statement about American citizens with the President. He approves. The President is getting ready to go out on his boat, *Fidelity*. On the pier, Gates says there are two problems working now: Navy has stopped an Iraqi tanker loaded with oil in the Gulf of Oman. Won't stop. One shot has been fired across its bow. Also, the Kuwait International Hotel has been sealed off. We don't know how many Americans are inside.

I go back to the Shawmut to issue the statement. My staff calls to say hold the release till 11:00 a.m., when Saddam Hussein is supposed to make a statement. At 10:25 the President calls me on a secure phone line from *Fidelity*.

"Do you know about the problems in the Gulf?" he asked, not wanting to be specific over this boat phone.

"Yes," I said. A tanker was going to run our blockade.

"This could be serious," the President said. "Talk to Gates when he gets back."

Gates said the President was briefed on this matter about the ships. The Navy Captain says he can't shoot the rudder off because it's too low in the water. He suggests taking off the superstructure. The President authorizes "whatever force is necessary to stop the ship."

Actually, there are two ships—one in the Persian Gulf, one in the Gulf of Oman. Both refused to stop. Both lied, saying they were carrying ballasts. In fact, they are loaded with oil.

The President goes to Coast Guard Cutter *Manomy* to use their communications system. He calls Scowcroft. Communications break down two or three times and the President is cussing the communications system.

At 12:00 I decide to call my own sources. I call Bill Harlow, my military adviser in the Situation Room, to review matters. Harlow, later to become PAO for the Pentagon and the CIA in the Clinton and Bush 43 Administrations, has a sharp but low-key sense of humor. He says, "We've got everything under control. As long as they turn around, we're showing great courage."

In fact, I think our military wants to go. The two guided missile cruisers in the Gulf want to sink the Iraqi oil tankers. Admiral Jeremiah says the desert is target rich. (Admiral Jeremiah was Vice Chairman of the Joint Chiefs of Staff. He later became a close and warm personal friend, a man of integrity and wisdom.)

In conversation on the pier this morning, Gates said the war would only last "a couple of weeks. The Air Force will take out their air defenses first, then their armor. Iraq has never seen anything like a B-52 raid."

"That would mean Baghdad," I said. He just smiled.

AUGUST 18, 1990

Passage of UNSC Resolution 664 that condemns Iraq and demands, "Iraq permit and facilitate the immediate departure from Kuwait and Iraq of the nationals of third countries."

AUGUST 18, 1990
MY DIARY

Biddeford, Maine. Katherine Holt, a member of my staff, invited me to Biddeford for a cocktail party with her family and friends. It was a very warm gathering. Twenty or thirty people treating me like a celebrity. For the first time in days, I could take my mind off the approaching war.

Among the guests were Dick LeBlond, Doro's former father-in-law. He gave me cards to give the President that say, "I'm a virgin, but this is a very old card."

My mind went back to the Gulf, where three ships, two tankers, and a freighter, were threatening to break the blockade. The plan is to blow the superstructure off the ships at daybreak. Our guided missile cruisers don't think their guns are right to do a clean job. A destroyer will be brought in during the night to do the job. Gulf time is seven hours ahead. These three ships could start the war.

AUGUST 18, 1990

Announcement is made by Iraq in an open letter read on Baghdad Radio that in return for the withdrawal of coalition forces, Iraq will release "the foreign guests." Saddam Hussein blames the United States and Britain for his stance on detaining foreign nationals as a "human shield" to "prevent military aggression." Saddam decrees "every citizen, regardless of nationality, harboring foreigners—who are forbidden to leave the country—would be sentenced to death."

SUNDAY AUGUST 19, 1990
THE WHITE HOUSE
Statement by Press Secretary Fitzwater:

On several occasions since the Iraqi invasion and subsequent occupation of Kuwait, the President has stated publicly his interest in the well-being of American citizens and all foreign nationals in both Iraq and Kuwait. The President thus views yesterday's statement by the Speaker of Iraq's National Assembly, that Iraq will "play host to the citizens of these aggressive nations as long as Iraq remains threatened in an aggressive war," to be totally unacceptable. He is deeply troubled by the indication that Iraqi authorities intend to relocate these individuals within Iraq against their will. The President is also deeply concerned about today's announcement by the Government of Iraq that foreign nationals may not have access to adequate quantities of food.

The use of innocent civilians as pawns to promote what Iraq sees to be its self-interest is contrary to international law and, indeed, to all accepted norms of international conduct. We urge that Iraq immediately reconsider its refusal to allow any foreign national desiring to leave to do so without delay or condition. We would also hope that Iraq would take note of yesterday's statement by the UN Security Council President expressing the Council's concern and anxiety over the situation of foreign nationals in Iraq and Kuwait and calling upon the Secretary-General to take all appropriate steps. The United States intends to consult with other governments with citizens being held in Iraq and Kuwait to determine what additional measures ought to be taken.

AUGUST 19, 1990
MY DIARY

I call the Situation Room in Washington. The tankers are still steaming to port. We are following. There must have been a change of orders; perhaps we are buying time. It turns out we have four to five days before the ships arrive at their port. We are trying for a UN endorsement of some kind before we act.

AUGUST 19, 1990
MY DIARY

Dinner in the residence of the White House with the President, General Scowcroft, UN Ambassador Pickering, General Powell, Deputy Sec. of State Eagleburger, General Atwood, to discuss military readiness. Not enough forces there yet to launch an invasion. We can hold and inflict punishment but we need another week.

Powell says tankers are seventy-two hours, not ninety-six hours, from port. Pickering is told to delay UN consideration of the resolution endorsing action.

MONDAY AUGUST 20, 1990
MY DIARY

Kennebunkport. The President calls PM Özal in Turkey. Özal still thinks Iraq will be in economic trouble soon, ten days to two weeks. Özal says one of his ministers just returned from Iran. He reports that Iran will observe the UN sanctions in spite of Iraq's post-war overtures. They will speak harshly of the US, but observe the sanctions.

President called Senator Byrd in Amsterdam to ask him to say thanks to Özal. He does not tell him of the Iran news. Typical George Bush small gesture of letting Özal know through Byrd how much we care about his relationship.

AUGUST 20, 1990
MY DIARY

The President makes "hostage speech."

AUGUST 20, 1990
THE PRESIDENT

Excerpt from speech at the Veterans of Foreign Wars 91st Annual Meeting, the President sends a message to Iraq:

The President: We have been reluctant to use the term 'hostage,' but when Saddam Hussein specifically offers to trade the freedom of those citizens of many nations he holds against their will in return for concessions, there can be little doubt that, whatever these innocent people are called, they are in fact 'hostages.'

I will hold the Government of Iraq responsible for the safety and well-being of American citizens held against their will.

AUGUST 20, 1990
MY DIARY

Kennebunkport. President Bush calls Prime Minister Mitterrand and thanks him for a firm response. We are concerned about hostages. Mitterrand suggests some kind of international statement. President says OK. President says: "We are in a position to severely punish Hussein for this type of thing."

The President hangs up and says: "Francois is rock solid. Totally committed. Like de Gaulle, he'll be there if we need him."

AUGUST 20, 1990
MY DIARY

Kennebunkport. Ships will be in Yemen territorial water at 9:00 a.m. Tuesday. We actually have twelve hours. Gates discovers this in close questioning of Bob Kimmit on deputies conference call from KBP at 5:00 p.m. Monday. Pickering cancels plan to pick up award from VFW in Baltimore Monday evening, rushes to New York to call a meeting of the Permanent Five. He tells them of 9:00 a.m. Tuesday deadline, or US will take unilateral action.

In KBP, Gates tells the President of this time change. The

President's instructions are: "Take it out" if there is no UN action by 9:00 a.m.

TUESDAY AUGUST 21, 1990
MY DIARY

Kennebunkport. In the middle of night, the Yemen delegate to the UN stops debate. He says he's ready to resolve the issue by complying with UN sanctions against letting the oil be shipped to Iraq. Yemen will take the ship into port, but not off load. Pickering stands by, looks over the Yemen Ambassador's shoulder as he calls home to confirm this with the Foreign Minister. We say OK and let the ship sail safely into Yemen port.

WEDNESDAY AUGUST 22, 1990
THE WHITE HOUSE
Statement by Press Secretary Fitzwater:

The President today authorized the Secretary of Defense to call Reserve units of the Armed Forces to active duty. The order permits the Secretary of Defense to call to duty selected members and units of the Reserve components of the Army, Navy, Air Force, and Marine Corps as needed to support United States and multinational operations now underway. The President signed the order after the Secretary of Defense advised him that the effective conduct of military operations in and around the Arabian Peninsula may require augmentation of Active components of the Armed Forces. The actual number of Reserve personnel to be called to active duty will depend upon the operational needs of the Armed Forces, but at this time, we do not anticipate approaching the full 200,000 authority provided by law. . . .

AUGUST 22, 1990
MY DIARY

Some irony. I called up the reserves to fight in Desert Storm in a written press statement. I then called Art Howard to say: "We may need extra manpower." (Art and I were Air Force munitions specialists called up as reservists by President Johnson in 1968 to seek the return of spy ship *Pueblo* from North Korea. In fact, we were called up to go to Viet Nam, although Art and I spent the entire deployment stateside.)

AUGUST 22, 1990
MY DIARY

Presidential Press Conference; Kennebunkport. I had Bill Harlow call Colin Powell to tell him to wear his uniform. Later at Walker's Point he said he remembered my words from years ago: "Always wear a tie. Never let them see you sweat." He was in uniform.

AUGUST 22, 1990
THE PRESIDENT

Excerpt from the President's 58th news conference, on the Persian Gulf Crisis, that took place at his home in Kennebunkport:

The President: First, Secretary Cheney and General Powell have just given me a very full and, I would say, encouraging briefing on the status of our deployment to the Persian Gulf. This has been a very complicated mission calling for precision, calling for maximum coordination with Saudi Arabia and the other nations providing forces. The process has gone smoothly, and we've now moved what amounts to a medium-sized American city completely capable of sustaining itself all the way over to the Middle East.

And the Secretary reports that the men and women in the Armed Forces have performed with extraordinary ability, their morale is high, and they've accepted the challenge of their mission with extraordinary dedication to duty. And I'm very proud of each and every single one of them, and I want them to know that the American people are behind them 100 percent, supporting them strongly.

And it's also crucial that everyone understand that we are not in this alone. We stand shoulder to shoulder right there in the Middle East with the Armed Forces of twenty-two other nations from the Middle East, from Europe, and around the world.

Secretary Dick Cheney reports an impressive alliance of multinational forces that stands behind the United Nations resolve that Iraq completely and unconditionally withdraw from Kuwait with the restoration of the legitimate government in that country. The United Nations has provided generous leadership to the whole world community in pursuing this objective and voting the sanctions necessary to carrying it out. And let's be clear: As the deployment of the forces of the many nations shows and as the votes in the United Nations show this is not a matter between Iraq and the United States of America; it is between Iraq and the entire world community, Arab and non-Arab alike. All the nations of the world lined up to oppose aggression.

And as our forces continue to arrive, they can look forward to the support of the finest Reserve components in the world. We are activating those special categories of reservists that are essential to completing our mission. The United States considers its Reserve forces to be an integral part of the total military command. These essential personnel will soon be joining the cohesive organization required to support the military operations in and around the Arabian Peninsula, and I have the highest confidence in their ability to augment the Active forces in this operation.

We continue to pursue our objectives with absolute determination. I might add that I talked to the four leaders of Congress today, and I am very pleased that they are giving us the strong support they have been—the Speaker, Senator Mitchell, Senator Dole, Congressman Michel. And the world simply cannot waiver in its opposition to the threat that Iraq has placed on the doorstep of all nations who cherish freedom and the rule of law.

AUGUST 22, 1990
MY DIARY

Kennebunkport. We had lunch on the patio at Walker's Point overlooking the Atlantic. Picture perfect day for the President, Gates, Sununu, Powell, Cheney, myself. Cheney gave a trip report. Powell gave a status report on tankers, and their coordinates. President wants to enforce the sanctions. As George W. (Jr.) said two days earlier, "Dad is ready to go. He knows what he wants to do."

President calls Baker in Wyoming. He said wait. The Soviets want till Friday. Eagleburger says they may want time to get Soviet citizens out of Iraq. President wants to set a 4:00 p.m. Friday deadline.

Eagleburger says that will threaten the Soviets, and could make them withdraw support for the UN resolution on use of military to enforce the sanctions. President decides to say, "until sometime later in the week."

AUGUST 22, 1990
MY DIARY

Sig Rogich calls from Las Vegas to say he's not the source of a *New York Times* story about recreation at Kennebunkport. He is, of course. He even wrote a memo last week to Governor Sununu on the horrible pictures of the President in his golf cart.

AUGUST 22, 1990
MY DIARY

At lunch, the President chides Governor Sununu about his comment on August 21 in the golf cart, that Saudi Arabia has the world's largest sand trap. I say the *Times* was going to write: "President today ordered up the Reserves from his golf cart to go fight in the world's largest sand trap."

AUGUST 22, 1990
MY DIARY

We're walking as a group along the Walker's Point sea wall to the press conference, when the President bolts over the sea wall and heads for the water. "Sir," I call out, "we don't have time for a swim." He returns with a shell, apparently from where he had collected them as a boy. We proceed on. I had written his press statement, and it went over well.

AUGUST 22, 1990
MY DIARY

Admiral Murphy, former Chief of Staff to Bush as Vice President, called to say Saudi Arabia wanted him to go to Saudi Arabia to teach them about press relations.

THURSDAY AUGUST 23, 1990
MY DIARY

Dan Goodgame of *Time* magazine asked me about Sununu's trip to Moscow from August 27 to September 3. "Is he stopping in London to see Thatcher about the hostages?"

"No," I replied, "he's talking about the environment, global warming."

"That's not what others are back-grounding," Dan said. By others, he met Sununu's assistant, Ed Rogers. (Rogers was telling the press privately that Sununu was really going to Moscow and London to conduct war diplomacy.)

I had heard General Scowcroft say that Sununu, under no circumstances, should be trying to conduct diplomacy in Moscow or London. Indeed, the President this morning said he did not want Sununu talking to Gorbachev and really should not even be going.

I called Card about all this. He called Rogers. Rogers called me to deny he had ever talked to Goodgame, but he had talked to Michael Duffy yesterday. I called Goodgame back. He was upset that I had told Rogers he was the source. But he said Duffy had the clear impression from Rogers that Sununu was going to talk about hostages.

I asked Rogers when the Dan Balz, *Washington Post*, story would be coming out (knowing Rogers was calling everybody). He said he had never talked to Balz. However, yesterday I was with Andy Card when Rogers told him he had talked to Balz about the trip. (Rogers can't remember his own leaks.)

AUGUST 23, 1990
MY DIARY

Dan Rather, CBS News, called from Saudi Arabia to express his concern about the President's press conference comments Tuesday that he hoped we would get some objective reporting from Baghdad. Rather had three concerns: #1 His patriotism had been challenged. He wanted to "let grudges and bygones be bygones." He supports our President. #2 A *New Republic* story quoted me as saying something nasty about his coverage. #3 An Oman security officer had complained about his coverage, and he felt it was White House inspired.

I denied #3, apologized for #2, and said the President wasn't trying to single him out. We had been concerned about TV interviews with Ted Koppel at the Rashid Hotel that had caused Iraq to move the Americans and make them hostages. Rather said he was gratified by my comments. Ironically, the President called while I was on the phone with Rather. I called him back to report the conversation. "Maybe his reporting will improve," the President said.

AUGUST 23, 1990
MY DIARY

The President's staff have gathered at the Walker's Point landing zone waiting for *Marine One* to land after the President had made a quick trip to Washington. George Bush Jr., wearing a two-day beard, ranger jacket, jeans, and a ball cap, is angry. "Tell Maureen Dowd she's crazy. Dad desires a vacation. It doesn't matter anyway; he's not going to run again." I was flabbergasted. George W. walked away without explanation. I believe he knew what he was saying and didn't want to have to explain. I'm not sure he will run again either.

FRIDAY AUGUST 24, 1990

Iraqi troops surround and threaten US Embassy in Kuwait City, stating electricity and water will be cut and diplomats will be forcefully removed. Iraqi official says, "This is the last night, and after that there will be no embassies in Kuwait; diplomatic immunity will be stripped and there will be no delays."

AUGUST 24, 1990
MY DIARY

I went on camera with a statement (of concern) about Kuwait Embassy employees held in Baghdad, and a cynical appearance by Saddam Hussein with British hostages. Wrote it myself. Gates said later it was perfect.

AUGUST 24, 1990
MY DIARY

I joined Secretary of the Treasury Nick Brady, Director of OMB

Dick Darman, Governor Sununu, and Andy Card for a budget meeting on Walker's Point. Darman estimates that with 160,000 troops in Saudi Arabia, it will cost about $3 billion for six months, assuming no fighting. If intense air power is used and limited ground forces, the cost would double.

Darman outlined Gingrich's deficit reduction plan. He thinks it is a plan to prevent a deal. We will portray it as a right-wing fringe plan. President to address a joint session of Congress on September 12. "It won't be showing leadership if I don't," the President said. "I think I have to take it to the people and say, 'here's what we have to do.'"

SATURDAY AUGUST 25, 1990
MY DIARY

The United Nations Security Council has passed Resolution 665 calling for enforcement measures to maintain the comprehensive sanctions against Iraq. The unanimous vote further underlines the deep concern of the world community regarding the blatant aggression by Iraq against Kuwait. The resolve of the international community is strong. The vote exhibits the commitment of the world to act effectively to achieve the complete, immediate, and unconditional withdrawal of Iraq from Kuwait. The United States pledges its complete support of the United Nations action.

AUGUST 25, 1990
MY DIARY

President Gorbachev's statement yesterday supporting the United Nations sanctions was a very important development. We welcome his voice to the world condemnation of the aggression by Saddam Hussein. The United Nations resolution passed last night further strengthens the world resolve to force Iraq out of Kuwait. We are encouraged by the progress of events at the United Nations and by President Gorbachev's strong support.

WEDNESDAY AUGUST 29, 1990
MY DIARY

The President went back to DC for Congressional briefings on the war. Staying two extra days, till Thursday, to help with the vacation image. I take Wednesday off to renew my driver's license. At 3:00 p.m., Roman Popadiuk, my Deputy, calls me at home.

"Marlin, we have a major PR problem. At my briefing, I was asked about a *Newsday* story that a former high-administration official has given a secret peace plan from Iraq to B. Scowcroft."

I didn't know anything about it, so I waffled, saying we get these type of feelers all the time. "I won't comment on any specific one, but there is no new peace plan. This idea was dismissed immediately. There's nothing to it."

Afterward, I checked with Brent. He said there was an idea from Richard Helms, CIA director under President Nixon, but nothing came of it. Your answer was just right, Roman said.

An hour later, Roman called back, "Another problem. Margaret Tutwiler at State's briefing said there was no such plan. She had checked with Baker and Kimmit, and they had never heard of it. Obviously, Brent had never told Baker. Actually, there was no plan, just an idea. (An irrelevant problem. Indeed, everyone said the right thing, but it shows how fragile information flows in Washington.)

AUGUST 29, 1990
MY DIARY

Oval Office meeting with CIA, State, DoD experts on Iraq, 10:30 a.m. April Glaspie, US Ambassador to Iraq, is very impressive. Plain face. No makeup, white shirt.

April: "Saddam thinks we're soft, and will not attack with hostages in Iraq. He thinks time is on his side. He waits for the ball to bounce his way—Jordan will fall, or the embargo will fail, or Israel will move.

"I do believe Saddam will turn around; he can change his position. We have a very good chance for the embargo to work over several months.

"Saddam can be flattered. He brags about getting a message from

George Bush. Any personal message you might send will be heeded.

"Saddam thinks Iran will smuggle him food across the border, for a price. He believes the Arabs will join him and desert us, especially after casualties. He remembers the truck bomb in Lebanon and how we left. He thinks we will leave if we suffer any casualties.

"Above all, Saddam wants to win. He knows he can't beat the US and Israel in a war. He will look for other ways.

"Remember, Mr. President, the Arabs (Saudi Arabia and Kuwait) cannot resist the impulse to pay. At some point, they will be willing to pay off Iraq, and you can't stop it.

"Only Morocco can mediate.

"Saddam wants to string us out. He doesn't think the American public will stay the course. He has said to me: 'I took 10,000 casualties in one day (in Iran) and another 10,000 the next. The US could never suffer 10,000 casualties a day like I did.'"

Of King Hussein, April says: "His Arab dignity is at stake. The Jordanian army turn down by Congress five years ago was 'searing' for Hussein. He said at the time that the VP Bush relationship was all he had. Don't demand a 100 percent embargo from him. Let 30 percent go through. Give him some dignity."

(In retrospect, April Glaspie was right on almost every point.)

THURSDAY AUGUST 30, 1990
MY DIARY

Wyatt Andrews, CBS, came to my office at 8:30 a.m. to say they have a good source saying Bush is going to Saudi Arabia. They want to go on the air. I go to the Oval and meet Brent coming out. He says we're not going. But since I knew that we had been planning to go—that's why the new *Air Force One* was rushed to Andrews and was doing refueling training on flight to Hawaii—I thought maybe Brent was giving me one of his famous narrow interpretations, i.e. we're not going today but maybe next week. I tell Wyatt no, but he doesn't believe me. He says his source is high. I'm doubtful, so I decide to go to the President. He's in his study.

I relate the situation, and he swears (a very seldom occurrence). By coincidence, Margaret Tutwiler had just called me to say the

Israelis had reported the President is going to Saudi Arabia, Egypt, and Turkey. They were upset Bush was not going to Israel. I told the President that must be the source. (It often is, by the way. Foreign governments leak this kind of thing to influence the President. They make it look like a US government source.)

"Brent," the President said, "I think we have to publicly announce we're not going to Saudi Arabia. Otherwise, the press will run the story, then Saudi Arabia will be upset and the trip will never happen."

"Let's just let CBS run it," Brent said, "and let them be wrong."

"If we do that," the President said, "then we violate the agreement with Saudi Arabia. No. You better call Bandar, tell him we're not coming and we're going to say it publicly."

I go back and give Wyatt a firm no, on the word of the President. (This is another case where the press is used to influence the government. Everybody responds in good faith, but a lot of energy is expended to satisfy all parties.)

AUGUST 30, 1990
MY DIARY

I learn the mysterious peace plan came from an Iraqi businessman of Lebanese descent, who gave it to Helms, who gave it to Scowcroft over lunch at Maison Blanche. (Much ado about nothing. Everybody wants to get in the game. The media is an easy mark.)

AUGUST 30, 1990
MY DIARY

The President had a picnic for the press at Walker's Point, hot dogs and hamburgers. (All press corps with spouses are invited. Most bring their children to get pictures taken with President and First Lady.) Dan Goodgame, *Time*, uses the occasion to say their Moscow bureau reporting that Bush would meet with Gorbachev in Helsinki on September 8. I asked Brent, who was at the picnic, and he said yes, on September 9, but "don't admit it." The Soviets didn't want to announce the trip until September 8. (This is classic. The Soviets have no press, so they can announce anything anytime, and no one minds.)

Brent says there is no special reason for the meeting, but the President wanted to have the meeting before he gives the Joint Session of Congress speech on September 12. My guidance was: "We're thinking of several trips, but we have nothing to announce." Later, Agence France Presse got the same story from Moscow. Then Craig Hines, in T-shirt and shorts, and Carl Leubsdorf and Susan Paige found me on the front porch of the Nonantum. I refused to deny the story and gave them the guidance from above. My refusal to deny was enough for them to go with the story. (These are typical journalistic word games to use when governments want to deny the undeniable, for no good reason, and yet we want to do the right thing. On the basis of my guidance, the press knows that we're going to Moscow, probably on September 8 or 9, but we can't say it because the Soviets say no. And we may never know why.)

AUGUST 30, 1990
MY DIARY

Kennebunkport. Margaret Tutwiler calls to say Jesse Jackson is bringing 237 American hostages home. President Bush and Secretary Baker want a magnanimous, generous response. I give it.

SUNDAY SEPTEMBER 2, 1990

Iraq begins allowing Western, Japanese, and Kuwaiti nationals detained as human shields to leave Iraq (included in the first wave of departures are 163 Americans).

TUESDAY SEPTEMBER 18, 1990
MY DIARY

Press Office. Roman came in breathless from running across the street from the Eisenhower Office Building. "Did you know General Duggan got fired? Cheney fired him at 8:00 a.m. this morning."

"No shit," I exclaimed. "Not since MacArthur."

"The President doesn't know. Cheney meets with our regional reporters at 12:30 and the President meets with the regional press at 2:00. Should they hold it (the announcement) till after that?"

"Yes. But what is Cheney going to say? Why?" I asked.

Roman called Pete Williams, Assistant Secretary of Defense. He was writing a statement to release at 2:30. At 11:00 a.m., David Martin of CBS, called Roman with the story. We called Williams. The press was gathering outside my door: Helen Thomas, Charlie Bierbauer, Tom Raum, Gene Gibbons—wires. I told Williams he needed to get Cheney's statement out immediately, so we could respond that the President concurs. Otherwise, we would be the first to comment and the announcement would come from the White House. I couldn't keep walking through these reporters without responding.

Williams faxed us the statement. It didn't say why Duggan was fired. I called him back, "Cheney has to make a statement at 12:30. We'd say the President concurs, and will have no further comment pending Cheney's statement. Cheney came on Williams' line. He didn't want to go into the reasons for the firing with the White House press. So he suggests another press conference on Wednesday for DoD press."Dick," I said, "the story is today. You have to do it today."

"OK, at 2:30," he said. Thus, the strategy was set. First, a three-line written DoD statement to be issued at 11:00 a.m. Second, a Cheney TV statement at the Regional Reporters briefing at 12:30. Third, a President Bush comment at the Regional Reporters briefing at 2:30. Fourth, Cheney before the DoD press corps at 2:30 with a full explanation. It worked perfectly. (That's how White House planning often happens in press relations.)

THURSDAY SEPTEMBER 20, 1990
MY DIARY

Washington, DC. Melinda Andrews called with a personal item. She said her college was going to have lunch with my friend Andy Card, Deputy to the Chief of Staff, on Friday. As she put it, "We want President Mitterrand of France to address the new American Institute of Architects dinner in April.

Author's Note: Melinda Andrews worked in the White House from 1980 to 1986 and is now my wife, since January 23, 1999.

FRIDAY SEPTEMBER 21, 1990
THE PRESIDENT
Excerpt from the President's 61st news conference, from the South Portico:

The President: I have just a few brief remarks before departing. First, I had a very good and useful meeting this morning with the congressional leaders. We talked about the situation in the Gulf. I made clear that sanctions remain our strategy for resolving this crisis. At the same time, I pointed out my deep and growing concern over what Iraq is doing to Kuwait and to the Kuwait people, and to American citizens and foreign nationals, more generally. And I also pointed out that Iraq support for terrorism would indeed have serious consequences.

I also asked the congressional leaders for the prompt approval of key aspects of our policy; in particular, I urged that the supplemental funds needed to cover defense operations be passed quickly. Similarly, I emphasized just how critical it is that Congress agree to forgive the FMS [foreign military sales] debt of our stalwart ally Egypt. And I also informed the congressional leaders that it is essential that we continue to meet Saudi Arabia's legitimate defense requirements.

Let me just say that I appreciate the support that Congress is giving to the Administration during this situation. It's good, and it's strong. And for my part, I pledge to continue to consult fully, consult regularly with the Congress. The United States stands determined and united in its quest to see the Iraqi forces withdraw from Kuwait fully and unconditionally.

FRIDAY SEPTEMBER 28, 1990
THE PRESIDENT
Remarks following discussions with the Amir of Kuwait, from the South Portico of the White House:

The President: Well, it is my great pleasure to welcome His Highness Sheik Jabir Sabah to the United States. His Highness is visiting Washington for the first time. What normally would be a pleasurable occasion instead is a time for sobriety and sorrow. Our meeting has taken place with the backdrop of the tragedy that has been vested on Kuwait and its people by a ruthless and ambitious dictator.

Iraqi aggression has ransacked and pillaged a once peaceful and secure country, its population assaulted, incarcerated, intimidated, and even murdered. Iraq's leaders are trying to wipe an internationally recognized sovereign state, a member of the Arab League and the United Nations, off the face of the map.

To them and to the world, I will state what I told His Highness, the Amir. Iraq will fail. Kuwait—free Kuwait—will endure. And I have reaffirmed to the Amir that America's resolve to end this aggression against Kuwait remains firm and undiminished. Kuwait's sovereignty and territorial integrity will be restored, the stability and security of the Persian Gulf region is assured, and the safety of all innocent citizens is secured. . . ."

MONDAY OCTOBER 15, 1990
THE WHITE HOUSE

President Mikhail Gorbachev of the Soviet Union has been a courageous force for peaceful change in the world. I want to offer my congratulations on behalf of the American people for his selection to receive the Nobel Peace Prize. He has brought historically significant change, both political and economic, to the Soviet Union and to Eastern Europe. East-West relations hold greater promise for peace and world stability today than at any time in the last forty-five years. The United States continues to work with the Soviet Union to promote regional and international peace. Barbara and I send our warmest regards to President and Mrs. Gorbachev in receiving this international honor.

WEDNESDAY OCTOBER 17, 1990

Estimated figures for coalition forces stationed in the Gulf region: 200,000 American; 15,000 British; 11,000 French troops.

MONDAY OCTOBER 22, 1990

France calls for a broader settlement to the Middle East crisis and announces a plan for a peaceful resolution. Saddam Hussein announces that all French hostages will be allowed to leave, with France having, "rejected Bush's aggressive methods."

SATURDAY OCTOBER 27, 1990
THE PRESIDENT
Excerpt from the President's exchange with reporters at 12:15 p.m. in the East-West Center, Honolulu, Hawaii:

The President: I think Saddam Hussein really felt that nobody was going to move against his aggression in Kuwait. I also believe that he really intended to threaten Saudi Arabia. Or else, why did he move all his armor south to the Saudi border? I think as he sees the US forces moving in conjunction with many Arab country forces, in conjunction with many European country forces on land and on the sea, that he's taking another look. Because we are deadly serious. I want to see these economic sanctions work.

I'm not too good at the emotional side of it, but when you talk to the parents and spouses of our kids halfway around the world, it makes a real impact on you. I remember when I got off the plane at the Marine base, and they were saying, "Take care of my husband." And yet, "We back you 100 percent." So I don't think that's a conflict exactly, but I want to take care of every young man and woman that's serving the United States halfway around the world. But they want, and I want, to see that Saddam's aggression is unrewarded and, indeed, repudiated. So, the moving of US force up to now has sent a strong signal to him. We have the finest, most highly motivated, best trained, best equipped Armed Forces in the world. And they're right there. They're right there in substantial numbers—land, air, and sea.

Now, Mr. Saddam Hussein, get out of Kuwait with no condition. This talk of some condition—that is unacceptable not just to the United States but to the other countries around the world.

THURSDAY NOVEMBER 1, 1990
THE PRESIDENT
From remarks by President Bush at a rally in Mashpee, Massachusetts:

The President: Subsequently, the United Nations Security Council passed ten resolutions of condemnation and disapproval. And on August 5th, I said that Saddam Hussein's aggression will not stand. And today I am more determined than ever in my life: This aggression will not and must not stand.

This morning, this very morning, over three hundred Americans, innocent civilians, are held against their will in Iraq. Saddam Hussein calls them 'guests.' They are held in direct contravention of international law, many of them reportedly staked out as human shields near possible military targets. . . .

Many more Americans are in hiding in Kuwait, their lives at stake. A number imprisoned in the United States Embassy in Kuwait City, the Embassy surrounded by Iraq forces. They're cut off from food. They are cut off from other supplies. They're surrounded. And our flag still flies. . . .

NOVEMBER 1, 1990
THE PRESIDENT
President Bush speaks regarding the hostage situation at his 64th news conference, in Orlando, Florida [excerpt]:

The President: The United States and the rest of the world are united in the condemnation of Iraq's invasion of Kuwait. We have no quarrel with Iraqi people. Our problem is with Iraqi's dictator, Saddam Hussein.

I want a peaceful resolution to this crisis. We're giving the United Nations sanctions imposed on Iraq time to work. But let me be very clear: There will be no compromise on the stated objectives for the United Nations Security Council resolutions.

Iraq's brutality against innocent civilians will not be permitted to stand. And Saddam Hussein's violations of international law will not stand. His aggression against Kuwait will not stand.

This canard of calling people that are held hostage—calling them 'guests' when they're hostages—is turning off the whole world. And further, the reports that are coming out from some of these French hostages coming home, of their understanding of the way the Americans are being treated, is just terrible. And the whole concept of staking out people next to what might become military targets is also unconscionable.

SUNDAY NOVEMBER 4, 1990
Saddam Hussein orders British hostages to phone home and

invite their loved ones to visit for the Christmas holidays.

Thursday November 8, 1990

The United States sends about 100,000 additional troops to the Gulf region to support the existing 220,000 troops in the region.

November 8, 1990
The President

Excerpt from the opening statement of the President's 64th news conference at 4:04 p.m. from the Briefing Room:

The President: To achieve these goals, we and our allies have forged a strong diplomatic, economic, and military strategy to force Iraq to comply with these objectives. The framework of this strategy is laid out in ten United Nations resolutions, overwhelmingly supported by the United Nations Security Council. In three months, the US troop contribution to the multinational force in Saudi Arabia has gone from 10,000 to 230,000 as part of Operation Desert Shield. General Schwarzkopf reports that our forces in conjunction with other coalition forces, now have the capability to defend successfully against any further Iraqi aggression.

After consultation with King Fahd and our other allies, I have today directed the Secretary of Defense to increase the size of US forces committed to Desert Shield to ensure that the coalition has an adequate offensive military option should that be necessary to achieve our common goals. Toward this end, we will continue to discuss the possibility of both additional allied force contributions and appropriate United Nation actions. . . .

Wednesday November 14, 1990
My Diary

The White House. Sunday night the President returned from Camp David at 2:00 p.m. and had dinner in the residence with Baker, Sununu, Scowcroft, Gates, Powell, and Cheney to discuss Desert Storm war strategy.

FRIDAY NOVEMBER 16, 1990

"Imminent Thunder," the first American-Saudi military exercise, is carried out south of the Kuwait border.

SUNDAY NOVEMBER 18, 1990

Saddam Hussein announces that he will release all hostages between December 25 and March 25.

MONDAY NOVEMBER 19, 1990

Iraq sends 250,000 troops to Kuwait.

NOVEMBER 19, 1990

THE PRESIDENT

Excerpts from remarks and an exchange with reporters in Paris, France:

The President: There won't have to be a shot fired in anger if he does what he's supposed to do, which is to comply fully, without condition, to the United Nations resolutions. That's the way to get the peaceful solution to this question, and that is the only way to get a peaceful solution because it's not going to go on forever. It simply cannot go on forever and won't go on forever. . . .

I've seen the different negotiation efforts. I've seen people try for a so-called Arab solution. And they all fall short. The reason they fall short is that, in the final analysis, Saddam Hussein tells every single person that tries to be in a negotiating role, Kuwait is a province of Iraq. That is unacceptable. That is unacceptable to the United Nations. Clearly, it is unacceptable to the United States. And that's why it fails.

You can't negotiate with a terrorist. . . .

NOVEMBER 19, 1990

MY DIARY

President George Herbert Walker Bush, our 41st President, arranged to meet with Soviet Union Chairman Mikhail Gorbachev in the US Embassy residence in Paris to discuss support for the United Nations resolution ordering Iraq to pull out of Kuwait, and authorizing a coalition of nations to force the withdrawal. Gorbachev had indicated the possibility of a historic support for this resolution by the Soviet Union. It was to be a quiet dinner, but hopefully, Gorbachev would support the UN resolution.

Gorbachev and Bush arrived at the Embassy residence and went to an upstairs room to discuss the issue. United States and Soviet reporters gathered in a downstairs room to await the standard press briefing after the meeting, either by the principals or the press secretaries. However, after about ten minutes, Bush and Gorbachev came downstairs together and left without any comment. No notice was given to the staff waiting below, or to the press. I was left to explain why. The press immediately assumed trouble, most likely some disagreement, possibly a heated exchange.

General Brent Scowcroft, who had been in the meeting, tells me that Gorbachev is not ready to talk, due to hard-line opposition in Moscow. But I can't tell the press. It is clear to me that, in fact, Gorbachev wants to create stories that say the two leaders could not reach agreement and, indeed, left the meeting after just a few minutes.

I quickly ask for Vitali Ignatenko, Gorbachev's press secretary, to see what the Soviets want to say. They don't really care, of course, because they don't feel any responsibility to explain themselves to the press, and in fact, they probably want a story that says the meeting broke up unexpectedly. Ignatenko is not in the Embassy; he has gone to dinner with Soviet staff. I locate the Soviet protocol chief, who looks like the actor Cesar Romero, and ask him to find Ignatenko and order his return to the Embassy residence immediately to join me in briefing the press. I want a joint appearance to allay the appearance of disagreement. I assume the President wants to give Gorbachev his story for the hardliners back home, but take the edges off so it doesn't look like a total rejection of the US initiative.

I sit at the dining room table and write a statement for the press, emphasizing our joint cooperation, our interest in working with the Soviets, and our objectives in opposing Saddam Hussein. But the Soviet leader has had to leave quickly to address other problems. Very general, few specifics. I figure the Soviets could stiffen the language for their press back in the Soviet Embassy.

As I finish the statement, Vitali returns. He had plenty of wine before dinner—red eyes, slurred speech—and no guidance from his advisers. I suggest we issue my statement as a joint statement, so he will not have to take questions, and that I would emphasize his inability to speak English. He was in no condition to talk anyway. He reads my statement and agrees to this plan.

I read the statement to the press, speaking for both countries, and take a few questions. One US reporter, speaking Russian, asks Vitali a question. Vitali indicates he agreed with what I had said. We ended the press briefing with a minimum of damage.

I believe Vitali was eternally grateful. I probably saved his job. After the war, and after the dissolution of the Soviet Union on December 25, 1991, Vitali visited me in the White House. We never discussed the incident from 1990. At this point, we expected a Soviet evolution toward democracy and friendship with the United States. Under Gorbachev and his successor, Boris Yeltsin, that occurred for several years. But after Vladimir Putin became president of Russia, the country began returning to dictatorial rule. Vitali Ignatenko became Director General of the Russian News Agency TASS, the official Communist news service, and received a medal from Vladimir Putin for outstanding service to the motherland.

But for one evening in Paris, I had been the official spokesman for both superpowers, the United States and the Soviet Union, when hopes for peace and friendship were high.

NOVEMBER 19, 1990
THE PRESIDENT
Excerpt from a statement at the US Ambassador's residence, Paris, France:

The President: The fact that the Soviet Union and the United States could work together not only to achieve an arms control agreement but to start looking into the future with harmony and in cooperation is very, very promising for the new world order, for a Europe whole and free, and for peace in the world. . . .

TUESDAY NOVEMBER 20, 1990
WHITE HOUSE
Statement by Press Secretary Fitzwater:

President Bush held a wide-ranging discussion for approximately one hour with President Özal of Turkey this afternoon, with particular attention to the Persian Gulf. Their discussion was characterized by the same close cooperation that we have enjoyed with Turkey. President Bush noted that Turkey is showing real leadership in the international response to Iraq's aggression against Kuwait and that the United States is committed to helping Turkey to deal with the effects of that situation on Turkey. . . .

WEDNESDAY NOVEMBER 21, 1990
THE PRESIDENT
Excerpts from remarks and a question-and-answer session with reporters in Paris, France at the US Ambassador's residence:

The President: This was very encouraging to me that the world is still strongly together. And member after member came up to me and said, Thank God for the United States leadership in standing up against this aggression. And it just happened all the time. . . .

The deadline should have been the day the UN passed its first resolution or, in my view, the day he first went in. But I have no specific deadline in mind. But we are just going to keep ratcheting up that until the man does what he should have done long ago. . . .

. . . It's Thanksgiving, and gosh, we have a lot to be thankful for at this time of year—this particular year, too. And so, I will be trying as best I can, right from the heart, to express my thanks to the young men and women that are serving over there. It is a time for prayer; it is a time when we all thank God for our blessings. And I will try through this visit, perhaps only symbolically, to tell every single man and woman over there that we thank them and we thank God for the blessings that we have and that we are going to prevail. They're not there on a mission impossible. . . .

His Highness the Amir told me of the atrocities and acts of destruction that are being committed daily against Kuwaiti people by the forces of Saddam Hussein. It is a moving and touching and horrible story. And I come away from this conversation more committed than ever to seeing this cruel occupation come to an end and those responsible for this violence called to account. . . .

He showed me some pictures that are so cruel and so brutal, the treatment of Kuwaitis so cruel and so brutal that it just turns your stomach. . . . And justice demands that the world listen and understand exactly the kind of brutality that Saddam Hussein has wrought upon innocent kids and families in Kuwait. And what he is doing to hostages in Kuwait today is appalling.

WEDNESDAY NOVEMBER 22, 1990
MY DIARY

The build-up of troops in Saudi Arabia is going well and the President wants to visit the troops already in the desert on Thanksgiving. We arrive on a C130, with web seats, and wearing fatigues provided by the Army, then truck out to the tents that are the base. Hundreds of troops have gathered under camouflage tenting to be served a Thanksgiving dinner. The President walks into the middle of this picture, starts greeting troops individually, then sits down at the table to share the turkey. I'm told by a military aide that the President has a call from Mrs. Thatcher in London. I take the call and tell the London operator that the President is with the troops, but he will get back to her very soon. I go back to the dinner tent and tell the President that Mrs. Thatcher is calling. He soon interrupts his meal and goes to a communications tent to take the call. Mrs. Thatcher tells him she has been removed from office by her party.

This is a very sad day for America because Mrs. Thatcher has been the closest of friends with our country, and with Presidents Reagan and Bush. We release a statement by the President praising the prime minister. (Remarkably, her successor, John Major, and President Bush developed a warm and supportive relationship that existed for the rest of their lives.)

NOVEMBER 22, 1990
THE PRESIDENT
Excerpt from an exchange with reporters near Dhahran, Saudi Arabia:

The President: You know of my high regard for Prime Minister Thatcher. We will obviously work with the next Prime Minister, and I expect that, knowing the fiber there, that they'll stay right on course with us. But on a very personal sense, I would send my best to her at this difficult time. She's been a staunch friend and ally. She's a woman of principle; she's stood for what she believes. You always know where she was and what she believed. I think everybody in America would agree that Margaret Thatcher has been an outstanding ally for the United States. I'm certain that this will continue with the United Kingdom. But on a personal basis, I'll miss her because I value her counsel, I value her long experience—the wisdom that comes from her long experience. She has been an outstanding prime minister for the United Kingdom and an outstanding friend to the United States.

WEDNESDAY NOVEMBER 28, 1990
MY DIARY
The President called me to his study to ask that I consider a speech to the nation on Friday to discuss the UN resolution (678) on use of force in the Persian Gulf. Later, Scowcroft and Haass stop by my office to ask about timing—Friday, Saturday, or Sunday?

THURSDAY NOVEMBER 29, 1990
Passage of UNSC Resolution 678, authorizing the use of "all means necessary" to remove Iraqi forces from Kuwait. Iraq must withdraw from Kuwait before January 15, 1991, or face military action.

NOVEMBER 29, 1990
THE WHITE HOUSE
Statement on the United Nations Security Council Resolution Authorizing the Use of Force Against Iraq:
The United Nations Security Council vote underscores the unity and determination of the international community to end Iraq's illegal occupation of Kuwait. We are pleased to note the common stance and determination of the world in this endeavor. The United States will continue working with all countries for the express purpose of

having the United Nations Security Council resolution fully implemented. We continue to favor a peaceful settlement of this crisis; at the same time, and as the Security Council vote demonstrates, there is growing resolve that Saddam's occupation of Kuwait not be allowed to stand and that all necessary means be employed to ensure this is the case.

FRIDAY NOVEMBER 30, 1990
MY DIARY

I advised President Bush that a Friday afternoon press conference would be better than a prime-time speech because there is no real news in the message. The press briefing is scheduled for 11-30-1990 at 11:00 a.m. One hour before, the President calls me to his study to show a one-page insert announcing the offer of talks between Tariq Aziz, Foreign Minister of Iraq, and Secretary of State Baker. We should have done it on prime time. This is big news. But we (Demerest and I) weren't told about the Aziz insert. Secrecy has robbed us again. I could never understand why the President and Sununu would ask us if a speech should be televised if they wouldn't tell us what was in the speech.

NOVEMBER 30, 1990
THE PRESIDENT

Excerpt from the President's 66th news conference from the Briefing Room of the White House:

The President: I have a statement, and opening statement, that is a little longer than normal; and I'd ask your indulgence. And then I will be glad to respond to questions.

We're in the Gulf because the world must not and cannot reward aggression. And we're there because our vital interests are at stake. And we're in the Gulf because of the brutality of Saddam Hussein. We're dealing with a dangerous dictator all too willing to use force who has weapons of mass destruction and is seeking new ones and who desires to control one of the world's key resources all at a time in history when the rules of the post–Cold War world are being written.

Our objectives remain what they were since the outset. We seek

Iraq's immediate and unconditional withdrawal from Kuwait. We seek the restoration of Kuwait's legitimate government. We seek the release of all hostages and the free functioning of all embassies. And we seek the stability and security of this critical region of the world.

We are not alone in these goals and objectives. The United Nations, invigorated with a new sense of purpose, is in full agreement. The United Nations Security Council has endorsed twelve resolutions to condemn Iraq's unprovoked invasion and occupation of Kuwait, implement though economic sanctions to stop all trade in and out of Iraq, and authorize the use of force to compel Saddam to comply.

Saddam Hussein has tried every way he knows to make this a fight between Iraq and the United States, and clearly, he has failed. Forces of twenty-six other nations are standing shoulder to shoulder with our troops in the Gulf. The fact is that it is not the United States against Iraq. It is Iraq against the world. And there's never been a clearer demonstration of a world united against appeasement and aggression.

Yesterday's United Nations Security Council resolution was historic. Once again, the Security Council has enhanced the legitimate peacekeeping function of the United Nations. Until yesterday, Saddam may not have understood what he's up against in terms of world opinion, and I'm hopeful that now he will realize that he must leave Kuwait immediately.

I'm continually asked how effective are the UN sanctions put into effect on August 6th. I don't know the answer to that question. Clearly, the sanctions are having some effect, but I can't tell you that the sanctions alone will get the job done. And thus, I welcome yesterday's United Nations action.

The fledgling democracies in Eastern Europe are being severely damaged by the economic effects of Saddam's actions. The developing countries of Africa and in our hemisphere are being victimized by this dictator's rape of his neighbor Kuwait. Those who feel that there is no downside to waiting months and months must consider the devastating damage being done every day to the fragile economies of those countries that can afford it the least.

As Chairman Alan Greenspan [Board of Governors, Federal Reserve System] testified just the other day, the increase in oil prices resulting directly from Saddam's invasion is hurting our country, too. Our economy, as I said the other day, is at least in a serious slowdown, and if uncertainty remains in the energy markets, the slowdown will get worse.

I've spelled out once again our reason for sending troops to the Gulf. Let me tell you the things that concern me most. First, I put the immorality of the invasion of Kuwait itself. No nation should rape, pillage, and brutalize its neighbor. No nation should be able to wipe a member state of the United Nations and the Arab League off the face of the earth.

I'm deeply concerned about all the hostages—innocent people held against their will in direct contravention of international law. Then there's the cynical and brutal policy of forcing people to beg for their release, parceling out human lives to families and traveling emissaries like so much chattel.

I'm deeply concerned about our own Embassy in Kuwait. The flag is still flying there. A handful of beleaguered Americans remain inside the Embassy unable to come and go. This treatment of our Embassy violates every civilized principle of diplomacy. It demeans our people; it demeans our country. And I am determined that this Embassy, as called for under Security Council Resolution 674, be fully replenished and our people free to come home. What kind of precedent will these actions set for the future if Saddam's violation of international law goes unchallenged?

I'm also deeply concerned about the future of Kuwait itself. The tales of rape and assassination, of cold-blooded murder and rampant looting, are almost beyond belief. The whole civilized world must unite and say: This kind of treatment of people must end. And those who violate the Kuwaiti people must be brought to justice.

I'm deeply concerned about Saddam's efforts to acquire nuclear weapons. Imagine his ability to blackmail his neighbors should he possess a nuclear device. We've seen him use chemical weapons on his own people. We've seen him take his own country, one that should be wealthy and prosperous, and turn it into a poor country all because of insatiable appetite for military equipment and conquest.

I've been asked why I ordered more troops to the Gulf. I remain hopeful that we can achieve a peaceful solution to this crisis. But if force is required, we and the other twenty-six countries who have troops in the area will have enough power to get the job done.

In our country, I know that there are fears about another Vietnam. This will not be a protracted, drawn-out war. The forces arrayed are different. The opposition is different. The resupply of Saddam's military would be very different. The counties united against him in the United Nations are different. The topography of Kuwait is different. And the motivation of our all-volunteer force is superior.

I want peace. I want peace, not war. But if there must be war, we will not permit our troops to have their hands tied behind their backs. And I pledge to you: There will not be any murky ending. If one American soldier has to go into battle, that solder will have enough force behind him to win. And then get out as soon as possible, as soon as the UN objectives have been achieved. I will never—ever—agree to a halfway effort.

Let me repeat: We have no argument with the people of Iraq; indeed, we have only friendship for the people there. Further, I repeat that we have no desire to keep one single American soldier in the Gulf a single day longer than is necessary to achieve the objectives set out above.

No one wants to see a peaceful solution to this crisis more than I do. And at the same time, no one is more determined than I am to see Saddam's aggression reversed.

Lastly, people now caution patience. The United States and the entire world have been patient. I will continue to be patient. But yesterday's UN resolution, the 13th by the Security Council, properly says to Saddam Hussein: Time is running out. You must leave Kuwait. And we've given you time to do just exactly that.

Many people have talked directly to Saddam Hussein and to his Foreign Minister Tariq Aziz. All have been frustrated by Iraq's iron-clad insistence that it will not leave Kuwait. However, to go the extra mile for peace, I will issue an invitation to Foreign Minister Tariq Aziz to come to Washington at a mutually convenient time during the latter part of the week of December 10th to meet with me. I'll invite Ambassadors of several of our coalition partners in the Gulf to join me at that meeting. In addition, I'm asking Secretary Jim Baker to go to Baghdad to see Saddam Hussein. And I will suggest to Iraq's President that he receive the Secretary of State at a mutually convenient time between December 15th and January 15th of next year.

Within the mandate of the United Nations resolutions, I will be prepared, and so will Secretary Baker, to discuss all aspects of the Gulf crisis. However, to be very clear about these efforts to exhaust all means for achieving a political and diplomatic solution. I am not suggesting discussions that will result in anything less than Iraq's complete withdrawal from Kuwait, restoration of Kuwait's legitimate government, and freedom for all hostages.

DECEMBER 6, 1990
THE WHITE HOUSE
President Bush in a question-and-answer session with reporters that began at 1:55 p.m. at President Azocar's residence, Santiago, Chile [excerpt]:

Q: Mr. President, do you view this promise by Saddam Hussein to release the hostages as credible, and will it affect the US war footing in the Persian Gulf?

The President: One, I hope it is credible. Two, no single hostage should have been taken in the first place. And I hope that it shows that the strategy is working and that Saddam understands that his hostage policy has incurred the condemnation of the whole world. And we've got to continue to keep the pressure on. And this would be welcomed, if true, but it will not change my thinking on his need to comply 100 percent, without condition, to the UN resolutions.

THURSDAY DECEMBER 6, 1990
MY DIARY
Air Force One en route Caracas from Santiago, Chili, six-hour thirty-minute flight. Twenty minutes left in flight. I call Bill Harlow in Washington. Not there. Steve Hart says, "Did you get the State guidance that we're closing the Kuwait Embassy?" "What!" I exclaimed. "That can't be. Get me everything you've got before we get

off this plane."

I turned to Gates. He did not know about the closing. The President did not know. Gates called Scowcroft, who said it wasn't true. But it was. The President was livid. He kept saying the flag would not come down. Now we were leaving it.

DECEMBER 6, 1990

Saddam Hussein announces he is releasing all 3,000 foreign hostages from Iraq and Kuwait.

SATURDAY DECEMBER 8, 1990
MY DIARY

In Washington, I told him [Bush] the Embassy people were coming home Thursday. "That was a mistake," he said.

MONDAY DECEMBER 10, 1990

Iraq releases hundreds of British hostages; 156 former American hostages return to the US.

TUESDAY DECEMBER 11, 1990
MY DIARY

Gates visits former presidents to brief on the Gulf situation. Reagan says, "Did you know Saddam's mother was arrested when he was born? Violation of the toxic dumping rules." (Classic Reagan. He had a gag line for it, and his position was clear.)

DECEMBER 11, 1990
MY DIARY

Laurel Cavazos, Sec. of Education, faxed in a one-sentence resignation, from the Don Regan school of resignations. Jim Cicconi asks for a better letter.

Cavasoz had been offered (Ambassador) to Costa Rica, said no, packed his bags and drove to Boston on December 9, 1990. He left his Chief of Staff to announce his resignation at Education.

THURSDAY DECEMBER 13, 1990
THE PRESIDENT
Excerpts from an exchange with reporters prior to a meeting with seven former hostages (and their families) released by Iraq, in the Cabinet Room at the White House:

The President: But what this man put the world through, I just can't express it. And I think you all have expressed it, coming home, with a clarity that has brought this home to the American people. I'm very anxious to hear from each of you, how you read it, and what you think is happening there. . . .

Q: Should you give something in return for their freedom?

The President: Hell, no! Not one thing! You don't reward a kidnapper. You don't reward somebody that has done something that he shouldn't have done in the first place. . . .

FRIDAY DECEMBER 14, 1990
THE PRESIDENT
Excerpt from remarks and a question-and-answer session with reporters from the South Lawn of the White House:

Q: You said the deadline is real. Does that mean you think you have carte blanche to start a war after January 15th, or on January 15th?

The President: "I'm saying that the United Nations resolution is very clear as it regards January 15th. And I will continue now to work for a peaceful solution."

MONDAY DECEMBER 17, 1990
THE PRESIDENT
Excerpts from remarks from a session with reporters from the Rose Garden at the White House:

The President: What you see here is living proof that the international coalition arrayed against Saddam's aggression remains deep and wide. We're talking now about some twenty-eight countries that have committed their forces of one kind or another to this extraordinarily historic effort. Every country represented agrees that the twelve Security Council resolutions that are now on the books make clear what is required: Iraq's complete, immediate, and unconditional withdrawal from Kuwait. These same countries—and there are more than two dozen represented here today. I think maybe all twenty-eight of us—are contributing over 200,000 individuals to the military effort against Iraq. Tens of thousands more are on their way. As has been the case from August 2d on, it is not simply the United States against Iraq; it is really Iraq against the world.

And again, none of us wants war, but none of us is prepared to accept a partial solution. It is for this reason that we all welcome Security Council Resolution 678 and its authorization that all necessary means be used after January 15th to bring about Iraq's full compliance with all that the United Nations has demanded.

Let us just add that I also used this occasion inside to brief our coalition partners on our efforts to meet directly with Iraqi officials. And thus far, Iraq's behavior underscores what I think is its lack of interest in a peaceful settlement of this crisis. For our part, we remain open to having these meetings if mutually acceptable dates can be agreed upon. And if meetings are held, I want to reiterate publicly what I said inside: namely, that what we want to do is impress upon Iraq the consequences of its aggression and the need for all Iraqi forces to leave every square inch of Kuwait. There can and will be no negotiations for concessions and no rewards for aggression. . . .

. . . the United States remains steadfast and will remain steadfast in its determination to see every single United Nations resolution on this subject fulfilled without concession, without yielding one single inch . . .

Tuesday December 18, 1990
My Diary
Morning, in the White House. Teeter calls. Says President has asked his help. Wants to talk.

Saturday December 22, 1990
The President
Camp David, Maryland; following a meeting with British Prime Minister John Major at 8:20 a.m. on the helipad:

The President: Well, let me just say that this meeting with the Prime Minister has been very fruitful, at least from the United States standpoint. As you all know, we have had a very special relationship with the United Kingdom. And I am totally convinced that not only will that relationship continue, we will work to enhance it in every way possible. And so, I feel, Mr. Prime Minister, that we've gotten off to a wonderful start, and I want to thank you for coming at this terribly busy time of year for you, just coming into office and then, of course, with the holidays just over the horizon. So, thank you for coming. And I do think it shows exactly the right sense in terms of this special relationship.

We talked about the Gulf. We talked about the changes in the Soviet Union that have dominated so much of the international news lately. We talked about the importance of resuming and successfully concluding the GATT [Generalized Agreement on Tariffs and Trade] talks. We talked about NATO and its continuing importance. And we talked about South Africa, both sides expressing encouragement on developments. So, I found common ground with Prime Minister Major on these very, very important issues. . . .

DECEMBER 22, 1990
MY DIARY

Camp David. President meets with the new British Prime Minister, John Major. Major is a very funny guy, understated sense of irony. We met in the Conference Room at Laurel Lodge, Camp David. President raised the GATT issue. Major said he had met our negotiator, Ambassador Carla Hills, while he was Chancellor of the Exchequer. "The bruises have nearly healed," he said.

On Shamir, Major said he had a good meeting with him. "Everyone said he was in the best of moods. I would hate to have met him in his worst."

Great dinner following the meeting. My table was PM Major, Mrs. Bush, Scowcroft, Charles Powell, Mrs. Thatcher and Major's national security advisor, Robin Butler, the PM's cabinet secretary,

Mrs. Bush kept up a constant conversation. She said she had three great girls on her staff in 1989 who got engaged or married. She didn't mention Carol Powers, her photographer. So I did. She said she was trying to be sensitive since I had once been engaged to Carol.

The US Army chorus sang before dinner. They were great. President knew each member personally. They always sang at the VP's house; woe be unto the staff person who didn't pay attention. Mrs. Bush would let you know.

The Gulf War was seldom mentioned. Everyone wanted to get away from it over Christmas.

MONDAY DECEMBER 24, 1990 (CHRISTMAS EVE)
THE PRESIDENT
Christmas Message to the American Troops:

The President: Merry Christmas and happy holidays to you who are standing watch around the world. Never have I been prouder of our troops. Never have I been prouder to be your Commander in Chief. Because in this season of peace, it is your commitment and your courage that makes peace possible.

We think of you in the snowy fields and runways of Europe, where thanks to you millions are celebrating Christmas and Hanukkah openly for the first time in forty-five years. We think of you off the coast of the Philippines and Japan and the DMZ in Korea. We think of you in Panama, where lightning success last Christmas ended the reign of a despot and brought peace to a people. We think of you in the air, on the high seas, and at bases and Embassies around the world, who kept our country untouched and at peace throughout the long winter darkness of the Cold War.

Back home, some talk of the cost of war, but it is you who understand the price of peace. Each Christmas Day, we close our eyes in prayer and think of what Harry Truman called the humble surroundings of the Nativity and how from a straw-littered stable shone a light which for nearly twenty centuries has given men strength, comfort, and peace.

It's distant in time, but close within our hearts, because on this Christmas Day, hour by hour, hand in hand, Americans will send their prayers eastward across the ocean and halfway across the world not only to the town of Bethlehem but to the sands and shores where you stand in harm's way.

We're in the Gulf because the world must not reward aggression, because of the brutality and danger of Saddam Hussein. We're there backed by twelve United Nations resolutions and the forces of twenty-five other countries.

Barbara and I spent Thanksgiving with our men and women over there. And when we got back, I spoke to the American people, told them of your bravery and reminded them why we're there. First, I put the immorality of the invasion of Kuwait itself. I said I was deeply concerned about what has happened and is happening there, concerned about a ruthless despot's attempt to dominate a volatile and critical region, concerned about his efforts to acquire nuclear arms, and concerned that a promising era is threatened by an international outlaw. And I told the American people something else: that we want peace, not war, and that I will do my level-best to bring you home without a single shot fired.

And let me say one other thing: The sacrifices you make will never be forgotten. America is behind you, the world is behind you, and history is behind you. When you come home—and we hope it's soon—you'll be welcomed as what you are: all-American heroes.

Today at the White House and all across America, candles burn in remembrance of you and all our troops across the country and around the world. There is no way Americans can forget the contribution you are making to world peace and to our country. Whenever we see Old Glory snapping in the breeze, we think of you. Whenever we hear the inspirational words of "The Star-Spangled Banner," we think of you. And whenever we enjoy the boundless opportunities of a free country, we think of you.

History may make men, but you are making history. I think of Lieutenant Mary Danko, the flight nurse who volunteered for Saudi Arabia. Her husband, a C-130 navigator, was already flying in support of Desert Shield. And when asked if leaving their baby with relatives was a hard thing to do, Mary said, "It's the right thing to do. We're needed." And when asked, "Now, what about the kid?" Mary explained, "We're doing it for the kid." Well, she's right. Mary's right. She knows that when peace and freedom triumph, it's not a triumph for one particular country or one particular people but a triumph for our children, a triumph for all humankind.

And so it is with the holidays, for tonight the star of Bethlehem and the candles of the menorah will cast their light in American outposts around the world with a timeless message of hope and renewal that radiates to people of all faiths. Each of you is precious. Each life is important because it touches so many other lives. And while you may be out of America's sight, rest assured no matter where you serve you will never be out of America's heart.

Merry Christmas and happy holidays to you all. God keep you and watch over you. And God bless America."

DECEMBER 24, 1990
MY DIARY

Camp David. 10:30 p.m. Dan Balz, *Washington Post,* calls to say the *NYT* reports Cheney/Powell told President Bush at Camp David that General Waller was right: US ground troops are not ready to attack Iraq. I call Brent at home. He said the military wants more time to get troops in place, train and organize them. He says to point to Cheney comments in Saudi Arabia on Waller. I know that won't hold. I tell Balz, "We believe the military is ready to respond. The building continues." I hope that last phrase will imply we have more troops to get in place. The question all this raises is: will readiness impact the decision to attack and will we have to wait until February or later? Probably, but I don't know for sure.

THURSDAY DECEMBER 27, 1990
THE PRESIDENT
Excerpt from an exchange with reporters that began at 1:45 p.m. from the South Lawn of the White House:

The President: I really just want to wish you all a happy New Year.

Q: What about a message for Saddam Hussein?

The President: No, we have no message for him.

Q: What do you mean by rabbit trails running through the snow?

The President: I mean there are a lot of false leads out there. As a matter of fact—

Q: Are you upset about the report, sir?

The President: No, but as a matter of fact, I think it would be useful if from the president and others there were fewer comments about readiness. And I don't plan to make any comments about it at all. And I did make a comment earlier. And I feel very comfortable with the briefing I had from the Chairman of the Joint Chiefs, Colin Powell, and the Secretary of Defense. I mentioned to some earlier, I talked to General Schwarzkopf over the holidays, and there has been enough said about readiness. And I don't plan to continue to add to the debate at all. I'm very comfortable with the briefing. And the briefing I had was quite different than most of the stories I'm reading in the last day or two. So, that's what I mean about rabbit trails. . . . "

WEDNESDAY JANUARY 2, 1991
MY DIARY

Ellen "Bumblebee" Warren and three other reporters, including Randall Pinkston, CBS, ran into President Bush Sunday afternoon following his return from Camp David. Bush made a few comments on tape for Ellen, then walked on. Randall, who wasn't close enough to get the passing remarks, starts after Ellen shouting, "I must have that tape." Ellen turns on him, takes his hand, and says, "I don't believe we've met. You've got to know my name before you fuck me." Randall was dumbfounded and backed away sheepishly. He just learned how tough it is in the White House press corps.

JANUARY 2, 1991
MY DIARY

The President called me in at 8:49 a.m. to discuss communications between now and January 15. He's smarting from the *Time* magazine (Men of the Year.) "I don't care what the press says. I only care what Saddam thinks. I have an audience of one. And he must not see any flexibility, any waiver of our commitment."

FRIDAY JANUARY 4, 1991
THE PRESIDENT
Excerpt from remarks made beginning at 3:39 p.m. from the South

Lawn of the White House, regarding a Geneva meeting between Baker and Aziz:

The President: Iraq has accepted my initiative for a meeting between Secretary Baker and Foreign Minister Aziz. The meeting will take place on Wednesday, January 9th, in Geneva. And this is a useful step.

I hope that Iraq's acceptance of the meeting indicates a growing awareness of the seriousness of the situation and a willingness to heed the international community's will as expressed in twelve United Nations Security Council resolutions. And so, it is now for Saddam Hussein to respond to the international community's plea for reason.

I took this initiative yesterday with the view of going the extra mile to achieve a peaceful solution to the current crisis in the Gulf. Secretary Baker's mission to Geneva is to convey to Iraq the gravity of the situation and the determination of the international community to overcome Iraq's aggression against Kuwait.

Iraq knows what is necessary: The complete and unconditional and immediate withdrawal of all Iraqi forces from all of Kuwait, and the restoration of the legitimate government of Kuwait. . . .

Q: Mr. President, what is in the letter you are sending to Saddam Hussein? And are you willing to have Secretary Baker go on to Baghdad if that proves an option?

The President: Well, the answer to your question is that letter has not been finalized yet. I'm working on it. I have a copy I'm carrying with me now. I want to talk to the Secretary of State some more about it. And the second part of the question is no."

Q: Mr. President, you said you wanted Secretary of State Baker to speak eye to eye with Saddam Hussein. And he was willing to meet you on the 12th. You're willing to talk on the 9th. Why not wait three days and have that direct meeting?

The President: Because we have exhausted that option. We put forward fifteen different dates. And I believe that the message that both Secretary Baker and I want to convey can be done in this matter.

JANUARY 4, 1991
MY DIARY

President offered to have Baker meet with Aziz in Geneva January 1–7. I announced on camera at 7:30 a.m. in the Briefing Room. The questions focused on whether or not Baker might go on to Baghdad and meet with Hussein. I told this to the President and he said, "I don't think I want him (Baker) to go to Baghdad. That option is closed."

"I closed that off yesterday," Brent said. (In a background interview with White House TV correspondents.)

Back in my office, Roman cautioned me that Baker was leaving the door open. He gave me a cable from State to Gulf Embassy showing Damascus and several European cities as possible stops. I went to Brent privately for guidance. He looked me in the eye. "Marlin, we don't want to give him any excuses to string this thing out. Clearly, the decision for war had been made. The President is just waiting.

On Friday January 4, the *NYT* story by Tom Friedman said Baker might go to Baghdad. Brent and I mentioned the story to the President who said, "I don't want him to go."

When Aziz accepted the meeting offer about noon, the President decided to talk to reporters at 3:30 p.m. en route to Camp David. The first question was about Baker going on to Baghdad. The President said simply, "No."

January 5, 1991, the *Washington Post* headline was: Iraq Accepts Geneva Meeting, Bush Rejects Baghdad Talks.

Often the best way to cut off discussion, or end a debate, is to use the press. The President said simply, "No."

SATURDAY JANUARY 5, 1991
THE PRESIDENT
Excerpt from radio address to the nation recorded January 4 in the Oval Office at the White House and broadcast at 12:06 p.m. on January 5:

The President: As the new year begins, new challenges unfold—challenges to America and the future of our world. Simply put: 1990 saw Iraq invade and occupy Kuwait. Nineteen ninety-one will see Iraq withdraw—preferably by choice; by force, if need be. It is my most sincere hope 1991 is a year of peace. I've seen the hideous face of war and counted the costs of conflict in friends lost. I remember this all too well, and have no greater concern than the well-being of our men and women stationed in the Persian Gulf. True, their morale is sky-high. True, if they are called upon to fight the aggressors, they will do their job courageously, professionally and, in the end, decisively. There will be no more Vietnams.

But we should go the extra mile before asking our service men and women to stand in harm's way. We should, and we have. The United Nations, with the full support of the United States, has already tried to peacefully pressure Iraq out of Kuwait, implementing economic sanctions and securing the condemnation of the world in the form of no less than twelve resolutions of the UN Security Council.

This week, we've taken one more step. I have offered to have Secretary of State James Baker meet with Iraqi Foreign Minister Tariq Aziz in Switzerland. Yesterday, we received word that Iraq has accepted our offer to meet in Geneva. This will not be secret diplomacy at work. Secretary Baker will restate, in person, a message for Saddam Hussein: Withdraw from Kuwait unconditionally and immediately, or face the terrible consequences.

Eleven days from today, Saddam Hussein will either have met the United Nations deadline for a full and unconditional withdrawal, or he will have once again defied the civilized world. This is a deadline for Saddam Hussein to comply with the United Nations resolution, not a deadline for our own Armed Forces. Still, time is running out. It's running out because each day that passes brings real costs. . . ."

TUESDAY JANUARY 8, 1991

President Bush gave a message to the Allied Nations on the Persian Gulf Crisis to share "views of the aims and objectives that must guide us in the challenging days ahead."

President Bush delivered a letter to Congressional leaders on the Persian Gulf Crisis requesting that "the House of Representatives and the Senate adopt a resolution stating that Congress supports the use of all necessary means to implement UNSC Resolution 678."

JANUARY 8, 1991

MY DIARY

The President meets with Arab experts including April Glaspie, former Ambassador to Iraq. She said, "Saddam thinks he is Iraq. He feels as long as he survives, Iraq survives. Therefore, he is willing to sacrifice his people and his country. He doesn't think he can win, but he can keep you from winning by holding on until you suffer so many casualties that the US leaves."

The President: "How will it end?"

April: "Forces will surrender. He just won't be able to fight."

President: "You mean no surrender on board the *Missouri*, no white flag, no surrender talks?"

April: "No. For him, surviving is success. He will bill himself as the only Arab to stand up to the West and survive. The only one since Nasser."

President: "Do any of you think he will pull out on the 15th?"

All: "No. He may try a stalling tactic, some diplomatic offer. No way he will pull out. He is ready for war. Civil defense drills. Troops dug in for thirty days at least."

President: "If he loses, will there be dancing in the streets?"

April: "No. The people are hypnotized. They are conditioned not to celebrate."

After the meeting, Colin Powell stopped by my office for a cigar. I gave him two of my JR 122s.

"Is the President ready?" I ask. "Does he understand the consequences?"

"He's been ready since August 4," Colin said.

"Yes," I say, "but more since Christmas. But those questions today indicate he thinks it might be easy or quick."

"It won't be," Colin said. "When I go, Marlin, everything goes. We're taking out everything, Marlin."

He waved his hand in a wide sweeping motion to indicate, in my mind, that Iraq and Baghdad will be gone. Colin didn't mean that, but he meant full force.

WEDNESDAY JANUARY 9, 1991

Secretary of State James Baker meets Foreign Minister Tariq Aziz at the Geneva Conference Hotel InterContinental; their attempt to find a peaceful resolution is unsuccessful.

JANUARY 9, 1991

THE PRESIDENT

Excerpt from an exchange with reporters that began at 2:05 p.m. in the Cabinet Room at the White House:

Q: Mr. President, are you encouraged by what you've heard from Secretary Baker, sir?

The President: "Encouraged, you say? No."

Q: Why, sir?

The President: "Because I think Iraq has demonstrated no flexibility whatsoever. And I think the meeting we're having here today no takes on even greater importance because I would like to see the Congress send a strong signal that they want to see these United Nations resolutions fully supported. And given the position taken by Iraq at the Geneva meetings—it lasted several hours, the meetings did—but I've talked to the Secretary of State and I've told these friends in the United States Congress of his reaction, and his reaction was they were not flexible at all and showed no propensity to comply with the United Nations resolutions. . . . So, Baker could not report any progress at all."

JANUARY 9, 1991

THE PRESIDENT

Excerpt from the President's 68th news conference that began at 3:55 p.m. in the Briefing Room of the White House:

The President: I have spoken with Secretary of State Jim Baker, who reported to me on his nearly seven hours of conversation with Iraqi Foreign Minister Tariq Aziz. Secretary Baker made it clear that he discerned no evidence whatsoever that Iraq was willing to comply with the international community's demand to withdraw from Kuwait and comply with the United Nations resolutions.

Secretary Baker also reported to me that the Iraqi foreign minister rejected my letter to Saddam Hussein—refused to carry this letter and give it to the president of Iraq. . . .

I can't misrepresent this to the American people. I am discouraged.

I am going to say, if Saddam doesn't move, we are going to fully implement Resolution 678. And it will be fully complied with.". . .

SATURDAY JANUARY 12, 1990

Congress passes a joint resolution authorizing the use of military force in Iraq and Kuwait (Senate votes 52–47; House of Representatives 250–183).

Soviet special envoy Yevgeny Primakov meets with Saddam Hussein in Baghdad.

JANUARY 12, 1991
MY DIARY

Congress voted to approve the resolution in support of the President and the United Nations resolution. Roman wrote the POTUS statement with this great line: "We didn't plan war, we didn't seek war, but if war is thrust upon us, we are ready and we are determined."

Sununu took the third "war" out and made it "conflict," thereby taking some of the poetry out. I still thought it was good enough to check the Nexus computer to be sure it wasn't taken from Churchill, Chamberlain, or worse, some dictator. No reference found. POTUS delivered it with strength.

Demerest told me he had been secretly working on a war speech for four months. It would be given on National TV when the war started. He gave it to the President on Friday. Another speechwriter did a shorter version to give when the first shots are fired. It went to the President Friday also.

I convinced the President to release his letter to Saddam Hussein. It had leaked anyway to the BBC and *NYT*.

Going out to his press conference, the President stopped in the Oval doorway and asked if he looked OK. He looked older. I was almost shocked. The lines were deeper than I remembered. I swallowed deeply and said yes, he looked fine.

JANUARY 12, 1991

THE PRESIDENT

Excerpt from the President's 69th news conference that began at 4:00 p.m. in the Briefing Room of the White House:

The President: I am gratified by the vote in the Congress supporting the United Nations Security Council resolutions. This action by the Congress unmistakably demonstrates the United States commitment to the international demand for a complete and unconditional withdrawal of Iraq from Kuwait. This clear expression of the Congress represents the last, best chance for peace. . . .

Let there be no mistake: Peace is everyone's goal. Peace is in everyone's prayers. But it is for Iraq to decide. . . ."

JANUARY 12, 1991

THE WHITE HOUSE

Statement by Press Secretary Fitzwater on President Bush's letter to President Saddam Hussein of Iraq:

We do not believe it is appropriate as a general matter to release diplomatic correspondence. However, the President's letter to Saddam Hussein has now appeared in the news media. Stories containing large segments of the letter have appeared on major wire services. This published letter is not, however, the final letter as presented to Foreign Minister Aziz.

Therefore, we are today releasing the President's actual letter to Saddam Hussein:

```
Mr. President:


We stand today at the brink of war between Iraq
and the world. This is a war that began with your
invasion of Kuwait, this is a war that can be
ended only by Iraq's full and unconditional com-
pliance with UN Security Council Resolution 678.


I am writing you now, directly, because what is
at stake demands that no opportunity be lost to
```

avoid what would be certain calamity for the people of Iraq. I am writing, as well, because it is said by some that you do not understand just how isolated Iraq is and what Iraq faces as a result. I am not in a position to judge whether this impression is correct; what I can do, though, is try in this letter to reinforce what Secretary of State Baker told your Foreign Minister and eliminate any uncertainty or ambiguity that might exist in your mind about where we stand and what we are prepared to do.

The international community is united in its call for Iraq to leave all of Kuwait without condition and without further delay. This is not simply the policy of the United States; it is the position of the world community as expressed in no less than twelve Security Council resolutions.

We prefer a peaceful outcome. However, anything less than full compliance with UN Security Council Resolution 678 and its predecessors is unacceptable. There can be no reward for aggression. Nor will there be any negotiation. Principle cannot be compromised. However, by its full compliance, Iraq will gain the opportunity to rejoin the international community. More immediately, the Iraq military establishment will escape destruction. But unless you withdraw from Kuwait completely and without condition, you will lose more than Kuwait. What is at issue here is not the future of Kuwait—it will be free, its government will be restored—but rather the future of Iraq. This choice is yours to make.

The United States will not be separated from

its coalition partners. Twelve Security Council resolutions, twenty-eight countries providing military units to enforce them, more than one hundred governments complying with sanctions—all highlight the fact that it is not Iraq against the United States, but Iraq against the world. That most Arab and Muslim countries are arrayed against you as well should reinforce what I am saying. Iraq cannot and will not be able to hold on to Kuwait or exact a price for leaving.

You may be tempted to find solace in the diversity of opinion that is American democracy. You should resist any such temptation. Diversity ought not to be confused with division. Nor should you underestimate, as others have before you, America's will.

Iraq is already feeling the effects of the sanctions mandated by the United Nations. Should war come, it will be a far greater tragedy for you and your country. Let me state, too, that the United States will not tolerate the use of chemical or biological weapons or the destruction of Kuwait's oil fields and installations. Further, you will be held directly responsible for terrorist actions against any member of the coalition. The American people would demand the strongest possible response. You and your country will pay a terrible price if you order unconscionable acts of this sort.

I write this letter not to threaten, but to inform. I do so with no sense of satisfaction, for the people of the United States have no quarrel with the people of Iraq. Mr. President,

UN Security Council Resolution 678 establishes
the period of January 15 of this year as a "pause
of good will" so that this crisis may end without
further violence. Whether this pause is used as
intended, or merely becomes a prelude to further
violence, is in your hands, and yours alone. I
hope you weigh your choice carefully and choose
wisely, for much will depend upon it.

George Bush

Note: Foreign Minister Tariq Aziz of Iraq refused to deliver the letter, which was dated January 5.

SUNDAY JANUARY 13, 1991
MY DIARY

The President returned from Camp David to make a statement
on arrival about the Soviets moving to crush Lithuania. Going into
the residence, he turns at the elevator to say, "Another damn thing to
worry about."

Then he goes upstairs to meet with NSC advisors about the Gulf.
Communication plan going well.

MONDAY JANUARY 14, 1991
MY DIARY

"Any moment after 15th is borrowed time."

TUESDAY JANUARY 15, 1991

UN deadline for Iraqi withdrawal; Iraq ignores UN resolutions.
Kuwait has 540,000 troops in the region; the coalition has 580,000
troops in the Gulf region.

JANUARY 15, 1991
MY DIARY

The President sent a note during my 11:00 a.m. briefing to invite
me to join him for lunch. I went to the Oval, and from there to the

mess. Boyden Gray was alone at the next table and the President invited him to join us. Small talk lunch. No mention of the Gulf. I couldn't help remembering that we had dinner together the night we went into Panama. Afterward, we walked back to the Oval and he asked me to come in a minute. He ushered me to the white chair in front of the fireplace. The fire was crackling.

"Marlin," he said. "I haven't told anybody but the security guys. We're going to do this tomorrow. What are your thoughts on a speech?"

"I think you have to speak from the Oval. It's the only symbol that will instill confidence."

"I understand," he said, "but can I just give one speech. It'll be tomorrow evening."

"Yes," I said, "if it's in the afternoon, we can put out a brief written statement that you will speak to the nation at 9:00 p.m."

"OK," he said. "I just wanted you to be ready." He seemed calm, older somehow, very concerned.

JANUARY 15, 1991
MY DIARY
The President called to ask me why Bernard Shaw, CNN, wasn't out of Baghdad. I called Carol Crotty, CNN Producer in the White House, and I asked her to pass along to CNN management my advisories that all journalists be out of Baghdad by the 15th. She promised she would.

JANUARY 15, 1991
MY DIARY
President is praying for guidance.

JANUARY 15, 1991
MY DIARY
Just before departure for Kennebunkport (KBP), Roman brought me a statement condemning Israel Ambassador Shoval in very personal terms for his comments about Sec. Baker and the United States objecting to $400 million for settlements.

"Baker and Scowcroft agreed to this, Marlin," Roman said, "and you can't change it."

"The President won't do this," I said. "This is crazy. It kicks Shoval out of this country. What the hell did he do?"

"Gates will show it to the President on the chopper," Roman said. "Talk to him then."

On *Marine One* to Andrews, the President read the statement with consternation. He didn't think it was appropriate. He asked if any President had ever done such a thing before, especially to the Ambassador of a friendly country. None of us could think of a precedent.

On *Air Force One*, I told the President that *Evans & Novak, US News*, and the *NY Times* are all writing stories that Baker's influence is waning due to the Bessmyrtnik (Soviet Deputy Foreign Minister) communiqué screw-up. The President got the picture. He knew Baker was very defensive and wanted a White House statement backing his private reprimand of Shoval.

Mrs. Bush leaned over on *Marine One* and said, "He always says to me, 'If you're not comfortable with it, don't do it.'"

Later, at Walker's Point, the President called Jim Baker about it again. He had already called Baker while on *Air Force One*, and Baker had agreed to rewrite the statement. But the rewrite said the same thing, just a shorter version.

After a twenty-minute talk, the President agreed. I was given the statement to issue about 5:00 p.m. It made all the networks. (And the newspapers).

The next morning, February 16, the President said, "Marlin, you got your name in the paper on this Israel thing."

"Mr. President," I said, "We always said that some day we would have to take on the Israeli lobby, but you didn't say I had to go first."

He laughed. "Don't worry, Marlin. I'm right behind you." He laughed again, and he wished me well on my ski trips to Mt. Abraham.

WEDNESDAY JANUARY 16, 1991
THE PRESIDENT
Letter to Congressional leaders transmitting a report pursuant to the

Resolution authorizing the use of force against Iraq:

```
Dear Mr. Speaker (Dear Mr. President)

Pursuant to section 2(b) of the Authorization
for Use of Military Force Against Iraq Resolution
(J.J. Res. 77, Public Law 102-1), I have con-
cluded that:

1. The United States has used all appropriate
diplomatic and other peaceful means to obtain
compliance by Iraq with UN Security Council
Resolutions 660, 661, 662, 664, 665, 666, 667,
669, 670, 674, 677, and 678, and

2. That those efforts have not been and would
not be successful in obtaining such compliance.

Enclosed is a report that supports my decision.

Sincerely,
George Bush
```

Note: Identical letters were sent to Thomas S. Foley, Speaker of the House of Representatives; Robert C. Byrd, President pro tempore of the Senate; George J. Mitchell, Senate majority leader; Robert Dole, Senate Republican leader; and Robert H. Michel, House Republican leader.

JANUARY 16, 1991

The liberation of Kuwait, Operation Desert Storm, begins at 7:00 p.m. Washington, DC, (3:00 a.m. January 17 in Kuwait) when the first Apache air attacks of Operation Desert Storm are launched.

Coalition forces, led by the United States, begin deploying to Kuwait via the Persian Gulf and Saudi Arabian border.

JANUARY 16, 1991

The air campaign begins with Operation Senior Surprise, which became known as "Secret Squirrel." On the 14,000-mile round trip combat sortie, seven B-52G Stratofortresses fly from Barksdale Air Force Base, Louisiana, to the Middle East. They launch thirty-five conventional air-launched cruise missiles at strategic targets in Iraq.

JANUARY 16, 1990

As part of its "scorched earth" policy to destroy the oil infrastructure of Kuwait, Iraq sets on fire the first Kuwaiti oil wells, starting at Wahfra field and moving north.

JANUARY 16, 1991
THE WHITE HOUSE
"The Liberation of Kuwait Has Begun"
Statement by Press Secretary Fitzwater on Allied Military Action in the Persian Gulf, from the Briefing Room of the White House at 7:08 p.m.:
I have a statement by the President of the United States:

```
The liberation of Kuwait has begun. In conjunc-
tion with the forces of our coalition partners,
the United States has moved under the code name
Operation Desert Storm to enforce the mandates
of the United Nations Security Council. As of
7 p.m. Eastern Standard Time, Operation Desert
Storm forces were engaging targets in Kuwait
and Iraq.
```

President Bush will address the Nation at 9:00 p.m. tonight from the Oval Office. I'll try to get you more as soon as we can.

In a televised speech to the Nation, President Bush announces Allied military action for the liberation of Kuwait has begun in the Persian Gulf.

"WE WILL NOT FAIL"

Just two hours ago, allied air forces began an attack on military targets in Iraq and Kuwait. These attacks continue as I speak. Ground forces are not engaged.

This conflict started August 2nd when the dictator of Iraq invaded a small and helpless neighbor. Kuwait—a member of the Arab League and a member of the United Nations—was crushed; its people, brutalized. Five months ago, Saddam Hussein started this cruel war against Kuwait. Tonight, the battle has been joined.

This military action, taken in accord with United Nations resolutions and with the consent of the United States Congress, follows months of constant and virtually endless diplomatic activity on the part of the United Nations, the United States, and many, many other countries. Arab leaders sought what became known as an Arab solution, only to conclude that Saddam Hussein was unwilling to leave Kuwait. Others traveled to Baghdad in a variety of efforts to restore peace and justice. Our Secretary of State, James Baker, held an historic meeting in Geneva, only to be totally rebuffed. This past weekend, in a last-ditch effort, the Secretary-General of the United Nations went to the Middle East with peace in his heart—his second such mission. And he came back from Baghdad with no progress at all in getting Saddam Hussein to withdraw from Kuwait.

Now the twenty-eight countries with forces in the Gulf area have exhausted all reasonable efforts to reach a peaceful resolution—have no choice but to drive Saddam from Kuwait by force. We will not fail.

As I report to you, air attacks are underway against military targets in Iraq. We are determined to knock out Saddam Hussein's nuclear bomb potential. We will also destroy his chemical weapons facilities. Much of Saddam's artillery and tanks will be destroyed. Our operations are designed to best protect the lives of all the coalition forces by targeting Saddam's vast military arsenal. Initial reports from General Schwarzkopf are that our operations are proceeding according to plan.

Our objectives are clear: Saddam Hussein's forces will leave Kuwait. The legitimate government of Kuwait will be restored to its rightful place, and Kuwait will once again be free. Iraq will eventually comply with all relevant United Nations resolutions, and then, when peace is restored, it is our hope that Iraq will live as a peaceful and cooperative member of the family of nations, thus enhancing the security and stability of the Gulf.

Some may ask: Why act now? Why not wait? The answer is clear: The world could wait no longer. Sanctions, though having some effect, showed no signs of accomplishing their objective. Sanctions were tried for well over five months, and we and our allies concluded that sanctions alone would not force Saddam from Kuwait.

While the world waited, Saddam Hussein systematically raped, pillaged, and plundered a tiny nation, no threat to his own. He subjected the people of Kuwait to unspeakable atrocities—and among those maimed and murdered, innocent children.

While the world waited, Saddam sought to add to the

chemical weapons arsenal he now possesses, an infinitely more dangerous weapon of mass destruction—a nuclear weapon. And while the world waited, while the world talked peace and withdrawal, Saddam Hussein dug in and moved massive forces into Kuwait.

While the world waited, while Saddam stalled, more damage was being done to the fragile economies of the Third World, emerging democracies of Eastern Europe, to the entire world, including to our own economy.

The United States, together with the United Nations, exhausted every means at our disposal to bring this crisis to a peaceful end. However, Saddam clearly felt that by stalling and threatening and defying the United Nations, he could weaken the forces arrayed against him.

While the world waited, Saddam Hussein met every overture of peace with open contempt. While the world prayed for peace, Saddam prepared for war.

I had hoped that when the United States Congress, in historic debate, took its resolute action, Saddam would realize he could not prevail and would move out of Kuwait in accord with the United Nation resolutions. He did not do that. Instead, he remained intransigent, certain that time was on his side.

Saddam was warned over and over again to comply with the will of the United Nations: Leave Kuwait, or be driven out. Saddam has arrogantly rejected all warnings. Instead, he tried to make this a dispute between Iraq and the United States of America.

Well, he failed. Tonight, twenty-eight nations—countries from five continents, Europe and Asia, Africa, and the Arab

League—have forces in the Gulf area standing shoulder to shoulder against Saddam Hussein. These countries had hoped the use of force could be avoided. Regrettably, we now believe that only force will make him leave.

Prior to ordering our forces into battle, I instructed our military commanders to take every necessary step to prevail as quickly as possible, and with the greatest degree of protection possible for American and allied service men and women. I've told the American people before that this will not be another Vietnam, and I repeat this here tonight. Our troops will have the best possible support in the entire world, and they will not be asked to fight with one hand tied behind their back. I'm hopeful that this fighting will not go on for long and that casualties will be held to an absolute minimum.

This is an historic moment. We have in this past year made great progress in ending the long era of conflict and cold war. We have before us the opportunity to forge for ourselves and for future generations a new world order—a world where the rule of law, not the law of the jungle, governs the conduct of nations. When we are successful—and we will be—we have a real chance at this new world order, an order in which a credible United Nations can use its peacekeeping role to fulfill the promise and vision of the UN's founders.

We have no argument with the people of Iraq. Indeed, for the innocents caught in this conflict, I pray for their safety. Our goal is not the conquest of Iraq. It is the liberation of Kuwait. It is my hope that somehow the Iraqi people can, even now, convince their dictator that he must lay down his arms, leave Kuwait, and let Iraq itself rejoin the family of peace-loving nations.

Thomas Paine wrote many years ago: "These are the times

that try men's souls." Those well-known words are so very true today. But even as planes of the multinational forces attack Iraq, I prefer to think of peace, not war. I am convinced not only that we will prevail but that out of the horror of combat will come the recognition that no nation can stand against a world united, no nation will be permitted to brutally assault its neighbor.

No President can easily commit our sons and daughters to war. They are the Nation's finest. Ours is an all-volunteer force, magnificently trained, highly motivated. The troops know why they're there. And listen to what they say, for they've said it better than any President or Prime Minister ever could.

Listen to Hollywood Huddleston, Marine lance corporal. He says, "Let's free these people, so we can go home and be free again." And he's right. The terrible crimes and tortures committed by Saddam's henchmen against the innocent people of Kuwait are an affront to mankind and a challenge to the freedom of all.

Listen to one of our great officers out there, Marine Lieutenant General Walter Boomer. He said: "There are things worth fighting for. A world in which brutality and lawlessness are allowed to go unchecked isn't the kind of world we're going to want to live in."

Listen to Master Sergeant J.P. Kendall of the 82nd Airborne: "We're here for more than just the price of a gallon of gas. What we're doing is going to chart the future of the world for the next one hundred years. It's better to deal with this guy now than five years from now."

And finally, we should all sit up and listen to Jackie Jones, an Army lieutenant, when she says, "If we let him get away with this, who knows what's going to be next?"

I have called upon Hollywood and Walter and J.P. and Jackie and all their courageous comrades-in-arms to do what must be done. Tonight, America and the world are deeply grateful to them and to their families. And let me say to everyone listening or watching tonight: When the troops we've sent in finish their work, I am determined to bring them home as soon as possible.

Tonight, as our forces fight, they and their families are in our prayers. May God bless each and every one of them, and the coalition forces at our side in the Gulf, and may He continue to bless our nation, the United States of America.

Note: President Bush spoke at 9:01 p.m. from the Oval Office. The address was broadcast live on nationwide radio and television.

THURSDAY JANUARY 17, 1991
THE PRESIDENT
Excerpt from an exchange with reporters on the Persian Gulf Conflict, at 9:40 a.m. from the Cabinet Room at the White House, prior to a meeting with congressional leaders:

Q: Mr. President, based on what you've been told this morning, what are your thoughts at this point on how severely the Iraqis have been damaged, how long this may last, and at what cost?

The President: "Well, again, I don't want to go into questions here because of the moment. I will say that was covered very well by Secretary Cheney and Colin Powell. And the way we're going to handle this is, I will not be commenting on the ups and downs—and there will be some downs—or the trauma of the moment—there's a lot of trauma of the moment. But I think it is fair to say—and I will be repeating this to the leaders here—that we are pleased with the way things have gone so far. We're determined to finish what we've set out to do. . . ."

JANUARY 17, 1991

In response to Operation Secret Squirrel, Iraq fires Scud missiles at Israel and Saudi Arabia.

The US deploys the first successful use in combat of the MIM-104C Patriot missiles. The Patriot disables or destroys incoming ballistic missiles by detecting, targeting, and detonating near them. First American air attacks launch from Turkey into Dhahran, Saudi Arabia.

Saddam Hussein declares: "The great showdown has begun! The mother of all battles is under way."

JANUARY 17, 1991

Twenty-four hours after US air assault begins, Iraq attacks Tel Aviv, Israel, with up to eight Scud missiles, injuring and killing Israelis. Israel vows to defend itself.

The US tells Israel not to retaliate, fearing the escalation of war and collapse of the Arab coalition.

JANUARY 17, 1991

THE WHITE HOUSE

Statement by Press Secretary Fitzwater confirming Iraqi missile attacks on Israel and Saudi Arabia:

The Department of Defense has confirmed the firing of missiles from Iraq into Israel and Saudi Arabia. Damage assessments are being made.

President Bush was informed of the action by NSC Adviser Brent Scowcroft earlier this evening. The President has also discussed this matter with Secretary of State Baker and Secretary of Defense Cheney. The President is outraged at, and condemns, this further aggression by Iraq.

Coalition forces in the Gulf are attacking missile sites and other targets in Iraq.

FRIDAY JANUARY 18, 1991
THE PRESIDENT
Opening remarks from the President's 70th news conference, from the Briefing Room of the White House:

The President: We're now some thirty-seven hours into Operation Desert Storm and the liberation of Kuwait, and so far, so good. US and coalition military forces have performed bravely, professionally, and effectively. It is important, however, to keep in mind two things: First, this effort will take some time. Saddam Hussein has devoted nearly all of Iraq's resources for a decade to building up this powerful military machine. We can't expect to overcome it overnight—especially as we want to minimize casualties to the US and coalition forces and to minimize any harm done to innocent civilians.

Second, we must be realistic. There will be losses. There will be obstacles along the way. War is never cheap or easy. And I said this only because I am somewhat concerned about the initial euphoria in some of the reports and reactions to the first day's developments. No one should doubt or question the ultimate success, because we will prevail. But I don't want to see us get overly euphoric about all of this.

Our goals have not changed. What we seek is the same as what the international community seeks—namely, Iraq's complete and unconditional withdrawal from Kuwait and then full compliance with the Security Council resolutions.

I also want to say how outraged I am by Iraq's latest act of aggression—in this case, against Israel. Once again, we see that no neighbor of Iraq is safe. I want to state here publicly how much I appreciated Israel's restraint from the outset, really from the very beginning of this crisis. Prime Minister Shamir and his government have shown great understanding for the interests of the United States and the interests of others involved in this coalition.

Close consultations with Israel are continuing. So, too, are close consultations with our coalition partners. Just a few minutes ago I spoke to Prime Minister Brian Mulroney of Canada. And in that vein, I also had a long and good conversation this morning with

Soviet President Gorbachev in which we thoroughly reviewed the situation in the Gulf. And, of course, I took the opportunity from that call to express again my concern, my deep concern, over the Baltics and the need to ensure that there is a peaceful resolution to the situation there.

Let me close here by saying how much we appreciate what our fighting men and women are doing. This country is united. Yes, there's some protest, but this country is fundamentally united. And I want that message to go out to every kid that is over there serving this country.

I saw in the paper a comment by one who worried—from seeing demonstrations here and there in this country on television—that that expressed the will of the country. So, to those troops over there, let me just take this opportunity to say your country is supporting you—the Congress overwhelmingly endorsed that. Let there be no doubt in the minds of any of you: You have the full and unified support of the United States of America. So, I salute them. They deserve our full support, and they are our finest.

JANUARY 18, 1991

By Executive Order 12743 President Bush orders the Ready Reserve of the Armed Forces to Active Duty [Filed with the Office of the Federal Register, 10:59 a.m. January 22, 1991].

JANUARY 18, 1991
THE WHITE HOUSE
Statement by Press Secretary Fitzwater on the Activation of the Ready Reserves:

At the request of the Secretary of Defense, the President today authorized the Department of Defense and the Department of Transportation to order members of the Ready Reserve of the Armed Forces to active duty under the provision of section 673 of title 10, United States Code. This step is necessary to support the continued operations of US forces in Operation Desert Storm. This authority will enable reservists to remain on active duty for longer than 180 days and will also permit the call to active duty of personnel in excess of the 200,000 previously authorized.

SATURDAY JANUARY 19, 1991
MY DIARY

Camp David meeting with the President. He calls PM Shamir, saying afterwards, "I must say, that little guy is very cooperative."

Flying back with Cheney and Powell on a Marine chopper, I joked that he and Cheney were ready for a 1996 run for the Presidency and Vice Presidency. This was after I told them ABC news was reporting an 83 percent approval rating for George Bush and the war.

"The only question," Colin joked, "is how Dick will like living at the Naval Observatory?" We all laughed uproariously. The *Post* reported today that I am a veteran of five military campaigns, and Colin engineered them all, with Reagan and Bush.

JANUARY 19, 1991
MY DIARY

The White House. In an 11:30 a.m. phone conversation with the President, PM Shamir agreed to hold off on retaliation as long as possible. He cared less about retaliation than just about eliminating the Scud missiles in order to protect his cities. He wants to send in lower level helicopters to look for mobiles. We don't think it will work because the human eye can see less than our aerial surveillance planes. Also, we fear a chopper would go down and then we would have to rescue Israeli pilots. Then Israel would be in the war. Arens tells Cheney the choppers could cross Jordan, undetected, but we're skeptical. Shamir agrees to hold off since we sent Patriot missiles. But clearly, one more Scud attack and they are going in. They can retaliate later, but they want those Scuds now. The President offers to send Eagleburger, Wolfowitz, and Armitage to coordinate US/Israel policy on the spot. Eagleburger was going home to Charlottesville for the weekend. Baker calls him at 11:45 a.m. to send him to Israel. They are to leave immediately, Saturday afternoon. Sununu passes me a note. "Another FOTEM." (Failure Of The Eagleburger Mission.) We kidded Larry unmercifully Thursday night in Scowcroft's office when a TV anchorman referred to the failed Eagleburger mission.

"If Israel stays out," Larry said, "It better be called the "Successful Eagleburger Mission."(Israel did stay out of the war.)

The President is not happy today. Tired from being up all night. He snaps at Sununu once when the Governor started to interrupt. I showed him the ABC-TV poll showing 83 percent support for the President, and 86 percent do not support the protesters. Even that didn't cheer him up. I think the President is getting nervous that all this bombing—5,000 sorties—hasn't produced much visual destruction. He asks how we detected Scud attacks on Israel. Colin says our satellites system picked up the mobile firing, registered it on Colorado Springs computers, transmitted it to the Pentagon and Israel simultaneously. The President can't understand how we can do that and still not find the Scud launchers.

In the chopper on the way back to Washington, Colin and Dick are pretty confident. I tell Colin that so far we've a new war each Christmas—Panama and Iraq.

"Are you with me in '96?" Colin jokes.

"You bet," I say. God, I hope we're still able to joke this time next year.

JANUARY 19, 1991
MY DIARY

Camp David. Jack Kemp called me out of lunch with the President to ask if the NFL should play its games this weekend, and Superbowl the next week. I told him yes, the President feels the nation's business and recreation must go on. Life goes on. I returned to the table and told the President.

"Of course," he said. "We should have the games." I told the press later at the White House, and Kemp told NFL commissioner Paul Tagliabue.

SUNDAY JANUARY 20, 1991
MY DIARY

11:00 a.m. Tom Johnson, president of CNN, called to say he is meeting Bernard Shaw and John Holliman at the airport in DC this afternoon. "Thanks for your help," he said. "I could hear it in your voice last week that you had our personal welfare in mind." I had called Johnson, at the President's request, last Wed. January 16, to advise CNN to leave Baghdad. I had given private advice to that effect on January 10, 14, 15 and 16. It was a last chance because I knew the bombs would start falling at 7:00 p.m. on the 16th. Earlier CNN told us they were leaving on the 14th. Johnson called me on the 18th to say Shaw and Holliman were leaving by car; on the 19th to say other CNN staff leaving; on the 20th to say Peter Arnett had decided to stay with a shortwave radio. I asked if the Iraq authorities approved. He said yes.

JANUARY 20, 1990

Deputy Secretary of State Lawrence Eagleburger and Undersecretary of Defense of Policy Paul Wolfowitz arrive in Tel Aviv, Israel, to coordinate military strategy.

First Kuwaiti oil wells set on fire by Iraq, starting at Wahfra field and moving north.

JANUARY 20, 1991

Iraq fires ten Scuds at Saudi Arabia; nine Scuds are intercepted and one goes offshore.

JANUARY 20, 1991
MY DIARY

The President meets with Bernard Shaw, Scowcroft, Sununu, and me in his office in the private quarters of the residence. At one point, the President says to no one in particular, "What will it take to make this guy say uncle?"

"I don't think he ever will," Bernie Shaw says. "I think he will either die a martyr to the Arab cause, or his military men will say, 'enough is enough' and kill him."

JANUARY 20, 1991
MY DIARY

TV anchormen are having to learn what it means to respond fast and make mistakes (as war coverage starts). Peter Jennings has made many mistakes, after opposing his correspondents (Jack McWethy and Sam Donaldson). (Jennings after the war did a documentary that focused on five reasons for the war. All five were wrong. Worst [news] story of the war.)

MONDAY JANUARY 21, 1991

President Bush officially designates areas in which the Armed Forces of the United States are and have been engaged in combat: the Persian Gulf; the Red Sea; the Gulf of Oman; that portion of the Arabian Sea that lies north of 10 degrees north latitude and west of 68 degrees east longitude; the Gulf of Aden; and the total land areas of Iraq, Kuwait, Saudi Arabia, Oman, Bahrain, Qatar, and the United Arab Emirates.

JANUARY 21, 1991
THE WHITE HOUSE
Statement by Press Secretary Fitzwater on the Designation of the Arabian Peninsula as a Combat Zone:

The President today signed an Executive order designating the Arabian Peninsula areas, airspace, and adjacent waters as a combat zone. This designation means that for Federal tax purposes military pay received by enlisted personnel while serving in the combat zone will be exempt from income tax. For commissioned officers in the combat zone the exclusion is limited to $500 a month.

In addition, members of the armed forces in the combat zone will not have to file their income tax returns until at least 180 days after they depart the Persian Gulf.

JANUARY 21, 1991

The US conducts more than 8,000 sorties in the first five days of the war; Scud missiles remain a threat.

Iraq continues to use human shields as defense, saying it has scattered prisoners of war at air targets.

JANUARY 21, 1991

Tariq Aziz accepts the Soviet peace plan. President Bush refuses the plan.

TUESDAY JANUARY 22, 1991

Iraq fires six Scud missiles on Saudi Arabia; five fall without doing damage; one is destroyed by a Patriot.

THURSDAY JANUARY 24, 1991

Saddam Hussein claims the coalition bombed a baby formula factory near Baghdad. The White House and the Pentagon strongly deny the report. Marlin Fitzwater says, "That factory is in fact a production facility for biological weapons . . . behind a facade of baby milk production as a form of disinformation."

JANUARY 24, 1991

Coalition forces capture the small island of Qaruh, Kuwait.

US officials say allied sorties are over 15,000.

FRIDAY JANUARY 25, 1991

Iraq dumps millions of gallons of crude oil into the Persian Gulf.

Two are killed in Iraqi Scud missile attacks on Israel and Saudi Arabia.

JANUARY 25, 1991

THE PRESIDENT

President Bush speaks from the Briefing Room of the White House at 3:02 p.m. in Q-and-A session with reporters [excerpts]:

The President: Now, Helen [Helen Thomas, UPI]

Q: Mr. President, what can you do about the Iraqi dumping of oil in the Gulf? Is there any way you can offset it?

The President: Well, there's a lot of activity going on right now trying to figure out what the best course of action is to clean this mess up, to stop this spill.

Saddam Hussein continues to amaze the world. First he uses these Scud missiles that have no military value whatsoever. Then he uses the lives of prisoners of war, parading them and threatening to use them as shields; obviously, they have been brutalized. And now he resorts to enormous environmental damage in terms of turning loose a lot of oil. No military advantage to him whatsoever in this. It's not going to help him at all. . . .

Q: Mr. President, the reports from Israel now indicate that the injuries to civilians, perhaps deaths, may have been caused by Patriot missiles themselves not striking their targets or at least if they struck them parts of them fell back on the civilian population, which raises anew the question of the sufficiency of the Patriot missile and the question about whether you are now contemplating additional measures to try to deal with this obviously persistent problem?

The President: We are certainly dealing with that all the time and we want to find ways to stop it. We want to find ways to stop these brutal, senseless nonmilitary-value attacks on civilian populations.

Q: . . . why wouldn't it be entirely military appropriate to target Saddam Hussein?

The President: Because we are not in the business of targeting Saddam Hussein. I've set out our goals, and I think that—I will say this, as I said the other day in echoing my support for what Prime Minister Major of the United Kingdom said, no one will weep when he's gone. But having said that, we have spelled out our objectives and I will stay with them.

Saturday January 26, 1991

Iran seizes Iraqi planes that landed in Iranian territory. US F-15s shoot down three Iraqi MiG-23s. USS *Louisville* is first submarine to launch cruise missile. No casualties reported from Scuds fired by Iraq at Israel and Saudi Arabia.

TUESDAY JANUARY 29, 1991

The United States and the Soviet Union offer Iraq a cease-fire on the condition of total withdrawal of all its troops from Kuwait, an "unequivocal commitment" to withdraw.

Iraq forces invade Khafji, Saudi Arabia. Saudi Arabian and Qatari troops, with the help of a battalion-size force of US Marines, fire artillery, mortars, and TOW missiles at Iraqi bunkers in Kuwait, engaging the Iraqi forces in the largest ground battle yet. No US casualties.

JANUARY 29, 1991
THE PRESIDENT
At 9:09 p.m. in the House Chamber of the Capitol, President Bush's address a joint session of the Congress on the State of the Union.

"WE STAND AT A DEFINING HOUR"

Mr. President and Mr. Speaker and Members of the United States Congress:

I come to this House of the people to speak to you and all Americans, certain that we stand at a defining hour. Halfway around the world, we are engaged in a great struggle in the skies and on the seas and sands. We know why we're there: We are Americans, part of something larger than ourselves. For two centuries, we've done the hard work of freedom. And tonight, we lead the world in facing down a threat to decency and humanity.

What is at stake is more than one small country; it is a big idea: a new world order, where diverse nations are drawn together in common cause to achieve the universal aspirations of mankind—peace and security, freedom, and the rule of law. Such is a world worthy of our struggle and worthy of our children's future.

The community of nations has resolutely gathered to condemn and repel lawless aggression. Saddam Hussein's unprovoked invasion—his ruthless, systematic rape of a peaceful neighbor—violated everything the community of nations holds dear. The world has said this aggression would not stand, and it will not stand. Together, we have resisted the trap of appeasement, cynicism, and isolation that gives temptation to tyrants. The world has answered Saddam's invasion with twelve United Nations resolutions, starting with a demand for Iraq's immediate and unconditional withdrawal, and backed up by forces from twenty-eight countries of six continents. With few exceptions, the world now stands as one.

The end of the cold war has been a victory for all humanity. A year and a half ago, in Germany, I said that our goal was a Europe whole and free. Tonight, Germany is united. Europe has become whole and free, and America's leadership was instrumental in making it possible.

Our relationship to the Soviet Union is important, not only to us but to the world. That relationship has helped to shape these and other historic changes. But like many other nations, we have been deeply concerned by the violence in the Baltics, and we have communicated that concern to the Soviet leadership. The principle that has guided us is simple: Our objective is to help the Baltic peoples achieve their aspirations, not to punish the Soviet Union. In our recent discussions with the Soviet leadership we have been given representations which, if fulfilled, would result in the withdrawal of some Soviet forces, a reopening of dialog with the Republics, and a move away from violence.

We will watch carefully as the situation develops. And we will maintain our contact with the Soviet leadership to encourage continued commitment to democratization and reform. If it is possible, I want to continue to build a lasting basis for US-Soviet cooperation—for a more peaceful future for all mankind.

The triumph of democratic ideas in Eastern Europe and Latin America and the continuing struggle for freedom elsewhere all around the world all confirm the wisdom of our nation's founders. Tonight, we work to achieve another victory, a victory over tyranny and savage aggression.

We in this Union enter the last decade of the twentieth century thankful for our blessings, steadfast in our purpose, aware of our difficulties, and responsive to our duties at home and around the world. For two centuries, America has served the world as an inspiring example of freedom and democracy. For generations, America has led the struggle to preserve and extend the blessings of liberty. And today, in a rapidly changing world, American leadership is indispensable. Americans know that leadership brings burdens and sacrifices. But we also know why the hopes of humanity turn to us. We are Americans; we have a unique responsibility to do the hard work of freedom. And when we do, freedom works.

The conviction and courage we see in the Persian Gulf today is simply the American character in action. The indomitable spirit that is contributing to this victory for world peace and justice is the same spirit that gives us the power and the potential to meet our toughest challenges at home. We are resolute and resourceful. If we can selflessly confront the evil for the sake of good in a land so far away, then surely we can make this land all that it should be. If anyone tells you that America's best days are behind her, they're looking the wrong way.

Tonight I come before this House and the American people with an appeal for renewal. This is not merely a call for new government initiatives; it is a call for new initiatives in government, in our communities, and from every American to prepare for the next American century.

America has always led by example. So, who among us will set the example? Which of our citizens will lead us in this next American century? Everyone who steps forward today—to get one addict off drugs, to convince one troubled teenager not to give up on life, to comfort one AIDS patient, to help one hungry child.

We have within our reach the promise of a renewed America. We can find meaning and reward by serving some higher purpose than ourselves, a shining purpose, the illumination of a Thousand Points of Light. And it is expressed by all who know the irresistible force of a child's hand, of a friend who stands by you and stays there, a volunteer's generous gesture, an idea that is simply right.

The problems before us may be different, but the key to solving them remains the same. It is the individual—the individual who steps forward. And the state of our Union is the union of each of us, one to the other—the sum of our friendships, marriages, families, and communities.

We all have something to give. So, if you know how to read, find someone who can't. If you've got a hammer, find a nail. If you're not hungry, not lonely, not in trouble, seek out someone who is. Join the community of conscience. Do the hard work of freedom. And that will define the state of our Union.

Since the birth of our nation, "We the People" has been the source of our strength. What government can do alone is limited, but the potential of the American people knows no limits.

We are a nation of rock-solid realism and clear-eyed idealism. We are Americans. We are the Nation that believes in the future. We are the Nation that can shape the future. And we've begun to do just that, by strengthening the power and choice of individuals and families.

Together, these last two years, we've put dollars for child care directly in the hands of parents instead of bureaucracies; unshackled the potential of Americans with disabilities; applied the creativity of the marketplace in the service of the environment, for clean air; and made home ownership possible for more Americans.

The strength of a democracy is not in bureaucracy. It is in the people and their communities. In everything we do, let us unleash the potential of our most precious resource—our citizens, our citizens themselves. We must return to families, communities, counties, cities, States, and institutions of every kind the power to chart their own destiny and the freedom and opportunity provided by strong economic growth. And that's what America is all about.

I know that tonight, in some regions of our country, people are in genuine economic distress. And I hear them. Earlier this month, Kathy Blackwell, of Massachusetts, wrote me about what can happen when the economy slows down, saying, "My heart is aching, and I think that you should know your people out here are hurting badly."

I understand, and I'm not unrealistic about the future. But there are reasons to be optimistic about our economy. First, we don't have to fight double-digit inflation. Second, most industries won't have to make big cuts in production because they don't have big inventories piled up. And third, our exports are running solid and strong. In fact, American businesses are exporting at a record rate.

So, let's put these times in perspective. Together, since 1981, we've created almost 20 million jobs, cut inflation in half, and cut interest rates in half. And yes, the largest peacetime economic expansion in history has been temporarily interrupted. But our economy is still over twice as large as our closest competitor.

We will get this recession behind us and return to growth soon. We will get on our way to a new record of expansion and achieve the competitive strength that will carry us into the next American century. We should focus our efforts today on encouraging economic growth, investing in the future, and giving power and opportunity to the individual.

We must begin with control of Federal spending. That's why I'm submitting a budget that holds the growth in spending to less than the rate of inflation. And that's why, amid all the sound and fury of last year's budget debate, we put into law new, enforceable spending caps, so that future spending debates will mean a battle of ideas, not a bidding war.

Though controversial, the budget agreement finally put the Federal Government on a pay-as-you-go plan and cut the growth of debt by nearly $500 billion. And that frees funds for saving and job-creating investment.

Now, let's do more. My budget again includes tax-free family savings accounts; penalty-free withdrawals from IRA's for first-time home buyers; and to increase jobs and growth, a reduced tax for long-term capital gains.

I know there are differences among us—[laughter]—about

the impact and the effects of a capital gains incentive. So tonight, I'm asking the congressional leaders and the Federal Reserve to cooperate with us in a study, led by Chairman Alan Greenspan, to sort out our technical differences so that we can avoid a return to unproductive partisan bickering.

But just as our efforts will bring economic growth now and in the future, they must also be matched by long-term investments for the next American century. That requires a forward-looking plan of action, and that's exactly what we will be sending to the Congress. We've prepared a detailed series of proposals that include: a budget that promotes investment in America's future—in children, education, infrastructure, space, and high technology; legislation to achieve excellence in education, building on the partnership forged with the fifty Governors at the education summit, enabling parents to choose their children's schools and helping to make America number one in math and science; a blueprint for a new national highway system, a critical investment in our transportation infrastructure; a research and development agenda that includes record levels of Federal investment, and a permanent tax credit to strengthen private R&D and to create jobs; a comprehensive national energy strategy that calls for energy conservation and efficiency, increased development, and greater use of alternative fuels; a banking reform plan to bring America's financial system into the twenty-first century so that our banks remain safe and secure and can continue to make job-creating loans for our factories, our businesses, and home buyers.

You know, I do think there has been too much pessimism. Sound banks should be making sound loans now, and interest rates should be lower, now.

In addition to these proposals, we must recognize that our economic strength depends on being competitive in world markets. We must continue to expand American exports. A successful Uruguay round of world trade negotiations will create more real jobs and more real growth for all nations. You and I know that if the playing field is level, America's workers and farmers can out-work, out-produce anyone, anytime, anywhere.

And with a Mexican free trade agreement and our Enterprise for the Americas Initiative, we can help our partners strengthen their economies and move toward a free trade zone throughout this entire hemisphere.

The budget also includes a plan of action right here at home to put more power and opportunity in the hands of the individual. And that means new incentives to create jobs in our inner cities by encouraging investment through enterprise zones. It also means tenant control and ownership of public housing. Freedom and the power to choose should not be the privilege of wealth. They are the birthright of every American.

Civil rights are also crucial to protecting equal opportunity. Every one of us has a responsibility to speak out against racism, bigotry, and hate. We will continue our vigorous enforcement of existing statutes, and I will once again press the Congress to strengthen the laws against employment discrimination without resorting to the use of unfair preferences.

We're determined to protect another fundamental civil right: freedom from crime and the fear that stalks our cities. The Attorney General will soon convene a crime summit of our nation's law enforcement officials. And to help us support them, we need tough crime control legislation, and we need it now.

And as we fight crime, we will fully implement our national strategy for combating drug abuse. Recent data show that we are making progress, but much remains to be done. We will not rest until the day of the dealer is over, forever.

Good health care is every American's right and every American's responsibility. And so, we are proposing an aggressive program of new prevention initiatives—for infants, for children, for adults, and for the elderly—to promote a healthier America and to help keep costs from spiraling.

It's time to give people more choice in government by reviving the ideal of the citizen politician who comes not to stay but to serve. And one of the reasons that there is so much support across this country for term limitations is that the American people are increasingly concerned about big-money influence in politics. So, we must look beyond the next election to the next generation. And the time has come to put the national interest above the special interest and to totally eliminate political action committees. And that would truly put more competition in elections and more power in the hands of individuals.

And where power cannot be put directly in the hands of the individual, it should be moved closer to the people, away from Washington. The Federal Government too often treats government programs as if they are of Washington, by Washington, and for Washington. Once established, Federal programs seem to become immortal. It's time for a more dynamic program life cycle. Some programs should increase. Some should decrease. Some should be terminated. And some should be consolidated and turned over to the States.

My budget includes a list of programs for potential turnover totaling more than $20 billion. Working with Congress and the Governors, I propose we select at least $15 billion in such programs and turn them over to the States in a single consolidated grant, fully funded, for flexible management by the States.

The value, the value of this turnover approach is straightforward. It allows the Federal Government to reduce overhead. It allows States to manage more flexibly and more efficiently. It moves power and decision making closer to the people. And it reinforces a theme of this administration: appreciation and encouragement of the innovative powers of States as laboratories.

This nation was founded by leaders who understood that power belongs in the hands of people. And they planned for the future. And so must we, here and all around the world.

As Americans, we know that there are times when we must step forward and accept our responsibility to lead the world away from the dark chaos of dictators, toward the brighter promise of a better day. Almost fifty years ago we began a long struggle against aggressive totalitarianism. Now we face another defining hour for America and the world.

There is no one more devoted, more committed to the hard work of freedom than every soldier and sailor, every marine, airman, and coastguardsman, every man and woman now serving in the Persian Gulf. Oh, how they deserve—[applause]—and what a fitting tribute to them.

You see—what a wonderful, fitting tribute to them. Each of them has volunteered, volunteered to provide for this nation's defense, and now they bravely struggle to earn for America, for the world, and for future generations a just and lasting peace. Our commitment to them must be equal to their commitment to their country. They are truly America's finest.

The war in the Gulf is not a war we wanted. We worked hard to avoid war. For more than five months we—along with the Arab League, the European Community, the United Nations—tried every diplomatic avenue. UN Secretary-General Perez de Cuellar; Presidents Gorbachev, Mitterrand, Özal, Mubarak, and Bendjedid; Kings Fahd and Hassan; Prime Ministers Major and Andreotti—just to name a few—all worked for a solution. But time and again, Saddam Hussein flatly rejected the path of diplomacy and peace.

The world well knows how this conflict began and when: It began on August 2d, when Saddam invaded and sacked a small, defenseless neighbor. And I am certain of how it will end. So that peace can prevail, we will prevail. [Applause] Thank you.

Tonight I am pleased to report that we are on course. Iraq's capacity to sustain war is being destroyed. Our investment, our training, our planning—all are paying off. Time will not be Saddam's salvation.

Our purpose in the Persian Gulf remains constant: to drive Iraq out of Kuwait, to restore Kuwait's legitimate government, and to ensure the stability and security of this critical region.

Let me make clear what I mean by the region's stability and security. We do not seek the destruction of Iraq, its culture, or its people. Rather, we seek an Iraq that uses its great resources not to destroy, not to serve the ambitions of a tyrant, but to build a better life for itself and its neighbors.

We seek a Persian Gulf where conflict is no longer the rule, where the strong are neither tempted nor able to intimidate the weak.

Most Americans know instinctively why we are in the Gulf. They know we had to stop Saddam now, not later. They know that this brutal dictator will do anything, will use any weapon, will commit any outrage, no matter how many innocents suffer.

They know we must make sure that control of the world's oil resources does not fall into his hands, only to finance further aggression. They know that we need to build a new, enduring peace, based not on arms races and confrontation but on shared principles and the rule of law.

And we all realize that our responsibility to be the catalyst for peace in the region does not end with the successful conclusion of this war.

Democracy brings the undeniable value of thoughtful dissent, and we've heard some dissenting voices here at home—some, a handful, reckless; most responsible. But the fact that all voices have the right to speak out is one of the reasons we've been united in purpose and principle for two hundred years.

Our progress in this great struggle is the result of years of vigilance and a steadfast commitment to a strong defense. Now, with remarkable technological advances like the Patriot missile, we can defend against ballistic missile attacks aimed at innocent civilians.

Looking forward, I have directed that the SDI program be refocused on providing protection from limited ballistic missile strikes, whatever their source. Let us pursue an SDI program that can deal with any future threat to the United States, to our forces overseas, and to our friends and allies.

The quality of American technology, thanks to the American worker, has enabled us to successfully deal with difficult military conditions and help minimize precious loss of life. We have given our men and women the very best. And they deserve it.

We all have a special place in our hearts for the families of our men and women serving in the Gulf. They are represented here tonight by Mrs. Norman Schwarzkopf. We are all very grateful to General Schwarzkopf and to all those serving with him. And I might also recognize one who came with Mrs. Schwarzkopf: Alma Powell, the wife of the distinguished Chairman of the Joint Chiefs. And to the families, let me say our forces in the Gulf will not stay there one day longer than is necessary to complete their mission.

The courage and success of the RAF pilots, of the Kuwaiti, Saudi, French, the Canadians, the Italians, the pilots of Qatar and Bahrain—all are proof that for the first time since World War II, the international community is united. The leadership of the United Nations, once only a hoped-for ideal, is now confirming its founders' vision.

I am heartened that we are not being asked to bear alone the financial burdens of this struggle. Last year, our friends and allies provided the bulk of the economic costs of Desert Shield. And now, having received commitments of over $40 billion for the first three months of 1991, I am confident they will do no less as we move through Desert Storm.

But the world has to wonder what the dictator of Iraq is thinking. If he thinks that by targeting innocent civilians in Israel and Saudi Arabia, that he will gain advantage, he is dead wrong. If he thinks that he will advance his cause through tragic and despicable environmental terrorism, he is dead wrong. And if he thinks that by abusing the coalition prisoners of war he will benefit, he is dead wrong.

We will succeed in the Gulf. And when we do, the world community will have sent an enduring warning to any dictator or despot, present or future, who contemplates outlaw aggression.

The world can, therefore, seize this opportunity to fulfill the long-held promise of a new world order, where brutality will go unrewarded and aggression will meet collective resistance.

Yes, the United States bears a major share of leadership in this effort. Among the nations of the world, only the United States of America has both the moral standing and the means to back it up. We're the only nation on this Earth that could assemble the forces of peace. This is the burden of leadership and the strength that has made America the beacon of freedom in a searching world.

This nation has never found glory in war. Our people have never wanted to abandon the blessings of home and work for distant lands and deadly conflict. If we fight in anger, it is only because we have to fight at all. And all of us yearn for a world where we will never have to fight again.

Each of us will measure within ourselves the value of this great struggle. Any cost in lives—any cost—is beyond our power to measure. But the cost of closing our eyes to aggression is beyond mankind's power to imagine. This we do know: Our cause is just; our cause is moral; our cause is right.

Let future generations understand the burden and the blessings of freedom. Let them say we stood where duty required us to stand. Let them know that, together, we affirmed America and the world as a community of conscience.

The winds of change are with us now. The forces of freedom are together, united. We move toward the next century more confident than ever that we have the will at home and abroad to do what must be done—the hard work of freedom.

May God bless the United States of America. Thank you very, very much.

WEDNESDAY JANUARY 30, 1991

The coalition starts its first land-based operations in Southern Iraq and Kuwait. Thousands of Iraqi troops, along with tanks, advance into Saudi Arabia. They are met by US Marines, Saudi, and Qatari troops. Eleven marines die in combat.

Gen. Schwarzkopf declares air supremacy, and says, "The Iraqi early warning system has completely failed."

THURSDAY JANUARY 31, 1991

Saudi and Qatari troops, backed by US artillery, successfully retake Khafji, Saudi Arabia.

FRIDAY FEBRUARY 1, 1991

Allies bomb a ten-mile-long Iraqi armored column as it is headed into Saudi Arabia, driving Iraqi forces out of Saudi Arabia.

FEBRUARY 1, 1991
MY DIARY

Traveling to Military Bases. Dr. Burton Lee, the President's physician, said the Pres. told him privately this week that the war would be over in days not weeks. Also the President said he had taken the decision about how to respond to chemical weapons used by Saddam, "out of the hands of the military. I will make the decision." As we start the ground war, that possibility draws closer. Traveling between Cherry Point and Seymour Johnson AFB, I mention the length of the war to the President, sitting at his desk aboard *Air Force One*. Brent Scowcroft and Governor Sununu and I are sitting on the couches.

"All the Pentagon guys tell me it will be days, not weeks or months," the President said. "Isn't that what they tell you, Brent?"

Brent nodded in agreement. He didn't say whether or not he believed it. I don't. It has now been three weeks and we haven't killed many Iraqis yet. I believe two or three months of fighting, at least. (I was wrong.)

FEBRUARY 1, 1991
MY DIARY

I rode with the President in his limousine for the fifty-minute drive from West Palm Beach airport to his mother's home on Hobe Sound. The President was pumped up by the three military base visits. We talked about individual reporters. He mentioned again his dislike for Evan Thomas and Gary Trudeau (*Doonesbury*), but he mentioned the fur coat sequence, so he does read him. The President tuned in some Country and Western music and started humming. It was dark so the President couldn't see the smile on my face as he was humming along. His weekend guest at Camp David is Moe Bandy, the Country and Western singer.

FEBRUARY 1, 1991
THE WHITE HOUSE

In the morning, the President traveled to Cherry Point Marine Corps Air Station in North Carolina to address Marine Corps families and attend a reception with spouses of deployed personnel. He then traveled to Seymour Johnson Air Force Base to attend a picnic with base families and support personnel.

In the afternoon, the President went to Fort Stewart, Georgia, to address Army families and attend a reception with spouses of deployed personnel. He then traveled to Hobe Sound, Florida, to visit his mother.

In the evening, the President went to Camp David, MD, for the weekend.

SATURDAY FEBRUARY 2, 1991

Scud attacks continue. No reported casualties when two Scuds hit central Israel. Two reported injured in Scud attack, which is downed by Patriot missile over Saudi Arabia.

SUNDAY FEBRUARY 3, 1991

Officials report approximately 40,000 air-to-ground sorties in the coalition air campaign, involving nearly every type of US fixed-wing aircraft.

MONDAY FEBRUARY 4, 1991

For the first time in combat since the later part of the Korean War, the battleship USS *Missouri* (on whose deck the Japanese surrendered to, marking the end of WWII) fires its 16-inch guns, attacking Iraqi positions inside occupied Kuwait.

TUESDAY FEBRUARY 5, 1991
THE PRESIDENT

Excerpt from the President's 71st news conference that began at 11:35 a.m. in the Briefing Room of the White House:

Q: Mr. President, your new budget contains relatively little money for the Persian Gulf war, which some analysts think could cost as high as $1 billion a day if it goes into a ground conflict. If the war goes on for months, how will you pay for it with an economy that's in a recession and a deficit that's climbing past $300 billion?

The President: Well, I think that in the budget some $15 billion is included. And I think what people that are concerned about this have not realized is that we are getting significant support committed from overseas. And I'm confident that what we have in there will take care of it—will be testimony on this up on the Hill, but we're talking about having commitments of close to—I think it's $50 or $51 billion from others added to the $15 billion that we have budgeted. That's $66 billion, and we believe it should be sufficient.

Q: Would you under any circumstances consider a surtax to pay for the war if it goes on?

The President: Too hypothetical, but I can see no reason for a war surtax. I don't think it's necessary, and I've heard very little call for that, as a matter of fact, because I think people realize that these cost estimates are pretty accurate. . . .

WEDNESDAY FEBRUARY 6, 1991
MY DIARY

A *People* magazine article on me is out this week. Lady Di is on the cover. It was quite flattering. No one at the White House commented, except Carol Powers, who complimented me. I contrast this with a *Washington Times* article two weeks ago that said I was testy and defensive. On this one the President gave me a thumbs up and said it was fine. People in the White House never compliment each other or wish each other well. It's too competitive.

FEBRUARY 6, 1991
THE PRESIDENT

From an exchange with reporters aboard Air Force One *en route from Washington, DC, to New York City:*

Q: Mr. President, King Hussein says that the war is unjust and you've exceeded the limits laid out by the UN What do you say to that?

The President: Well, I'm afraid that we have a major disagreement on that. It's not true.

Q: Will America's offer of assistance for refugees still stand—to Jordan?

The President: Well, we tried to make clear to Jordan that we have no argument with Jordan, I think they've made a mistake to align themselves so closely with Saddam Hussein against the rest of the world. But on the other hand, I've tried to understand the pressures that King Hussein is under. So, we will obviously try to keep open lines of communication. That's about as far as I'd want to go.

But you have to listen to the rhetoric and then understand why it's being used out in that part of the world.

Q: Your conversation with Mitterrand today—

The President: We just stay with the course here. There will be no cease-fire; there will be nothing of that nature until this man commences a credible unilateral withdrawal. And then we'll see what happens. But there's no interest in the other. I mean, there's talk about it, but most of the people I've talked to in that part of the world feel that Saddam simply has got it wrong and doesn't have the word on what he might do, so—

Q: The notice on the diplomatic threat—have you seen that from Iraq; that Iraq has broken diplomatic ties?

The President: I saw a notice about it. I don't think we've had official notice. I saw something in the paper about it. We have no people over there, so I don't know what he's proving by that.

Q: You talked to President Özal and Mitterrand, and presumably, the Iranian "initiative" came up in both calls. Is there, in fact, an Iranian initiative for a peace proposal?

The President: Not that we know of.

Q: Any kind of mediation effort underway?

The President: No. I think they've indicated they might be available. But somebody asked me yesterday whether there was some plan, and I said no, and there isn't. But I think they're conducting themselves very well right now—Iran.

Q: The Iranians?

The President: I think so. But there's no peace plan, or I know of no initiative. And we've talked to the French—Mr. Scheer, who is back in Paris now and was supporting—supposedly he was on some peace plan, and apparently that's not correct at all. So, maybe General Scowcroft can fill you in. I have to go back and fix my seat belt. [Laughter]

Mr. Scowcroft: I don't need one.

FEBRUARY 6, 1991
MY DIARY

A *Boston Globe* article by Mary Curtis today said an Administration official said POTUS was upset with Margaret Tutwiler's comments on Iran's offer to mediate the war. "What's to mediate," she said. She told me Baker had dictated the phrase to her. Indeed, it was sent to the White House as official State Department guidance.

In their 8:00 a.m. meeting with the President, he asked Scowcroft, Sununu, and the Vice President where that (phrase) came from. Sununu said, "Marlin back-grounded on that." I didn't, of course. Sununu is trying to set me up. I went to Andy Card and the President to say: Sununu was wrong.

FRIDAY FEBRUARY 8, 1991

Defense Secretary Dick Cheney travels to Saudi Arabia, indicating that war may be drawing to a close.

MONDAY FEBRUARY 11, 1991

THE PRESIDENT

Remarks at 3:45 p.m. from the Rose Garden at the White House:

The President: Let me just say that we had a very thorough briefing from Secretary Cheney and from Chairman Powell. They had a very good visit out there to the Gulf area, talking to our commanders. I am very satisfied, having heard their briefing, with the progress of the war. The air campaign has been very, very effective, and it will continue for a while. We're not talking about dates for further adding to the air campaign—put it that way.

But I would simply want to say to the American people that the war is going well. I am very pleased with the people that are running the war; they have my full confidence. We are going to take whatever time is necessary to sort out when a next stage might begin. And I will not be discussing it any further than that. And I can guarantee you that there should be no further discussion of that for a lot of reasons, including the safety of our own troops—and that comes first as far as I'm concerned—and the coalition forces. Their safety is paramount in my mind.

But I would be remiss if I didn't reassure the American people that this war is being fought with high technology. There is no targeting of civilians. It has gone far better in terms of casualties than

I'd hoped—though we mourn the loss of every single member of our armed forces and the coalition forces, of course.

My heart still goes out to the families. I might say to the families of those who are over there; the report from General Powell and from Secretary Cheney is very reassuring in terms of the morale of our people over there. They know why they are there. They are gung ho about it. They know its importance. They know that it's right and just. And so, I have great confidence in them.

And altogether, I feel much better after this briefing. I've always felt confident we were on the right path, I feel even more so now after this briefing from Secretary Cheney and General Powell.

So, we will just continue down this road. We're the ones that are going to set the time for how this war—the time for any action that is taken. We are not going to suit somebody else's timetable, whether he lives in Baghdad or anyplace else. And that's exactly the way it should be.

And so, I will rely heavily on the advice of our Secretary of Defense, of our Chairman, of our generals out here—General Schwarzkopf and others. Then if they come to me and say there needs to be another phase, then I will then make that decision—because that is a decision for the President of the United States.

Having said that, I have total confidence that we are on the right path, and with no further ado, I want to thank them for this arduous trip—but it was well worth it.

TUESDAY FEBRUARY 12, 1991

Largest battlefield action so far as coalition forces open a combined barrage against Iraqi forces in Kuwait, by land, sea, and air.

WEDNESDAY FEBRUARY 13, 1991

Two laser-guided precision bombs are dropped by US Stealth fighters on a well-known military target, an underground facility five miles from the center of Baghdad that had been transmitting military signals, according to US intelligence. Iraqi officials claim 500 people, including women and children, were killed. Tariq Aziz calls it a "planned attack against civilians." (The final death toll is 314.)

FEBRUARY 13, 1991
THE WHITE HOUSE
Statement by Press Secretary Fitzwater on Allied bombing in Baghdad, read to reporters at 11:47 a.m. in the Briefing Room of the White House:
Last night, coalition forces bombed a military command and control center in Baghdad that, according to press reports, resulted in a number of civilian casualties.

The loss of civilian lives in time of war is a truly tragic consequence. It saddens everyone to know that innocent people may have died in the course of military conflict. America treats human life as our most precious value. That is why even during this military conflict in which the lives of our service men and women are at risk, we will not target civilian facilities. We will continue to hit only military targets. The bunker that was attacked last night was a military target, a command and control center that fed instructions directly to the Iraqi war machine, painted and camouflaged to avoid detection, and well-documented as a military target. We have been systematically attacking these targets since the war began. We don't know why civilians were at this location, but we do know that Saddam Hussein does not share our value in the sanctity of life. Indeed, he, time and again, has shown a willingness to sacrifice civilian lives and property that further his war aims.

Civilian hostages were moved in November and December to military sites for use as human shields. POWs reportedly have been placed at military sites. Roving bands of execution squads search out deserters among his own ranks of servicemen. Command and control centers in Iraq have been placed to top of schools and public buildings. Tanks and other artillery have been placed beside private homes and small villages. And only this morning we have documentation that two MiG-1s have been parked near the front door of a treasured archaeology site which dates back to the 27th century B.C.

His environmental terrorism spreads throughout the Persian Gulf, killing wildlife and threatening human water supplies. And finally, Saddam Hussein aims his Scud missiles at innocent civilians in Israel and Saudi Arabia. He kills civilians intentionally and with purpose.

Saddam Hussein created this war. He created the military bunkers. And he can bring the war to an end. We urge him once again to save his people and to comply with the UN resolutions.

FRIDAY FEBRUARY 15, 1991
THE WHITE HOUSE
Statement by Press Secretary Fitzwater on the offer by Iraq to withdraw from Kuwait at 8:32 a.m. from the Briefing Room of the White House:

We have not yet examined a full official text of the Revolutionary Command Council's statement, but it clearly contains conditions for Iraqi withdrawal from Kuwait. The United Nations Security Council resolutions are clear in their insistence that the withdrawal be complete and unconditional. Promises alone are not sufficient. There must be not only agreement to comply with all United Nations Security Council resolutions but also immediate and concrete action on the ground.

FEBRUARY 15, 1991
THE PRESIDENT
Excerpt from remarks at 9:58 a.m. to the American Association for the Advancement of Science:

The President: I do want to make a few comments on the statement that came out of Baghdad early this morning. When I first heard that statement, I must say I was happy that Saddam Hussein had seemed to realize that he must now withdraw unconditionally from Kuwait, in keeping with the relevant United Nations resolutions.

Regrettably, the Iraq statement now appears to be a cruel hoax, dashing the hopes of the people in Iraq and, indeed, around the world. . . .

FEBRUARY 15, 1991
THE PRESIDENT
Excerpt from an exchange with reporters in Andover, Massachusetts, on the offer by Iraq to withdraw from Kuwait; 12:40 p.m. in the Andover Room of the assembly building at the Raytheon Missile System Plant:

Q: Mr. President, is there any indication that Iraqis are turning around and going home?

Q: Do you think this is words only—this Iraqi statement?

The President: What statement? You mean this morning?

Q: Yes.

The President: Oh, there's no evidence of any withdrawal. I mean, as I said down in Washington, it's a cruel ploy. What he did was reiterate some conditions and add some new ones. And it's totally unacceptable to everybody.

You know, my heart goes out to the people in Iraq that you saw kind of jumping with joy early on, firing their weapons—which is I guess their sign of joy—in the air, and only to recognize when the fine print came out that it was a step backwards.

So, there's no sign of any withdrawal. I wish there were. So did the whole world.

Q: —members of the coalition, sir?

Q: What do you think the use of the word "withdrawal" means? It's the first time we've heard that.

The President: I don't know. It doesn't mean compliance with the United Nations resolutions. Until that happens, regrettably, there will not be a cessation of hostilities. There will be no pause, there will be no cease-fire, there will be no reliving experiences in the past that were unhelpful to a peaceful, satisfactory conclusion of the war. And so, there's nothing in this thing to offer hope. I wish I thought there was; there's not.

Q: Any sign that this tempts any members of the coalition?

The President: No, they're all—the ones we've talked to are all solid and got on this thing the minute they saw the declaration coming out of Baghdad, pronounce it—it was an initiative—pronounced it dead on arrival because there wasn't anything new or significant. There was just some more conditions, including asking the American taxpayer to pay for damage in Iraq. It's the other way around—there—reparation sanctions are called for under the United Nations. Reparations for Iraq—undoes the damage that it's done to its neighbors. I don't know how to repay for the loss of human life in Kuwait, the brutality, the fifteen-to-twenty-year-old Kuwaitis just this last week. You can't make amends for that.

But this was a cruel ploy. And the world saw it as such, including the coalition, which is just as solid today as it's ever been.

FEBRUARY 15, 1991
THE PRESIDENT
From remarks to Raytheon Missile Systems Plant Employees in Andover, Massachusetts, at 1:45 p.m. in the fabrications building:

The President: I view it as an honor to be here, to come to Raytheon, the home of the men and women who built the Scudbusters. We're very, very grateful.

Earlier today, maybe your hopes were lifted, maybe mine—mine were—and I think some hopes were lifted in downtown Baghdad with the statement. And I expressed, earlier on, regret that that Iraqi statement that first gave rise to hope in fact turned out to be a cruel hoax. Not only was the Iraqi statement full of unacceptable old conditions, Saddam Hussein has added several new conditions.

Let me state once again: Iraq must withdraw without condition. There must be full implementation of all the Security Council resolutions. And there will be no linkage to other problems in the area. And the legitimate rulers, the legitimate government, must be returned to Kuwait. And until a credible withdrawal begins, with those Iraqi troops visibly leaving Kuwait, the coalition forces in compliance with United Nations Resolution 678 will continue their efforts to force compliance with all those resolutions, every single one of them.

Compliance with the resolutions will instantly stop the bloodshed. And there's another way for the bloodshed to stop, and that is for the Iraqi military and the Iraqi people to take matters into their own hands and force Saddam Hussein, the dictator, to step aside, and then comply with the United Nations resolutions and rejoin the family of peace-loving nations. We have no argument with the people of Iraq. Our differences are with that brutal dictator in Baghdad.

Everyone here has a friend or a neighbor, a son or daughter, or somebody he knows in the Gulf. And to you, let me say this, and to the American people: The war is going on schedule. Of course, all of us—all of us—want to see this war ended, the limited loss of life. And it can if Saddam Hussein would simply comply unconditionally with all the resolutions of the United Nations. But let me say this to you: I am going to stay with it, we are going to prevail, and our soldiers are going to come home with their heads high.

Now, I just had the thrill of sitting in the command post of an Engagement Control System—ECS to you. [Laughter] And I've heard about the years of painstaking work that produced the split-second accuracy of the Patriot missile defense system. Let me tell you, I'm impressed with the technology. But especially after today, even more I'm impressed with the people behind the machines.

Just days after Saddam Hussein took the offense against an unde-fended Kuwait, the people of this plant went into overdrive and took the offense. And since mid-August, it's been an around-the-clock ef-fort, three shifts a day, seven days a week. And I know many of you gave up your own Thanksgiving and Christmas even to be right here, to keep these lines moving.

In the last month, the world has learned why. Patriot works, and not just because of the high-tech wizardry. It's because of all the hours, all the attention to detail, all the pride, and all the profession-alism that every one of you brings to the job. Patriot works because of patriots like you. And I came again to say thank you to each and every one of you.

You see, what has taken place here is a triumph of American technology. It's a triumph taking place every day, not just here at Raytheon but in the factories and firms all across America, wherever American workers are pushing forward the bound of progress, keep-ing this country strong, firing the engines of economic growth. What happens right here is critical, absolutely critical, to our competitive-ness now and then into the next century.

Let me focus for a moment not simply on high-tech workers like yourselves who build these Patriots but on the highly skilled service men and women who operate Patriot in the field. We hear so often how our kids, our children, our schools fall short. I think it's about time that we took note of some of the success stories, of the way the brave young men and women who man the Patriot stations perform such complex tasks with unerring accuracy. They, along with the children in our schools today, are part of a generation that will put unparalleled American technology to use as a tool for change.

As I was touring the plant a few minutes ago, I saw a sign out there that said: "Patriot—a Revolution in Air Defense." Well, we are witnessing a revolution in modern warfare, a revolution that will shape the way that we defend ourselves for decades to come. For years, we've heard that anti-missile defenses won't work, that shooting down a ballistic missile is impossible—like trying to "hit a bullet with a bullet." Some people called it impossible; you called it your job.

They were wrong, and you were right. Thank God you were right.

The critics said that this system was plagued with problems, that results from the test range wouldn't stand up under battlefield conditions. You knew they were wrong, those critics, all along. And now the world knows it, too. Beginning with the first Scud launched in Saudi Arabia, right onto Saudi Arabia—and the Patriot that struck it down—and with the arrival of Patriot battalions in Israel, all told, Patriot is 41 for 42: 42 Scuds engaged, 41 intercepted. And given the fact that this Scud missile has no military value, simply designed to devastate cities and wipe out population, imagine what course this war would have taken without the Patriot.

No, I'm sure that some experts here would say Patriot's not perfect. No system is; no system ever will be. Not every intercept results in total destruction. But Patriot is proof positive that missile defense works. I've said many times that missile defense threatens no one, that there is no purer defensive weapon than one that targets and destroys missiles launched against us.

We know that this is a dangerous world. Today, our cold war concern about a large-scale nuclear exchange—thank God it is more remote than at any point in the post-war era. At the same time, the number of nations acquiring the capability to build and deliver missiles of mass destruction—chemical, even nuclear weapons—is on the increase. In many cases, these missiles will be superior to Scuds, smaller, capable of flying farther and faster—in short, more difficult targets. Between now and the year 2000, in spite of our best efforts to control proliferation, additional nations may acquire this deadly technology. And as we've been taught by Saddam Hussein, all it takes is one renegade regime, one ruler without regard for human decency, one brutal dictator who willfully targets innocent civilians.

Well, we now know that some of the adversaries we face today—and Saddam Hussein is a prime example—are more rash than rational, less impressed by theories than by a nation with the means and will to defend itself. And thank God that when those Scuds came in, the people of Saudi Arabia and Israel and the brave forces of our coalition had more to protect their lives than some abstract theory of deterrence. Thank God for the Patriot missile. Thank God for that missile.

And so, when you all go home at night, you can say with pride that the success of Patriot is one important reason why Operation Desert Storm is on course and on schedule. And we're going to continue to fight this war on our terms, on our timetable, until our objectives are met. We will control the timing of this engagement, not Saddam Hussein.

Make no mistake about it: Kuwait will be liberated. The people who build Patriot have every reason to be proud. Because of you, the world now knows that we can count on missile defenses. And because of you, a tyrant's threat to rain terror from the skies has been blunted; it's been cut short. And because of you—and this one is special—innocent civilians, priceless human lives, have been spared.

When we think of war, we think first, of course, of the soldiers in the field, the brave men and women now serving half the world away. But Woodrow Wilson once said that in war there are "a thousand forms of duty." In this room today stand thousands of reasons why our cause shall succeed.

You—and people like you all across the country—have given our brave men and women in the Gulf the fighting edge that they need to prevail and, what's more, to protect precious lives. . . .

FEBRUARY 15, 1991
MY DIARY
One month to the day since the war began, Saddam Hussein said he would withdraw from Kuwait. At 6:15 a.m. my home phone rang. I knew it would be a morning TV reporter. Usually I don't answer. It was James Allen Miklaszewski, NBC.

"Have you heard? Saddam just announced on Baghdad radio that he's willing to withdraw."

"No shit."

"Unconfirmed report. Do you have any comment?"

"No."

"When will you?"

"I'm leaving now."

At the White House, I met Roman. He had only bare wire stories. I went to the Oval at 7:20 a.m. President Bush was in his study watching CNN with Scowcroft, Gates, Sununu, and Baker.

"Marlin," the President said, "Do we have a full text? Get me the article text."

We didn't have anything. Even the wires didn't have text.

"What if it's real?" The President asks. "Are there conditions?" No one knew. We watched in silence. Everyone was silent, thinking through their respective options.

"Well," Baker said, "we have the criteria in our plan: Out of Kuwait City in twenty-four hours, moving away from the front lines in twenty-four hours, leave the equipment where it is. We could put all that out."

It was too early. No one picked up the discussion.

"What do you suppose he's up to?" the President asked.

"I think he finally realizes he's losing," Scowcroft said.

"Look at these people celebrating in Baghdad," the President said. "They think it's over."

A report on CNN said the Soviets said this was a hopeful sign. "We don't know whether it is or not," the President said. "Marlin, check again for the text. Gates picked up the phone to call CIA for a full text. They didn't have one.

Patty Presock came in to say Bandar (Saudi Ambassador) was calling Gates. He took the call in the study. Hanging up, he said, "That's encouraging." He looked up and added, "Bandar says there are conditions. Linkage."

The President laughed, "That's encouraging." He laughed again, noting the irony that we found the withdrawal conditions to be "encouraging." Clearly, we didn't want this. Our fear all along has been that Saddam would actually pull back, claiming victory, and we couldn't prevent it.

Charles Powell, PM Major's security advisor, called for Brent. He said it looked like there were conditions, be cautious. PM Major would not comment until we did.

"That's why we've got to get a statement on CNN soon," the President said. "Everyone wants to comment. They need to know our reaction."

Roman brought me a wire story with the conditions. I handed it to the President at about 8:00 a.m.

"He has all these conditions in here," the President said, reading. We can't accept any of this. Marlin, say we're disappointed. It has more conditions than before."

The VP was coming in as I left to go draft a statement. I called Lynn and Roman in, dictated a paragraph and went back to the Oval.

Baker had handwritten a statement when I arrived. I gave mine to the President. But Baker said, "This is what we should say." We all turned our attention to it.

8:15 a.m. "Go do it, Marlin," The President said. "We need to get this out fast."

After I read the statement to the press, I returned to the Oval. The President said it went fine. Then I went to my office to background the press on the preceding hour. They thought the statement left the door open because it didn't say: reject.

"Do you reject this or not?" Miklaszewski asked.

"I will say that there's nothing new here. More conditions than before."

"That sounds harder than your on-camera statement," Bierbauer said.

"Well, now we know a little more. There's nothing here," I said. Bierbauer ran from the room. I knew he would be on air in minutes, so I headed for the Oval. Cheney was now there. They had moved to the dining room and were watching CNN.

"Mr. President," I said, "The press thinks our statement was soft, so I closed the door. OK."

"Yes," he said, "Hell, they even want us to pay the damages."

"Should I say something at this speech?" the President asked.

"Yes," I said, "All the nets will carry it live."

That would give everyone presidential words to replace mine. That was my strategy in the January 16 announcement too: that I get out first and fast with the message for the world, and all US spokesmen. Then the President would follow up soon with formal words in a controlled forum. It worked great both times.

The President wrote the speech insert himself, including the "cruel hoax on the Iraqi people" line that led the insert. He also wrote in the line that "it was time for the Iraqi people to take care of Saddam." The President had handwritten a similar passage into his Reserve Officers Speech a week earlier, but Baker urged him to take it out. He also had a long essay on CNN, the press, and Peter Arnett in that speech. I suggested he take that out. Later he thanked me for "that piece of good advice."

Sunday February 17, 1991

The President

Excerpts from an exchange with reporters in Kennebunkport that began at approximately 11:00 a.m. on the beach in front of the President's home:

The President: The American people are strongly in support not only of the troops but of these objectives. And, of course, that is a very important point because it is my hope that when this is over we will have kicked, for once and for all, the so-called Vietnam syndrome. And the country's pulling together, unlike any time—in this kind of situation—any time since World War II. And that's a good thing for our country. And that sends a strong signal for the future—that we're credible, we're committed to peace, we're committed to justice, and we are determined to fulfill our obligations in trying to bring about a more peaceful world order.

That's what I've been thinking about today. . . .

Q: Is it a goal to topple Saddam?

The President: The goals have been spelled out by me and by the coalition partners, and the goals remain the same. But I would answer like the Prime Minister: I wouldn't weep if they put him aside.

Monday February 18, 1991
My Diary

Oval Office. We returned from Kennebunkport, Maine about 4:00 p.m. President convenes National Security Council meeting in the Oval at 4:30, lasts two-and-a-half hours, to discuss Soviet peace plan for Tariq Aziz to give to Saddam. Baker reports, reading from his yellow legal pad, large black handwritten notes, from his phone conversation with Soviet Embassy. Cable text in Russian being translated. Four point plan: (1) withdraw from Kuwait; (2) no firing on departing forces. I can't hear 3 and 4. We are concerned. The President said privately in KBP, before we had seen the plan, that "We better not pull defeat from the jaws of victory."

The decision was made to issue a brief public statement of no comment, but the war continues. Privately, Baker notifies the Allies though, that we are negative because the Soviet proposal does not deal with: (l) restoration of Kuwait government; (2) reparations; (3) stability in the region and all UN resolutions.

Two hours of discussion. Cheney says, "We should reject now or pressure will build to accept. We should be just as negative as we were on Iraq's proposal of February 15."

Scowcroft suggests we tell Allies that "Iraq has ninety-six hours to get out, no attack on troops, and restoration of Kuwait government. This would require them to leave their front line artillery. We want to get rid of that artillery."

Gates asks Colin if he has a two-minute drill.

"You bet we do," Colin says. "We want to get heavy artillery, ammo dumps, storage facilities, truck repair garages, etc."

The ninety-six-hour suggestion is agreed to, but later rejected. The group comes back to it after watching the films (of bombing).

Baker: "I can't remember. Why did we think the ninety-six-hour idea was good?" No one recalled, so it was dropped.

Cheney suggested: "Why don't we publicly announce that the ground war begins in seventy-two hours and Saddam has to get out before then. Everybody in Saudi Arabia thinks the ground war is starting now anyway. I don't know what the chairman thinks." He sheepishly looks at Colin. Colin was reluctant but not negative.

"I don't want to turn off the Soviets," the President said. "I think the main thing about all this is that they want in the game. They always complain we don't tell them what's happening."

Cheney: "I just hope they don't screw things up."

Baker: "I don't think Saddam will accept this. He thinks the bazaar is open. He will want to bargain, to get more. Two days ago he was asking for us to pay him damages. If we reject this out of hand, he might think it's the best he can do and accept it. We all agree, don't we, that we want him to reject this."

Everyone agreed. It's clear we want to fight and to take out Saddam's forces. At 6:30 the group moves to the dining room to watch Colin's films of aerial attacks. The show has pilots picking off buried tanks like flies. They are buried under the sand. But the sun heats their tops and they show up under infrared rays. The planes are picking them off 1-2-3. Other film shows helicopters at night finding mobile Scuds. This looks like the Israeli technique. This is how they wanted to do it.

The film showed one lone man going into what looked like an outhouse. The plane targeted him and dove down to twenty feet. "He's now cleaning his pants," Scowcroft said.

Tuesday February 19, 1991
My Diary

After a morning meeting in the Oval with POTUS and Sununu, the President asks me to stay behind.

"Close the door," he said (to outer office). "I want you to know that we're going in Saturday night at 8:00 p.m. Just so you don't get crossways on this. Please don't say anything to anybody. If you have questions, ask me. Not everyone knows, even some you might think know.

"I'm going on to Camp David, but I'll come back."

"Will you go on television?" I ask.

"We haven't thought about it. Think about it."

WEDNESDAY FEBRUARY 20, 1991
MY DIARY

6:15 p.m. The President walks into my office. "How are the overnights?"

"Great," I say.

"Well," he says. "I'd like to get in it. Kick some butt." He left.

THURSDAY FEBRUARY 21, 1991

Meeting at the White House between CIA and Pentagon officials over battle-damage assessment.

FEBRUARY 21, 1991
THE WHITE HOUSE

Statement by Press Secretary Fitzwater from the Briefing Room of the White House, on remarks made by President Saddam Hussein:

Let me just read a few sentences in response to Saddam Hussein's speech.

The statement by Saddam Hussein this morning is disappointing. He repeats the same invective and disregard for the United Nations mandate that we have heard so often since August 2d. In vowing to continue the war, he once again demonstrates his determination to maintain the aggression against Kuwait and the absence of compassion for his people and his country.

For our part, the coalition forces remain on the course set by the twelve United Nations resolutions. Our forces remain on a steadfast course. The liberation of Kuwait continues.

FRIDAY FEBRUARY 22, 1991

President Bush rejects the Soviet's plan for withdrawal because it sets conditions.

The President issues an ultimatum: To avoid the start of a ground war, Iraq must withdraw from Kuwait in twenty-four hours (by noon Feb. 23).

FEBRUARY 22, 1991
THE PRESIDENT
Remarks on the Persian Gulf Conflict at 10:43 a.m. from the Rose Garden at the White House:

The President: Good morning.

The United States and its coalition allies are committed to enforcing the United Nations resolutions that call for Saddam Hussein to immediately and unconditionally leave Kuwait. In view of the Soviet initiative—which, very frankly, we appreciate—we want to set forth this morning the specific criteria that will ensure Saddam Hussein complies with the United Nations mandate.

Within the last twenty-four hours alone we have heard a defiant, uncompromising address by Saddam Hussein, followed less than ten hours later by a statement in Moscow that, on the face of it, appears more reasonable. I say "on the face of it" because the statement promised unconditional Iraqi withdrawal from Kuwait, only to set forth a number of conditions. And needless to say, any conditions with be unacceptable to the international coalition and would not be in compliance with the United Nations Security Council Resolution 660's demand for immediate and unconditional withdrawal.

More importantly and more urgently, we learned this morning that Saddam has now launched a scorched-earth policy against Kuwait, anticipating perhaps that he will now be forced to leave. He is wantonly setting fires to destroy the oil wells, the oil tanks, the export terminals, and other installations of that small country. Indeed, they're destroying the entire oil production system of Kuwait. At the same time that that Moscow press conference was going on and Iraq's Foreign Minister was talking peace, Saddam Hussein was launching Scud missiles.

After examining the Moscow statement and discussing it with my senior advisers here late last evening and this morning, and after extensive consultation with our coalition partners, I have decided that the time has come to make public with specificity just exactly what is required of Iraq if a ground war is to be avoided.

Most important, the coalition will give Saddam Hussein until noon Saturday to do what he must do—begin his immediate and unconditional withdrawal from Kuwait. We must hear publicly and authoritatively his acceptance of these terms. The statement to be released, as you will see, does just this and informs Saddam Hussein that he risks subjecting the Iraqi people to further hardship unless the Iraqi Government complies fully with the terms of the statement.

We will put that statement out soon. It will be in considerable detail. And that's all I'll have to say about it right now.

FEBRUARY 22, 1991
THE WHITE HOUSE
Statement by Press Secretary Fitzwater on the Persian Gulf Conflict, read to reporters at 12:48 p.m. from the Briefing Room of the White House:

The Soviet announcement yesterday represents a serious and useful effort which is appreciated. But major obstacles remain. The coalition for many months has sought a peaceful resolution to this crisis, in keeping with the UN resolutions. As President Bush pointed out to President Gorbachev, the steps the Iraqis are considering would constitute a conditional withdrawal and would also prevent the full implementation of relevant UN Security Council resolutions. Also there is no indication that Iraq is prepared to withdraw immediately.

Full compliance with the Security Council resolutions has been a consistent and necessary demand of the international community. The world must make sure that Iraq has, in fact, renounced its claim to Kuwait and accepted all relevant UN Security Council resolutions.

Indeed, only the Security Council can agree to lift sanctions against Iraq, and the world needs to be assured in concrete terms of Iraq's peaceful intentions before such action can be taken. In a situation where sanctions have been lifted, Saddam Hussein could simply revert to using his oil resources once again, not to provide for the well-being of his people but instead to rearm.

So, in a final effort to obtain Iraqi compliance with the will of the international community, the United States, after consulting with the Government of Kuwait and her other coalition partners, declares that a ground campaign will not be initiated against Iraqi forces if, prior to noon Saturday, February 23, New York time, Iraq publicly accepts the following terms and authoritatively communicates that acceptance to the United Nations:

First, Iraq must begin large-scale withdrawal from Kuwait by noon New York time, Saturday, February 23. Iraq must complete military withdrawal from Kuwait in one week. Given the fact that Iraq invaded and occupied Kuwait in a matter of hours, anything longer than this from the initiation of the withdrawal would not meet Resolution 660's requirement of immediacy.

Within the first forty-eight hours, Iraq must remove all its forces from Kuwait City and allow for the prompt return of the legitimate government of Kuwait. It must withdraw from all prepared defenses along the Saudi-Kuwait borders, from Bubiyan and Warbah Islands, and from Kuwait's Rumaylah oil fields within the one week specified above. Iraq must return all its forces to their positions of August 1st, in accordance with Resolution 660.

In cooperation with the International Red Cross, Iraq must release all prisoners of war and third-country civilians being held against their will and return their remains of killed and deceased serviceman. This action must commence immediately with the initiation of the withdrawal and must be completed within forty-eight hours.

Iraq must remove all explosives or booby traps, including those on Kuwaiti oil installations, and designate Iraqi military liaison officers to work with Kuwaiti and other coalition forces on the operational details related to Iraq's withdrawal, to include the provision of all data on the location and nature of any land or sea mines.

Iraq must cease combat aircraft flights over Iraq and Kuwait except for transport aircraft carrying troops out of Kuwait, and allow coalition aircraft exclusive control over and use of all Kuwaiti airspace.

It must cease all destructive actions against Kuwaiti citizens and property and release all Kuwaiti detainees.

The United States and its coalition partners reiterate that their forces will not attack retreating Iraqi forces and, further, will exercise restraint so long as withdrawal proceeds in accordance with the above guidelines and there are no attacks on other countries.

Any breach of these terms will bring an instant and sharp response from coalition forces in accordance with United Nations Security Council Resolution 678.

That's the conclusion of our prepared statement.

Let me just add a couple of points—first of all, that a copy of this document was provided to Iraqi diplomats here in Washington about noon today. President Bush and Secretary Baker spoke with President Gorbachev for over an hour and fifteen minutes this morning to discuss this situation, Secretary Baker spoke with Soviet Foreign Ministry officials both yesterday and today. And we have consulted with all of our allies and coalition partners last night or this morning. The coalition remains strong and united.

FEBRUARY 23, 1991
THE WHITE HOUSE
Statement by Press Secretary Fitzwater on the Persian Gulf Conflict:

CENTCOM reports that they have detected no military activity, which would indicate any withdrawal of Saddam Hussein from Kuwait. Similarly, there has been no communication between Iraq and the United Nations that would suggest a willingness to withdraw under the conditions of the coalition plan. Iraq continues its scorched earth policy in Kuwait, setting fire to oil facilities. It's a continuing outrage that Saddam Hussein is still intent upon destroying Kuwait and its people, still intent upon destroying the environment of the Gulf, and still intent upon inflicting the most brutal kind of rule on his own population, yet appears to have no intention of complying with the UN resolutions. Indeed, his only response at noon was to launch another Scud missile attack on Israel.

The coalition forces have no alternative but to continue to prosecute the war.

As we indicated last night, the withdrawal proposal the Soviets discussed with Tariq Aziz in Moscow was unacceptable because it did not constitute an unequivocal commitment to an immediate and unconditional withdrawal. Thus, the Iraqi approval of the Soviet proposal is without effect.

President Bush today spoke with Prime Minister Kaifu of Japan, President Özal of Turkey, and President Gorbachev of the Soviet Union. The phone call from President Gorbachev occurred at 11:15 a.m. and lasted for approximately twenty-eight minutes. President

Gorbachev informed the President that he asked for a UN review of his proposal and said that he had talked to Prime Minister Major and President Mitterrand about his plan. Both of the allied leaders indicated full support for the coalition withdrawal plan. President Bush thanked President Gorbachev for his extensive efforts and reflected our general disappointment that Saddam Hussein has chose not to respond positively.

FEBRUARY 23, 1991.

Satellite images show extensive smoke from oil wells burning in Kuwait. (Estimates of more than 750 of Kuwait's 943 oil wells are damaged or destroyed.)

FEBRUARY 23, 1991
THE WHITE HOUSE
Statement on the Persian Gulf Conflict:

We regret that Saddam Hussein took no action before the noon deadline to comply with the United Nations resolutions. We remain determined to fulfill the UN resolutions. Military action continues on schedule and according to plan.

SATURDAY FEBRUARY 23, 1991

Coalition ground offensive begins at 8:00 p.m. EST (February 24 at 4:00 a.m. Saudi time).

Phase II:

—The Ground War —

Operation Desert Storm

Saturday February 23, 1991
The President
Presidential address to the Nation announcing Allied military ground action in the Persian Gulf Conflict at 10:00 p.m. from the White House Briefing Room.

"The Liberation of Kuwait

Has Now Entered Its Final Phase"

The President: Good evening. Yesterday, after conferring with my senior national security advisors, and following extensive consultations with our coalition partners, Saddam Hussein was given one last chance—set forth in very explicit terms—to do what he should have done more than six months ago: withdraw from Kuwait without condition or further delay, and comply fully with the resolutions passed by the United Nations Security Council.

Regrettably, the noon deadline passed without the agreement of the Government of Iraq to meet demands of United Nations Security Council Resolution 660, as set forth in the specific terms spelled out by the coalition to withdraw unconditionally from Kuwait. To the contrary, what we have seen is a redoubling of Saddam Hussein's efforts to destroy completely Kuwait and its people.

I have, therefore, directed General Norman Schwarzkopf, in conjunction with coalition forces, to use all forces available, including ground forces, to eject the Iraqi army from Kuwait. Once again, this as a decision made only after extensive consultations with our coalition partnership.

The liberation of Kuwait has now entered a final phase. I have complete confidence in the ability of the coalition forces swiftly and decisively to accomplish their mission.

Tonight, as this coalition of countries seeks to do that which is right and just, I ask only that all of you stop what you doing and say a prayer for all the coalition forces, and especially for our men and women in uniform who this very moment are risking their lives for their country and for all of us.

May God bless and protect each and every one of them. And may God bless the United States of America. Thank you very much.

FEBRUARY 24, 1991
MY DIARY

4:30 p.m. The President and Will Farish stop by my office before the 5:00 p.m. meeting. I'm watching TV.

"What's Saddam say," Farish asks.

"He says he's winning," the President says. "I guess that's how you do it in war. Ever heard of anyone saying he's getting his ass kicked. He's losing."

FEBRUARY 24, 1991
MY DIARY

5:00 p.m. Cheney and Powell briefed the President on the first day of [ground] war. The plan is going great. Incredibly, only one confirmed casualty.

I had appealed the news blackout Sunday morning before church to Sununu. He argued, but must have mentioned it to the President.

He asked Colin about resuming the briefings. Cheney said Norm briefed this morning and would brief again tomorrow. I must have gotten through.

At the end of the briefing, Colin said he was embarrassed to ask, but he would like to hit the arch in Baghdad that Saddam had built in honor of his Iran war, and a statue of Saddam. President asked, "Do they have any religious significance." No. "Can you do it without hurting anyone?"

"Yes," Cheney said. "We do it in the middle of the night." The President never actually gave his approval. Sununu asked if they could wait and make it "an exclamation point on the war." Everyone looked at the floor.

The President asked about rumors of anthrax in British troops caused by sheep. Colin said they had checked it out. Turns out the Bedouins move their sheep by crowding them in trucks, so some die. When they do, the drivers just throw them out in the desert. Thus it wasn't anthrax at all. It was pneumonia that the Brits had.

MONDAY FEBRUARY 25, 1991

Coalition forces are outside Kuwait City.

Iraq launches a Scud missile attack on barracks in Al Khobar, Dhahran. Barracks are hit by Scud (28 US soldiers killed, 98 wounded).

Reports on Baghdad Radio state that Saddam Hussein has ordered troop withdrawal according to the terms of the Soviet peace proposal.

In two days of ground assaults, US 4 killed, 21 wounded; Iraqi 20,000 taken prisoner and 270 tanks destroyed.

FEBRUARY 25, 1991
MY DIARY

About 6:00 p.m. The wires reported Baghdad Radio saying Saddam is offering to withdraw. I went to Brent and Bob Gates for a statement. We wrote that Saddam had not contacted us or the UN so we had no comment and no change in policy. I returned to my office and the President called. I read the statement and he said, "Add that a war is on. Things are changing. We have troops at risk. Their safety and security is our first concern."

"That means, Mr. President, that the February 22 terms no longer apply. We've moved beyond that." I said.

"We have. We're at war," he said.

"OK," I said, hung up, and called Baker to coordinate with him.

"We can't go beyond the UN resolutions," he said. "Can't we say that we don't accept this because it meets the Soviet plan, and that plan is unacceptable?"

"I'll call back," Baker said. He called back to say the Soviet Embassy says Saddam's not accepting their plan. He accepted our plan, so you have to take that out."

I called the President, in dinner with Mrs. Bush and Brent.

"Why haven't you issued the statement," the President demanded.

"Secretary Baker says we can't say this. The Soviet Plan doesn't apply. We can't go beyond the UN resolution."

"Don't say that," the President said. "Just say the war has changed things and let others interpret."

"The group feels that won't work," I said.

"The group," the President said, clearly agitated. "I'm saying do it."

I called Baker back. "The President has ordered me to release this. I'm going to do it." I said.

"OK," Baker said. "I'll call the President." He called me back to say, "The NSC will meet with the President at 8:00 p.m. Hold the statement till then."

In the meeting, the President said, "Saddam wants to get his forces out of Kuwait and back into Iraq. Then he can tell us to get out of Iraq. That's as clear as the ass of a goat."

"We've got to show a win," the President said. "One side surrenders to another."

Cheney/Powell were adamant against acknowledging a withdrawal.

Baker wrote a sentence saying we learned at Khafji not to trust his surrender moves. We fashioned a statement saying we saw no evidence of a withdrawal. The plan was to issue that statement tonight and a longer one tomorrow that laid out our terms, just like we did on the 22nd.

9:15 p.m. The President went home. We went to Brent's office. A strong argument broke out about not letting Saddam off the hook. Kimmit reported that Verontsov (Soviet) was calling for a night (10:00 p.m.) meeting to discuss the withdrawal offer.

Gates suggested adding to our statement tonight to answer the two key questions: would we attack retreating troops—no; and what does Saddam have to do to comply—Bob's paragraph said Saddam must "personally and publicly" call for withdrawal. Baker convinced Cheney that Saddam would never do it. If he did, it would constitute public humiliation, and maybe the closet thing we would get to surrender. The President wants surrender.

MONDAY FEBRUARY 25, 1991
THE WHITE HOUSE
Statement by Press Secretary Fitzwater on the Persian Gulf Conflict that was read to reporters at 10:30 p.m. in the Briefing Room of the White House:

We continue to prosecute the war. We have heard no reason to change that. And because there is a war on, our first concern must be the safety and security of United States and coalition forces.

We don't know whether this most recent claim about Iraqi withdrawal is genuine. We have no evidence to suggest the Iraqi army is withdrawing. In fact, Iraqi units are continuing to fight. Moreover, we remember when Saddam Hussein's tanks pretended to surrender at Khafji, only to turn and fire. We remember the Scud attacks today, and Saddam's many broken promises of the past. There are at least an additional twenty-two dead Americans tonight who offer silent testimony to the intentions of Saddam Hussein.

The statement out of Baghdad today says that Saddam Hussein's forces will fight their way out while retreating. We will not attack unarmed soldiers in retreat. But we will consider retreating combat units as a movement of war.

The only way Saddam Hussein can persuade the coalition of the seriousness of his intentions would be for him personally and publicly to agree to the terms of the proposal we issued on February 22. And because the announcement from Baghdad referred to the Soviet initiative, he must personally and publicly accept explicitly all relevant UN Security Council resolutions including especially UN Security Council Resolution 662, which calls for Iraqi recision of its purported annexation of Kuwait, and UN Security Council Resolution 674 which calls for Iraqi compensation to Kuwait and others.

That's the end of the statement. I might just add that the President met with his national security advisors for approximately an hour and fifteen minutes this evening to consider this matter, and the President has returned to his residence.

FEBRUARY 25, 1991
MY DIARY

I read the statement at 10:30 p.m. The President called me immediately afterward.

"Great job, Marlin," he said. "You said it just right. You obviously added to the statement after I left."

"I'm sitting in the john," he said, "kinda like LBJ." He laughed and it was good to hear.

"Thank you, Sir," I said.

TUESDAY FEBRUARY 26, 1991

Battle of 73 Easting underway, in which VII Corps battles Saddam Hussein's Republican Guard.

Iraqi troops flee Kuwait City.

Iraq's withdrawal from Kuwait is announced on Baghdad Radio: "Orders have been issued to our armed forces to withdraw in an organized manner to the positions they held prior to 1 August 1990. This is regarded as a practical compliance with Resolution 660. The spokesman emphasized that our armed forces, which have proven their ability to fight and stand fast, will confront any attempt to harm it while it is carrying out the withdrawal order."

FEBRUARY 26, 1991
THE WHITE HOUSE
Statement by Press Secretary Fitzwater on the Iraqi Statement on Withdrawal From Kuwait:

Saddam Hussein's radio statement last night contained the same diatribe as previous comments, with no commitment to complying with the twelve United Nations resolutions. His speech changes nothing. It does not annul the annexation of Kuwait or meet any of the coalition's other terms. The war goes on.

FEBRUARY 26, 1991
MY DIARY

During the night, Saddam announced withdrawal. Calls started at 5:00 a.m. from the press. I called the Situation Room and headed for the White House. The President was in the Oval well before I arrived. I went to his study at 7:15 a.m.

"Do you want to comment?" I asked.

"This speech is an outrage," he said. "It changes nothing. Same diatribe. You should get that out so our coalition friends know."

10:00 a.m. The President wants to deliver a response on the colonnade steps. He writes the speech that begins this "speech is an outrage."

I tell him it's a "Jesus" opening. When the press hears it, they say "Jesus." He loved it.

FEBRUARY 26, 1991
THE PRESIDENT
Full address broadcast live on nationwide radio and television to the Nation at 9:45 a.m. from the Rose Garden at the White House on the Iraqi statement on withdrawal from Kuwait:

The President: I have a brief statement to make today. Saddam's most recent speech is an outrage. He is not withdrawing. His defeated forces are retreating. He is trying to claim victory in the midst of a rout, and he is not voluntarily giving up Kuwait. He is trying to save the remnants of power and control in the Middle East by every means possible. And here, too, Saddam Hussein will fail.

Saddam is not interested in peace but only to regroup and fight another day. And he does not renounce Iraq's claim to Kuwait. To the contrary, he made clear that Iraq continues to claim Kuwait. Nor is there any evidence of remorse for Iraq's aggression or any indication that Saddam is prepared to accept the responsibility for the awful consequences of that aggression.

He still does not accept UN Security Council resolutions or the coalition terms of February 22, including the release of our POWs— all POWs—third-country detainees, and an end to the pathological destruction of Kuwait. The coalition will therefore continue to prosecute the war with undiminished intensity.

As we announced last night, we will not attack unarmed soldiers in retreat. We have no choice but to consider retreating combat units as a threat and respond accordingly. Anything else would risk additional United States and coalition casualties.

The best way to avoid further casualties on both sides is for the Iraqi soldiers to lay down their arms as nearly 30,000 Iraqis already have. It is time for all Iraqi forces in the theater of operation, those occupying Kuwait, those supporting the occupation of Kuwait, to lay down their arms. And that will stop the bloodshed.

From the beginning of the air operation nearly six weeks ago, I have said that our efforts are on course and on schedule. This morning I am very pleased to say that coalition efforts are ahead of schedule. The liberation of Kuwait is close at hand.

And let me just add that I share the pride of all of the American people in the magnificent heroic performance of our Armed Forces. May God bless them and keep them.

FEBRUARY 26, 1991
MY DIARY

1:30 p.m. Cheney/Powell briefing the President. Colin showed a Sam Donaldson, Prime Time, film of Iraqi troops surrendering to three American soldiers. He said he had shown it to the Black Caucus.

"I played the Mutual radio tape of Iraqi troops surrendering to a radio technician by chanting, "George Bush. George Bush." The

President smiled but maintained his reserve.

The President asked again, "How does it end?" He asks this at every meeting. He still wants a surrender on the decks of the *Missouri*. He wants Saddam to have to surrender.

Later, en route to General Max Thurmund's retirement ceremony, he says he asked Turkey's Özal why he couldn't demand a surrender. Bandar says it's terrible in the Arab world to say surrender. Özal says he will look into it.

At the end of the 1:30 p.m. meeting, Gates suggested a joint session of Congress speech to declare victory when the withdrawal is complete—when Iraq is out of Kuwait. "You may never get a chance later," he said.

"It may be," I suggested, "that the 1990s equivalent of the *Missouri* deck is a TV studio." The President grimaced. He wants that old-fashioned "hand over your sword" surrender. He did address the Congress.

FEBRUARY 26, 1991

Iraqi forces are reported to be in "full retreat." As US Marines push into Kuwait City, thousands of Iraqi soldiers are retreating and laying down their arms in surrender.

The US Embassy in Kuwait is back under US control.

WEDNESDAY FEBRUARY 27, 1991

United States Marines and Saudi Arabian troops enter Kuwait City. The 101st Airborne Division nears Baghdad. The coalition announces they have destroyed almost half of all Iraqi division. A half-million Iraqi troops are taken as POWs.

PHASE III:

—THE LIBERATION OF KUWAIT—

THE WAR IS OVER

FEBRUARY 27, 1991
MY DIARY
Big Nine Meeting, Oval Office. Victory In Hand.

A Big Nine meeting (the nine leaders who met almost daily to decide the war: President, Vice President, Baker, Cheney, Scowcroft, Gates, Powell, Fitzwater, and Sununu.) Colin gives the President the Schwarzkopf briefing given earlier in Riyadh. He says fighting is virtually over. Fighting last Republican Guards near Basra. He says Iraqi troops are fleeing Kuwait through Iran and Basra. Little organized combat resistance left.

"By tomorrow," Colin says, "It could be embarrassing. We will be killing for little reason because all their armor will be destroyed. It will just be troops in trucks and cars they've stolen."

"When can I say we've won?" the President asks. "Tomorrow?"

Foreign Minister Hurd of the United Kingdom arrives for ten minutes with the President. They discuss the war. The President doesn't raise the end or cease-fire possibility. He says, "I'm old fashioned, I guess, I'd still like to see a clear finish, like on the deck of the *Missouri*." Hurd just shakes his head.

After Hurd leaves, the Big Nine resumes discussions. During Hurd meeting, I move to sit at the Oval Office desk in the President's chair. He has two typewritten phrases under the glass of the desk, lower righthand corner: THEY DON'T KNOW NOTHING, AND THEY GOT THAT TANGLED UP. And: IF WE'RE GONNA SEE A RAINBOW, WE'LL HAVE TO STAND A LITTLE RAIN. No attributions.

President raises the deck of the *Missouri* again. Colin said again it was over.

President: "Maybe we could meet on the border, Schwarzkopf and the Revolutionary Council guys, and exchange prisoners. "The

President had finally found the idea to duplicate the *Missouri*.

Pres: "Could we end it tonight, Colin? Call for an end to the hostilities. I don't want to keep this going any longer than necessary."

Colin: "I'll have to check with Norm."

In typical Bush style, the President says, "Call him up. Use my phone here in the desk."

Scowcroft walks over to show Colin the phone in the bottom left-hand drawer of the desk—direct to Norm. He picks up the phone and gets through immediately. He talks in low tones for two minutes, and returns to the couch.

"Norm can handle all this," Colin said, at 2:40 p.m. (The war is over.)

"Then I want to do it tonight," the President said.

We set 9:00 p.m. as the time (for President's speech). I would announce (the speech) at 6:30 p.m. I later moved that (announcement) up to 6:15 p.m. so it would make the first evening news feeds taping in New York.

Walking out of the Oval, we were happy. The relief was starting. "Colin, are you in the two-minute drill," Gates asked, referring to the bombing of military targets saved till the last.

"You boys better get some teak wood for the Oval Office," Colin laughed, referring to the deck of the *Missouri*.

Author's Note: I privately referred to the Big Eight meeting as the Big Nine, in order to include myself. In the first Oval Office meeting after the August 1 invasion and after our return from Aspen, Scowcroft identified the participants on the President's schedule as President, Vice President, Sec. of Defense, Sec. of State, Chief of Staff, National Security Adviser, Deputy National Security Adviser, Chairman of Joint Chiefs of Staff, and Press Secretary to the President. This was the group to meet almost daily with the President from August until the war was over in February 1991.

But after the first meeting, General Scowcroft came to me privately and said some of the Pentagon generals were complaining that I was in the first meeting, in effect taking a space that should go to the military. I responded that public statements on the war were crucial, and we would have to make decisions daily on statements, speeches, etc. Scowcroft says, "Yes, but all the Generals see your name on the President's schedule and they want in."

I said, "Fine, take my name off the schedule." When I showed up for every meeting, to my knowledge no one complained. First, they soon saw that a portion of nearly every meeting was spent on press statements and timing, and presidential speeches. Second, one day after about three meetings, I was about two seconds late. I walked into the Oval just as the group was sitting down. The President was sitting in front of the fireplace. He looked up at the group and said, "Let's wait till Marlin gets here." No one ever questioned my presence again. And I adopted the ten-minute rule: Always go to the Oval ten minutes in advance. I didn't want to lose my special status.

FEBRUARY 27, 1991
THE PRESIDENT
At 9:02 p.m. from the Oval Office at the White House, President Bush addresses the Nation on the suspension of Allied offensive combat operations in the Persian Gulf,

"KUWAIT IS LIBERATED"

Kuwait is liberated. Iraq's army is defeated. Our military objectives are met. Kuwait is once more in the hands of Kuwaitis in control of their own destiny. We share in their joy, a joy tempered only by our compassion for their ordeal.

Tonight, the Kuwaiti flag once again flies above the capital of a free and sovereign nation, and the American flag flies above our embassy.

Seven months ago, America and the world drew a line in the sand. We declared that the aggression against Kuwait would not stand; and tonight America and the world have kept their word.

This is not a time of euphoria, certainly not a time to gloat, but it is a time of pride, pride in our troops, pride in the friends who stood with us in the crisis, pride in our nation and the people whose strength and resolve made victory quick, decisive, and just.

And soon we will open wide our arms to welcome back home to America our magnificent fighting forces. No one country can claim this victory as its own. It was not only a victory for Kuwait, but a victory for all the coalition partners. This is a victory for the United Nations, for all mankind, for the rule of law, and for what is right.

After consulting with Secretary of Defense Cheney, the Chairman of the Joint Chiefs of Staff, General Powell, and our coalition partners, I am pleased to announce that at midnight tonight, Eastern standard time, exactly one hundred hours since ground operations commenced, and six weeks since the start of Operation Desert Storm, all United States and coalition forces will suspend offensive combat operations. It is up to Iraq whether this suspension on the part of the coalition becomes a permanent cease-fire.

Coalition, political, and military terms for a formal cease-fire include the following requirements:

– Iraq must release immediately all coalition prisoners of war, third-country nationals, and the remains of all who have fallen.

– Iraq must release all Kuwaiti detainees.

– Iraq also must inform Kuwaiti authorities of the location and nature of all land and sea mines.

— Iraq must comply fully with all relevant United Nations Security Council resolutions. This includes a rescinding of Iraq's August decision to annex Kuwait, and acceptable— and acceptance in principle of Iraq's responsibility to pay compensation for the loss, damage, and injury its aggression has caused.

The coalition calls upon the Iraqi Government to designate military commanders to meet within forty-eight hours with their coalition counterparts at a place in the theater of operations to be specified to arrange for military aspects of the cease-fire. Further, I have asked Secretary of State Baker to request that the United Nations Security Council meet to formulate the necessary arrangements for this war to be ended.

This suspension of offensive combat operations is contingent upon Iraq's not firing upon any coalition forces and not launching Scud missiles against any other country. If Iraq violates these terms, coalition forces will be free to resume military operations.

At every opportunity I have said to the people of Iraq that our quarrel was not with them but instead with their leadership, and above all with Saddam Hussein. This remains the case. You, the people of Iraq, are not our enemy. We do not seek your destruction. We have treated your POW's with kindness. Coalition forces fought this war only as a last resort and look forward to the day when Iraq is led by people prepared to live in peace with their neighbors.

We must now begin to look beyond victory in war. We must meet the challenge of securing the peace. In the future, as before, we will consult with our coalition partners. We've already done a good deal of thinking and planning for the post-war period, and Secretary Baker has already begun to consult with our coalition partners on the region's challenges. There can be and will be no solely American answer to all these challenges, but we can assist and support the countries of the region, and be a catalyst for peace. In this spirit Secretary Baker will go to the region next week to begin a new round of consultations.

This war is now behind us. Ahead of us is the difficult task of securing a potentially historic peace. Tonight though, let us be proud of what we have accomplished. Let us give thanks to those who risked their lives. Let us never forget those who gave their lives.

May God bless our valiant military forces and their families; and let us all remember them in our prayers.

Good night, and may God bless the United States of America.

THURSDAY FEBRUARY 28, 1991

President Bush announces a cease-fire has taken place at 8:00 a.m. Riyadh time (Wednesday midnight EST), marking the liberation of Kuwait and defeat of the Iraqi Army. Schwarzkopf announces, "We've almost completely destroyed the offensive capability of the Iraqi forces in the Kuwaiti theater of operations."

FRIDAY MARCH 1, 1991

In Safwan, Iraq, Schwarzkopf and Iraqi generals meet to negotiate a cease-fire plan. On March 3, 1991, commander of UN coalition forces, Gen. Norman Schwarzkopf, met with Hussein's generals at the Safwan Airfield in Iraq to discuss the terms of the cease-fire,

The American Embassy in Kuwait officially reopens.

MARCH 1, 1991
MY DIARY

11:00 a.m. in the Oval Office. The Big Nine met in the Oval to discuss post-war plans and Baker's trip. After much discussion, the considerations were: "We wanted no permanent ground combat presence in the Gulf." The President was adamant that we hold to our promise not to have a "big new permanent presence."

Cheney said the Arabs wanted some presence. Kuwait and Saudis want the security of the US. He suggested a training center operation where US forces go TDY (temporary duty) and we could leave tanks and equipment there for them to use in training. We will have an air presence in Saudi Arabia, perhaps a tactical fighter wing in Bahrain.

"Whatever you want," Baker said to Cheney, "now is the time to address it. Give me a list."

Baker added, "We need to build down arms in the region. An arms sales ban is crucial."

MARCH 1, 1991
THE PRESIDENT

Excerpt from the 72nd Presidential press conference that began at 12:45 p.m. in the Briefing Room of the White House:

The President: Good afternoon. In the hours since we suspended military operations in the Kuwaiti theater of war, considerable progress has been made in moving towards a cease-fire and postwar planning. As our forces moved into Kuwait City, and as the faces of these jubilant Kuwaiti citizens have warmed our hearts, the coalition leaders started the arduous task of addressing the next stages of the Persian Gulf situation.

As a first order of business this afternoon, I want to thank the American people for the affection and support that they have shown for our troops in the Middle East. In towns and cities across this nation, our citizens have felt a sense of purpose and unity in the accomplishment of our military that is a welcome addition to the American spirit. And as our service men and women begin coming home, as they will soon, I look forward to the many celebrations of their achievement.

In the meantime, we are focused on the many diplomatic tasks associated with ending this conflict. General Khalid, General Schwarzkopf, and other coalition military leaders of our forces in the Gulf will meet with representatives of Iraq tomorrow afternoon, March 2nd, in the theater of operations to discuss the return of POWs and other military matters related to the cease-fire. We will not discuss the location of the meeting for obvious security reasons. But this is an important step in securing the victory that our forces have achieved.

Work is proceeding in New York at the United Nations on the political aspects of ending the war. We've welcomed here in Washington this week the envoys of several of our close friends and allies. And shortly, Secretary Baker will be leaving for a new round of consultations that I am confident will advance planning for the war's aftermath. Again, and as I said Wednesday evening, the true challenge before us will be securing the peace.

MARCH 1, 1991
MY DIARY

The President does a press conference at 12:45 p.m. At the end of the press conference, he turned and walked away from the podium for the first time ever. No lingering. No extra questions. He clearly had a new confidence. Also, he had now seen Fitzwater and Schwarzkopf do it throughout the war.

Author's Note: I had always urged President Reagan and President Bush to end their press conferences by turning away from the podium and not look back. It looks decisive and commanding to the TV audience. But politicians have a tough time turning away from people shouting their name and asking for one more question. Norman Schwarzkopf changed that.

MARCH 1, 1991
MY DIARY

At home about 7:00 p.m. Charles Bierbauer calls me to say the cease-fire meeting between Schwarzkopf and the Iraqis was delayed. He wanted confirmation.

7:02 p.m. I call the Situation Room. They have no information.

7:10 p.m. Roman calls from Brent's office. Colin has called Pete Williams, the Pentagon Spokesman, who called Roman, who called me. He confirms a twenty-four-hour delay. I instruct Roman to have Pete announce the change at the Pentagon, as "a technical change."

7:45 p.m. The Situation Room calls to say they still have no confirmation from the Joint Chiefs of Staff of a change in plans.

Must be the fog of post-war.

SATURDAY MARCH 2, 1991

UNSC Resolution 686 pasess, demanding Iraq's acceptance of all previous resolutions.

SUNDAY MARCH 3, 1991

At the Safwan Airfield, Iraq, Gen. Schwarzkopf and Iraqi generals meet to negotiate a cease-fire plan.

WEDNESDAY MARCH 6, 1991
THE PRESIDENT
The President speaks before a joint session of Congress at 9:12 p.m. in the House Chamber at the Capitol. This address on the cessation of the Persian Gulf Conflict is broadcast live on nationwide television and radio.

"KUWAIT IS FREE"

Speaker Foley: Mr. President, it is customary at joint sessions for the Chair to present the President to the Members of Congress directly and without further comment. But I wish to depart from tradition tonight and express to you on behalf of the Congress and the country, and through you to the members of our Armed Forces, our warmest congratulations on the brilliant victory of the Desert Storm Operation.

Members of the Congress, I now have the high privilege

and distinct honor of presenting to you the President of the United States.

The President: Thank you, Mr. Speaker. Mr. Speaker, thank you, sir, for those very generous words spoken from the heart about the wonderful performance of our military.

Mr. President, Mr. Speaker, Members of Congress: Five short weeks ago, I came to this House to speak to you about the State of the Union. We met then in time of war. Tonight, we meet in a world blessed by the promise of peace.

From the moment Operation Desert Storm commenced on January 16, until the time the guns fell silent at midnight one week ago, this Nation has watched its sons and daughters with pride—watched over them with prayer. As Commander in Chief, I can report to you: Our Armed Forces fought with honor and valor, and as President, I can report to the Nation—aggression is defeated. The war is over.

This is a victory for every country in the coalition, and for the United Nations, a victory for unprecedented international cooperation and diplomacy, so well led by our Secretary of State James Baker. It is a victory for the rule of law and for what is right.

Desert Storm's success belongs to the team that so ably leads our Armed Forces—our Secretary of Defense and our Chairman of the Joint Chiefs: Dick Cheney and Colin Powell.

And of course, this military victory also belongs to the one the British call the Man of the Match—the tower of calm at the eye of Desert Storm—Gen. Norman Schwarzkopf.

And let us, recognizing this was a coalition effort, not forget Saudi General Khalid, or Britain's General de la Billiere, or General Roquejoffre of France, and all the others whose leadership played such a vital role. And most importantly, all those who served in the field.

I thank the Members of this Congress—support here for our troops in battle was overwhelming. And above all, I thank those whose unfailing love and support sustained our courageous men and women: I thank the American people.

Tonight, I come to this House to speak about the world—the world after war. The recent challenge could not have been clearer. Saddam Hussein was the villain; Kuwait the victim. To the aid of this small country came nations from North America and Europe, from Asia and South America, from Africa and the Arab world—all united against aggression. Our uncommon coalition must now work in common purpose to forge a future that should never again be held hostage to the darker side of human nature.

Tonight in Iraq, Saddam walks amidst ruin. His war machine is crushed. His ability to threaten mass destruction is itself destroyed. His people have been lied to—denied the truth. And when his defeated legions come home, all Iraqis will see and feel the havoc he has wrought. And this I promise you: For all that Saddam has done to his own people, to the Kuwaitis, and to the entire world—Saddam and those around him are accountable.

All of us grieve for the victims of war, for the people of Kuwait and the suffering that scars the soul of that proud nation. We grieve for all our fallen soldiers and their families, for all the innocents caught up in this conflict. And yes, we grieve for the people of Iraq—a people who have never been our enemy. My hope is that one day we will once again welcome them as friends into the community of nations. Our commitment to peace in the Middle East does not end with the liberation of Kuwait. So tonight, let me outline four key challenges to be met:

First, we must work together to create shared security arrangements in the region. Our friends and allies in the Middle East recognize that they will bear the bulk of the responsibility for regional security. But we want them to know that just as we stood with them to repel aggression, so now America stands ready to work with them to secure the peace. This does not mean stationing US ground forces on the Arabian Peninsula, but it does mean American participation in joint exercises involving both air and ground forces. It means maintaining a capable US naval presence in the region, just as we have for over forty years. Let it be clear: Our vital national interests depend on a stable and secure Gulf.

Second, we must act to control the proliferation of weapons of mass destruction and the missiles used to deliver them. It would be tragic if the nations of the Middle East and Persian Gulf were now, in the wake of war, to embark on a new arms race. Iraq requires special vigilance. Until Iraq convinces the world of its peaceful intentions—that its leaders will not use new revenues to rearm and rebuild its menacing war machine—Iraq must not have access to the instruments of war.

And third, we must work to create new opportunities for peace and stability in the Middle East. On the night I announced Operation Desert Storm, I expressed my hope that out of the horrors of war might come new momentum for peace. We have learned in the modern age, geography cannot guarantee security and security does not come from military power alone.

All of us know the depth of bitterness that has made the dispute between Israel and its neighbors so painful and intractable. Yet, in the conflict just concluded, Israel and many of the Arab States have for the first time found themselves confronting the same aggressor. By now, it should be plain to all parties that peacemaking in the Middle East requires compromise. At the same time, peace brings real benefits to everyone. We must do all that we can to close the gap between Israel and the Arab States—and between Israelis and Palestinians. The tactics of terror lead absolutely nowhere. There can be no substitute for diplomacy.

A comprehensive peace must be grounded in UN Security Council Resolutions 242 and 338 and the principle of territory for peace. This principle must be elaborated to provide for Israel's security and recognition, and at the same time for legitimate Palestinian political rights. Anything else would fail the twin tests of fairness and security. The time has come to put an end to Arab-Israeli conflict.

The war with Iraq is over. The quest for solutions to the problems in Lebanon, in the Arab-Israeli dispute, and in the Gulf must go forward with new vigor and determination. I guarantee you: No one will work harder for a stable peace in the region than we will.

Fourth, we must foster economic development for the sake of peace and progress. The Persian Gulf and Middle East form a region rich in natural resources with a wealth of untapped human potential. Resources once squandered on military might must be redirected to more peaceful ends. We are already addressing the immediate economic consequences of Iraq's aggression. Now, the challenge is to reach higher—to foster economic freedom and prosperity for all people of the region.

By meeting these four challenges we can build a framework for peace. I have asked Secretary of State Baker to go to the Middle East to begin the process. He will go to listen, to probe, to offer suggestions, and to advance the search for peace and stability. I have also asked him to raise the plight of the hostages held in Lebanon. We have not forgotten them. We will not forget them.

To all the challenges that confront this region of the world, there is no single solution, no solely American answer. But we can make a difference. America will work tirelessly as a catalyst for positive change.

But we cannot lead a new world abroad if, at home, it's politics as usual on American defense and diplomacy. It's time to turn away from the temptation to protect unneeded weapons systems and obsolete bases. It's time to put an end to micromanagement of foreign and security assistance programs, micromanagement that humiliates our friends and allies and hamstrings our diplomacy. It's time to rise above the parochial and the pork barrel—to do what is necessary, what's right, and what will enable this Nation to play the leadership role required of us.

The consequences of the conflict in the gulf reach far beyond the confines of the Middle East. Twice before in this century, an entire world was convulsed by war. Twice this century, out of the horrors of war hope emerged for enduring peace. Twice before, those hopes proved to be a distant dream, beyond the grasp of man. Until now, the world we've known has been a world divided—a world of barbed wire and concrete block, conflict and cold war.

Now, we can see a new world coming into view, a world in which there is the very real prospect of a new world order, in the words of Winston Churchill, a world order in which 'the principles of justice and fair play protect the weak against the strong . . . ,' a world where the United Nations, freed from cold war stalemate, is poised to fulfill the historic vision of its founders, a world in which freedom and respect for human rights find a home among all nations. The Gulf War put this new world to its first test. And my fellow Americans: We passed that test.

For the sake of our principles—for the sake of the Kuwaiti people—we stood our ground. Because the world would not look the other way, Ambassador Al-Sabah, tonight, Kuwait is free. We are very happy about that.

Tonight, as our troops begin to come home, let us recognize that the hard work of freedom still calls us forward. We've learned the hard lessons of history. The victory over Iraq was not waged as 'a war to end all wars.' Even the new world order cannot guarantee an era of perpetual peace. But enduring peace must be our mission. Our success in the Gulf will shape not only the new world order we seek, but our mission here at home.

In the war just ended, there were clear-cut objectives, timetables and, above all, an overriding imperative to achieve results. We must bring that same sense of self-discipline, that same sense of urgency, to the way we meet challenges here at home.

In my State of the Union address and in my budget, I defined a comprehensive agenda to prepare for the next American century.

Our first priority is to get this economy rolling again. The fear and uncertainty caused by the Gulf crises were understandable. But now that the war is over, oil prices are down, interest rates are down, and confidence is rightly coming back. Americans can move forward to lend, spend, and invest in this, the strongest economy on Earth.

We must also enact the legislation that is key to building a better America. For example: In 1990, we enacted an historic Clean Air Act. Now we've proposed a national energy strategy. We passed a child care bill that put power in the hands of parents. Today, we're ready to do the same thing with our schools, and expand choice in education. We passed a crime bill that made a useful start in fighting crime and drugs. This year we're sending to Congress our comprehensive crime package to finish the job. We passed the landmark Americans With Disabilities Act. Now we've sent forward our civil rights bill. We also passed the aviation bill. This year we've sent up our new highway bill. And these are just a few of our pending proposals for reform and renewal.

So tonight, I call on Congress to move forward aggressively on our domestic front. Let's begin with two initiatives we should be able to agree on quickly: transportation and crime. And then, let's build on success with those and enact the rest of our agenda. If our forces could win the ground war in one hundred hours, then surely the Congress can pass this legislation in one hundred days. Let that be a promise we make tonight to the American people.

When I spoke in this House about the State of our Union, I asked all of you: If we can selflessly confront evil for the sake of good in a land so far away, then surely we can make this land all that it should be. In the time since then, the brave men and women of Desert Storm accomplished more than even they may realize. They set out to confront an enemy abroad, and in the process, they transformed a nation at home. Think of the way they went about their mission—

with confidence and quiet pride. Think about their sense of duty, about all they taught us, about our values, about ourselves.

We hear so often about our young people in turmoil; how our children fall short; how our schools fail us; how American products and American workers are second class. Well, don't you believe it. The America we saw in Desert Storm was first-class talent.

And they did it using America's state-of-the-art technology. We saw the excellence embodied in the Patriot missile and the patriots who made it work. And we saw soldiers who know about honor and bravery and duty and country and the world-shaking power of these simple words. There is something noble and majestic about the pride, about the patriotism, that we feel tonight.

So, to everyone here, and everyone watching at home, think about the men and women of Desert Storm. Let us honor them with our gratitude. Let us comfort the families of the fallen and remember each precious life lost.

Let us learn from them as well. Let us honor those who have served us by serving others. Let us honor them as individuals— men and women of every race, all creeds and colors—by setting the face of this Nation against discrimination, bigotry, and hate. Eliminate them.

I'm sure many of you saw on the television the unforgettable scene of four terrified Iraqi soldiers surrendering. They emerged from their bunker—broken, tears streaming from their eyes, fearing the worst. And then there was the American soldier. Remember what he said? He said: 'It's OK. You're all right now. You're all right now.' That scene says a lot about America, a lot about who we are. Americans are a caring people. We are a good people, a generous people. Let us always be caring and good and generous in all we do.

Soon, very soon, our troops will begin the march we've all been waiting for—their march home. I have directed Secretary Cheney to begin the immediate return of American combat units from the Gulf. Less than two hours from now, the first planeload of American soldiers will lift off from Saudi Arabia headed for the USA. That plane will carry men and women of the 24th Mechanized Infantry Division bound for Fort Stewart, Georgia. This is just the beginning of a steady flow of American troops coming home. Let their return remind us that all those who have gone before are linked with us in the long line of freedom's march.

Americans have always tried to serve, to sacrifice nobly for what we believe to be right. Tonight, I ask every community in this country to make this coming 4th of July a day of special celebration for our returning troops. They may have missed Thanksgiving and Christmas, but I can tell you this: For them and for their families, we can make this a holiday they'll never forget.

In a very real sense, this victory belongs to them—to the privates and the pilots, to the sergeants and the supply officers, to the men and women in the machines, and the men and women who made them work. It belongs to the Regulars, to the Reserves, to the National Guard. This victory belongs to the finest fighting force this Nation has ever known in its history.

We went halfway around the world to do what is moral and just and right. We fought hard, and—with others—we won the war. We lifted the yoke of aggression and tyranny from a small country that many Americans had never even heard of, and we ask nothing in return.

We're coming home now—proud. Confident—heads high. There is much that we must do at home and abroad. And we will do it. We are Americans.

May God bless this great nation, the United States of America.

FRIDAY MARCH 8, 1991
MY DIARY

Boyden Gray tells me the President wants more credit for Brent. President had asked me the day before to get some credit for Brent. I took the Reuters News Service into the Oval for a five-minute interview on Brent. Boyden says in fact, the President said, the first military ground plan for Iraq called for a head-to-head frontal invasion. It was Lt. General Brent Scowcroft who suggested "the amphibious diversion," and the wide swing around the Western flank of Iraq forces. Thus cutting off supply lines from Baghdad and all routes of escape. Schwarzkopf got most of the credit for this, but it was Scowcroft's plan.

SATURDAY MARCH 8, 1991
MY DIARY

The President stopped by my office at 6:00 p.m. Just had a haircut. Looked great, about forty-five years younger. The puffiness of the war was gone. At the end, his face looked like it was molded in clay, with great globs. Two fishing trips and the old youth was back.

MARCH 9, 1991
MY DIARY

Camp David. The President tapes nearly five hours of interview with David Frost on the war. Both the President and Mrs. Bush have exhaustive diaries in white loose-leaf notebooks. Mrs. Bush uses her laptop computer and the President uses a recorder (to record the diaries.) There are no astounding revelations except that the first ground invasion date was February 21, then changed to February 23.

We had dinner Friday night at one huge round table (Pres., Mrs. Bush, Roger Ailes, David Frost, Fitzwater, Scowcroft). Very warm. Great dessert—peeled grapefruit with liquor topping. David Frost wants to get these tapes for commercial use. President is adamant no. I bet they're out in two years.

Lunch after the taping at one long table. Had Carolyn Deaver salad, sesame seeds in Chinese noodles and sliced chicken. I sat by Carim Frost. Very nice, attentive, smart. After lunch, I entrusted the tapes, seven from each of three cameras, to Don Rhoads. (This means the President's personal possession.)

TUESDAY MARCH 12, 1991
MY DIARY

King Hussein of Jordan has written the President a letter begging to be taken back into the fold. No response yet. Apparently, he also asked to come to Washington to meet with the President. We sent word back, no. So the King asks if his brother, Crown Prince Hassan, could come. We said he could come meet with other US officials. They want to be part of the Arabs now considering the future of the Gulf region. The President is unwilling.

MARCH 12, 1991
MY DIARY

White House. Cabinet meeting at which nine members give a three-minute report on their activities. Boring. I nod off. The President sends Brent a note saying: 'Marlin is mounting a challenge for the Scowcroft award."

Brent responds: "His case does not merit consideration."

I sent Brent a note, which he gives to the President. "The death rate from Cabinet Room boredom is 1 per 9, three times the rate of the Persian Gulf War." The President smiles.

MONDAY MARCH 25, 1991
MY DIARY

Bureau chiefs come in to say they want to pool their tapes. This is my proposal a year ago. Then (a year ago) Bill Headline, CNN Bureau Chief, told the *Washington Post* it was "censorship." Today, Headline makes the proposal. Must be financial hardship.

TUESDAY MARCH 26, 1991
MY DIARY

More secrecy. I asked the President about doing an ABC documentary on the war. He said OK.

"In fairness," I said. "Sig is opposed. He says it would conflict with his documentary with pictures that could be used in the campaign."

The President gives me a blank stare. His head turns away, as if searching for an answer. I had stumbled on a secret. One day earlier he had taped a one-hour show with Sununu on the war. Sununu would ask the questions and show pictures of various meetings during the war. "Oh, I thought you knew," he said. I looked at Sununu. He looked away. Then he looked at the President, searching for an answer as to whether or not to admit the taping. They never did. (It was for the campaign.)

"The ABC project won't conflict with that," the President said in partial recognition.

MARCH 26, 1991
MY DIARY

Tonight we learned that Brent and Richard Haass are going on a secret two-day mission to Saudi Arabia. We don't know why. Maybe State doesn't know.

MARCH 26, 1991
MY DIARY

Big Nine meeting in the Oval at 10:00 a.m. Cheney says 540,000 troops now down to 413,000. By April 19, 10,000 to 12,000 troops a day will be coming home. It will take twenty-one days to get a troop from southern Iraq to Saudi Arabian port to heading home.

We changed policy on withdrawal. It had been: We will withdraw from Iraq when Iraq accepts the UN cease-fire. Today the President changed it to: We start withdrawal when the UN adopts cease-fire resolutions and we complete it when the UN observer force takes up position along the Kuwait/Iraq border. The President wants out of Iraq fast.

The sequence is:
1. Passage of UN cease-fire resolution.
2. Arrival of UN Observer force.
3. US pulls out of Iraq.
4. Sanctions remain on while Iraq considers cease-fire.
5. We fly the aerial recon missions.
Our permanent station will include:
1. Leave enough equipment in GCC countries to support fifteen tactical fighter squadrons.
2. Conduct air exercises that would keep planes rotating in and out of Gulf on a more or less continuous basis.

WEDNESDAY MARCH 27, 1991
MY DIARY
Decided today not to do any presidential interviews. That had been my instinct ever since the war ended. Schwarzkopf interviewed Barbara Walters and David Frost. Both caused trouble. This is a good example of a time when limiting access pays. We won. We're at 91 percent. Why say anything that would detract. Stay with press conferences. As I said in my November 1988 memo to the President, frequent press conferences will cover a multitude of sins. During the Reagan years, the press built press conferences up as the sole measure of an open administration.

WEDNESDAY APRIL 3, 1991
UNSC Resolution 687 passes, declaring a formal cease-fire and ending the war.

SATURDAY APRIL 6, 1991

Iraq accepts and signs the UN Security Council's cease-fire. Saddam Hussein agrees to give up all weapons of mass destruction and pay damages for its seven-month occupation of Kuwait. Stated in Iraq's twenty-three page letter, delivered to the UN Secretary-General, Iraq "found itself facing only one choice: to accept this resolution."

SATURDAY APRIL 13, 1991
MY DIARY

Pentagon to announce withdrawal from Iraq. President was fishing at Ray Scotts Bass Ranch near Montgomery, Alabama. I ask Pete Williams to hold it till Sunday a.m. so Cheney could explain that 10:30 on *Meet the Press*—and so the story wouldn't be part of the President's pictures holding up a fish.

APRIL 13, 1991
THE PRESIDENT

Excerpt from remarks at Maxwell Air Force Base War College in Montgomery, Alabama:

The President: It falls to all of you to derive the lessons learned from this war. Desert Storm demonstrated the true strength of joint operations: not the notion that each service must participate in equal parts in every operation in every war but that we use the proper tools at the proper time. In Desert Storm, a critical tool was certainly air power. And every one of you can take pride in that fact. Our technology and training ensured minimal losses, and our precision—your precision—spared the lives of innocent civilians.

But our victory also showed that technology alone is insufficient. A warrior's heart must burn with the will to fight. And if he fights but does not believe, no technology in the world can save him. We and our allies had more than superior weapons; we had the will to win. . . .

But what defines this nation? What makes us America is not our ties to a piece of territory or bonds of blood; what makes us American is our allegiance to an idea that all people everywhere must be free. This idea is as old and enduring as this nation itself—as deeply rooted, and what we are as a promise implicit to all the world in the words of our own Declaration of Independence. . . .

TUESDAY APRIL 16, 1991
MY DIARY

President is on the phone calling Prime Minister Majors, Pres. Mitterrand, Prime Minister Özal, and UN Secretary-General. One call after another, juggling phone, making notes, phone tucked under his chin: He looks up and says to Gates. "Just like the old days."

MONDAY AUGUST 22, 1991
MY DIARY

I sit behind Isaac Stern in the East Room watching Mstislav Rostropovich play the base violin. It was special—one of those incredible White House experiences that we take for granted, and then go back to work.

THURSDAY MAY 2, 1991
MY DIARY

President Bush was taken to Bethesda Naval Hospital from Camp David after collapsing with an atrial fibrillation while jogging.

On May 2, about 6:30 p.m., I was told by Dr. Burton Lee, the President's physician, and Governor Sununu, that the President could go under anesthesia at 6:00 a.m. the next morning if the medication he was given did not work. I couldn't believe it. Staff had gathered in my office: Andy Card, C. Boyden Gray, Sean Walsh, Judy Smith, Bill Harlow, Natalie Wozniak, and Diane Tomb. I called the Governor at the hospital.

"You can't do this," I said. "People will wake up tomorrow morning to a new President. (Assuming the 25th Amendment will be activated if the President goes under anesthetic, and Vice President Quayle will be acting President.) They'll be afraid for the President. Markets will drop. Foreign leaders will be frightened. We have to tell America tonight that this could happen."

"We can't," he said. "The doctors don't want the pressure. They don't want second guessing."

"Tell the doctors to do what's right medically," I said. "We have to do what is right for the Presidency."

I wrote a statement, faxed it to Sununu and the President at the hospital. He took out most of the Twenty-Fifth Amendment debate. "Just say the VP will take over. He'll only be out for a few minutes."

"OK," I said, and went on nationwide television live at 9:00 p.m. to explain the situation. During the night the medication worked, the President went into normal sinus rhythm, and we didn't have to apply the 25th Amendment.

FRIDAY MAY 17, 1991
MY DIARY

President meets at 12:00 noon to get Baker's report on the Mid East. He calls me in about 12:45. Sununu, Scowcroft also in the President's private dining room off the Oval. Baker says be optimistic. If Jordan accepts a peace conference, Israel can't not go. He calls Hosni Mubarak. Egypt operator holds for Mubarak. Muzak plays.

"This sounds like clerical music," the President says, holding his hand over the receiver.

"I think it's ours," Scowcroft says, "the Camp David operators."

"I don't think Hosni can hear it," Baker says.

"Maybe I can get them some Country and Western," the President says. "Hello, Hosni."

"George, how are you?" Hosni says.

"How are your teeth?" the President quips.

"My what?"

Scowcroft and I are howling in laughter. Hosni has no idea what the President is talking about.

"The music, Hosni, sounds like one of our dental offices," the President says.

"Oh," Hosni says.

"Hosni, you have to tell King Hussein to go to the peace conference. The King is going to see Assad tomorrow. You should call him today."

"George, can't you do something for Gaddafi? Anything?"

"I don't know, Hosni. He's so crazy."

Baker says, "I have let him know he has to renounce terrorism and get rid of Abu Nidal, and stop his terrorist training bases."

"He needs something," Hosni says.

After the President hangs up, he, Baker, and Scowcroft agree to offer Gaddafi something if he agrees to the above three items. At 1:30 p.m. Baker calls Hosni back to tell him to tell Gaddafi our offer.

At 1:45 p.m., the President leaves for Camp David and tells the press there is "reason for optimism in the Mideast peace process."

SATURDAY JUNE 8, 1991

The National Victory Celebration parade is held in Washington, DC. General Norman Schwarzkopf Jr., commander of the Desert Storm forces, leads the parade, which includes 8,000 US troops. A crowd estimated at 800,000 shows up to celebrate the end of the Gulf War and return of the troops.

PART IV

—POST-WAR DAYS—
MY STORIES AND MEMORIES

Introduction to Part Four

AFTER THE WAR, I wrote some stories about isolated events. They range from the Clarence Thomas nomination for the Supreme Court to the campaign of 1992. They tend to show the highs and lows of events, or the absurdities of various situations. But they are all part of the fabric of the presidency.

JULY 1, 1991

Kennebunkport. The President announced Clarence Thomas as his nominee for the Supreme Court. He flew in an Air Force plane to Pease AFB, New Hampshire. We picked him up in a funeral parlor van, borrowed from CBF Brothers Funeral Home of Saco, Massachusetts. It was the only one we could find with dark windows. It slipped unnoticed onto Walker's Point. But because TV telephoto lenses were focused on the Bush compound, Thomas was transferred to another car behind the swimming pool privacy fence, and driven to the back of the house. Thomas must have known then that he was in for a rough time.

JULY 9, 1991

Oval Office. The President holds a meeting on the reappointment of Alan Greenspan to be Chairman of the Federal Reserve Board. [Treasury Secretary Nicholas F.] Brady and [White House Budget Director Richard G.] Darman want the President to solicit a commitment to growth before reappointment. Darman says appoint first, then question. Brady has a four-point question—part of which is: What is the Federal Reserve role in the Savings and Loans, and banks, bailout? Darman says 1 percent more growth means twenty billion a year and no tax increase. He wants a commitment to 3 percent growth a year.

"Well, you can't replace something with nothing. Do any of you have an alternative?" the President asks. All are quiet. Greenspan will be reappointed.

JULY 27, 1991

Inside Washington, CBS News issues show, applauds the Administration for withdrawing from pushing for Israel decision on peace talks by Monday. I did that in my briefing Tuesday, saying this is too important—Mideast peace talks—to ask for a deadline of any kind. The *Inside* group played it like a serious matter and a considered Administration action. I just thought it made good sense. Sometimes you stumble into a good idea.

AUGUST 21, 1991

Oval Office, 7:02 a.m. I arrive at the White House and go immediately to the Oval. The President is in his study, working at his computer, with his back to the door. I sit on the blue chaise lounge in the small study, and wait. He pulls two blue presidential notebook pages from his desk and hands them to me. It has eight single-spaced items to be done immediately after the Kuwait invasion by Iraq. What a lesson in crisis management. This is why there was never any question about who was in charge in the Bush White House. My heart jumped as I noticed item two: "Get Marlin back to Kennebunkport."

The full list was: (1) Assess the situation. Meet with NSC at 9:00; (2) Get Marlin back to KBP; (3) Call Gonzales (Spain) and Perez (Venezuela); (4) Keep message steady and strong; (5) Pay personal attention to Yeltsin; (6) No '92 politics. Don't respond to charges; (7) Keep our defenders informed (Lugar, etc.); (8) Change KBP. Part recreation, part work.

AUGUST 22, 1991

I sit behind Isaac Stern in the East Room watching Mstislav Rostropovich play the bass violin. It was special—one of those incredible White House experiences that we take for granted, and then go back to work.

AUGUST 25, 1991

Kennebunkport. Hamburgers on the patio behind Walker's Point home. Prime Minister Mulroney of Canada is about to arrive. I advise the President that we're a little behind other world leaders in commending the fall of communism.

The President is wearing a heavy grey-and-brown wool sweater, with deer running across the top. It's 75 degrees and sunny. I'm in shirtsleeves. He puts his feet on the table and asks what other world leaders are saying. In mid-sentence, Scrowcroft says to me, "I think we lost him."

At 12:52, during my most insightful presentation, the President qualified for a "Scowcroft" nomination. Sound asleep. Brent and I become silent, seeing if he would be out long enough for a clear recognition. He was—about two minutes.

SEPTEMBER 11, 1991

Wyoming. At 11:45 p.m. on August 19, 1991, Sean Walsh called me at Brinkerhoff Lodge in Jackson Hole, Wyoming, to say a news report says, "Gorbachev has been forced out." I told him to make sure Gary Foster, my Deputy, in Kennebunkport knew, and that Roman Popadiuk should check it with General Scowcroft. All were in Kennebunkport.

The next morning, Sean called to say it was true, and the President had held a press conference to deplore it. A plane was being sent to California to pick up Ambassador Strauss and would stop in Wyoming to get Baker. (Andy and Kathi Card and son Drew, and my friend Melinda Andrews and my son, Brad, and daughter, Courtney, we're vacationing together at the Lodge.) Andy and I arranged to get on the plane at Parkdale, Wyoming, near Baker's ranch.

I left Melinda with my children in Wyoming to return the next day with Kathi Card and her children. (Melinda and I were dating at the time, and later married. But it was a shock to her to be left in charge of getting my family home.)

Andy and I got to Parkdale at 3:00 in the afternoon, and Ambassador Strauss was there in minutes. Baker came an hour later.

In the little airport lounge, consisting of a desk, a couch, a candy vending machine, a few bags of chips, and two cowboys, Strauss was in rare form. He said he had talked to the President and Baker.

"Goddamn, Marlin," he said. "I don't know whether I'm the man for this job or not. I was supposed to bring Capitalism to Russia, and now we're back to the Cold War. The President may not want me now."

"No," I laughed. "You're the perfect man for the job. Who better to tell those Commies to shape up?"

"I'm going to call Andreas," Strauss said. "He'll know what's happening." Strauss goes to a pay phone near the door leading to the hangar where small private planes are awaiting repairs. After a few minutes, he hangs up and reports: "Andreas (Chairman of Archer Daniels Midland) says he talked to Dobrinski (Anatoli, long time USSR Ambassador to Washington), and Anatoli says, 'It's only the first inning. There's going to be four or five more innings to go before we know if this coup holds.'" We get to DC about 11:30 p.m.

SEPTEMBER 14, 1991

John Magaw, the President's Secret Service detail leader, came to see me with the following story. A Right to Life leader who had been a nurse at Walker's Point for the Bush family rented a limousine in Oregon to take her to a Right to Life meeting. When the limo arrived, she said that she was Doro Bush, the President's daughter, and asked the driver to pretend he was a Secret Service agent.

She said her real agents were traveling incognito. At the meeting, she stood up in the audience, made a speech as Doro Bush, and read a letter from her mother, Mrs. Barbara Bush (a forgery).

In the meantime, her driver became suspicious because he couldn't see the real agents. He went to a cop who was outside the meeting hall and told his story. The cop calls the Secret Service in Portland and tells the driver to resume his duties. The imposter leaves before the Secret Service arrives.

Before leaving, she gives the so-called Mrs. Bush letter to a California girl who was at the meeting as a Right to Life poster child— a little girl who was supposed to have been aborted, but somehow was spared. When the Secret Service arrived at the little girl's home in California days later, she was preparing to go on TV, *The 700 Club*, to read her letter. The Secret Service confiscated the letter. The little girl was disappointed. The imposter was banned from Walker's Point and put on the Secret Service "watch" list. But in spite of all this, she violated no laws.

SEPTEMBER 26, 1991

Washington, DC, about 6:00 p.m., [Assistant to the President for Media Affairs] Dorrance Smith came to my office to discuss the Satellite three-minute speech at 4:15 p.m. the next day. The subject is Iraq. I argue that we shouldn't talk about Iraq because we're not taking action; it will scare people about resuming the war. I call General Scowcroft to talk him out of it. He says it won't be Iraq; it will be a follow-up to a National Defense speech to be given at the War College at 1:15 p.m. "That's even worse," I say, "because the satellite speech will be old news and worthless." He said he would tell me more later. I relate this to Dorrance, and he heads for Sununu's office.

In minutes, Sununu calls on his direct line to demand why I oppose the satellite speech. "It's old news," I say. "It renders the satellite meaningless in the eyes of the press. It's like a radio actuality taken from the speech. Big deal."

"What if the speech announces we're eliminating some nuclear weapons," he asks.

"Yeah, right," I say.

I head for my car. At the guardhouse, Scowcroft comes running out of the White House in shirtsleeves. "Wait," he says. "I want to tell you. The speech will say we're unilaterally giving up all tactical nucs, all sea-launched tactical nuclear weapons, and others."

"Christ," I say, "that's huge. We should be giving a prime-time speech to the nation."

"That's what Cheney said,"

"Then why not?" I asked.

"Sununu said we couldn't wait till next week."

"Why wait. Do it tomorrow night," I said.

"Dorrance told the President Friday is a bad night."

"Well, it's better than Friday afternoon."

"I'll go talk to Sununu." Scowcroft and I walk to the door together. I call Andy and Dorrance and ask them to come to my office.

"Do you guys know what this speech says?" I ask. They nod hesitantly that they know something.

"Well, this is historic," I say. "It should be prime time. Why didn't Sununu tell us?"

"He's afraid of leaks," Andy said.

"Once again his paranoia has almost led to a terrible mistake. Let's go see Sununu."

We go to his office. He's getting into a tux for King Hassan state dinner.

"Governor," I say, "I asked the General for details and he told me what this satellite speech is about. I believe this should be a prime-time TV address tomorrow night."

"Why?" he asked.

"The audience for an evening news show is five to seven million. At prime time it's fifteen to twenty million. Figure on four networks.

We lose at least thirty to forty million viewers who will see the entire speech, not just ninety seconds worth. Plus, this is history. The President should get credit."

"What if the Democrats get it and they criticize it?" he asked.

"They don't need to get it," I said, "and so what, are they going to favor keeping nuclear weapons? Our Demo critics want us to disarm more, not less."

"OK," he says. "I just don't want to wait till next week."

"Nobody wants to," I said. "We want to do it tomorrow."

At home about 10:00 p.m., Thursday night, Pete Williams calls, "Can't we get some enthusiasm for this speech?" he asks.

"How about prime time?" I say.

"That's what we always wanted," he said.

"Call me in the morning," I say. Obviously, Cheney had told him more than Sununu told us. I'm depressed.

OCTOBER 6, 1991
Madison County, Virginia. I have taken my son and daughter to Camp Hoover in the Shenandoah Mountains for the weekend. It's a small fishing camp at least a couple miles off the main road. Ranger George of the Park Service welcomes us back. He says I was called to the phone by Nancy Reagan in 1987 about a *Washington Post* story on her dresses. (Apparently, he had to drive the two miles into the camp, and then drive me out to a telephone, then drive me back. Now he was doing it again, four years later.)

This time I was being called by Roman [Popadiuk] about a Gorbachev response to the President's nuclear disarmament proposals. Better than dresses.

OCTOBER 8, 1991
Washington, DC. The vote on Judge Clarence Thomas's nomination is set for 6:00 p.m. At 3:00 p.m., it looks like Senators are starting to back away. But I draft three statements—win, lose, and draw.

I go to Roman's office in the Old Executive Office Building to escape the confusion in the press office. Fred McClure calls from the Hill about 4:00 p.m. and says we're losing—prepare a statement of outrage about sleaze, character assassination, etc. I dictate to Elaine in Roman's office.

5:00 p.m., I go to Andy Card's office. I call the President at 6:30 p.m., after the vote has been delayed, to read the statement. He objects to "character assassination," wants to take the high road. I go back to boilerplate statement prepared at 3:00 p.m. (Thomas is later approved by the Senate.)

OCTOBER 9, 1991
The President calls Yeltsin to urge him to sign the Soviet Economic treaty. He says he will. We keep it secret, because it's an extraordinary intervention in Soviet internal affairs.

OCTOBER 10, 1991
POTUS meets secretly in the residence with the Chinese Ambassador. His message was that Baker is going to China next week as they want, but we better get some results—human rights reforms, etc.

Brit Hume asks who the "mystery guest" was, thinking it was Clarence Thomas.

OCTOBER 12, 1991
Last week at a fundraiser, the President met a man with no arms. He shakes hands with his feet. As the President came through, the man kicked off his loafers and raised his foot to shake. The President grabbed his toe and shook.

OCTOBER 21, 1991
The press asked me today if President Reagan knew of the diversion of funds in Iran-Contra, based on Ollie North's new book. How ironic. For five years they have called Ollie a liar. Now he attacks Reagan, so they want to believe him. Moral: Always attack someone the press already hates more than yourself.

OCTOBER 22, 1991
Outside the Oval, Bob Gates told me of trying to prepare his son Brad for defeat by the Senate in his quest to be CIA Director.

"I could still lose this," Bob explained. "But if I do, it's not the end of the earth. We would probably move to the Northwest. We could go fishing together. You could live where there is a lot of trees. There's ocean and the mountains."

Brad, twelve, paused, looked up at his father, and said, "What do we get if you win?"

Indeed! Gates became CIA Director, President of Texas A&M, and Secretary of Defense before the family made it back to the Northwest.

OCTOBER 31 – NOVEMBER 2, 1991
THE PERFECT STORM AT WALKER'S POINT
Atlanta, Georgia. It was a couple days after the Perfect Storm, the one that wiped out fishing boats, homes, and people. The one they made a movie about. And it was also the one that destroyed the President's home in Kennebunkport, Maine. Took it right down to the foundation. And if that wasn't painful enough, the Secret Service permanently stationed at their Walker's Point home had filmed the destruction from start to finish. And the videotape was on its way to Atlanta, Georgia, where the President was campaigning.

The showing of the film for the President and his family was set up in a special room at the hotel. I was getting questions from the press about the President's reaction to the storm and about when he would go home to see the destruction. I walked into the room and the family had gathered. The President and Mrs. Bush sat on a couch. Others were in the room, but it was quiet. No one knew what to say. I took a corner chair behind the Bushes.

The President and Mrs. Bush, of course, knew the damage. They had received a report from the Secret Service. Yet I was certain it would be difficult for them to fully comprehend the overwhelming force of the giant waves. Certainly, I had no inkling. Except for the quiet in the room. Everyone took their lead from the President, and he was sullen, sober, as if focused on all the bills coming due, all the arrangements to be made for new construction, new furniture, huge costs. And then the video began to play.

There were some preparatory photos of the raging storm, the

angry waves that seemed to be coming from the wrong direction, not rolling into the rocks that define Maine's coast. Then I realized the waves hid the rocks; they buried them. But as the camera pulled back, the house stood firm, boarded up as it had been for the winter.

Suddenly there appeared behind the house a gargantuan shadow that rose above the chimney, and for an instant it consumed the house, the entire living room with windows that looked out to sea, the entire stone fireplace that anchored the house to Walker's Point, the fireplace that defied intrusion from the elements, and stood guard against all destructive forces.

Our eyes squint to see it, and we realize it is the wave; it's not at the house, yet it is about to hit it. It is coming at train-wrecking speed. And then it is sucked into the end of the house, around the fireplace, and it disappears like unwanted guests. Then the sides of the entire house begin to swell, till it looks like a turtle holding its breath, and then it explodes, and the entire back side of the house is blasted out to sea. The ocean has reclaimed its wave. And the house is empty, as furniture, pictures, plates, virtually everything on the first floor is lost forever in the vastness of the sea.

I glance at the President as he holds Mrs. Bush, and I know that I should not be in the room. I leave without a word.

Several days later the President is free to inspect Walker's Point. We fly to Walker's Point; none of us know what to expect. A press pool is with us. I hold them at a point away from the house so they cannot see the President as he takes his first look at the damage. No pictures.

The President, myself, Andy Card, and Bob Gates walk up to the foundation and first floor. The house is gone. We stand in the middle of the living room with only a green carpet remaining on the floor. We look out to sea. We just stand and look around. There is nothing. Then we walk out to what had been the yard. The President seems in a daze. He just walks around looking for family items. He is remembering a desk, gone; a chair, gone; and he looks for pictures, gone. Then he spots a picture laying in the grass, spotted with water stains, but unbroken. His father. He picks it up and holds it to his chest. Then Dave Valdez, the President's Photographer, asks if he can take the picture and have it restored. The President is reluctant to separate from the picture, but he slowly hands it over. It is virtually the only surviving personal item from the house.

But there is that green carpet, caked in mud and rumpled in a corner. The President walks over to it and says his only words, "Help me." He picks up up the edge of the carpet, and it is too heavy to move. The rest of us join him, and we pull it away from the house to a split-rail fence nearby. The President directs us to put it over the fence, and he asks for a broom; apparently, one was left by the Secret Service. And he started beating the carpet. Water would squirt out after each smack. Then the President asked again, "Help me, guys." Andy and I picked up shovels. They were the only tools available. And we all start beating the carpet.

I glanced at the President and he was pale, but concentrated. I thought he might be going into shock. Andy and I watched him out of the corner of our eyes. He paused for a moment, and we suggested maybe we should go. We didn't say it, but it was hopeless. The carpet could never be saved. The only value it had was as an outlet for the President's frustration and sadness.

I asked the President if I could bring in the press after he was gone. I just wanted the press to see the destruction, to have to describe it in their stories, to have to record it in their cameras. But their comments of record never matched my sadness for the President.

We all just wanted to get back on the plane and return to Washington, DC. There was nothing we could do about the overwhelming destruction but to seek out the solace of friends.

NOVEMBER 6, 1991
I write an opening statement for the President to give on departure concerning Thornburg becoming Attorney General, Gates becoming CIA Director, and the Duke soccer players. On *Air Force One*, Sununu reads Ann Devroy's article in the *Washington Post* about our canceling the Asia trip. It quotes two "political operatives" who say cancelation was a mistake, shows we're scared, and the Democrats are winning.

Sununu is angry, demands to know the source. He goes through the plane asking Demerest, Sig Rogich, and others who the source is. So I tell him, the source is among the guys you met with at 5:00 (campaign political operatives). "They were mad because you had a meeting on political spin, Thornburg spin, travel spin, and yet you didn't tell them. So when the press called them, they lashed out at the decision—your decision." He denied it. "Fine," I said. "You asked. I'm telling you."

Later in Rome, I ran into Ann McDaniels of *Newsweek*, Jim Gerstenzang of the *LA Times*, and John Harwood of the *Wall Street Journal* at St. Peter's Basilica. Ann said the political consultants were mad at Sununu's secrecy because it showed again that he never shares information. He can't run a political campaign without sharing.

NOVEMBER 19, 1991

The NSC meets on Libya and Pan Am 103. We're consulting with Britain, France, and Italy. Ted McNamara [Special Assistant to the President and Senior Director for African Affairs] is working it. We will notify Libya of indictments soon.

Announced actions: sanctions, freeze assets, stop civil aviation, arms embargo, oil embargo, expel diplomats. All four countries should act together.

NOVEMBER 19, 1991

The President talked to Thomas Sutherland, released hostage, about Desert Storm. He said, "We followed the Gulf War every day. I bet our captors we'd win in five days. When we won in one hundred hours, things changed. We were treated much better."

NOVEMBER 30, 1991

I'm reading *PrairyErth* by William Least Heat-Moon, about Kansas. It reminds me to make a list of short story subjects that I might write about.

—Coyote hunt
—Killing the dog in chicken house
—Cheveree for Alfred Howie

—Snip Hunt at Sunny Side School
—Thanksgiving at the Seatons
—Squirrel hunting along Holland Creek at Seatons
—Dad the blacksmith
—Making the hen house a roller rink
—Climbing the Silo
—The '51 flood, fish in the cornfield
—Granddad Seaton's ticking clock and Chinese marbles
—Grandma Seaton's bonnet, strawberry patch
—Grandma Fitzwater and the arrowheads
—The Smokehouse pool and fear at the bar
—Howie place, DDT, porch pot, outhouse blueberries, hair wash and the cold rinse, cistern on porch
—Tornado, class reunion, in basement
—Hedgerows. What are they? Page 280 of *PrairyErth*
—Last day on the farm, Minneapolis Moline tractor, and spring-tooth
—Jim Simmons robs liquor store before Ike's funeral, arrested by SS
—"Piss on the fire, call in the dogs" campfire song, Green River with Doug Costle
—*Lindsborg News-Record*, setting headlines
—College, two-room basement, Thurston Street
(Most of these stories made it into my book *Call the Briefing*.)

DECEMBER 13, 1991
Baker, Margaret Tutwiler, and I have lunch in the mess, after his Soviet Relations press conference. "I predict the Soviet Union will be in civil war in six months," I said. "This guy Yeltsin is shooting from the hip. He has no idea where he's going." (I was wrong.)

DECEMBER 25, 1991
Soviet Union dissolved today. Yesterday I recommended that a pool go to Camp David to record the President's views of Gorbachev's resignation speech.

Skinner calls me at home to say Teeter suggests a TV speech to the

Nation on the eve of end of the Cold War. I heartily agree. Sam had reached me at Sears, buying some new khaki pants in the "Working Man" section. They are only $10.95, for a size 44 waist, 29 length. Sam is surprised that I shop at Sears. He suggests a conference call with the President, Scowcroft, Teeter, and me at 9:00 a.m.

On the conference call, I suggest moving the speech from Thursday to Wed. for its news value, and I volunteer to go to the office at 9:00 on Christmas day to coordinate.

In the office, today, December 25 at 8:30 a.m., Nick Burns has a draft text on my desk. Looks great. Teeter calls at 9:00 a.m to say OK. The situation room tells me Gorbi is calling the President at 10:00 a.m. I call Scowcroft to suggest a post-call statement and announce the speech. OK.

Yeltsin comes on CNN with Steve Hurst. He says nuclear suitcase will be passed today. Gorbi calls the President, and I issue a statement. Everything is set. I leave for Texas where my parents spend the winter.

January 8, 1992
Pandemonium in Japan

Dr. Burton Lee was the President's personal physician from the Sloan-Kettering Hospital in New York City. They met when the President's daughter Robin was being treated as a child for leukemia. Like all Presidents, Bush was allowed to select a personal physician to work in the White House. "Burt," as he was called, was a perfect choice to work in this collegial atmosphere. He traveled with the Presidential party around the world, prescribing a few sips of cola to solve most upset stomachs and occasionally recommending a local hospital or physician to treat staffers with more serious illnesses.

For the healthy among us, we loved traveling with Burt because he was funny, saw the irony in world affairs, loved good food and fine restaurants, was a terrific traveling companion, and was an outstanding doctor who could diagnose an illness from a mile away.

So when the President traveled to Japan for a dinner with their Prime Minister, Dr. Lee knew the President was not feeling well and no doubt had the flu. He recommended that the President skip the dinner, but President Bush said no. Nevertheless, Burt Lee was keeping a close eye on the President when he saw Mr. Bush's head start to drift downward onto the shoulder of the Japanese Prime Minister. Then the President started to vomit down the front of the Prime Minister, followed by the President sliding out of his chair and onto the floor. Pandemonium ensued. The Secret Service moved to the President's side, arriving about the same time as Dr. Burt Lee. Mrs. Bush knelt down and took the President's head in her lap.

Burt said later that he knew what the problem was and that not much could be done medically at that point. But he did want the President moved out of the crowded room. One of the White House nurses traveling with the President mentioned to Dr. Lee, "Loosen his tie."

Burt reached for his tie, but it was already loose, so he started to loosen the President's pants. As he reached for the President's fly, President Bush raised his head and said, "Burt, what the hell are you doing down there."

Burt later said, "That's when we knew he was all right."

JANUARY 14, 1992

Skinner asks me to take over as Counselor to the President for Communications and Press Secretary. I had said no three times already, but Jim Lake and Tom Griscom have turned it down. (This time Skinner yelled at me: "You're lazy, you just don't want to work this hard; you're not good enough." So I said yes. Skinner was scared to death he couldn't find anyone to take the job, and it would be his failure.)

At 6:00 p.m., the President called to see if I really wanted the job. Also, he didn't want me to give up the press briefings, and he wanted to be sure I could do both jobs. I said, "If I can't, we'll do something else. I'll give it a try."

"I don't want to lose your relationship with the press," he said. "It's not broke, and I don't want to break it."

At 6:20 Skinner called to say the President would be calling. "He already has," I said.

"He wants to make sure I didn't twist your arm, that you really want this," Skinner said.

"Don't worry, everything will be all right."

JANUARY 17, 1992

At home, Andy Rosenthal of the *NYT* calls. He's doing a process story on the State of the Union preparations.

"Is your problem really communications?" he asked.

"We should have a good message on the 28th," I say.

"Did Darman say in a Skinner meeting yesterday that if the State of the Union fails, it will be communications' fault?"

This is a typical Darman leak. He calls up reporters, tells them what he said in a meeting, then it's reported without attribution. He thinks his ideas are so great they should be reported to the world. Tomorrow, he will go around the White House complaining about people who leak his comments to the media.

JANUARY 21, 1992

Washington, DC. Visiting with the President in the Oval, his feet up, relaxed. "Andy Card to Transportation is a good move," I say. "This is a case where we underestimate those we know, those we see every day and work with."

"I don't know what it gets us (politically)," he says, "but it lets people know that loyalty counts. That's not a bad point to make around here," Obviously a little disgusted about something. I suspect it's Skinner's attempt to throw out all the Bush people.

(Sununu tried this also. I don't know why new Chiefs of Staff always want to eliminate the President's people. In the end, they lose.)

JANUARY 24, 1992

I called Demerest about my new job. He said Peggy Noonan had submitted a totally new State of the Union speech, "all fluff, but the President likes it." In his earlier call to me, he said my first job would be to smooth over the Noonan situation.

FEBRUARY 1, 1992

Yeltsin is at Camp David for a Summit Meeting. After lunch, Bill Farish, the President's friend from Kentucky, calls me at Laurel Lodge to say that Jack Kemp, on the *Evans and Novak* CNN show, says the Bush State of the Union speech was all gimmicks, except for the capital gains tax cut. I tell Skinner. He goes ballistic, wants to know why I approved. I don't approve what Cabinet officers say in interviews.

Skinner calls me at home, after the Camp David Summit, on a conference call with Teeter. They have talked to Kemp. "He was belligerent at first, then apologetic. He said he would issue a statement."

Skinner said, "Maybe Kemp would say something tomorrow, like 'Kemp is no economist.'"

Teeter: "Kemp called me this morning before the show for advice."

Skinner: "I told him to issue a statement. To say he was taken out of context, and he supports the President's program, all of it."

Skinner told me to see that it happens. He also said, get some economists who support the President. We may want to use them.

I call John Herr, in *News Summary,* and ask for an *Evans and Novak* transcript to be delivered to Skinner's home; and for a compilation of quotes from economists.

I call Mary Anton in the Library to run a Nexus on economist quotes by noon Sunday. I call Mary Burnett, Kemp's Public Affairs Director, to get a statement from Kemp and issue it. She calls Roman at 8:00 p.m. to say she's doing it.

Roman says Kemp called him at 7:00 to say he should issue the statement. Roman has the presence of mind to say no, that he should do it. Thus, I call Mary Burnett.

Kemp should be fired. But we think he wants political martyrdom, a new platform to run against the President.

FEBRUARY 10, 1992

Dinner with Andy and Kathi Card at the restaurant, Santa Fe East. Talking about his confirmation meetings with Senate staff considering his Secretary of Transportation nomination. I'm asking him questions that might come up.

"Any CDs?"

"No."

"Any stocks and bonds?"

"No."

"Any charity giving?"

"Five or ten too many."

Andy Card had no conflicts, ever. He's a committed public servant.

FEBRUARY 11, 1992

My communications group met at 4:00 p.m. to discuss the President's candidacy announcement. Sig said the campaign had arranged for Mrs. Bush to introduce the President, then go off stage to stand with the Cabinet and the Vice President and Mrs. Quayle. After the President spoke, the three would join the President for a group picture.

We changed it so all three would go on stage at the beginning. Mrs. Bush would introduce the President, and all three would stay on stage while the President spoke.

At 7:30, Mary Matalin called to ask why I had changed things. Skinner, Teeter, and the President had made the arrangement. OK, I said, go back to plan A. I hated this job.

FEBRUARY 11, 1992

NASA head Admiral Dick Truly is forced to resign because of differences with the Vice President over space policy. I recommended a praising letter from the President and lavish praise from staff. Always take the high road.

FEBRUARY 18, 1992

The White House, 4:00 p.m., Skinner, Teeter, Moore, and I go to the Oval to show the President the exit poll results [for the New Hampshire Primary] showing his winning by 52 to 46 percent over Pat Buchanan. The President is stunned by the closeness. "Why didn't we know about this?"

We did. Fred Steeper, our pollster, had been saying all along it would be close, and voters were saying, "anybody but Bush."

5:00 p.m., I go to Skinner: "President should go into the Briefing Room to say he got the message." We go to the Oval. President is at the dentist. I call and he has just taken a shot of Novocain. Who but G.B. would put a dental appointment on top of his New Hampshire primary.

"Can you give a press conference at 7:00?" I asked. "Sure," he said, "call me at 6:00 to see."

FEBRUARY 19, 1992

The White House, 7:40 a.m. We're going to Knoxville, Tennessee, for a campaign event. I meet the President outside the Oval. He's angry. "We'll talk on the plane about message."

On *Air Force One*, the President keeps saying, "18 points would be a landslide. I won."

I wrote a card of talking points for the inevitable press conference later in the day:

–18-point win

–Strong enough to take a heck of a pounding from six candidates

–We must turn the economy around

–Must take on Buchanan and Democrats

At the press conference, he said, "At least I'm not for voluntary Social Security."

What? I said to myself.

The attacks were on. Later, I issued the 1983 column by Buchanan favoring voluntary Social Security.

FEBRUARY 20, 1992

Washington Post runs another Style Section story on how Andy Rosenthal, *NYT*, screwed the President with his story on the food store checkout scanner. After Rosenthal's original story, I considered attacking him directly but held off. After a few days, it became clear and beyond doubt that Andy was wrong and the press knew it. So I made the worst charge a press secretary can make about a reporter— falsification. I said the press, particularly Andy, had manufactured and maintained this story. It made them mad. So Chris Connell, Associated Press (AP), checked out the facts. He called National

Cash Register and found out the President was right. It was new technology that had never been seen before. It was amazing scanning technology that would electronically repair a check torn into several pieces, record it, and approve the check for disbursement. Chris wrote it. Charles Osgood, CBS Morning News, also carried the story that the *NYT* had made a mistake. I also found a videotape of the scanner incident and sent it to TV outlets, showing the new technology.

(Once before, in 1981, I accused a White House correspondent of making up a story about Bush people bad-mouthing Reagan. It turned out I was wrong. The reporter never forgave me. This time I was right. But it was still a high-risk charge.)

And in the two or three days it took us to confirm the facts, get testimonials from NCR, get videotape proof from the grocery manufacturers, and then make the charge against the *NYT*, it was too late to change the public mind. Over the years, people came to realize the story was not true. But in terms of the campaign, it hurt the President.

FEBRUARY 23, 1992
The President's Study, The White House. The President remarked, "One year ago at this moment we started the ground war." He looked tired, drawn, and was impatient.

Vice President Quayle joined us to talk about Buchanan. He argued vigorously for the President not saying anything about Buchanan. I suggested one sentence, "Buchanan is a fringe spokesman. But the people will see through him." It was roundly rejected by the VP, but endorsed by Teeter.

I read my insert for the group on the tax pledge: "I will not make that mistake again" language. Quayle did not like most of it. We decided not to do it tomorrow at the Chamber of Commerce speech because it would look like a direct response to Buchanan. Maybe on March 20. I called Demerest after the meeting to take the tax language out.

MARCH 25, 1992

Dr. Burton Lee stopped me in the parking lot at 6:30 p.m. to say he is going to privately tell the President he must slow down, take a vacation, or he won't make it. "He's sixty-seven and he needs a rest. He looks terrible."

MARCH 28, 1992

GRIDIRON DINNER

I went to the residence at 6:15 p.m to accompany the President and Mrs. Bush to the Gridiron Dinner. He was sitting in the living room, wearing his white tie under a white windbreaker. He was reading the skit he and I were going to do: "Tarmac the Magnificent." It was a spoof of the old Johnny Carson routine "Carnac the Magnificent." We went over the lines, with me giving the answers, then he would give the question. We laughed uproariously at ourselves.

Mrs. Bush came in wearing her bathrobe after a dip in the small pool behind the West Wing. She changed into a beautiful gold gown and joined us. We were still reading the jokes.

"You two are having too much fun," she said. We were. And at the show later in the evening, we did again. The President even started ad-libbing about me being a "suffering snowball of succotash." It was a smashing success.

(We repeated the show in 1998 at a dinner roast to raise money to build the Fitzwater Center for Communication at Franklin Pierce University, in New Hampshire. The dinner was at the Reagan Building in Washington. Mrs. Bush also spoke, and was very funny. We made several hundred thousand dollars and the Center was dedicated in 2002, with the President attending.)

APRIL 2, 1992

Chelston, Bermuda. Chelston is the guesthouse of Consul General and Mrs. Ebersole Gaines. (I have come here for a short vacation before starting the President's campaign of 1992.) It is peaceful and tranquil. I keep telling them I want nothing but sleep and beach, from a yellow chaise lounge on the porch of the beach gazebo. The guesthouse sits high over Grape Bay. There are two landings, walled off with

Bermuda stone, to give the appearance of a Mediterranean castle. The stone walls are covered by vines and bright flowers. It's an Emily Bronte garden, the kind one never wants to leave. Beyond the landing, the lawn drops down to the water, perhaps three hundred yards.

From my porch, I watch the days float by and lose a little of my press anguish each day. Although last night I dreamed the press at home were portraying my stay here as another government perk, of the kind the Congress is charging us with right now. So not all my hates are gone. I will probably have these dreams the rest of my life.

APRIL 1992
THOSE LAZY BASTARDS

During hard-fought campaigns, the days all run together, morning till midnight, several cities a day.

I knew I needed a rest when [on March 6, 1991] I called the press a bunch of lazy bastards in Oklahoma, at a Christian university, of all places. We had completed four days of tough campaigning. Bad stories every day of sparse crowds, unenthusiastic supporters. Some were. It seems that people are turned off this year. No real excitement. But the press is more cynical than ever, and trying to build up Pat Buchanan to establish a conflict.

[On March 4, 1991] at the Hialeah, Florida, football stadium, Bush had a great rally. The Cuban community had turned out for him. But the press filing center was in a hotel miles away. Ann Devroy, *Washington Post*, and Andy Rosenthal, of the *NYT*, stayed in the filing center, never actually seeing the huge crowd. They wrote the crowds were "lackluster," at least partially because they hadn't seen them. This was on my mind the next day in Oklahoma City.

We arrived at the university by motorcade about 9:00 a.m. I immediately walked through the main building to the event site in back. When I opened the door, the crowd was spectacular, 20,000 people, as far as the eye could see. There were banners and bands, and a bright warm Oklahoma winter sun. I walked back into the building, to the press filing center, not twenty feet from that magical crowd. There sat thirty or forty members of the press, in an auditorium, listening to the speech over a public address system. I appeared at the top of the seating with Ron Kaufman, political advisor on our staff [Assistant to the President and White House political director], saw the press in casual repose, and exploded. My blood pressure was up and surging. I can only remember my good friend Tim McNulty of the *Chicago Tribune* sitting in the front row, laughing as I shouted. "It's a great day," I screamed. "Everyone out of the filing center. C'mon, off your asses and outta here."

The press thought I was laughing, having a little fun. But I was mad. And some inner trip wire told me to get out of there. I was losing control. I turned and walked down the hall. Kaufman was laughing and screaming, "Yes. You did it. Great."

Judy Smith, my Deputy, walked up to ask what the commotion was all about. I told her, still mad.

"Judy, we should turn the PA system off. Make them listen." She and Ron could see I was angry, so they didn't argue. Instead, she turned to go carry out my command.

Within minutes, Rita Beamish, AP, and Kathleen deLaski, ABC, appeared to complain. How unfortunate for me. Rita has always been on my case. She opposes us on abortion, welfare, war, every liberal/conservative litmus-test issue. She's a dedicated Democrat, married to Paul Costello, flack for Rosalyn Carter, Kitty Dukakis, and DC Mayor Sharon Pratt Kelly.

Delaski was new to the White House. On her first assignment, to cover the President at a housing/economic visit to a Baltimore housing development, she asked the President about something I had said about Congress. "Do you agree that Congress is a weasel?" She asked, trying to get the President to make the same insult, which had upset House Ways and Means Chairman Dan Rostenkowski. It's a cheap trick that most reporters avoid. Lou Cannon once did it to me with Reagan, and I never forgot it. Both President's defended me by saying something like, "I have great confidence in Marlin."

Anyway, when deLaski and Beamish appeared, I lost it. "I'm sick of you lazy bastards," I said. "Go out and cover the events."

"We have somebody out there," Rita said. "And I need more filing time," said Kathleen, a notoriously slow worker.

They both spun on their heels. Rita knew she had me. She rushed to the filing center and announced to all, "Marlin called us lazy bastards."

In minutes, it was on the wires speeding around the world. I spent the rest of the day ducking cameras and interviews. I will always have to answer for that back-hallway comment to Rita Beamish and Kathleen deLaski. (Although, in the Clinton Administration, deLaski became Assistant to the Secretary of Defense [Public Affairs]. She was terminated after a brief tenure.)

I woke up, still in Bermuda.

APRIL 2, 1992

Chelston, Bermuda. I walked down the hill from Chelston and visited the studio of Alfred Birdsey, a well-known artist on Bermuda. His home and studio was a small wood-frame home, hidden by vines and bougainvillea. At eighty, he was very talkative. Likes Bush. Clinton not very sincere man. He showed me his silkscreen process. It consisted of a homemade press made of used 1 x 2s, bedsprings, and wires. He looks like Norman Rockwell operating the press.

I brought an original silkscreen and a watercolor. His paintings were light and airy, highlighted by heavy distinctive outlines of the Bermuda landscape, with plenty of white space to dramatize the Caribbean sky and water.

APRIL 2, 1992

Chelston, Bermuda, 7:00 p.m., Judy Smith called to say, "Get your pink little cheeks back here."

"Not on your life," I said.

She said that Ann Devroy was writing a Friday story on Sam Skinner, Hensen Moore, and Clayton Yeutter. She's writing that I blew up in a long-range scheduling meeting. Further, that I had gone to the President and abruptly left on vacation because of it.

I told her she could deny it.

In fact, I had complained that we should be looking long-range weeks—six to eight weeks, not one or two weeks. These short-term items are already scheduled anyway. I certainly never complained to the President.

Also, I went on vacation just because it seemed like a slow time, and my last chance before the campaign. Indeed, many reporters, including Ann Devroy, had taken time off during this period to get ready for the campaign.

It didn't matter, of course. Devroy wrote the original story.

APRIL 7, 1992

Family Quarters, The White House. The President invited me to dinner with George W. and Rich Bond, Chairman of the RNC, in the Family Dining Room, where I previously had dinner with the President before Panama and lunch before Desert Storm. We watched the news on all three networks. Over dinner we discussed the campaign, keeping the President on the high road, responding to Hillary Clinton's gossip by staying above it, general chitchat. The President invited Susan Biddle to join us, after taking our pictures. She did.

After dinner, we watched the White House communications agency rerun of our Gridiron skit, "Tarmac the Magnificent." We laughed uproariously at ourselves. At 8:30 p.m., we went to the Kennedy Center to see Ann Murray in concert. The President had ordered one of her records by calling a CNN 800 number. She found out and invited him to her performance. At intermission, we went to the green room to meet her. There was a piano in the room. Ann was late. The President sat down and played a number, very impressively. It was "Swanee River." In my seven years with the President, I had never seen him play the piano. Didn't even know that he could. Amazing.

APRIL 20, 1992

Washington, DC. Met Bob Teeter for dinner at the Hay-Adams Grill. He wanted my ideas on making the staff process work. He wants Bob Zoellick to come to the campaign to work on speeches.

APRIL 21, 1992

The White House. The campaign group met in the Roosevelt Room at 5:00 p.m. for two hours to discuss strategy. Fred Steeper gave polling data showing the recession to be responsible for a drop of nearly 95 percent of our favorable rating. Darman thinks we should attack Perot now. Teeter feels that would drive him into the race. Teeter thinks he will drop out in June if it's not clear that he can win.

APRIL 30, 1992

Washington, DC, 6:30 a.m., I receive a phone call from an unknown reporter. There has been a night of rioting in Los Angeles following the acquittal of policemen involved in the Rodney King affair. I stay in bed, thinking of a plan. Generally, it involves a statement urging calm, a meeting with the Attorney General of the United States Bill Barr, a statement concerning the Department of Justice's civil rights investigation, and a speech in Columbus, Ohio, voicing Federal concerns. I get up.

I arrive at the White House at 7:15 a.m. Elaine, my secretary, meets me at the door and says the President wants me immediately. I join Skinner in the President's study. He asks about a statement. I outline my plan. The President agrees and picks up the phone to talk with the Attorney General. Barr says the civil rights investigation will be accelerated.

I suggest an 11:30 a.m. meeting with the Attorney General and other Federal officials. After that we leave for a speech in Columbus; and we cancel a physical fitness appearance previously scheduled for Columbus, Ohio, with Arnold Schwarzenegger. We were to leave at 11:05 a.m., now move that back to 12:55. No pictures of the President in a jogging suit. The President agrees.

I leave the Oval at 7:45 a.m, dictate a statement, clear it with POTUS and Skinner at 8:00 a.m., and begin dictating a statement for after the 11:30 a.m. meeting. Attorney General Barr makes changes in the statement during the meeting. I edit and deliver a final draft to POTUS at 11:55 a.m. The President goes on camera at 12:02 in the Briefing Room. I tell him to deliver it and walk off the stage like Norman Schwarzkopf. He does.

The evening news shows the President strong, concerned, and leading.

At our last event in Columbus, a fundraiser, Teeter and Skinner call to say cancel or shorten the speech. I ask why. No reason given. POTUS says no. He delivers a brief speech fine. We leave for DC at 10:00 a.m. A terrible tragedy in Los Angeles, but a good day of leadership for the President.

MAY 9, 1992

The President calls Yeltsin to fill him in on the [President] Kravchuk, Ukraine, visit. Yeltsin twice says he could hug the President. It was late evening in Moscow—could have had one too many vodkas.

MAY 9, 1992

The White House Correspondents' Dinner. Charles Bierbauer, CNN, is President of the Association. Without a script, he didn't seem to know how to start the evening. But the incoming President, Karen Hosler, *Baltimore Sun*, ended the evening by calling for a "a two-hole potty" in the Briefing Room.

MAY 12, 1992

Arrived at 7:15 a.m. to find a draft statement written by staff for a 5-point plan for urban areas: weed & seed, HOPE, Enterprise Zones, Education Reform, and Welfare Reform. I gave it a title: "For A New America," and sent it to Tim McBride to make a two-foot by three-foot chart, suitable for television. I went to the Oval to show it to the President. He liked it.

MAY 20, 1992

The Murphy Brown story breaks. (Vice President Quayle had given a speech in which he says Murphy Brown, a fictional character in a television show, was not a good mother because of her comments on single mothers and certain liberal issues.) I immediately defend the Vice President as simply making a point on the advantages of two-parent households.

JUNE 17, 1992
YELTSIN ARRIVAL CEREMONY
The White House. Naomi Nover, Nover News Service, was in the Rose

Garden for the arrival. A *Life* magazine photographer spotted her. She'll probably get a full-page spread. The bag ladies of the White House strike again. (Naomi qualified to be in the press corp as representative of the Nover News Service, which was a one-person bureau started by her husband, now deceased. Naomi, in her eighties, was quite cranky, most noted for poking Sam Donaldson with her umbrella, which she carried at all times in her large canvas bag. She also carried a small Kodak camera and constantly took pictures.)

JUNE 21, 1992

Campaigning. Just returned from California/Texas trips. The "Ask George Bush" sessions went well, except for an 800 number in the television pictures of the President. The number was for our event sponsor, Evergreen Environmental Sciences. Skinner went crazy in our morning staff meeting, saying that our advance team is no good. But it was his advance team, headed by his man, Ed Murnane.

In Newport Beach, I suggested the President walk on the beach. Nothing symbolizes California more than the beach. The front-page picture the next morning in the *LA Times* was POTUS on the beach. Great success, however small.

In Dallas last night, Bob Woodward of the *Washington Post*, called to say a story is coming that Ross Perot hired a law firm in DC to get dirt on President Bush. Big story this morning. Big break. I immediately called it "shocking intimidation."

JUNE 24, 1992

Oval Office. The President is discussing Ross Perot's call for an end to Secret Service protection. "Maybe I should tell about the man who went to Adlers (men's clothing store) for twenty-one days with a gun, just waiting for me to come back. When he was arrested, his mother said, 'Good, because he would have killed George Bush.'"

JUNE 24, 1992

CAMPAIGN STRATEGY MEETING

White House, 6:00 p.m., Teeter, Malek, Skinner, Darman, Matalin, and Findlay. Everyone is pleased by my "Perot is Paranoid" comment and Bond's attack on Perot on CNN's show with Bernie Shaw. We agree, however, to cool it for a day to see how things play.

June 25, 1992

4:30 p.m., I came home early. Roger Ailes called. "I know you Reagan folks need a nap in the afternoon. Keep the pressure on Perot. I'm afraid our folks will turn to mush. Say, methinks he doth protest too much. People believe that old cliché. Say he is acting like a spoiled brat."

June 30, 1992

6:00 p.m., Bush dropped to third in *Washington Post* poll: Clinton 33 percent, Perot 31 percent, Bush 28 percent. Teeter and Steeper are in good spirits. They say Perot is stopped and dropping. Clinton benefits, and will be up as he picks a Vice President, gets his DNC convention bounce. Then we will take them. Everyone feels very strong, even blasé.

July 23, 1992

On the G-20 out of Washington to Dayton, Nurse Kim and Doctor Lee tell the President not to play softball at the Brookville Community Picnic. Apparently, he went jogging at 5:00 a.m. and had another atrial fibrillation. His blood pressure is low.

The President tells me before getting off the plane, "If I get weak, come get me with a phone call about Iraq." The doctor says to watch for slurred speech, faintness, or stumbling. I watch closely, but he makes it through the day without incident. He starts with a POW/MIA speech with protesters. Then he has a baking 95-degree sun for a family-values conversation in a park, a hot sun speech at the Ohio picnic, and a rally at some university field house. No problems. (But I nearly died from sun and heat. Don't know how he did it.)

August 12, 1992

Oval Office, 6:00 p.m., the President calls me in. "We want to announce Baker tomorrow at 10:15 a.m.," he said. "I'll announce it in the Briefing Room, but not take questions. Baker will make a speech at 11:00 a.m. at State. He will be chief of staff. Skinner will be national Republican chairman, the Laxalt job, and Margaret will come to the White House. Zoellick, Ross, and Mullins will come. Of course, I don't know if Skinner will take this."

"He'll take it," I said. "He's talked about this. He's expecting something. He's also talked to Henson and Clayton, but I don't know their reaction. I suspect they are ready for something."

Baker called. "Marlin," the President said, "Get on the other line."

"Marlin," Baker said. "Has the President laid this out for you?"

"Yes."

"Take a look at the statement. It says a lot of good things about me. You may want to cut it down."

"Sure," I said jokingly.

The President picked up on the kidding. "See if it says anything about me," he said.

"It gives him some credit," Baker teased.

"Marlin," Baker said, "Margaret wants out of the press. You've worked so closely with her. Can she take over Communications?"

"That's great," I said. "I want out of Communications."

"He's mostly out of it anyway," the President said.

"OK," Baker said, hanging up.

"Marlin, take this statement and read it."

I raised a paragraph on page three to the lead, so the President was making the announcement right at the top. No other changes.

Baker would be my seventh chief of staff in nine years in the White House. Baker first hired me in September 1983. (The seven includes Jim Baker, Don Regan, Howard Baker, Ken Duberstein, John Sununu, Sam Skinner, and Jim Baker again. We had come full circle.)

AUGUST 14, 1992

Last week Jack Kemp, Vin Weber, and Newt Gingrich released another memo to the President advocating tax cuts in his convention speech. In the Oval later, "Do you suppose it's too late to get rid of Kemp? Sort of Truman and McArthurish."

"Too late," I said. He's still reading the *Truman* book by David McCullough.

AUGUST 17–20, 1992
MRS. BUSH AND CIGARS

Houston, Texas. In 1992, we were in the Houston Convention Center for a major campaign event. It is a high-ceiling affair with huge ballrooms and meeting rooms, in addition to the main arena. I had been on my feet most of the day, and in midafternoon I decided I needed a smoke break. I had given up cigarettes in the 1960s, but I still smoked an occasional cigar, and I often carried one in my suit pocket for these high-pressure emergencies.

So I sought out a private location in this huge building where I would not bother anyone. It turned out that a back hallway with a forty-foot ceiling was the best I could do. At the very moment, I lit the cigar, around the corner ahead of me comes George W. Bush, the President's eldest son, who was helping with his father's campaign. Sometimes in trouble, sometimes drinking too much, and always presenting himself as his father's personal adviser, W. was kind of a rogue. He walked up to me and asked, "Got an extra one of those?"

"Sure," I said. I pulled one from my pocket and produced a match to light it. Just as we had both taken a puff or two, the most unexpected person we could ever imagine turned a corner into the hallway, not thirty yards from us. It was Mrs. Bush. Young George W. and I reacted exactly the same way. We said nothing and stuffed those lit cigars immediately into our suit pockets.

Mrs. Bush didn't like cigars, didn't like smokers, and had a no-smoking rule that everyone observed religiously. She walked directly up to W. and myself, never expressed a smile or a frown, and asked, "Which way to the arena?"

Without waiting for an answer, she turned to walk away. Took two steps, turned back and said, "Boys, your pants are on fire." Then resumed her walk. Mrs. Bush was one cool customer.

George and I pulled the cigars from our pockets and headed for a door.

Later, W. became Governor of Texas, and President of the United States. He invited me to the Oval Office on the afternoon before his invasion of Iraq. Despite the approaching military action, I couldn't help wondering if he still smoked cigars.

AUGUST 21, 1992

Branson, Missouri. Day after the GOP convention. Press subdued by our comeback. Evening news shows a huge Gulfport crowd; evening news says Bush on the move. CBS has it 48–46 percent. We're almost even coming out, far better than we expected. Press is friendly, not pressing for comment. That means we have the upper hand. No weaknesses to exploit. At Silver Dollar City rally, I bought a bag of peanuts at "Rural Life" kind of stand. I saw Loretta Lynn, in an all-white frilly dress over slacks. She pops into a Johnny On The Spot. Devroy and Rosenthal started two-week vacations today. What a relief.

AUGUST 23, 1992

New York Times this morning has all negative Bush stories. Even Terry Hunt, AP, asked if I've seen the *NYT*. POTUS is angry. He asks for the *NYT* front page from the day after the GOP convention. He asks for the December 18 and 19 papers. In his speech today he takes another jab at the press. They notice, and they don't like it.

AUGUST 27, 1992

Baker calls me to his office. Takes me into Zoellick's office and closes the door.

"We've got to have a way to respond to Clinton," he said. "Nobody seems to be able to break through (get press attention). But Clinton made a wire story: Clinton Calls Bush Pinocchio and a liar."

Zoellick: "We need to emphasize the double-speak, and use the Schwarzkopf-Powell statement. Clinton keeps saying Schwarzkopf wanted the war to go on. That's not true and we need to nail Clinton on it."

Baker: "Can you say that Marlin?"

"Sure," I say, "but the press will accuse me of being too political in the White House. Like they did in the Howie Kurtz story a few weeks ago."

Baker: "Can't you say this is personal? You've been with Bush a long time. He's called Bush a liar. You just have to speak out."

"OK," I say. I go to the wire service booths and start my spiel:

"I have this wire story of Clinton calling Bush Pinocchio. I've been with the President a long time and this is just outrageous. This guy's record for honesty and veracity is such that he shouldn't be calling anyone a liar. And look how he ignores the Powell statement yesterday saying both he and Schwarzkopf advised the President to end the war. Either Clinton doesn't know this, or he doesn't want to know. He's the King of double-speak."

There was silence. I turned and walked away.

AP, CNN, and Reuters used it. I showed the wires to Baker in a 5:00 p.m. meeting. He read the story out loud, very pleased.

I took a call from Dave Broder of the *Post* and gave it to him. My quotes appeared in the Saturday story in the *Post*.

AUGUST 29, 1992

George Will, who called Bush a lapdog in 1986, said it was unprecedented for a government spokesman to be this political. Tom Wicker, a knee-jerk liberal at the *New York Times*, who has always hated Bush, said on the Brinkley show he had never seen anything like it.

Brit Hume, ABC, who covers the White House and heard my original remarks, reminded the group that Clinton had called Bush Pinocchio and kept repeating the charge about ending the war too soon.

Most of the press continues to ignore the names Clinton is calling Bush, or they approve of it.

SEPTEMBER 4, 1992

6:00 p.m., The Baker core group includes Margaret Tutwiler, Janet Mullins, Bob Zoellick, Dennis Ross, Dick Darman, Fred Steeper, Fred Malek, Bob Teeter. Steeper polls show we're winning only five or six states; four or five states undecided; Clinton has the rest. Polls show we need a dramatic economic program; 81 percent would cut the White House and Congressional staffs. Most think we have no economic plan.

I write on blue five-by-seven papers, the Fitzwater Agenda Five plan. It includes: 5 percent cut in WH and Congressional salaries; 5 percent tax rate cut, across the board; balanced budget in 5 years.

I show it to Zoellick. He smiles.

I show it to Teeter. He smiles.

I show it to Baker. He shows it to Margaret. She lights up.

"This is it," Baker tells Zoellick who starts writing it down. He picks up my piece of blue paper and puts it in his pocket. I ask for it to destroy, and begin to fold it up. He takes it back, tears it into a dozen parts, and hands it back. Meeting breaks up.

SEPTEMBER 10, 1992

7:30 a.m., Sean Walsh comes to tell me the camera crew setting up in the Oval to film POTUS's campaign commercial is incompetent. "Marlin, even I can see these guys don't have the lights or the cameras to do this. They have one camera. They don't know what they're doing."

The production was hired by the campaign and directed by Dorrance Smith, so I didn't worry.

After returning from Detroit at 4:30, Margaret came to my office with Janet Mullins. "You have to look at these ads," she said. "They're terrible." We go to Janet's office to look. They are third-rate amateur. POTUS face is shadowed on one side. There is a hot spot on his left forehead, and shadows under his eyes. The film is cut so it jumps from sitting at his desk to standing, from close-up to distance. No dissolves. Nothing smooth. It's a mess.

SEPTEMBER 23, 1992

Ohio. We're [campaigning] at the Brookville Community Picnic near Dayton, Ohio. "Call the briefing!" I shouted. (Meaning gather the press, I will be briefing in a few minutes.) I ran into a brown park service type of wooden building in the Brookville Park. The President was pitching horseshoes, just before speaking. On the plane out here, the President and Scowcroft spoke by phone and decided to return to Washington after the speech, go directly to Camp David, and hold a Saturday NSC meeting at the Camp.

After the President's speech, I called Doug Davidson, a USIA officer assigned to my office, and asked him to get the State Dept. line on Iraq, then went to the press filing center about one hundred yards away. Past the antique tractors, the hot air balloons, and the Sno-Cone stands. En route, I met John Mashek of the *Boston Globe*. "Come with me," I said. "I can't tell you why." If I had told him, he would have told the other press before I could. Give away no edge. I wanted surprise on my side.

I rushed in, yelled to Judy Smith that I was ready, and ordered the stenographers to get ready to record. (I told them we were going home.)

SEPTEMBER 25, 1992

Camp David. Once again I am struck by the world leaders who have stayed in Dogwood Cabin at Camp David. I can't believe I slept in the same bed with some of the worst mass murderers in history. And some very good men as well.

I had dinner that evening with the President, his dear friend Lud Ashley and his son, Meredith, at the President's house, Aspen Lodge. We sat at the dining room table in Aspen, ate ribs and corn on the cob, red wine, fried grapefruit—and watched *Being There* with Peter Sellers. I told the President it was a classic movie. He didn't like it. Like a kid, he kept saying, "Is this it. Where's the action?" At the end, he said, "Is it over?"

(After dinner, I sat in the same lounge chair I used to sit in after dinner with the Reagans. The house was about the same. President Bush slid a footstool over for me, and treated me like any weekend guest. It was special.)

SEPTEMBER 26, 1992

Camp David. I'm sitting in the tennis court gazebo, smoking a cigar, listening to the rain. I get paged to call Timberwolf, the President's Secret Service code name. He invites me to lunch at Laurel Lodge with Jim Burke, President of Johnson & Johnson. He wants to make a statement to the press on arrival at the White House later about the drug program.

Burke gives me handwritten notes, and I draft a one-page statement, then join the group for lunch. Another page from my Deputy Laura Melillo tells me that Rolf Ekéus, the UN weapons inspector, is live on CNN. I go to the living room to watch. The President joins me, and we decide to make a statement on Iraq. I get one ready, with Admiral Howell in Washington.

The President delivers it on the lawn at 4:30. (I don't remember what happened to the drug statement.)

SEPTEMBER 26, 1992

Camp David. Howard Kurtz, *Washington Post*, called me about a profile on my partisan comments about Al Gore. He lists all my gaffs—drugstore cowboy, Looney Tunes, lazy bastards, Danish pastry, and Gore's Mr. Sellout America performance. I explain them all and deny being the GOP's pit bull. This would be a very bad story.

SEPTEMBER 26, 1992

White House Residence. After returning from a Michigan/Wisconsin campaign visit, the President and the NSC met in the President's office in the residence. Sitting beneath Lincoln's portrait to consider Iraq. All agree the immediate crisis is over with Iraq's agreement for US inspections of buildings.

Cheney wants to slow down some of the military preparations. The President approved. General Powell says the next time there is an inspection crisis, the inspectors should leave immediately. He said, "They should say, 'We're outta here. Our friends will get back to you.'" The friends are T-LAM missiles.

Baker agrees, says that crisis inspections will come. We should be ready to respond quickly. Baker warns that we cannot appear to act for political reasons. There must be a real and perceived crisis. POTUS agrees. I say we should tell the press, "We are monitoring. We want full compliance."

SEPTEMBER 26, 1992

I've been in a silent war with NBC since two months ago when Michael Gartner, NBC News president, told his correspondents to "go after Bush." Then Tom Brokaw told a Seattle, Washington, audience that Bush is weak and should lose. John Cochran has grown increasingly malicious in his reporting.

But I realize this must stop. I cannot ignore Cochran. His reports will only get worse. Enroute to Grand Rapids, Michigan, Cochran is in the pool on *Air Force One.* I go back and sit beside him. We talk about Iraq, Bush's new speech on trust. It seems to help. His report tonight is better. ABC and CBS also gave good reports—perhaps the best we've had in months. I think the press realizes they have gone soft on Clinton, certainly since his convention and bus trip.

Clinton today criticized Iraq and Yugoslavia policy. He sounded knowledgeable. Since most people don't understand events in Yugoslavia, I figured all he has to do is sound good. So I wanted to label him reckless and irresponsible. I praised his support on Iraq, but said his Hugo comments were reckless, ignored the role of the EC and the UN, and clearly show he's not ready to make presidential decisions on foreign policy.

It worked. NBC and ABC both used my comments.

SEPTEMBER 27, 1992

Bad briefing today. All on Iraq. The networks—John Cochran, NBC; and Susan Spencer, CBS—try again and again to get me to admit that Saddam won a victory by getting US inspectors off the UN team. Saddam has been using this as propaganda, and the US networks seem to want to help. Finally, I yielded just enough for them to nail me. It was a "gotcha" briefing. I hate them.

SEPTEMBER 29, 1992

En route to Austin Peay State University, the President calls me to his cabin, hands me two typewritten pages. "I'm going to deliver this at the next stop." This was Clarksville, Tennessee, in about ten minutes. It was in a college gym, in a county that had no elected Republicans. Yet it was packed, and rolling with energy. The two pages announced a challenge of four debates on four Sundays, between POTUS and Clinton; and two debates between the VP candidates. I thought he was joking. I read it again.

"Steve (speechwriter) has it. Do whatever you need to do."

I ran back in *Air Force One* to ask Steve about it. "Yes, it's true. Here it is." He said.

"What do you think?" I asked Mary Matalin.

"Ex-cell-ent," she said, emphasizing the syllables.

"What's our spin?" I asked. "Why are we doing it?"

"How about," she said, "We told you we wanted debates."

We hurried from the plane to make arrangements. This was gang-busters. It had to put Clinton on the defensive. It had to be a surprise, and hopefully one that was thrown at him by the press. No leaks, even at this late stage.

In our motorcade from the plane to the event site, I radioed ahead to Michael Bush and Judy Smith of my staff, asking them to meet me at the school. The minute we stopped, I jumped out and told Sean Walsh to get me Wendy Walker, senior producer for CNN. I told Judy and Mike we had a big announcement. I couldn't say what.

I ran to the top of the stairs in the gymnasium, and the first reporter I saw was Ann Devroy of the *Post. Oh no,* I thought. *She will call the Clinton campaign and tip them off. Or at least call Dave Maraniss, and he will tell them.*

I turned on my heels and headed for a door, any door. Sean brought Wendy.

"Wendy," I said. "POTUS is about to make the biggest announcement of the campaign. I recommend you take it live."

"What is it?" she asked.

I looked her right in the eye, and hesitated. "I can't say, trust me."

She ran off with less than ten minutes before speech time.

With five minutes to go, I got a page to call Baker. I ran to a signal phone in the holding room. "What is it?" the President asked, as I darted past him in the hallway.

"Baker," I said, and kept on moving.

"Marlin," he said, "Here's the spin. We wanted debates, but Clinton's people won't talk to us. We're not dealing with the Commission, so we propose a six-debate package. Now it's time for Clinton to talk to us. Got it?"

"Right," I said, and hung up. POTUS was now on the stage. I

went back to the press room, ran in, and said loudly to all reporters, "The President is going to make a major announcement at the top of his speech."

I ran from the room. Reporters running after me, to editing rooms, to telephones, or to see the President. I headed down the gymnasium steps and stopped about halfway down the steps to listen as POTUS begins. He led with the announcement, and the gym was rocking with thunderous applause. They were chanting, "Four More Years."

The White House pool camera was on the floor, and I noticed it was panning the crowd. I started cheering. Ann Compton, ABC, saw me and pointed her cameraman in my direction. I thrust my arms up, fists clenched, into the air, and screamed for high heaven. By God, they were going to see enthusiasm if they filmed me.

It all worked perfectly. The White House press was impressed by the announcement. We had turned tables on Clinton and seized the offense.

Clinton was speaking at the time and totally surprised. The press yelled at him after the speech, and he said in disbelief, "No comment. You people have tricked me into this before."

The press reported him as stunned, caught by surprise, and on the defensive.

All four networks led with the Bush proposal—showed me cheering wildly. Brit Hume, ABC, said in his piece, "Even Bush aides had something to cheer about."

That night we did a Grand Ole Opry Salute to George Bush in Nashville, and the President appeared on *Nashville Now* TV at about 10:00 p.m.—after five cities, eight speeches, five victories, ninety-two appearances. He did an imitation of Jimmy Dean selling sausage. It was all classic. The perfect end to a great campaign day.

OCTOBER 1, 1992

Learned another valuable lesson today: never take the press's word for it. Andy Rosenthal, *NYT,* and Doug Jehl, *LA Times,* told me today that Candidate Clinton said he "would bomb and strafe" in Bosnia. Rosenthal and Jehl had pulled me aside to proffer this information in

Grand Rapids, Michigan, in the darkened back room of the National Water Company. I should have been suspicious. Instead, I said it was "reckless." It turns out Clinton didn't say that. Howard Kurtz then said I was reckless. George Will said I was hapless. Both blamed me for commenting on wrong information. Neither of them blamed, or even named, the reporters who gave me the information.

This was the kind of mistake a press secretary just has to eat.

If I even say anything about this publicly, the press will say I'm thin-skinned or wrong, or both. The press always backs their own. (Or at least they used to twenty years ago in pre-blogger days. One advantage of current media is the competitiveness of the Internet, cable news, bloggers, etc., that probably would have identified the reporters and criticized them.)

OCTOBER 7, 1992

Kennebunkport. Had dinner with Ann Devroy, *Post*; John Mashek, *Globe*; and Judy Smith, my Deputy, at the Tides Inn on Goose Rocks Beach. Conversation was pleasant, but strained. Off the record. Judy and I listened while Ann and John criticized the President, Mary Matalin, and others. The next day, Mashek asked to be added to our expanded pool of twenty-eight reporters. We said OK, then Mashek and Devroy used off-the-record information from our dinner discussion to ask the President about Mary Matalin's apology for something the RNC said about the campaign. The press will double-cross you every time. (Best to eat at McDonald's.)

OCTOBER 8, 1992

Kennebunkport. After the press conference on Bosnia at his Kennebunkport office, I had an off-the-record session with reporters in our Shawmut Inn press office. It was clear they didn't understand what was happening in Bosnia or, in many cases, even where Bosnia was located. To explain how complex the issues and alliances in the region were, I drew a circle and showed the geographic relationship of Slovenia, Croatia, and Serbia. Then I showed where Muslim factions were located, or at least allied. Then we considered the history of the area, including Yugoslavia. I think it was very helpful, but I lived in fear that someone would misstate some of my lessons.

OCTOBER 9, 1992

Kennebunkport, 8:00 a.m., in the Nonantum Hotel, where the President's staff is staying, I'm getting a cup of coffee at the hospitality table. Frank Murray, *Washington Times,* walks by and says, "Good morning, Marlin."

"Out of coffee," I say.

"Yes," he says. "Can you tell me if the Bush/Rabin talks will assign different layers of funding for settlements?"

"I don't know, Frank," I said.

"How's your nose?" he asks.

"OK," I said, backing away. I can't even get a cup of coffee without a question. There is some inner code in all reporters that says: never let the press secretary pass without asking a question.

OCTOBER 9, 1992

On Friday, October 7, Margie Lehrman, NBC deputy bureau chief, called to complain that we didn't give them enough description of our press conference so they could decide whether or not to carry it live. In Colorado Springs Thursday, we said it was Bosnia; it was. In Washington on Friday, we said Bosnia and Iraq. We added a paragraph on the economy, but it was 90 percent Bosnia and Iraq. Yesterday, John Cochran said Gartner was upset by my complaint to Margie. I told her Gartner had ordered his correspondents to go after Bush two months ago. He has no right to tell me about fairness. "You haven't heard the last of this," he shouted vindictively. (He was fired from NBC in 1993.)

NOVEMBER 8, 1992
WE LOST.

PART V

—THE CALM AFTER—
OUTSIDE THE WHITE HOUSE

Introduction to Part Five

THESE STORIES REFLECT some of the most memorable of events after government service. I retired from government after the 1992 election and started writing. These stories range from the extraordinary circumstances in which the mayor of Abilene, Kansas, asked me to come home and receive a $50,000 donation from a former bank robber. It was demanded of me by the donor.

Then I was invited to give remarks honoring President Eisenhower at his Library in Abilene. Ike has always been my hero, as he is for everyone who lives in Abilene. As a boy, I dreamed of meeting Ike. I never did, but I walked in his footsteps in the White House, and these remarks were a great honor for me.

There is also a story about the Press Briefing Room podium, that I designed and White House carpenters built in 1987. It was retired in 2007, and several years after that I started a search for the podium, hoping to have it transferred to the Bush Library in College Station, Texas. After a decade or so, I found the podium in storage in the White House during the Obama Administration. It has been promised, but it never seems to be sent. For me, it's a sad story.

I've also written about President Bush's last tandem parachute jump, which he made at ninety years old. And I finish with my remarks after receiving an honorary doctorate degree from Kansas State University, and then with more remarks at the graveside of President Reagan. These two events are among my most rewarding experiences.

Pardon Me

Every Thursday night during the summer we went to the city band concert. My brother and I loved climbing into the back seat of our grey 1951 Dodge, with the seat covers that felt like a burr haircut, and driving into Abilene, Kansas, hopefully in time to find a parking space among the inner ring of cars. The band shell, so called because it was exactly that, a concrete stage and backdrop that looked exactly like an oyster shell, and presumably with acoustics that would throw a good trumpet solo all the way to the Smoky Hill River. Similarly, the lawn in front was shaped like the same oyster, elevated a foot or two above the street so the front wheels of parked cars were higher than the back ones, allowing a perfect view of the band, over the low-cut privet hedge and the people seated on the lawn in folding chairs.

There was a thoughtfulness about this design that is seldom replicated today, or so it seems. In 1950's Kansas, farmers were the most important segment of most small town populations. We had doctors and lawyers and bankers all right, but not too many. And they were all dependent on farmers for their business. So it was important for this bashful and independent breed of pioneer, the dirt farmer, to be able to park at the band concert, keep his small children in the back seat, a couple of windows cracked for sound and fresh air, and never have to mingle with the crowd. You could wear overalls if you liked, and maybe give your wife a special hug in the front seat, especially after the stars came out and the musicians settled into their third or fourth song. For our family, this was a perfect evening, made even more so because the First Christian Church, which we attended regularly, often made ice cream for sale behind the band shell. It was homemade, churned by the strong arms of sunburned fathers, and it never required toppings of peanuts or candy to provide special flavor. It was vanilla ice cream, cold as ice and rich with the cream of Holstein cows that had been milked only hours before. My brother and I, both in grade school, talked about the ice cream for days before the event. In terms of music, I only remembered the National Anthem, *America the Beautiful*, and the *William Tell Overture*, widely known as the *Lone Ranger* song.

But there was always a remarkable sense of place about the city band shell, like reading Willa Cather and being able to hear the prairie winds or smell apple pies resting in a kitchen window. Even today, I think of the band shell and feel the darkness, the mosquitoes making little thuds against the car windows, and lightning bugs so thick in the night that they seemed like sparklers from the Fourth of July. Sometimes we would jump out of the car and catch a couple fireflies, as we called them, then jump back in before Dad would have to retrieve us. And the bugs would crawl over our hands, their tails lighting up as they walked, and I could see each freckle on my skin as they moved past. If we caught enough fireflies, we put them in a jar that my mom always brought for this purpose. My mom loved the music, played the piano all her life, and prayed openly that the city band concerts would instill a similar appreciation in her children. In a way they did. I love music, but alas I have no talent.

Nevertheless, all of these memories came to the fore in July 1990 when the mayor of Abilene called me in the White House to ask a favor. I was Press Secretary to President George H. W. Bush and gave a daily press briefing, usually televised, in which I often mentioned Abilene. I loved my hometown and often contrasted my youth on the farm with life in the city. There may have been some farm youth who became journalists and were in the White House press corps, but not many. So when I started talking about cutting a chicken's head off, scalding it, plucking it, and begging my mother to cook the heart and gizzard until they were crispy, it often became part of Washington news stories. Certainly, the people of Abilene knew where to find me, although the mayor had never called before.

The mayor reminded me of the fire that destroyed the band shell, and the emptiness of Abilene not having this institution in its midst. He then said that, remarkably, in the city's time of need, a former bank robber named Delbert Dunmire had arrived in town trying to make amends for robbing $2,461 from the Commercial State Bank in 1958. It turned out that he was captured and spent two years in prison for his crime, during which he decided to give honest work a try. After his parole and release, he borrowed $1,000 to open a machine shop in Kansas City that later became Growth Industries, an airplane parts company that became the source of his wealth.

The mayor's story was a little sketchy here, but apparently at some point, the bucks started rolling in, and piling up in large quantities. Mr. Dunmire started using his money for widely proclaimed benevolent deeds. One of these was a return to Abilene and the Commercial State Bank, where he apologized to the banker he had robbed years earlier. Dunmire said he wanted to make amends for his affront to society, and wanted to share his later good fortune with the City of Abilene. According to the mayor, this all led to Mr. Dunmire's offering $50,000 to the city for the rebuilding of the city band shell, but only if the Press Secretary to the President of the United States, an Abilene native, would come home to accept the money in a public ceremony. The mayor was quite passionate on this point, and I agreed on the spot. But I did ask one question: Why me?

The mayor quoted Mr. Dunmire as saying he wanted to meet me, and this was his only requirement. The mayor also suggested that this eccentric gentleman was known for doing philanthropic things in exotic ways, such as buying new guns for an entire police department. Or taking his 35th high school reunion classmates, by private jet and cruise ship, to the Bahamas for a free trip that cost a half-million dollars, including entertainment fees for Connie Stevens and Evel Knievel. Or paying $90,000 in an auction to have lunch with Warren Buffet. But one of the constants in all of these gifts was huge publicity and public recognition of his good works. The mayor took the generous view that the objective was simply to make amends, publicly and privately. I was more skeptical, no doubt due to my years of work in the White House, so I asked: What's he want? I normally associate philanthropy with giving money to charities, or poor people, or tornado victims, etc. No one seemed to have a good explanation for Mr. Dunmire's brand of giving.

Even as the City of Abilene prepared to celebrate the 130th anniversary of the band in 2011, and the 20th anniversary of the new band shell, the local newspaper quoted Mr. Dunmire as saying "it was his way of paying back the city for his good fortune."

In any case, I arrived in Abilene on October 23, 1989, a bright sunny Kansas day, perfect for a public ceremony in Eisenhower Park, and a special helicopter fly-in by Del Dunmire to present a check to me and to the city. This was sounding more and more like a presidential visit planned by "advance men" and Secret Service agents. Sure enough, it was. The site was selected for its telegenic views of the park, and the private helicopter would allow Mr. Dunmire to emerge in all his glory, be met by his entourage, and walk to the microphones, all within full view of the television cameras from Wichita and Topeka. Just like a president. As I arrived at the park, the cameras were setting up.

This was turning out to be quite a colorful day for Abilene residents, including representatives of the city band, the bank that had been robbed, my family and friends, city officials, and several high school classmates. My old friends had gathered for the fun. Maybe a hundred or more people arrived at the appointed time and waited for the helicopter. Everyone marveled at the generosity of the gift, and discounted the eccentricities of Del Dunmire's giving as small imperfections on the face of great wealth, something few if any of us knew anything about. We milled around, admiring the park and the rose garden. I even walked my brother over to the limestone pergola and showed him my initials etched in one of the stone columns more than thirty years before. Of course, hundreds of initials were marked in the stone and my brother suggested a half dozen people he knew with the same initials. Nevertheless, I thought of the hundreds of Abilene youth who returned to the city on occasion to reclaim their initials and reprise their youth. It's a special treasure of most small towns in America that such monuments to history are preserved, and not destroyed. I thank the people of Abilene for that.

Within minutes, we heard the helicopter. At that point, a well-dressed middle-aged man introduced himself as a former Secret Service agent, who was now on Mr. Dunmire's staff. This set off bells with me because I knew many rich men who had hired Secret Service agents to be their bodyguards, or to plan their travel, or to do their legwork of various kinds. I admit that the wealthy classes who travel in helicopters and private airplanes, and have corporate meetings all over the world, often need special support. But I have also found that people who hire agents are usually hoping that the aura of the presidency will somehow settle on their shoulders. And it occurred to me that my presidential aura, however small it might be, might be thought to add some illumination at moments like these.

As the helicopter circled the field, which they routinely do to announce their arrival, the agent guided me over to the landing area to be at the head of the greeting party. As I moved into place in front of the mayor, I suspected he was now getting an inkling of what this show was all about. And my stomach had a degree of queasiness related to a similar realization. A lot of trouble and money had been spent just to set up this show. What was going to happen next?

The rotors shut down. Then the door began to open and slowly was lowered to the ground. The agent positioned himself at the bottom of the stairs, ready to respond to any wish from the great man, and to introduce Mr. Dunmire to the assembled greeting party.

And then he appeared, a smiling, middle-aged, short fellow with thick white hair and a well-trimmed white beard, wearing a tailored summer suit with bright tie, and his hand outstretched. He was tanned and affable, calling me Marlin, and greeting the entire party with aplomb. A natural politician. After the pleasantries, we started moving toward the microphones and the official ceremony.

The agent slipped into step with Mr. Dunmire and gave him a quick briefing on the ceremony and when he would speak. He asked the agent if he had the money. I assumed that meant the $50,000 check.

But when Mr. Dunmire was introduced, he called forth an aide carrying a large leather duffle bag. The gentleman carrier emerged from the entourage, opened the top of the bag, and stepped aside. The guest of honor said that before he presented the check to the city, he wanted to give a similar gift to the people of Abilene. At this point he stepped to the bag; reached in and grabbed two handfuls of $5, $20, and $100 bills, and threw them into the air. There was a gasp from the crowd as the bills floated to the ground, and some bills were grasped in the air as they undulated like feathers in a light breeze. Mr. Dunmire grabbed more bills and flung them into the crowd, repeating this maneuver until the bag was empty and he could turn it upside down to demonstrate the full measure of his generosity.

The rest of the ceremony was conducted according to plan, with remarks by the mayor, who was also president of the Abilene Municipal Band, and other local officials. I accepted the check from Mr. Dunmire with only a few brief thank yous, and passed it along to the mayor. I suspect it was on the way to the bank even before our guest's helicopter had cleared Abilene air space.

In any case, the ceremony ended quickly and we were all left in the midday sun to contemplate what had just happened. Those with $100 bills certainly felt the afternoon had been rewarding. City officials and band members were exuberant over prospects for a new band shell. I was delighted that Abilene citizens had responded to Mr. Dunmire's chicanery with such aplomb, although I still wondered why I was required to make this event happen. I must have been slotted for the Connie Stevens role as special entertainment.

In any case, I returned to my job in Washington, wishing Abilene and Mr. Dunmire all the best, and looking forward to a new band shell consistent with my childhood memories. It was a busy time in Washington. Two months later the Berlin Wall fell, signaling the end of the Cold War. And by December 1989, I was with the President of the United States in Malta, attending the first summit meeting with Mikhail Gorbachev on the future of American relations with the Soviet Union, the reunification of East and West Germany, and the future of the Eastern European counties that were pressing for their freedom. I never thought much about the new band shell until it was completed in 1991. And I never heard from Del Dunmire again.

As fate would have it, President Bush 41 lost his re-election bid for the Presidency in 1992. I was preparing to leave government on Inauguration Day, January 20, 1993, and perhaps write a book or begin searching for a job in the private sector. The White House historically has been rather efficient in this process. Many stories have been written about the last days of an administration, when all pictures of the outgoing President are removed from the walls, all office ornaments must be packed and gone, all books returned to appropriate libraries, and every single piece of paper—always in the millions—must be packed and sent to a huge warehouse, awaiting further distribution to a future Presidential Library. The walls of the

White House, including the press secretary's office, are painted. And all the President's staff must turn in their security passes by January 19, and will not be allowed in the building on Inauguration Day. The Press Secretary is allowed to be at work on January 20, in order to coordinate the movement of the press corps as it covers the traditional 10:00 a.m. coffee between the incumbent and the newly elected President, and their subsequent motorcade ride to the Capitol for the inauguration. Security in the building is very tight.

I arrived in the building about 9:00 a.m. and was stopped by the smell of fresh paint and the starkness of the walls. The West Wing was eerily empty. No secretaries, or computers with their screens ablaze, no voices, and most doors were closed and locked. I went to my office, expecting to see the veteran reporter Helen Thomas in the hallway. But no one was there. My inner door was unlocked and I pushed it open, wanting to soak up the atmosphere of this office where I had spent six years with two Presidents. I pondered the fireplace, now cold and sparkling clean, a far cry from that cold evening in 1991 when the flames soared as I announced, "The Liberation of Kuwait has begun."

My desk was horseshoe-shaped in one corner of the room, and I walked around the end to sit and contemplate the next few hours. I pulled out the chair and noticed a white envelope on the seat, marked only with my name typed on the front. I don't remember it being sealed. But I thought it very strange, and I asked myself for the first of many times, how did this get here? I sat, unfolded the letter, and began to read.

I don't remember the exact words, and I didn't make a copy, but the letter made a passionate argument that a Presidential Pardon be given to Del Dunmire. The letter cited all the philanthropic deeds of Mr. Dunmire, especially the money for a new band shell in Abilene, Kansas. Suddenly I knew why I had been required to accept the check. Four years had passed with never a thought about Del Dunmire. Now this letter, somehow was sneaked into the inner sanctums of the White House on Inauguration Day, signed by Mrs. Del Dunmire, and left on the seat of my chair.

I was stunned. I leaned back in my chair to consider how this had all come about, and what I should do about it. First, it was crazy to think that the President makes a decision to pardon anybody in the last hour of his presidency. It just could never happen. I suppose people read the newspapers about presidents pardoning people at the end of their term, even on the last day. But even if it was announced on the last day, it had to have been reviewed for days or weeks before that. President Clinton pardoned a political friend, Marc Rich, in the last week of his presidency; and he pardoned Patty Hearst on the last day, January 20, 2001. But both of these were approved by the Justice Department before the President acted.

The truly sad part is that Dunmire might have had a chance at a pardon if he had hired a Washington lawyer, pursued a Justice Department review, and given the review process time to work. Maybe he had tried that and failed. I never knew. But a letter on the chair is not the right approach. I left the letter in the White House for the new President, who at that moment was walking up the driveway with the new First Lady, Hillary Rodham Clinton.

Ike and Marlin in Abilene

THE DWIGHT EISENHOWER Presidential Library and Museum in Abilene, Kansas, holds an annual celebration of Ike's birthday, often while also honoring the youth of Abilene who attend the same public schools that Ike did. I was invited to keynote the event on October 11, 2001. As a boy, I was always aware of Ike's history. These remarks focused on Ike's small-town experiences and the irony that two boys from Abilene would spend so many years in the White House.

Today we come to this beautiful library and museum to mark the birthday of a remarkable man who, like us, grew up in Abilene, Kansas. And I would like to speak briefly this morning about why it's special for us to be a part of his experience, to share the values that he held, to have walked in his footsteps, and to follow his direction.

This is a very special audience for me because, in addition to family and friends, you represent essentially the youth of Abilene—the schools, the activities, the experiences of summer, the car rides up and down main street, little league baseball, the rodeo and the county fair, Fourth of July fireworks at Eisenhower Park, tractor pulls, farming, junior proms, school plays, track meets, and trying to get a date on Saturday night.

These are pretty much standard fare in mid-America, and indeed across the land. But you have one incredible advantage over most groups of kids: you have a role model who walked in your shoes and then became General of the Armies and President of the United States of America. And I remember how that affected me at your age.

I grew up on a farm out in the Holland Community, south of town, and rode the bus for six years to attend McKinley Grade School, here in town. The playground back then was all dirt, so when it rained, we had to stay inside or play in the street between the school and Zey's market. The biggest event of the year for me was the annual track meet between McKinley, Garfield, and Lincoln schools.

Although I don't look like it today, back then I was fast as greased lightning. And I looked forward to the spring track meet as an opportunity to win about five blue ribbons. But then it started to rain, and for three days it soaked all the school playgrounds to the point where they couldn't be used. So when the sun finally did come out, the principals decided to hold the track meet in the street.

Now Lincoln grade school, which stood about where the Information Center is now, was the smallest of the three schools.

And here's what we said about Lincoln school.

Stinkin' Lincoln,
What have you been drinkin',
Smells like water, tastes like wine,
Oh my gosh, it's turpentine.

We thought that was pretty clever. And I did win a lot of blue ribbons over Lincoln that day. But I always remember my mother saying afterwards, "Remember, Marlin, Dwight David Eisenhower went to that school."

Her lesson was: It doesn't matter where you go to school or how rich you are or where you live. Anybody can achieve greatness, or achieve whatever you want to achieve, if you exhibit the inner qualities of this extraordinary man from Lincoln school.

Eisenhower's life is well documented in this library and museum. The biographies of his youth tell about his daily responsibility to light the fire in the family fireplace. They tell about the 1903 flood when Ike and his brother Edgar found a rowboat on Mud Creek and started giving their friends rides, until they sank the boat from too much weight.

But you, the students of Abilene, know much more about Ike than anyone can read in the biographies. Look over there at the railroad tracks. Ike walked along those tracks every day of his life. He felt the same hot and heavy Kansas heat on his shoulders as you do. He walked out Third Street and threw stones into Mud Creek. He knew the brisk days of autumn that cover the streets of this town with orange and brown splendor. There was no miracle of advantage that lifted this man above the masses. But there were the lessons of responsibility, respect, honesty, courage, cooperation, and perseverance. He exemplified all these qualities. And because you know Eisenhower as just another boy from Abilene, you must also know that these qualities are available to everyone—including yourselves.

My second school in the 1950s was seventh and eighth grade at Abilene Junior High, a red brick structure located on the far corner of Garfield's present-day playground. I always took significance from the fact that Ike attended this school in the first year it was constructed, and I attended the last year before it was torn down. And more importantly, under my desk was carved the initials: DE. Now those initials could have been from Dick Evers, one of my classmates. But I prefer to believe they came from Dwight Eisenhower, one of my idols.

And I always remember the picture of Ike with his high school football team, wearing a sweater with no pads or a helmet. It looked like he was having great fun. In my last year in that old red building, I was a substitute quarterback on the eighth-grade team. We played Concordia, and we were winning thirty-six to nothing when a Concordia player ran for a touchdown. But his team committed a foul. When the referee asked me, as the quarterback of the Abilene team, if I wanted to take the penalty or the touchdown, I remembered my mother's admonition to always be kind to those less fortunate than me. So I looked at the scoreboard, calculated our thirty-six-point lead, and gave them the touchdown.

That was pretty much the end of my football career. But I learned another lesson—while it's important to be kind, sometimes you have to be strong, and maybe a little tough.

At the end of Eisenhower's career, after he led America and its allies to victory in World War II, and after eight years as President, he became known as a gentle man of peace. Eisenhower knew that there was a time to fight, and a time to lead with reason and collegiality. He responded to the threat against America in the 1940s with the fiercest retaliation against Hitler that our country could muster. And as President, he led the nation on a course of peace, and showed us the dignity and grace of gentle strength.

America would do well to remember those qualities today, as we confront the forces of terrorism around the world. I'm sure it is difficult for young people today to understand the violence and hatred that we saw in the World Trade Center bombings of September 11.

Similarly, you must be a little troubled by the dual responsibilities our country asks of you today: to conduct your lives with normalcy, yet be vigilant to the world around you.

You continue with school, your classes, your friends and teachers. Yet there will be occasions when you visit airports or sporting events or relatives in other cities, and you will see the military or the metal detectors or those who search your possessions.

Remember the life of Eisenhower at those times as well. There have always been those who would threaten our families and our country; just as we have always defended our rights, our freedoms, and our homes. The life of Eisenhower shows that we can manage those fears and responsibilities and still live important and interesting lives. We will resist the forces of terrorism and make America safe for travel and commerce and daily life. As children, do not be afraid to seek those assurances from your family. And as parents, do not be afraid to give them.

It has been my good fortune to serve nearly ten years in the White House as an Assistant to two Presidents, and I have thought about the Eisenhower legacy many times. He never seemed closer than when we were in the Cabinet Room, considering the Persian Gulf War or other issues. I could feel him sitting next to me, even as Ronald Reagan's hand was on my shoulder, or George Bush came to my office to watch the evening news. Ike was a presence in my White House years because he was a presence in my youth.

I knew him as a boy who had shared my upbringing. As I had worked at the *Abilene Reflector-Chronicle*, so had Ike gone to the *Reflector* editor Charlie Harger and asked for help. As I had planted tulips in the gardens around this museum, so had Ike helped his mother in her garden only a few feet away. As I had spent my summers in the wheat harvests of my father, so had Ike worked a harvest, at least enough to know the rural life. I'm not sure either of us liked it very much, but we learned a lot about ourselves.

The agriculture of Dickinson County, and the work ethic of our people, provided lessons of perseverance and endurance that helped Ike, that helped me, and will help you. For you are the inheritors of his life, just as he inherited the wisdom of your grandfathers and generations before.

It is our great blessing, from the youngest to the oldest among us, to know that our values and our wisdom can take us as far as we reach. We know that because Dwight David Eisenhower showed us it was so.

The Podium

MARCH 2, 1987 – July 11, 2007. The historic podium placed in the White House Press Briefing Room on March 2, 1987, was used by four Presidents and eleven Presidential Press Secretaries over the next nineteen years to announce and discuss the major activities and decisions of the Federal Government.

It was designed and built under the direction of Marlin Fitzwater, when he became Assistant to the President and Press Secretary to President Ronald Reagan in 1987. It was built by White House carpenters working in the basement of the Old Executive Office Building, as it was called at the time, and placed in the West Wing's Press Briefing Room, now named the Brady Press Room.

Marlin Fitzwater recalls his first press briefing for President Ronald Reagan on February 2, 1987:

> I walked to the podium in the Press Briefing Room, a legendary facility built on top of the indoor swimming pool most famously used by President John F. Kennedy. There had been many jokes over the years about angry Presidents dropping the press corps into the pool. But my fears that day were far greater: the sight of nearly fifty correspondents ready to pounce on every word.
>
> I had not given a second thought to the podium that awaited me. It was thin and mostly glass, with a reading platform at a fairly steep angle, suitable for reading statements and allowing direct eye contact with the many television cameras in the back of the room. It was the working podium for the Press Secretary's daily briefing.
>
> The President had his own podium, with blue velvet around the top, and the Presidential Seal stationed in the front for maximum exposure. When the President came to the Briefing Room, his podium was installed in front of a traditional blue backdrop with White House logo hanging prominently on the curtain. Press Secretaries, over the years, had used a variety of podiums according to their choosing, but without a Presidential Seal or any

special designation. At some point, my predecessor had opted for an all-glass version with a steep reading stand.

On my first day, I carried a manila folder filled with notes on the news subjects of the day, a couple of brief statements to read about the economy, and numerous pieces of "guidance" provided by the State and Defense Departments on news of the day. Add some memos and notes from my staff on issues of interest to the press, and presumably, I was ready.

As I placed the folder on the podium, I noticed the steepness of the glass, and I ran my finger along the bottom edge to measure the depth of the rail. It would catch the folder, but it might not be deep enough to catch the full depth of the papers. I kept my left hand on the folder.

Fortunately, the first day's briefing went well, but I returned to my office worried about my briefing papers, primarily how I would remember their contents. Most frightening was the realization that I could never pause in the middle of a briefing to actually read anything in the folder. The folder was like a security blanket, perhaps with dates or words I could reference in a second, but any lengthy reference would elicit ridicule from reporters. Most definitely, I could not be worrying about the folder falling on the floor.

The second day's briefing started smoothly, as I read the President's schedule for the day. Then I called on Helen Thomas, dean of the press corps by virtue of age and position, chief correspondent for the wire service, United Press International. Helen was a legend for having been in the front row for at least thirty years, usually wearing a red dress, and always armed with tough questions. She asked about a Presidential remark of the previous day. I knew I had a copy of the statement in my folder, and I released my tenuous finger clamp on the folder. The papers started sliding. I grabbed for them. Too late. At least a dozen pages floated to the floor, amid much laughter. The rookie had made his first mistake, roughly equivalent to a sight gag. Nothing damaging, but having to pick up papers off the floor was certainly

embarrassing. I collected the papers myself, continued the briefing, and ended with only the slightest evidence of sweat on my
lips.

When Helen ended the briefing by saying thank you, as was
tradition, I turned from the podium and went directly to my office, just steps from the Oval. My thought, *I can't suffer this kind
of embarrassment again.* And I began to think how I could replace
the podium. I made a quick sketch of a flat-topped podium with
high sides. My requirements were a large flat surface to hold the
papers, high rails to keep the press from seeing the notes, a flat
front to hide my shaking knees and wrinkled pants, and most
importantly a sturdy round-top rail that I could grab tightly during moments of anguish. Maybe a light and some kind of rollers
to allow quick removal when the President's podium replaced
mine. These were the design requirements I took to the White
House carpenters in the basement of the Old Executive Office
Building, as it was then called. They were legendary for building anything. And they promised the finished podium soon. I
checked their progress after a week, and the top was almost finished. But it still had a sloping angle for reading. I said no. It had
to be flat enough that any stack of papers would not slide off. No
problem they said.

I grabbed those railings many times over the next six years,
defending President Reagan during the Iran-Contra investigations, summit meetings with Soviet leader Mikhail Gorbachev
and the end of the Cold War, and Mrs. Reagan's breast cancer surgery. During the administration of President George H. W. Bush
(41), we announced at this podium the beginning of the war to
liberate Kuwait, the beginning of the invasion of Panama, the in-
troduction of the Americans with Disabilities Act, Amendments
to the Clean Air Act, and the Civil Rights Act.

President Bush 41 preferred to conduct full-length press conferences in the Briefing Room, and used this podium for many of
them. He often gave press briefings on a moment's notice, simply
saying it was time to talk with the press, and he would walk from
the Oval Office to the Briefing Room. We often had to ask him

to wait a few minutes until the press had left their desks, notified their editors and producers, and arrived in their seats.

President Reagan sometimes used this podium in the Briefing Room if he had stacks of papers, or on one occasion, a complete copy of the Federal budget. He often took the leadership of Congress to the Briefing Room to announce agreements, and this podium allowed four or five members of Congress to gather their papers comfortably.

President William J. Clinton and President George W. Bush (43), and their press secretaries, also used this podium. Both Presidents enjoyed casual relationships with the press and would use this podium for its informality, leaning on its railing and bantering with reporters. President Bush 43 and Ari Fleischer reassured America from this podium after the 9-11 terrorist attack on the Twin Towers in New York City.

In addition, seven Supreme Court nominees were introduced to America by four Presidents at this podium, including Justices Kennedy, Souter, Thomas, Alito, Roberts, Breyer, and Ginsburg. Sometimes they were introduced in the Rose Garden or a more formal setting, then subsequent appearances would be in the Briefing Room. The podium was placed in the Press Briefing Room in March of 1987, and it served eleven press secretaries on a daily basis until it was replaced on July 11, 2007. Marlin Fitzwater was the first and Tony Snow was the last. It was replaced during remodeling of the Briefing Room in 2007 to accommodate electronic updates, computer connections, video screens, and other communications equipment.

President Bush 41 used the podium so often that he developed a personal connection to it, and he requested that the podium be placed in the Bush Presidential Library/Museum at Texas A&M University, College Station, Texas.

Presidents and Press Secretaries who used the podium include:

Ronald Reagan: Marlin Fitzwater
George Herbert Walker Bush: Marlin Fitzwater
William Jefferson Clinton: George Stephanopoulos;

Dee Dee Myers; Michael McCurry; Joseph Lockhart;
Jake Siewert
George W. Bush: Ari Fleischer, Scott McClellan; Tony Snow

For another nine years after the podium was removed, it seemed to disappear. But in 2002, the Marlin Fitzwater Center for Communication was established in Franklin Pierce University, New Hampshire, and Press Secretary Fitzwater remembered his old podium:

> I suggested to former President Bush 41 it would be great to have my old podium in the new Fitzwater Center. Surprisingly, he responded, "I asked for the podium several years ago to be placed in the Bush Presidential Library, but now I don't know where it is."
>
> At that point, my remarkable search began. I too would like this historic podium to be rescued from obscurity and placed in the Bush Library. By coincidence, I was invited to a luncheon by the White House Historical Association, so I asked if they could help me find the podium, perhaps at one of the other Presidential libraries. A general inquiry was made and most libraries responded that they did not have the podium.
>
> But then a response came from the George W. Bush (43) Library including a photo of several podiums now stored in their Dallas warehouse. Incredibly, one of the pictures showed the former President standing at the podium, with a group of press secretaries. And I was in the group. It was clearly the "Fitzwater Podium."
>
> Enter my dear friend Nadine Smith, a businesswoman from Annapolis, and her son, Sam. I told my story of the podium to Nadine one evening after she and her firm, Bayside Bull Catering, had served my daughter's wedding. Sam was about to enter Southern Methodist University (SMU) as a freshman. One day she called to say, "Sam and I are at the Bush 43 Library at SMU in Dallas. President Bush and Laura are expected to join our tour. Can I ask them about the podium?"

"When?" I asked.

"In a few minutes," she said.

"No. Please don't," I said. "They know nothing about this. It could be embarrassing. Why don't you ask a staff person?"

"OK," she said, and hung up.

An hour later, she called back to say that she didn't speak to the President, but she did ask a docent about the podium. "He referred me to a library staff member, who told me to file a Freedom of Information request. He said it would take two weeks to get an answer."

"So what did you do?" I asked.

I immediately filed a request. Got some paper, wrote it down, and submitted it on the spot," she said.

My reaction was shock. Now we had started a legal process. But the next day, Nadine called me again from SMU to say, "The Library called to say they don't have the podium, and they would like to clear up the FOI tomorrow."

"How could that be?" I wondered. "They sent in a picture. I saw it." After some thought, I advised Nadine to drop the whole matter, and I decided to pursue the issue from a different angle in Washington.

The next day I called my dear friend Dana Perino, who was President Bush 43's last press secretary, and I asked if she remembered the reason for replacing the podium in 2007. She thought a new podium was constructed to accommodate the renovations of the entire Briefing Room in 2007, and she referred me to the White House Communications Agency (WHCA) that had designed the facility with TV screens, computer terminals, and other modern electronics.

When I reached Scott Sforza at WHCA, he confirmed that the podium had been replaced, and in fact, he knew exactly where it was located: in the WHCA storage facility in Washington. Furthermore, he had recently arranged for the podium to be used for a few days by a special events group. Indeed, he said, it's now being used to fill up newly renovated space in the Eisenhower Office Building near the White House.

I was excited and asked if I could see the podium. I also mentioned that I felt the podium had historical value, and I would like to see it preserved in the President Bush 41 Library and Museum. There was simply no accounting for the photo of the podium we received earlier from the Bush 43 Library. My guess is that because the podium was last used in the press office of the Bush 43 Administration, it was somehow identified as being located in the Bush 43 Library. Perhaps someone in that library answered the earlier request for information by simply sending a picture of the podium with President Bush 43 and several press secretaries, all standing at the podium. In any case, the mystery was now solved.

Except for at least one more twist: The WHCA called to say they couldn't arrange a visit to the podium. At the same time, they called the Chief of Staff to former President George H.W. Bush, Jean Becker, to suggest that further discussion about the podium should go to Valerie Jarrett, Senior Advisor to President Barrack Obama.

I am now sending a letter about the podium to the White House Historical Association, for forwarding to Ms. Jarrett, hopeful that she can rescue the podium for the preservation of history in the George H.W. Bush Library/Museum.

Ms. Becker was not particularly eager to raise this matter with Ms. Jarrett, who was reported in the press to be "crony without portfolio" to President Obama, an aide who could dip into any issue, from the nuclear weapons treaty with Iran to the guest list for White House social functions. Her mystery and access are two qualities that scare bureaucracies to death. So I suggested we enlist the help of the president of the White House Historical Association, Stewart McLaurin, who might have a legitimate avenue of access to Ms. Jarrett.

By coincidence, I was invited to a luncheon by the association at their Decatur House headquarters just across Pennsylvania Avenue from the White House. The purpose was to present their annual journalism scholarship in honor of journalist and former president of the Historical Association, Hugh Sidey. Sidey was for decades a premier writer for *Time* magazine, and had become a close friend of President George H.W. Bush (41). Mr. McLaurin asked me to say a few words about the Sidey legacy. I agreed and took the opportunity to ask Stewart if he would write a letter to Valerie Jarrett, informing her of the historical nature of the now essentially discarded podium, and asking if she would approve a transfer of the podium to the Bush Library and Museum in College Station, Texas. He agreed, by now becoming intrigued by the mysterious nature of my quest for the podium, and by its nearly twenty-year history.

I wrote a brief history of the podium, and Stewart sent it with his letter to Ms. Jarrett on November 2, 2015. No response was ever received.

I made the same request of Joe Hagin, Deputy Chief of Staff in the Donald Trump White House. Joe has worked in three administrations, George H.W. Bush, George W. Bush, and President Trump. He makes the trains run on time—administrative stuff for the Chief of Staff.

I thought sure he would rescue the podium from the storage rooms of the WHCA. But sadly, I never heard from him.

Then a friend, Theresa Burch, who does volunteer travel advance for the Trump White House, suggested she could help. She located the podium and talked to the WHCA people about gifting the podium. They agreed. But it hasn't happened yet. I'm still hopeful.

The Last Jump

JUNE 14, 2014, Sleepy Hollow, New York. Melinda and I visited Walker's Point on June 12, 2014, for the President's last parachute jump. Confined to a wheelchair, the President planned his last jump to be on his ninetieth birthday. We went to witness the event with the Bush Family and friends. I recorded the event, which is the last story I wrote in my old diaries.

We stayed at the Nonantum Inn on Ocean Avenue, where I stayed every August from 1989 to 1992 as Press Secretary to President Bush. I loved the place. Now, twenty-two years later, it is still the same hotel, modernized as required and offering stunning views of the ocean, Kennebunkport harbor, and a winding row of lobster boats at buoys in the middle of the Kennebec River. In 1990–91, I lay awake in this hotel with the moon casting shadows across these boats. They seemed so peaceful then, as our warships steamed across the Persian Gulf to enforce the blockade of oil and arms to Iraq. Two decades later, Operation Desert Storm is long over. But it's the same water. The same moon. The same Nonantum.

On the morning of our first day here in 2014, President Bush sends out a Tweet to all Library Board members. It reads: "Looks like a great day for a parachute."

Not to me. The whole day has been overcast and threatening rain. I thought you needed a clear day for a parachute jump. But it turns out you can jump under the clouds, if it's not windy. Wind is the most threatening factor because it will blow the chute. So I went to bed last night thinking the rumored jump will never occur on Friday morning, no matter how excited the President gets about the jump. The Army Knights won't allow it.

The next morning we were told: The jump is on. Be at St. Ann's Episcopal Church at 9:15 a.m. The minute the sky clears, or the wind is right, he's jumping in a tandem with Army Sergeant Mike Elliott, who he has jumped with before. Most likely, between 10:30 a.m. and noon.

Betsy Hemingway, Mrs. Bush's best friend, who lives across the inlet from Walker's Point, invited us to park in her driveway and walk the short distance to St. Ann's Church. We pulled in at 9:15 a.m., and Betsy had already left for the church. She was checking guests off at the gate. The Bush staff and friends had long ago learned to put guest lists together on a moment's notice. Send out email blasts to several hundred people, and work with the Secret Service and local police to set up checkpoints and account for every guest. Except for the crashers.

We were among the first to arrive, walking up the church drive to the landing zone, already marked on the lawn. It seemed awfully small, maybe fifty yards across. And if the jumpers missed, it would be "on the rocks." And the Maine rocks around the church look as threatening as the clouds. At 9:30 a.m. it was still dark and cloudy, but no wind.

Suddenly a helicopter dropped out of the clouds directly overhead, perhaps a couple thousand feet high. It hovered, a dot in the sky. And out dropped two jumpers. Their chutes deployed. Colored streams of smoke were released to check the wind direction. It was a test jump. The Army Black Knights floated straight down, all business, and landed within seconds right in front of us, on the target marked on the lawn. They hit the ground running, grabbed their chutes, and never stumbled a bit. Two perfect landings. (But I wondered how you land in tandem if one person can't walk).

The next jump would be the President. And suddenly three new jumpers appeared. Our crowd on the ground had grown to perhaps two hundred. Mrs. Bush arrived, her white hair shining in the crowd. Then former President George W. Bush, the other President, and his wife, Laura, appeared with Mrs. Bush. Several people asked for autographs; 43 enjoyed that. But everyone's eyes were glued to the sky.

President Bush's degenerative Parkinson's disease was taking over his body. I went to Walker's Point three years ago and his body was just starting to degenerate. He was using a cane for walking but had trouble climbing stairs to his office. We talked about my stage play, *Empires Fall*. We, Bob Lawson and I, showed him a miniature mockup of the stage set. He was intrigued. He asked some questions, and he asked if we wanted to say hello to his son, President Bush 43, George W. He was there for a summer vacation. We took some pictures of the two Bush boys standing together.

Now, on 41's ninetieth birthday, he was virtually confined to a wheelchair. His legs couldn't hold him up. His arms were OK. He could talk, but not often. Yet he wanted to jump.

As we watched, two army parachuters jumped from the helicopter, one with a camera, one for emergencies. They hovered below the chopper, circling in the wind, as if tied to the sky.

Then the President appeared in the door. Sergeant Elliott was tethered to his body, and holding him outside the chopper. Then Elliott stepped out with the President and they started down. I gasped. For a moment, the President's legs dangled in the air. I realized how helpless he was. Then, somehow, he seemed to get control, and we could see four legs hanging straight down. The chute string was pulled and the chute opened. They were floating. They seemed to be maneuvering the chute. First they floated sideways, then in a circle, then across the sky above us. It looked like they were having fun, viewing the crowd below. At a few hundred feet, they started to circle and level off. They came around us, circled back into the wind, then down very fast. They were right above us, and I feared they were coming into the crowd. But then they turned, and came into the target faster than the individual jumpers did. At the last second, Elliott rolled. He and the President landed on their shoulders. They rolled enough so that the President's face was up. His legs were straight out behind him. It was clear he was all right. Two Knights rushed over to them, unhooked the harness, and removed the President's helmet. He was smiling broadly. He raised his thumb. Mrs. Bush and George W. rushed out. Barbara gave him a kiss, and the crowd asked for a second kiss. 41 and 43 shook hands. And the President was lifted into his wheelchair.

I saw the President at dinner that night at Earth restaurant. He smiled broadly when he saw me, and we shook hands. I said, "Mr. President, you should see 'the overnights' on this event." In the White House, twenty-five years ago, he would start many days by asking, "How are the overnights, Marlin?"

"Great," I would say.

This was probably our last exchange about the overnights, ever. And my last diary entry.

Doctor Fitzwater, I Presume

REMARKS BY MARLIN FITZWATER, former Press Secretary to President Ronald Reagan and President George H. W. Bush, receiving his honorary doctorate in philosophy, Bramlage Coliseum, Kansas State University, Manhattan, Kansas, December 11, 2015.

Good afternoon, distinguished graduates and fellow K-Staters. I am delighted to be here. Thank you, President Schulz; Member of the Board of Regents, Joe Bain; Provost, April Mason; Dean of the Graduate School, Carol Shanklin; Dean of Arts and Sciences, Peter Dorhout; Dean of University Libraries, Lori Goetsch; other distinguished guests, faculty, parents, and friends.

I am honored to speak at your commencement exercises this afternoon. Congratulations on this singular achievement. If getting your bachelors degree was turning a corner in life, this must surely be setting a new course. I can feel you pulling the reins already, fearful that I might hold up your progress, or at worst, suggest some nutty change in your aspirations. I will try not to do either.

I am also very excited about receiving an honorary doctorate from Kansas State University. President Ronald Reagan, who some people thought was just a grade-B actor, once gave a commencement address at his alma mater. And he was awarded an honorary doctorate degree. President Reagan, who had a great sense of humor, responded that a lot of people thought his first degree was honorary.

My Spanish teacher may have felt that way at the time. But I was extremely proud of my first degree, and I am just as proud of this one. It validates my life's work. And I am enormously grateful to the leadership of this great university, and to all of you who are receiving graduate degrees today, because I know what you can only begin to suspect: that Kansas State University has given you a great education, a mountain of opportunities, and memories that will last forever.

I have all the usual stories about growing up on a farm near Abilene, Kansas, without running water or indoor plumbing. But I will focus instead on one of my first days at Kansas State University in 1960, more than a half-century ago. I walked into a little basement apartment on Bertrand Street, about four blocks from Goodnow Hall, that cost twenty-five dollars a month. I was scared and lonely. So I walked over to Farrell Library, sat down in this huge reading room, with a high ceiling and massive windows, examined the many students around me, and knew I had a sanctuary. Fifty-five years later, it's named Hale Library, and my personal papers from a lifetime of books and writing and White House experiences have been given sanctuary, again, in this beautiful library. Not since lunch with the Queen in Buckingham Palace have I known such an impressive building. And I take this public opportunity to say, "Thank you, Kansas State University, for this wonderful contribution to my life."

In preparing my remarks today, I went back and read some of the more famous commencement speeches of the recent past. Matthew McConaughey, the actor, said, "Life is not fair." Steve Jobs, the founder of Apple Computers, said, "Stay hungry and stay foolish." Those are all good pieces of advice, but put me down as slightly more optimistic, perhaps more practical, and more confident about the future. I say: "Don't be afraid to use your degree. Let your knowledge give you the courage to lead. And leadership with hard work will give you rewards."

I recall my first reporting class in K-State's Kedzie Hall, where I heard the story of a professor who waited until all his students were settled into their seats, then he lumbered into the room to begin his lecture. He faced the class and said these words: "Accuracy, Accuracy, Accuracy—and the greatest of these is Accuracy." Then he turned and walked out of the room. He knew his moment.

It was a story I never forgot. Not so much for the words, but for the focus and discipline and sense of purpose. Five years later I took my degree, with three hundred dollars and a cardboard suitcase that now resides in the Special Collections unit at Hale Library, and drove to Washington, DC. So began the great journey of my life.

And although my mother said I would run off the edge of the earth just north of Chicago, I had no doubts. I had the degree. I had the purpose. I wanted to be in journalism. And I had the courage to make the effort. You have all those qualities too, or you wouldn't be here today.

I went through a number of jobs in Washington, mostly in government. But one thing I learned is that very seldom does the tooth fairy pick you up and move you to the head of the line. You have to earn it, maybe toot your own horn, and probably spend some restless nights. But the opportunities for success in America are still there. Take them one small step at a time, and remember, you've got the time.

In 1987, Mikhail Gorbachev, communist leader of the Soviet Union, our Cold War nemesis, came to the United States for a Summit Meeting with President Reagan to discuss the arms race, nuclear weapons, and future relations. I was the President's Press Secretary at the time, and it was my job to brief the more than seven thousand journalists from around the world who had gathered for this meeting. I moved the White House Briefing Room to the ballroom of the Marriott Hotel, and invited my Soviet Counterpart, Gennady Gerasimov, to join me in daily press briefings before and during the Summit meetings. Gennady was a tall handsome fellow who spoke perfect English. The briefings were carried on television networks around the world. Gerasimov and I got along fine. Gorbachev and Reagan became friends and broke new ground in the quest to end the arms race and the Cold War.

Afterward, *Time* magazine reported that the Summit went well. But who would have guessed that the Soviet spokesman would look like Gary Grant, and the American spokesman would look like Nikita Khrushchev. I was reminded that looks seldom really matter. But substance does. Let your knowledge and the education you earned here give you the courage to lead.

When Saddam Hussein invaded the country of Kuwait on August 1, 1990, I was in Kansas. I flew to Aspen, Colorado, to meet President Bush 41 and the Prime Minister of Great Britain, Margaret Thatcher, who were there to give a speech. By January 17, 1991, we were ready to drive Saddam Hussein out of Kuwait as directed by a United Nations resolution.

The plan was for me to announce that Operation Desert Storm had started about 7:00 p.m., the coalition aircraft had struck at Baghdad, and for the first time in history, the attacks were shown live on television. At 9:00 the President would speak to the nation in a live broadcast from the White House. That afternoon I went to the Roosevelt Room, just across the hall from my office, and I sat at the huge conference table in front of the Nobel Peace Prize won by Teddy Roosevelt* in 1906. I wanted to write one or two sentences that would wrap up the situation and alert America to the President's speech that evening.

I looked at the Nobel Prize for inspiration. I thought about my parents, and my friends from Kansas. And I thought about that K-State professor saying, "Accuracy, Accuracy, Accuracy." And I realized that my sentence should be about purpose, about focus, about one sentence that would resonate with every American in a positive way. Finally, I wrote this simple statement: "The liberation of Kuwait has begun." It was recorded around the world.

I tell this story because I have always felt there is something in the values of Kansas that are extraordinary in America. I think they come from the earth. As a farm boy, I spent a lot of time thinking about how things grow, about my neighbors and their many kindnesses, about my parents and their love of country. And about my university, here at Kansas State, and about teacher after teacher who stood up for me in some way, and then gave me their greatest gift, an education.

As I was leaving the White House in 1992, the toughest and most committed reporter I ever knew, Helen Thomas, asked me a question. Helen was famous all over the world as the dean of the White House press corps. She asked if I had any parting words for the press. I said yes, "Be Kind."

And I say to you this afternoon, the future is brighter in America than it may seem. We still have the heart and soul for great adventures. We still have the freedom to pursue every dream. So let the journey begin. And "Be Kind." Thank you very much.

*Roosevelt helped negotiate peace in the Russo-Japanese War in 1904–05, and was awarded the Nobel Peace Prize in 1906.

Honoring President Reagan

February 6, 2016
Ronald Reagan's 105th Birthday
Reagan Presidential Library, Simi Valley, California
Graveside Remarks Honoring President Ronald Reagan

STANDING IN THE glowing dusk of a southern California shopping center in 1984, as President Reagan was ending the last appearance of his campaign, he was talking about how much he loved America. And he began to tell the story of a French mother during the liberation of Paris at the end of World War II. And the President's voice began to change. It grew strong and yet quiet, as he described a mother who had endured years of untold hardship. And then his voice became her voice, and she told of the liberation, and the young American soldier who appeared at her doorway to ask about her safety and welfare. She thanked America, and she thanked the American soldier.

"He was a big strappin' boy," she said. "I don't remember his name, but he came from a place called I-O-Way." And as the crowd teared up, and roared its approval at the same time, the President's Chief of Staff, James Baker, turned to me and said, "No other President could ever do that."

And if you think he could tell stories, you should have heard Ronald Reagan speak of his love of country, his appreciation for historic leadership in America, our Christian heritage, our concern and respect for women's rights, our belief in the rule of law, our interest in promoting freedom around the world, and the basic goodness of the American people. Ronald Reagan believed in all these values, and he spoke of them often. They were the bedrocks of his trust and confidence in America.

In perhaps the most decisive and crucial period of his public life, the Summit meetings with Mikhail Gorbachev in the last two years of his presidency, President Reagan again spoke of values.

I would like to focus briefly on just three days in President Reagan's life. They are May 29–31, 1988, in Moscow. I had been with

President Reagan during many of the most memorable moments of his presidency: the fortieth anniversary of D-Day in Normandy, at the Brandenburg Gate when he told Mr. Gorbachev to "tear down this Wall," in the Oval Office during so many late afternoons when he would write letters to friends, and so many other historic times. But my memories are strongest of those three days in May of 1988, when President Reagan went to Moscow, determined to speak to the Soviet people about freedom and life in America and the opportunities that could be theirs.

On the first day, our staff gathered in the lobby of the American Embassy residence to greet the President and Mrs. Reagan. The President had told our staff many times that he wanted to meet the Soviet people, and he wanted to do it now. Now, when the citizens of Moscow were all around him, just a few steps away, in a public square, and in huge apartment buildings within shouting distance. But the KGB and the Secret Service said they were skeptical about whether or not they could protect the President. Our advance team had no plan. The Secret Service was reluctant. But finally the Service was asked, can you protect us or not? Yes or no? The answer was yes. And the response from the Reagans was: we go, in fifteen minutes.

Bodies were flying out of that room like doves in a cornfield. We all rushed to mobilize our respective constituencies—the press, the Secret Service agents, the Embassy staff, the Soviet government, the local police. And moments later the President and Mrs. Reagan walked out the door and headed down the street to the Arbat shopping area. Street artists and vendor carts were in the square. People were strolling with children and baby carriages. The President of the United States and his wife walked into the middle of this crowd and started shaking hands.

Almost immediately, people started shouting, "Reagan, Reagan." I looked up to the eight- or ten-story apartments around us. Faces were in every window. Then I looked to the doors, and people were streaming out and running toward the President. I looked for the President and couldn't find him in the crowd. Then suddenly he appeared, standing on a vendor's cart. Smiling with enthusiasm and speaking to the people of the Soviet Union. This is what he came for.

He brought them greetings from the people of America. And suddenly it was a crowd of thousands, laughing, shouting, waving, and holding their babies high to see this American leader.

President Reagan had several more messages to deliver in the succeeding hours. He had built a mosaic of public events over the next three days to tell America's story. They started with a reception at the Embassy residence for more than ninety human rights advocates, dissidents, and refusniks who had been persecuted or jailed for their beliefs. President Reagan would add his voice to those who were speaking out. Perhaps never before had such a group gathered with an American President.

"If I may," he told the Soviet dissidents, "I'd like to share with you the main aims of our human rights agenda."

He had just demonstrated one in the Arbat, the freedom of assembly.

And in the Danilov Monastery, in a country that was officially atheist, he spoke of the freedom of religion:

> I'm hopeful the Soviet Government will permit all the peoples of the Soviet Union to worship their creator as they themselves see fit, in liberty.

He spoke of freedom of speech:

> It is my fervent hope for you and your country that there will soon come a day when no one need fear prison for offenses that involve nothing more than the spoken or written word.

Freedom to keep the fruits of one's own labor. Freedom of travel. He said:

> We hope that one freedom will lead to another and another; that the Soviet Government will understand that it is the individual who is always the source of economic creativity, the inquiring mind that produces a technical

breakthrough, the imagination that conceives of new products and markets; and that in order for the individual to create, he must have a sense of just that—his own individuality, his own self-worth. He must sense that others respect him and, yes, that his nation respects him—respects him enough to grant him all his human rights. This is our hope.

Then, the next day, President Reagan faced the challenge of presenting his ideas to youth, to the students of Moscow State University. And when I first walked in the hall, I saw that the Soviets had planned a special welcome for our President. His podium was placed squarely at the foot of a twenty-foot statue and bust of Vladimir Lenin, founder of the Russian Communist Party.

I was nervous, but delighted. Because I knew that Ronald Reagan would appreciate the special ironies presented by this location. Mr. Lenin, for more than an hour, would have to stare at the backside of perhaps the greatest political communicator in modern history. And our President was ready.

I give you one paragraph from that great speech:

But freedom is more even than this. Freedom is the right to question and change the established way of doing things. It is the continuing revolution of the marketplace. It is the understanding that allows us to recognize shortcomings and seek solutions. It is the right to put forth an idea, scoffed at by the experts, and watch it catch fire among the people. It is the right to dream—to follow your dream or stick to your conscience, even if you're the only one in a sea of doubters.

After the last working meeting of the Summit, President Reagan and Chairman Gorbachev agreed to a walk in Red Square, no doubt in front of Lenin's tomb, and most assuredly in front of the world. The television cameras were set, and Ronald Reagan knew exactly what he wanted to say.

He had only one message to deliver: The world is changing; I no longer believe the Soviet Union is the evil empire. He had been framing this message in his mind for some time. As he spoke to Soviet citizens in the Arbat, Christians in the monastery, Soviet students in the university, dissidents in the reception, and Mr. Gorbachev himself, he knew this was the time and place. And he did it.

There is a picture of a young blond male KGB agent in those groups of people in Red Square, and it looks like Vladimir Putin. He denies it. But I think it does symbolize the idea that uncertainty always lurks in the background. And Russia has changed much in the last twenty-five years. But Ronald Reagan's words remain strong and true, and I believe they will guide America's beliefs forever.

President Ronald Reagan always had a sense of timing that would catch the crest of history. And he did it with a strong and gentle voice that was always civil. He seldom condemned his critics. He always conducted himself as President of all the people.

When he sought to console the youth of America after the death of our astronauts on the Challenger space shuttle in 1986, he said: "I want to talk to our school children The future doesn't belong to the fainthearted; it belongs to the brave."

President Ronald Reagan lived among the brave, and he always will.

Thank you very much.

PART VI

—A SOFT LANDING—
FROM FACT TO FICTION

Introduction to Part Six

SOME PEOPLE TURN to gardening in retirement; I turned to fiction. My first fiction story was written in college. It was about a girlfriend and the pain of rejection. It was terrible, of course, and you will never see it. But I have written many stories over the years. In this section are just three.

Most short stories are reality-based, or at least they're sparked by personal happenings in the life of the writer. And sometimes they end up in faraway places. But they are all great fun, at least for this writer.

The Bug Man is about military regulations. *Too Old for Ice Cream* is about whether we can keep up when we're getting old. And *The Flamingo Line Dancer* is about living with that reality. We winter in Florida at a place called The Villages, where line dancing is a rejuvenating force. There is live music every night in the town square. And we go often.

The Bug Man

Art Hughes never really enjoyed squashing the entrails out of hard-shelled beetles, but as an alternative to fusing napalm bombs, it had its merits.

Art, originally trained as a weapons specialist, had been searching for a more human mission on the aerospace team ever since his June arrival in Vietnam. His discovery was Roads and Grounds, that section of the Air Force dedicated to maintaining a disciplinary image of Do Dat AFB by constantly cutting the grass.

No one actually knew the corollary between short grass and discipline, except that, to an enlisted man, a lawnmower evokes the same hatred as a shoeshine brush and a mouthful of spit. Art was never a great spitter, and the non-gloss on his shoes mirrored his attitude much better than it did his face. Nevertheless, Roads and Grounds did possess a singular attraction—in that its members could usually be found in the NCO club or asleep in the bunkers.

It was on page 1076 of the Roads and Grounds' *Job Classification Manual* that Art discovered the two-paragraph section entitled, "Insect Diagnosis." It read in part:

> It will be the responsibility of the Insect Diagnosis Specialist to investigate the presence, proper or improper, of all insects (see page 1077 for list of 346 insects common to Air Force barracks) not directly related to the Air Force mission, and to determine the appropriate corrective measures with regard to repellent, removal or destruction.

There was no listing of those insects directly related to the Air Force mission, but Art supposed they were named in some top secret document, probably connected with the germ warfare program. In any case, the training period for an Insect Diagnosis Specialist was only three days, to be spent in the jungle of the applicant's choice. Art signed up.

He was the first volunteer in seventeen years. His recruitment soon became cause for celebration in personnel circles. It had been difficult to find recruits who could approach the job, or who were not opposed to killing bugs on moral grounds. So the job had been vacant for seventeen years.

One boy, an atheistic Boston surgeon, had been recruited during that period. But his first day on the job, a giant land crab bit his scalpel finger. He not only asked for a transfer but also attempted to sue the Air Force for destroying his ability to perform surgery. He settled out of court for a three-day pass. But after that, the Air Force became very apprehensive about bug-man recruiting.

Art spent considerable time decorating his office. Immediately over his desk hung a ten-by-twelve inch drawing depicting two marines swatting giant mosquitoes in the Mekong Delta. Under the drawing, Art hung a bronze plaque engraved with the words, IF THIS IS YOU—BUG ME. Art won an award from the Public Information Office for best promotional effort on base. The award hung next to the drawing.

He also had a special red phone installed with a direct line to the flight line control office. The Bug Line had only been used once—a wrong number, by an airman second class trying to call a friend at the NCO club.

It wasn't until near the end of the day, August 31, 1969, that the Bug Line was first seriously used.

"Insect Diagnosis," Art said nervously into the receiver, "Sergeant Hughes here."

"This is Major Snake," the voice said, "one of our pilots has reported a large red-and-green bug crawling under his ejection seat. Get out here fast and take care of it."

"Yes, Sir," Art replied as he speculated on the major's name, "I'll be right there."

He slammed the receiver down, grabbed his magnifying glass, his eight-inch goose feather, and his flashlight, and headed for the flight line. Major Snake met him with a staff car and motioned him in.

Four F-100 fighter-bombers were lined across the end of the runway, their engines running, their open canopies exposing the white-helmeted pilots. Ground crews scampered nervously about the planes, fearing a long idling period which would necessitate refueling.

Three men with shoulder bronze stood directly below the cockpit of aircraft 731 and were shouting at the paralyzed pilot above them.

The pilot of 731 was none other than Wing Commander General Emil Gung-ho, a Korean War ace of Chinese descent who had risen through the ranks by virtue of his inscrutability. Whenever asked a question, Emil would frown, his eyes closing into narrow slits, with the answer remaining forever within the recesses of his mind.

It soon became widely accepted that Emil's refusal to answer questions was based on a pompously superior intellect. Thus, to avoid the embarrassment of having a higher ranking officer ask Emil a stupid question and receive no answer, Emil was rapidly promoted to the highest rank of all.

Emil had suffered only two traumatic experiences in his life. One was a black widow spider bite at age thirteen. The other was an ejection seat failure after his airplane was hit by sniper fire over Saigon. He survived both calamities. But the basic fears of both events remained with him, focusing sharply as the red-and-green bug crawled under the ejection seat.

A ladder was placed on the aircraft, and Art climbed cautiously to within a few inches of the controls. Emil pointed toward his feet. Art could see nothing in the cramped lower cockpit, so he asked for his flashlight. Still, he could see nothing. A careful probing with the goose feather also yielded no results. The only answer was to abort the mission.

Art ordered the engines of all four planes shut down and demanded complete quiet from all observers. The officers below grumbled about taking orders from a sergeant, but Emil's approving glance forced them to maintain silence.

The bug first appeared nearly ten minutes later. Its long yellow legs resting on the edge of Emil's left shoe. Art spotted it instantly and recognized it as the rare but deadly angora spider, which could kill a human in thirty seconds.

Unfortunately, the angora was also the number one weapon in the Air Force's arsenal of "Insect Viet Cong Killers," an elite group formed in 1950 by General Citrus LaDay and trained in fifteen-gallon milk cans by the most famous insect trainers in America. They had been written about in *Sports Illustrated* and *Playboy*.

Furthermore, it was against Air Force regulations to kill or otherwise harm the angora spider weapon. For the first time in his career, Art would have to consult his superiors in Washington.

After two wrong numbers and a busy signal, Art was put through to a Civilian Classification Clerk in the basement of the Pentagon. The CCC reported that the Pentagon's number-one bug specialist was temporarily assigned to eradicate an ant farm in a wine cellar belonging to a member of the House Armed Services Committee. It would be at least two days before he could finish that job and be flown to Vietnam.

Art decided that the only answer was to use a temporary anesthetic spray develop by a prostitute in suburban Cleveland for controlling unruly house guests. The can had come from an elderly janitor who had discovered it one day while cleaning the WAF's barracks. The janitor died from overexertion shortly after that, but his last act was to give the can to a young weapons specialist who happened to be on the scene in Art's time of need.

The first cloud of spray went to Emil, who was so profoundly thankful that he swore to submit Art's name for the Congressional Medal of Honor. The second burst of spray numbed the spider in a matter of seconds.

It was Art's plan to lift the spider out of the cockpit with page thirty-one of Emil's aircraft control checklist. Unfortunately, when Art leaned over to slide the page under the angora, he knocked the flashlight from its perch. It landed directly on the angora, opening a large gash above the heart, from which it never recovered.

The days that followed were filled with considerable confusion. On the one hand, since Emil was a man true to his word, Art was up for the Congressional Medal of Honor. On the other hand, Art was due to face a court-martial—for destroying a secret weapon that had cost millions of dollars to perfect.

The puzzle was finally solved by giving Art a commission and immediate promotion. Major Art Hughes was then asked to resign his commission (to clear the Air Force's good name) in return for a civilian job as an insect scientist at the Los Alamos proving grounds.

He accepted.

Too Old for Ice Cream

Dɪᴄᴋ Wɪꜱᴇ ᴅʀᴏᴠᴇ into one of the two parking spaces for Nancy's ice cream store, located on the small town's main street, right beside the only grocery store in Parkers. He shut down the pickup truck's engine, which automatically switched off the air-conditioner system, and tugged at the door handle. It moved but didn't seem to hit the latch; at least the door stood firm. Dick pulled again, this time throwing his shoulder into the door, and it gave instantly. Dick surmised that he had opened the door so often during the fifteen years he owned the truck, and had leaned his weight on the window to leverage himself out so frequently, that the hinge had bent and now stuck the latch. He knew it would never be fixed.

According to a fast calculation he made more and more often as he reached his sixty-fifth birthday, if he lived ten more years the truck should last, and it would no doubt be his last truck, so why fix the door. As long as he could get out with a little tug or push, no harm done.

Dick thought about going to the ice cream store several times when he visited the nearby grocery store. It was a small ice cream store, with a stand-up counter only big enough for one customer to order through the flap window, and maybe two more customers to wait in line. Little stick-on notes with customer instructions, like "Oᴜᴛ ᴏꜰ Sᴛʀᴀᴡʙᴇʀʀʏ," made it difficult to see Nancy through the window. Dick wanted to see Nancy because he wondered what kind of person would want to stand behind a three-foot counter all day, shoulder to shoulder with an ice cream dispenser, and only a small overhead fan to keep her company. He imagined her stepping out the side door about three times a day and screaming for release.

She never did. In fact, Nancy loved her business. Indeed, that's how she came to it.

Nancy had been dating the previous owner for more than a year, when one night they began to argue about the quality of their sex. Milton, who owned the ice cream store, was something of an entrepreneur in Parkers; he also owned the laundry mat, gas station, and bait shop. His business plans for all these investments seemed the same: hire one manager/employee who could run the place all day long; then be the substitute for the employee on sick days and vacations. But he had a propensity to treat his businesses like trinkets to take on and off at will, simply selling them at his pleasure, and always seeming to find some other entrepreneur willing to take a chance on a business. Often these were unemployed people who liked to work alone, and who could find a bank to be a willing partner, as long as there was a building or ice cream machine available as collateral.

Nancy had been dating Milton for three years and knew him pretty well. She suspected he was never going to marry her, but she thought he might be vulnerable to other forms of entanglement. So as they continued to discuss their sexual situation one night, Nancy blurted out, "I'll give you the best sex you've ever had, if you'll give me the ice cream shop."

Milton instantly liked this idea because it excited him, and he appeared to be the judge of his own fate. No one else but him could determine the quality of the event. "You're on," he shouted enthusiastically.

"In writing," she shouted back.

This set him back for a moment, but then he agreed, taking a pen out of his shirt pocket and nervously writing in a small note pad he always carried for business purposes: IF NANCY'S SEX IS THE BEST EVER, I GIVE HER THE ICE CREAM SHOP.

"Sign and date," Nancy said.

Milton was helpless by this point. He laid down his pen and turned to Nancy to reap the reward. Nancy responded with the most aggressive behavior he had ever known, pushing him down on the couch, ripping the buttons off his shirt, and grabbing his belt, without being too careful what she touched. Before long, Milton gasped and collapsed. He was dead as a doornail, as they say in Parkers.

Nancy was appropriately shocked, and began screaming and crying, realizing that the game had gone far beyond her intentions. She called the police and the rescue squad, then ran to her neighbor's house for help.

A few obstacles stood in her way, but after it was established that no one could legally challenge Milton's unorthodox deal with

Nancy, she was set up to scoop ice cream into cake cones in less than a month.

After all the publicity around its closing and the scuffle over the business transfer, not many customers were visiting her newly reopened ice cream shop. Then Nancy had a marketing idea. She hung a bold new sign over the carry-out window that read: NANCY'S, THE BEST YOU'VE EVER HAD.

Dick West stretched to steal a look at Nancy. He had read the local paper's stories about how she offered Milton the best sex he ever had in exchange for the store. Dick remembered seeing her picture as she pleaded with the judge to grant her the ice cream shop. The reporter described the exotic details of her arrangement with Milton. Dick even remembered a picture of her holding the famous note. Under the picture ran the headline: HOW SWEET IT WAS!

Nancy came to the window, and Dick stammered for a second, then ordered. "A small chocolate cone," he said.

Nancy turned to the soft serve machine, placed a cake cone under the dispenser, and pulled the lever. Chocolate ice cream emerged.

"Wait," Dick said. "That's not what I want."

"You said chocolate," Nancy said.

"Yes, but I meant the white ice cream with a chocolate covering. Like I get at Dairy Queen."

"Oh," Nancy replied. "You mean the chocolate dip. Don't worry, I'll just set this aside."

She set the cone on the counter, presumably to eat herself, took another cake cone, and began filling it with vanilla ice cream. She then took the cone gingerly by the bottom and quickly dipped it into the chocolate sauce, without spilling a drop. She handed it through the flap.

"That will be three dollars," she said, "for the best you've ever had."

Dick's hand was shaking so badly he could hardly hold the cone.

The Flamingo Line Dancer

SHE IS TALL, thin, and angular like a pink flamingo. She unwinds her body when the music starts. And she is always aware of herself. They are walking through the town square on a lively summer night when the music is loud, hundreds of people are seated around the square, some in casual conversation, but most are simply enjoying the music. A small crowd of couples in shorts and T-shirts are dancing, some of them moving in and out of the dance in such random fashion that they cannot be counted. And then their eyes catch the one person not moving. She is posing for herself and waiting for that moment of self-recognition when she catches the right note and it lifts her into the sky. They cannot move until she releases them. And then she starts. Her ponytail swings around her shoulder as her head jerks sideways, her straight nose is slightly lifted, and she holds her head royally. Then her body is carried by the notes, and she begins her trademark twirl, when her long thin legs lift high under her short skirt and her body turns in sync with her arms. She turns like a ballerina. It is so graceful, few realize she is wearing drug store bath sandals, no jewelry, nothing to interrupt the eye as it follows her motion. Everyone sitting in the white plastic lawn chairs on her side of the square is glued to her moves. It is The Villages, after all, where all are looking back at middle age.

As the next song starts, she conducts with the water bottle in her right hand. Like a scepter in the hands of Rostropovich, the bottle guides the sweeping themes of the music. Sometimes she raises it over her head; the crescendo is coming, the crashing climax to a stanza. Then it goes down, and she is off to a series of steps that seem to swing around her hips. Her fellow line dancers watch her out of the corner of their eyes, and move away imperceptibly to avoid her elbows that establish the diameter of her moves. They are happy to be in her aura. They feel the grace of her flamenco moves, and they are empowered.

Slowly, other women join her. They are oblivious to their own style, believing for just a moment that they, too, can float with the majestic beauty of their friend. For at least this dance, they are not old, or frumpy, or absorbed in bridge or nursing their husbands, or calling their grandchildren. They are alive and sensuous and proud of their ability to mimic the motions of the Flamingo Dancer. Their age-seventy husbands move slowly to their sides, pick up the steps, and their bodies move again as if some wi-fi router has fed them a silent source of energy.

Then the music changes to slow songs that feed the passion, and groups of bystanders move to partners old and new. It's The Villages legend: that everyone participates. The Flamingo Dancer never has a partner, but she offers herself to everyone. Her body begins to coast to the slow music, her hips turning like a revolving door, and her legs seem to fly out, expanding her circle as if she were wearing a chiffon ball gown. Her ponytail, always the ponytail, is like a tiara that signals the line dancing princess is performing.

Then just as the men in the crowd are reaching for a kiss during the final bars of slow music, it changes. The Flamingo Line Dancer is off. She takes a swig of water from her scepter, throws back her head, and suddenly her left hand rises over her head, her fingers snapping to the music, and the crowd changes. The passion pursuers move back to their seats, and the country music wives grab their husbands' hands, snap their fingers, and start the dosey doe. It is Florida, after all. The Villages ("The" is always part of the title) is three towns with a combined total of over 125,000 people living in over 60,000 individual homes—with banks, investment houses (ready to manage all the 401-ks), churches, every store and restaurant imaginable, and three town centers. The three town centers each have a town square with live music every night, seven days a week, and it has to be raining like hell to make them cancel. Even more remarkable, during a light rain, people bring umbrellas and still expect music. The Villages is in the middle of the state, roughly between Tampa and Orlando. It's rural, horse country, with an occasional patch of orange trees. A Chicago businessman named Schwartz bought up the rural land in the 1950s and started his new town with a Spanish motif and house trailers that could be expanded if necessary. Today, it is thousands of homes ranging from $135,000 dollars to over $1 million, with most of them in the lower range. The residents come from every walk of life, but there is a recurring story that you hear in ice cream parlors and on the par-three golf courses, a story of middle-class Americans who worked hard all of their lives in small businesses or schools or professions, sent their kids to college, then left their empty nests.

They sold their homes, which had appreciated a few hundred thousand dollars over the passing decades, bought smaller homes in The Villages, and combined their new nest egg with the Social Security check to enjoy a life of casual living among new friends and neighbors. They all say it: they are happier than ever in their lives. And they love the town squares, with free music and dancing, where farmers and judges and housewives and accountants can grab a white plastic chair, get a drink from the corner kiosk, and admire their good fortune. They all know Heather, who dances like a flamingo.

Sitting in the front row, just a dozen yards from the bandstand, is Herb Krakin, usually wearing a baseball cap with the Kansas City Royals insignia just above the bill. He looks younger than his sixty-five years, well tanned, with muscled legs below his blue shorts and above his Docksider shoes. His wife died three years ago in Minnesota, and he took up golf to nurture a new life, playing and watching all the big tournaments on television. That's where he first heard the catchy little theme song for The Villages, advertising free golf for the rest of your life, and a chance to live in a world of swimming pools, bocce ball, and pickleball, a new game apparently invented by an aging tennis player in The Villages.

Herb noticed the Flamingo Dancer on his first visit to the town square. He knew no one. But he took the first empty chair he could find and set about to study the ways of the people in The Villages. They seemed to arrive early, perhaps four o'clock in the afternoon, a full hour before the music was scheduled to begin (the music stops at nine at night). Herb wasn't sure he could last until that time, well after dark, but he considered it his luck to be there early, when residents were starting to take chairs from the stacks of plastic lawn chairs, and he could fall in line. He wondered who stacked the chairs at night, assuming there was a designated stacker, because everything was so well organized at The Villages.

Everyone seemed older than Herb, which made him uneasy, but

he reminded himself that this was an over–fifty-five community, so they should seem old. Age dictated many things in his life, but it was a new feeling to have aching knees, and some fear of 400-yard golf holes that used to mean a chance for par. Now they meant an extra shot with a hybrid three iron and more sand traps to worry about. In the square, youth seemed like an advantage, especially since he was so close to the minimum. Still, line dancing was new to him, and a hundred sets of eyes focused on every participant.

Herb had sold hardwood flooring in Minneapolis, owned his own store on Campbell Street, or at least he owned the stock. Actually, he only leased the store, and was given most of the display flooring by the manufacturer. All he had to do was sell it, which a naturally outgoing personality made easy.

Back in Minnesota, Herb would never have approached the Flamingo Dancer for a million dollars, not in public nor in front of friends, and he would have been totally dumbfounded about what to say. But here, he knew no one, and the crowd around him was not a threat. In fact, it was a shield. Hundreds of voices and screams and costumes and personalities that ignored his presence, and likely would never see him again. So he walked right up to her and asked, "Can I say hello and ask your name?"

She turned her head slowly to him, looked him up and down, and saw nothing threatening. "Yes," she said. "I'm Heather."

"Where are you from?" he asked.

"Minnesota," she said. Herb's heart jumped. *My home state,* he thought. I *have a hundred questions to ask.*

"I'm from Sweetwater," she said. "My husband and I moved here five years ago, and then he died."

"That's a suburb, right? Of Minneapolis."

"Yes. But it's a real town. A small town."

Heather wasn't giving more than she had been asked. She was cautious, having been approached by many men, always asking where are you from. That's an easy approach in an area where everyone comes from someplace else, and nobody has been here long. It was a former governor of the state who said Florida's biggest export is bodies, going home after a retirement sojourn. Most living in The

Villages are acutely aware of their longevity, in life or in relationships where widowers meet, marry, and depart for cemeteries planned long ago. And they talk about it openly.

"Are you happy here, Heather?"

"Of course," she said. "There's the music. I have to go." She started backing away toward the band.

Herb turned away quickly, not wanting to look like one of those poor losers looking for a date. He hesitated at his empty chair, but chose not to sit, not wanting to appear like a sitting stalker, just there to watch the Flamingo Dancer. So he walked away, through the crowd of people waiting for seats. An older woman, wearing black slacks and white tennis shoes, dodged around him and into the vacant seat. A few more steps and Herb was absorbed into The Villages residents, alone in the night.

The next day he was back at the community square, seeking lunch. He parked behind the movie theatre, and entered the first restaurant he encountered, Johnny Rockets. He couldn't remember ever seeing this restaurant before, certainly not in Minnesota, and he didn't know the menu. The picture flew across his mind of someone leaving the building, as he had left the square the night before. He remembered an ice cream cone, suggesting a fast food menu, perhaps in the hands of a family leaving through the corner door. He pushed it open and walked in, with wide eyes surveying the booths along the wall. And there she was. The Flamingo Dancer was paying her bill at the front counter.

Her hair was swinging the same ponytail she wore in the square. It cast her as young, energetic, and inquisitive. But her costume was different: blue jeans with a four-inch cuff, and a plaid flannel shirt. He figured she must have brought the shirt from Minnesota, although it looked fine in Florida in January.

Herb flipped around just inside the door and followed her out, determined not to let any opportunities slip away. "Heather," he shouted to catch her in mid-stride. She turned, and didn't recognize him.

"I'm Herb," he said with more emphasis than he planned. "I met you yesterday on the square."

"Oh yes," she said. "From Minnesota."

"Would you join me for coffee?" he asked.

"I just had breakfast," she said.

"I so admire your dancing," he offered.

She hesitated, always eager to talk about her dancing. For a moment she felt the old street-smart fears of Minnesota, where she never spoke to a stranger on the street, certainly not to someone who had mysteriously appeared two days in a row. But she looked him over carefully and reminded herself that this is The Villages, where everyone is over fifty-five, lives in a nice cottage, is probably retired and maybe lonely, but more likely is a widower who plays golf three times a week, and just wants to talk.

"OK," she said. "But I have to meet some friends soon."

Herb pulled out one of the black metal sidewalk chairs and held it for her. She couldn't remember if that was a good sign or not. Maybe a little forced. But Herb smiled, pulled another chair for himself, and ask if she was a member of the Minnesota Club.

So it began. He asked her to dinner. They went to a movie. He escorted her to the town square each evening. They dated for several weeks, exploring each other, and a possible life together in The Villages.

They joined the Minnesota Club and at first enjoyed meeting people from little towns across the state, folks they had never met, but who shared their background. They had been to the same stores, the same resorts; their kids had been to the same colleges. It was a degree of familiarity that made living in The Villages easy.

Heather was a physically creative person, and Herb suggested acting. They had gone to several plays and musical comedy performances at the Savannah Center, where every night was a new production. A few of the old stars showed up every year, like Kenny Rogers and Loretta Lynn, and regulars from Orlando or New Jersey who gave "tributes" to Frank Sinatra or Johnny Cash or the Smothers Brothers, or some other 1960's star who was incredibly popular in their time. And in The Villages, they were popular again. The house was always packed, and the residents often sat with their eyes closed, no doubt dreaming of tender moments from the past. And there was a group called The Toronto Stars, a young people's band with trumpets and trombones that rocked the building, and three beautiful girls with professional voices who could sing the most popular songs. It was another chance for the old to be young again, and Heather moved her hands and her head in time to the music. Herb sat beside her and could feel her body moving next to him. He was smitten.

The next day they tried golf. Neither of them played, but they had rented a house with a golf cart and two bags of old clubs. The age didn't matter because they wouldn't know the difference between a 50-yard shot and a 200-yard drive, as least in terms of the club's role. They had signed up for one of the thirty-five "Executive Courses," which were par-three courses where most of the holes were 100-yards long and reachable for the older, younger, and feeble alike. But the courses had one distinguishing feature: They were designed and maintained professionally with smooth, often lush, greens; and sand traps interspersed with small ponds that enhanced the challenge. Indeed, it was easy for beginners, at least, to imagine they were on a course designed by Arnold Palmer. And in fact, Nancy Lopez lived on one of the nine championship courses, made public appearances at the Nancy Lopez clubhouse and restaurant, and was generally beloved by everyone who met her. The food at her restaurant was generally considered the best, although the music was often so loud that Herb would only go on a weeknight when the band was off. Heather didn't seem to mind.

Herb and Heather were joined on the Lauren Bacall Executive Course by two elderly women from the Peach Blossom area of The Villages. The computer had put the foursome together, and Herb and Heather were happy to see them, on the theory that two eighty-year-old women were unlikely to complain about having to play with beginners. These two ladies were sweet as pie and never complained about Herb and Heather, although they did have to explain some of the rules of etiquette. And they teed off with a three wood or a driver on holes only 75-yards long. The remarkable thing was that their shots went straight, rose softly into the air for about 65 yards, then rolled gently on the green to about ten feet from the pin. Every time. Herb and Heather had fallen into the arms of two widows who had moved to The Villages in the 1970s, bought mobile homes in the first sections of The Villages, lost their husbands to cancer, inherited some money, and bought two-bedroom/two-bath cottages on one of the golf courses near Spanish Springs. They had played regularly for the last twenty years and said The Villages was like heaven on earth. They wouldn't even criticize the summer heat in central Florida.

After mid-afternoon golf, Herb and Heather went to the Fried Tomato restaurant, a favorite of Heather's. She didn't eat much meat, staying in shape for line dancing.

She could select her own salad and dressing at Fried Tomato, add some potato salad on the side, a piece of freshly baked bread, a bowl of summer fruit, any soft drink, and always some specialty item like a small blueberry muffin. Best of all, especially to Herb, was the soft ice cream right out of the dispenser in chocolate or vanilla, all you could eat. It was a great way to end the evening, except it wasn't the end for Heather.

By six o'clock every night, she wanted to be "on the line," as she said, meeting her friends for music in one of the three town squares. Heather had checked *The Villages Sun* that morning to see which band was playing in which square. She knew them all. And the one with the strongest beat would win her presence. Then she would call her friend Tom, who was the unofficial leader of the dancers, and he would take calls all day long on his cell phone advising other members of the group where Heather would be dancing each night. This group was a little possessive about Heather, but Herb convinced himself to live with it. He was not a jealous person as a general rule, and the dancers were as single-minded on this subject as Heather. They only wanted to dance.

The *Sun* was seldom wrong about the bands. They were paid to be on time, and to appear rain or shine. And the newspaper was seldom wrong. Indeed, the *Sun* was a role model for all those people in America who want "good news" in their paper. Only good things happen in the *Sun* news. Politics is a very even-handed affair in the *Sun*. Tragedies like hurricanes or terrorist attacks are in section C. The front page is local news, like antique car rallies or horse races in nearby Ocala. A full page is dedicated to meetings of local clubs, of which there are two thousand to report. Another page is dedicated to the movies in three theatres. And the rest of the paper is anchored by feature stories about the grandchildren of The Villages residents who won the lottery or achieved recognition in their jobs or had been photographed with the governor of a home state. People loved the *Sun*. Heather read it religiously, and Herb was learning. He occasionally bought a *New York Times* at the Starbucks in Sumter's Landing, but only if he was looking for a specific story like Hillary Clinton's email problems. Those wouldn't appear in the *Sun*.

When Herb and Heather arrived at the Square in Brownwood, the music was blaring and the line dancers were on the south side of the pavilion. The white plastic lawn chairs were lined along the side, and Tom had arranged the front row with sweaters and blankets on the seats. Two had been saved for Heather and Herb, who after a week or so of this special treatment were starting to feel pressures. At first he felt like royalty, but now he was beginning to yearn for freedom, the right to choose his own seat in his own location. This was a growing problem. A couple of his friends had joked that The Villages was their last chance to experience communism. The Villages management made everyone's decisions for them: their houses, the stores, the traffic laws for golf carts, liquor laws, everything. Most people just said, "I never thought I would like communism, but this place works." And it did. In fact, most residents of The Villages wanted someone else to make the decisions, especially if they were fair and reasonably priced. Few people complained. Even Herb told himself that where he sat was a small price to pay for security. So he took the seat Tom had picked for him, right between two attractive women he had never met before. Heather handed him her sweater and went directly to her place in the front line of dancers.

"I'm Margaret Farber," the lady on his right said, "Tom's cousin from Tennessee. I just moved here last week. Just getting settled."

"I'm Herb," he replied. "We just use first names here. I'm a friend of Heather's."

"Tom has told us about her," Margaret said. "Looks like a flamingo. Elegant and stands on one foot."

Herb was surprised. He realized now that Heather was his identity.

"Do you like it here?" Herb asked

"Oh, it seems nice," Margaret said. "Everyone is so busy doing things. I'm a more quiet person."

And so it began, that Heather started dancing with other people, and so did Herb.

PART VII

—IN MEMORIAM—
President George H.W. Bush

Introduction to Part Seven

On February 14, 2019, Jean Becker wrote me a note: "Ambassador McNamara gave me permission to share these wonderful essays with you. I hope you will take the time to read them." She attached a letter from Ambassador McNamara, which follows. I asked, and was granted permission, to include these wonderful remembrances in this book.

I attach a copy of those remembrances of President George H.W. Bush by some of his NSC staff and other senior officers, career and non-career appointees. It was my pleasure and honor to be the editor of, and a contributor to, this collection and to arrange to have it published in the online journal, "American Diplomacy." This quarterly reaches over fifty countries, has more than 300,000 readers annually, and is associated with the University of North Carolina.

Those of us who worked directly for him during his terms as vice president and president, have felt deeply and personally the loss of this great man and extraordinary statesman. We have chosen to express our thoughts and feelings about the person and the president through a collection of short essays in tribute to him.

Amb. Thomas E. McNamara (Ret.)
Adjunct Professor
The Elliott School of International Affairs
The George Washington University

President George H.W. Bush: the Man and the Statesman

February 2019
Edited by Thomas E. McNamara

President George H.W. Bush entered the office with more extensive foreign affairs experience than any other president except John Quincy Adams. After serving as ambassador to the United Nations, chief of the Liaison Office in Beijing, and eight years as vice president, Bush had exceptional understanding of foreign policy and diplomatic practice, and personal relationships with the most important world leaders. In his international accomplishments, Bush was, arguably, the most successful and consequential one-term president, and surpassed most two-term presidents.

Those of us who worked closely with him on foreign issues during his twelve years as vice president and president came to know and respect him and his international expertise. We mourn his passing.

What follows are reminiscences of over a dozen of his team, who worked closely with him in different situations in those twelve years. Some came into government from other professions and returned to them afterwards. Others are career diplomats who collectively served under eleven presidents. What all share is a deep admiration for the nation's forty-first president, a great statesman and a wonderful person, who loved the country he served so well.

From Central America to the Persian Gulf

— Thomas R. Pickering: Ambassador to El Salvador (1983–85); Ambassador to the UN (1989–92); Under Secretary of State for Political Affairs (1997–2000)

When I was ambassador to El Salvador, I was fortunate to work with George H.W. Bush. That nation suffered from civil war and a recent offensive by Marxist guerrillas that decimated several military units and destroyed an important bridge, cutting the country in half in 1983. The military's death squads reacted by capturing suspected FMLN sympathizers and murdering them in a vain attempt to stifle rebellion.

Hoping to squelch this death squad activity, I asked Vice President Bush to visit and read the riot act to Salvadoran military leaders. Addressing fifty senior military officers, through an interpreter with me next to him, Bush brilliantly varied his tone and content to fit his purpose and audience. He ended his short, sharply-worded talk and surprised everyone by threatening that unless death squad killings ended, Ronald Reagan and he could do nothing with the American Congress to preserve assistance programs. His words and demeanor suppressed death squad murders for a time.

Thanks to Bush's earlier experience as ambassador to the United Nations, he knew the organization very well. As his successor at the UN, I worked closely with him when he was president. Although Margaret Thatcher argued against going to the UN in response to Iraq's invasion of Kuwait, Bush insisted on UN approval to use force. He understood that the Security Council gave legitimacy to the 1991 Gulf War coalition and it was essential to Democratic support of a Congressional resolution for US participation in combat. These steps also assured he would not be hounded into fighting on into Baghdad. Just as when the Soviet Union fell, Bush remained calm and avoided doing too much.

George H.W. Bush worked for a world order of equality, fairness, justice, and democracy. This was part of his personality and leadership. That vision should go down as part of the growing positive history of his presidency.

Managing the End of the Cold War

— R. Nickolas Burns: NSC Director, Senior Director and Special Assistant to the President for Russian Affairs (1990–95); Professor of Practice of Diplomacy and International Politics at Harvard's Kennedy School of Government

Where does the late George H.W. Bush rank among American presidents? I admit to bias. I worked at the National Security Council in the White House for the last half of his presidency. I am convinced Bush was one of the greatest global leaders in foreign policy of all our presidents, certainly with achievements exceeding those of any president in fifty years.

He ended the Cold War peacefully. He was the central figure unifying Germany after the Berlin Wall fell. He organized a unique global coalition to defeat Saddam Hussein in the Gulf War. That year, he created the contemporary, two-track Israeli-Palestinian peace negotiations. He began hemispheric-changing NAFTA negotiations. Each achievement would be consequential for any president. Together, they represent an extraordinary legacy of successes for America and the world.

The Cold War was never predestined to end peacefully. KGB and Red Army leaders tried overthrowing Gorbachev and Yeltsin in 1991. Soviet nuclear weapons might have fallen into the hands of warlords or criminals, or cabals might have obstructed the freedom of former satellites in Eastern Europe. Bush's solid, trusted relationships with Gorbachev and Yeltsin reassured them and Russians that we would not take advantage in the Soviet Union's final months. It was not a given that Germany would unify peacefully until Bush supported Chancellor Helmut Kohl in uniting a Germany embedded in the NATO alliance. Nor was it automatic that an extraordinary US-led coalition would defeat Saddam Hussein without major casualties.

Bush was widely admired by those of us in the career foreign service and the military because he believed in us and in the power of government to do great things. He governed by seeking to unite us as Americans, not to divide us. Bush's combination of in-depth knowledge and sophistication about the world, along with his ability to connect to other leaders personally, was the key to his greatness in the presidency.

Delivering the Message in Central Europe

— Paula J. Dobriansky: NSC Director of European and Soviet Affairs (1981–87); Under Secretary of State for Global Affairs (2001–2009); Presidential Envoy to Northern Ireland (2007–2009)

As a member of the National Security Council staff handling East European and Soviet Affairs in the Reagan Administration, I had the privilege of working with then-Vice President George H.W. Bush on US policy toward Central European countries. This policy was laid out in Presidential Directive 54 (1982), which stated that, instead of treating Warsaw Pact members alike, the US would pursue a "policy of differentiation in East European countries and will render preferential treatment to those East European countries that do not support extensively Soviet ventures and foreign policies and have manifested increasing internal liberalization and Westernization . . ." This policy provided tangible incentives for East European countries to lessen their dependence on Moscow and set the stage for revolutionary transformations to come.

In September 1983, I traveled with Vice President Bush to Yugoslavia, Romania, Hungary, and Austria. In Vienna, he delivered a most inspirational speech, building upon the differentiation policy for countries "which assert greater openness or independence," and highlighting our "strong and unbreakable ties with the people of Central Europe," the legacy of our World War II alliance, and our common democratic bonds.

George H.W. Bush was a remarkable statesman. Having enunciated a vision of how to end peacefully the Cold War in Moscow-dominated East Europe, he succeeded in his quest to "once again make Europe whole." This took vision, fortitude, and superb statecraft. I was honored to be part of George H.W. Bush's historic effort.

Attention to Africa

— Frank Wisner: Ambassador to Zambia (1979–82); Deputy Assistant Secretary of State for African Affairs (1982–86); Undersecretary of State for International Security (1992–93)

I was privileged to be closely associated with George H.W. Bush as vice president. He made clear that his door was open to African leaders, even if others were not available to backup our Africa diplomacy. He did so with great effect. No American president or vice president devoted as much attention, and none has been as amply rewarded as George Bush in seeking support for his African objectives.

As Deputy Assistant Secretary of State for Africa, I took prominent Africans to call on him. The vice president was warm and generous with his time. He charmed visitors with his knowledge of their countries and of our relations with them. I remember a delegation from Zaire (Congo) when each Minister was given one of Bush's golf shirts. They were elated.

No Africa duty was too onerous. I was with him when he accompanied the body of Sekou Toure to Conakry for interment. He used the occasion to meet with the presidents of Egypt, Pakistan, Senegal, Benin, and the young prince (now, king) of Morocco. Despite the stifling heat, he walked in the funeral cortege and attended ceremonies in the football stadium and the national Mosque.

I traveled with him in Africa seeking support for our "constructive engagement" policies in opposition to apartheid, Cuban troop presence in Angola, and supporting Namibian independence. In Kenya, Zaire, and elsewhere he lobbied political leaders. I watched him compete with Mobutu of Zaire to catch the largest fish, and in Kenya down a Tusker beer. These gestures provided platforms for his political message, which he delivered gracefully and forcefully.

As president, he had Africa at his "beck and call." Africa's leaders understood that the United States cared and was willing to go out of its way to help.

Keeping Europe and the US United in NATO

— David Gompert: Deputy Director, Bureau of Political-Military Affairs (1977–81); Special Assistant to the President (1989–93); Deputy Director of National Intelligence (2009–11)

Many have noted that President George H.W. Bush was central to German reunification, when most Europeans resisted it. But few realize he was also critical to resolving an important follow-on NATO issue. Charged with European issues on the NSC staff, I saw his vision and determination prevail.

German unification fueled European interest in closer economic and political union. France was eager to constrain Germany within common structures and obligations. With a somewhat different perspective, George H.W. Bush was, also, intent on maintaining a US presence and voice in European security.

French President Francois Mitterrand saw a historic opportunity to end Europe's military dependence on the US by creating an EU-based military alliance of Europeans, mainly France, separate from NATO. In his conception, the United States and NATO would be a backup, an insurance policy, against a resurgent Russia. The Bush administration insisted it would assist in keeping peace in Europe only if it had a role in managing European security affairs.

This was a diplomatic logjam that only presidential leadership could break. In a series of bilateral and NATO summit meetings, Bush persuaded German Chancellor Helmut Kohl and Mitterrand to retain NATO as the mechanism to manage post-Cold-War European security. He stated that a European defense alliance apart from NATO would undermine American support for NATO and US troop presence. Europeans had to choose; they could not keep NATO as a backup against Russia, while also marginalizing the US from European security management. At the decisive meeting—the 1991 Rome NATO summit—Bush flatly challenged Mitterrand and Kohl to "tell us now" if they wanted to replace NATO. They stayed silent. The issue was resolved.

Cutting Down Qaddafi

— Thomas E. McNamara: Ambassador to Colombia (1988–91); Special Assistant to the President, NSC (1991–93); Assistant Secretary of State for Political-Military Affairs (1994–98)

In 1985, after Iran-Contra, I came to the National Security Council and worked closely with Vice President George H.W. Bush on Beirut hostages, terrorism, and drugs. I returned to the NSC after three years in Colombia to work on the PanAm-Lockerbie bombing, a tragedy that resulted from Reagan's unsuccessful military strikes against Libya. President Bush wanted a non-military option before deciding to act against Qaddafi.

The option I presented was to join the British and French (Qaddafi bombed a French airliner over Niger) in the UN Security Council, to get strong sanctions to end Qaddafi's support of terrorism. Bush and Brent Scowcroft were skeptical of UNSC capabilities and Mitterrand's cooperation. Relations with France were poor due to France's opposition on important European issues. Yet, as a professional diplomat, Bush understood, valued, and supported diplomacy.

Months of quiet, forceful diplomacy—Bush's hallmark method—produced powerful, worldwide UNSC sanctions on Libya that ended Qaddafi's terrorism and undermined his regime for years. Bush knew he would pay a price for this decision not to use military force. And he did. The Lockerbie Families group and others publicly denounced him as a "wimp" during his 1992 campaign. He was no wimp. It was the right decision.

Of twentieth-century presidents, only T. Roosevelt, Truman, and Nixon had as deep an understanding and powerful impact on foreign affairs as Bush 41. And of this group, he had the most successes and fewest setbacks. History will recognize his greatness as a statesman.

During a decade of working for him and Barbara, I can attest that they were persons who never let their positions lessen their humanity, humility, and kindness; who treated everyone with courteous respect; who never demeaned; who wore their laurels lightly; and who led with greatness of spirit for the benefit of the nation.

Defending Russia Policy

— Robert Hutchings: NSC Director for European Affairs (1989–92); Rostow Chair in National Security, LBJ School of Public Affairs, University of Texas

Many have spoken of President Bush's exemplary personal qualities: his modesty, kindness, decency, and unshakable integrity. I fully share those thoughts of the president I was privileged to serve. Let me share a vignette that shows a harder edge to this consummate statesman.

At the Helsinki Summit of July 1992, President Bush met with the three Baltic delegations. In discussing difficulties with Moscow over Russian troops withdrawals, Lennart Meri, Estonia's former foreign minister and future president, remarked offhandedly that he hoped the United States would not make the same mistakes with Russian President Boris Yeltsin that it had made with Mikhail Gorbachev. Before President Bush could reply, another of the Baltic leaders tactfully tried to change the subject, but Bush, despite being preoccupied with his re-election struggle, was having none of it.

"Wait," he said, "I want to finish this!" He asked what was meant. Meri opined that showing understanding or accommodation of Russian concerns only strengthens hardliners. Being tough demonstrates resolve and isolates hardline opponents—a preposterous bit of cheek given all the Bush administration had been through with Moscow over the previous three years.

Bush was as infuriated as I ever saw him. He reviewed our policies briefly, politely, but forcefully: the strategic and tactical planning; the measured use of power; combining firmness on principles with flexibility on tactics; and in the end, successfully liberating Eastern Europe (including Estonia!). He also added the unification of Germany and the collapse of Soviet communism, all achieved peacefully and on Western terms. He finished with: "We like to think we know a thing or two about dealing with Russian leaders." Typical of him, he avoided using the "I" word, which he hated.

A Hostage Release Phone Call

— Edward Djerejian: Ambassador to Syria (1988–91); Assistant Secretary of State for Mideast Affairs (1991–93); Ambassador to Israel (1993–94)

As the ambassador to Syria in President George H.W. Bush's administration, I was involved in gaining the release of three American hostages held captive in Lebanon. My job was to press the Syrian government to use its influence in Lebanon and Iran to get them released. Each time one was to be released, I was called to come see the foreign minister. I cabled Washington that a hostage might be freed and went to the minister's office and waited for the individual being freed—always a deeply emotional experience.

Once, as I drafted press remarks before a release, the telephone rang while the drafts were on my knees. It was a call from the White House and a strong, deliberate voice intoned: "The next voice you will hear will be that of the President of the United States of America." Impressed and respectful, I stood up, and, of course, my briefing notes scattered to the floor! President Bush came on the line: "Ed, I understand a hostage is being released. Do you know who it is?" I replied we thought it might be Robert Polhill, a professor at the Beirut University College. He asked about my press remarks, and I summarized what was strewn before me on the floor. He said, "Good. I'll be watching you on TV." He, also, asked to speak with Polhill, "but only if his health allows."

Afterwards, with Polhill at the residence and after a champagne toast with our wives, we made the call. Polhill had a brief, private conversation with the president, who warmly expressed his happiness at Polhill's liberation.

That was a special moment, a clear demonstration of Bush's compassion, which manifested itself so often. That quiet, private conversation to comfort a beleaguered American as soon as he could spoke loudly of George Bush's personal character and leadership.

Ending Apartheid

— Herman J. Cohen: NSC Senior Director and Special Assistant to the President (1987–89); Assistant Secretary of State for African Affairs (1989–93)

In 1989, white South Africans elected new leaders. President F.W. de Klerk believed that South Africa could not progress and industrialize without full participation of the majority black community. He decided to dismantle the apartheid system. This was bitterly opposed by the hardcore white community, who argued sanctions would never be ended in return for ending apartheid. By threatening violence, they tried to block approval of the agreement that de Klerk had negotiated with Nelson Mandela for a new South African political future.

When President George H.W. Bush heard of the stalemate, he acted, based on his authority to remove US sanctions when political progress had been made. He told de Klerk and Mandela, with both of whom he had good relationships, that he would lift US economic sanctions, thus, helping to get majority white approval for the constitutional pact. The US was the first to remove sanctions against South Africa.

Coalition and Alliance Builder

— Chester Crocker: Assistant Secretary of State for African Affairs (1981–89)

The George H.W. Bush administration had more success in foreign policy in four years than any other modern administration I can think of. The peaceful end of the Cold War; the restructuring of relationships with Russia and China; the freedom for Russia's neighbors; the reunification of Germany were all major achievements. An excellent use of American power was the 1991 Gulf War. Bush got strong UN Security Council and Congressional mandates to use force to liberate Kuwait. He did not crow or beat the drum about it. He just went out and did it.

Bush was a coalition builder. He understood the importance of building alliances. He built relationships based on mutual interests. Hence, he could rely on them when he contacted leaders in every region of the world. I saw this as I worked closely with him on Africa. At a critical point his intervention with de Klerk and Mandela, for example, removed a roadblock to ending apartheid in South Africa.

Another characteristic of the man was that he chose the best, most experienced people. He was comfortable with those who knew more about issues and regions of the world than he did, and from whom he could learn. This showed at the top level—his marvelous team of Brent Scowcroft, James Baker, Colin Powell—and lower down as well. He understood, reached out, and listened to career people. I saw this as I traveled around Africa with him.

He was a strong leader who did not flex his muscles for TV cameras. His leadership style was to quietly reach out to others to work with him. He did not appeal just to domestic audiences. He knew we needed to understand many overseas audiences also, and weigh them in the balance. He was comfortable within himself. This kind of leadership can be strong, effective, and successful. It was for him and for our country.

Human, Cheerful Style

— William Harrop: Ambassador to Kenya and Seychelles (1980–83), Ambassador to Zaire/Congo (1987–91); Ambassador to Israel (1992–93); Inspector General of the Foreign Service (1983-86)

We thought the world of George and Barbara Bush and are saddened by their deaths. Here is an anecdote about a visit we had from them when I was ambassador to Kenya that is quite typical of their human, cheerful style.

In 1982, George and Barbara Bush—he was then vice president—spent three days with Ann and me in Nairobi. They were the most gracious houseguests we ever had. One morning after breakfast, Barbara was about to set off with Phil and Loret (then Peace Corps Director) Ruppe, on a day trip to the highlands to visit Peace Corps volunteers. We realized that Phil was not warmly enough dressed. Visitors often forget how cool it can get in the Kenyan highlands even though they are on the equator. Ann asked our steward to get out one of my sweaters to loan him.

On the party's return that evening, Barbara said they had had a wonderful day but it was rather embarrassing since Phil Ruppe was wearing the most disgraceful sweater, full of holes. Then she realized, to her embarrassment, that the sweater was mine.

Two weeks later we received a handsome new sweater from Bermuda where they had stopped to refuel on the way back to Washington. The card read, "From Old Foot-in-the-Mouth Bush." On returning to Washington the Bushes telephoned each of our four sons to report that they had been with us in Kenya and we were fine.

A truly grand American couple we were honored to have known.

Commitment to Drug Enforcement

— Robert Bonner: DEA Administrator (1990–93); Commissioner of US Customs and Border Protection (2003–05)

As head of the Drug Enforcement Administration (DEA), I was struck in my meetings with George H.W. Bush by his genuine interest in drug enforcement. Twice he visited DEA headquarters and inspired and energized DEA. I was impressed by the depth of his knowledge and his geniality.

In June 1992, I had my most memorable interaction with him. He accepted my invitation to dedicate DEA's new field office in New York City. I flew with him on *Air Force One* and rode with him into the city. Passing through Greenwich Village, Bush pointed out the window and remarked heartily: "Would you look at that!"

I looked. On the sidewalk stood a crowd of people, two or three deep, about one-quarter of whom appeared to be flipping the President of the United States an obscene finger gesture. He took this in perfectly good humor. The crowd was undoubtedly reacting to what, in NYC, they called "Bush Lock" (traffic jams caused by presidential motorcades).

But as we spoke, there was a wistfulness in his comments. It was clear he would be very happy and at peace without a second term. He told me that Barbara would prefer that. He was neither behind in the polls at that point, nor did he think he would lose. I had the strong sense that his heart was not in running again. It wasn't until late September 1992, when faced with the prospect of losing to an upstart governor from Arkansas, that his competitive juices were stirred.

He was a great president. But few recognized how deeply committed he was to end what he rightly called "the scourge of drugs." He was a true friend and supporter of DEA and federal law enforcement. He had our backs at home and overseas.

Personal Relationship with Gorbachev

— Roman Popadiuk: Deputy Assistant to the President and Deputy Press Secretary for Foreign Affairs (1986–89). Parts of this essay appeared in the author's The Leadership of George Bush, *Texas A&M Univ. Press, 2009*

The passing of George H.W. Bush led to much public discussion and nostalgia about his personal qualities. Observers wistfully lament the absence of these qualities in today's political dialogue. Unnoticed, however, is the impact that they had on Bush's policies. For him, personal relations were both a personal responsibility and a policy mechanism that facilitated relationships. I experienced his personal decency frequently, including in his interaction with domestic and foreign leaders.

A few simple rules guided him. He avoided making policy debates personal, holding grudges, or demeaning adversaries. These could create enemies, undermine trust, or preclude cooperation—this last, the bedrock of politics. He sought to identify interests, so he might mesh them with US goals. He hoped these would translate into trust and cooperation.

His approach was very evident in his relationship with Soviet leader Mikhail Gorbachev. His impression was that the West could do business with Gorbachev. Bush set up a meeting with Gorbachev that became the 1989 Malta Summit, beginning a personal relationship and cooperation between the two countries. When Gorbachev resigned in 1991, Bush felt he had lost a friend.

Gorbachev shared these feelings. Years later, at Bush's eightieth birthday in Houston, Gorbachev said that "of all my counterparts in the world arena, George Bush was the best. He was a reliable partner; he had balanced judgement, and he had decency. He had qualities that were and are central to trust. And trust is what makes it possible to solve any international problem." His restraint opened communication and showed Bush to be a trustworthy partner, not an adversary exploiting events.

Bush brought together a rare combination of personal qualities and government experience that helped guide the United States through a tumultuous and historic period. Overall, he demonstrated the importance of personal relations and decency in the policy process and the world of diplomacy.

Shaping NATO's Nuclear Strategy

— W. Robert Pearson: NATO Deputy Assistant Secretary General for Political Affairs (1987–1990); Ambassador to Turkey (2000–2003); Director General of the Foreign Service (2003–2006)

The 1989 NATO summit in Brussels, only months after President Bush took office, presented him with an important, complex problem. As Deputy Assistant Secretary General for Political Affairs at NATO and Chair of NATO's Political Committee, my committee's job was to bring the Alliance's security policy up to date. Within that assignment, we needed to update the Alliance's nuclear strategy, including NATO's stance on intermediate range nuclear missiles based in Europe.

Over the two years leading up to the 1989 Summit, through several drafts, debates, and meetings, we closely observed how the US position was developing. When the Summit convened, the debate history and the pending issues as well as the various national positions, including German, British, and American, were well known. Once President Bush arrived at the summit, what he hoped to accomplish was clear to me—meet German concerns, reassure the Brits, maintain a clear stance on deterrence, and most importantly, demonstrate American leadership of the Alliance. He accomplished all of them.

In the course of the Summit it was obvious that the president's leadership, character, reputation, and personal acquaintance with NATO's senior leaders created the atmosphere necessary to reach a final agreement.

REFERENCES

Weekly Compilation of Presidential Documents, Vol. 26, 1990. Office of the Federal Register, National Archives and Records Administration, Washington, DC, 1991.

Weekly Compilation of Presidential Documents, Vol. 27, 1991. Office of the Federal Register, National Archives and Records Administration, Washington, DC, 1991.

Presidential Papers in Ronald Reagan Presidential Library, Simi Valley, California. Reagan Library Website: Ronald Reagan Presidential Library. "Chronology of Ronald Reagan's Presidency, 1979-89." https://reaganlibrary.gov/facts-ronald/reagan-post-presidency-chronology (accessed 18 May 2016)

Presidential Papers in George H.W. Bush Presidential Library, located on the campus of Texas A&M University in College Station, Texas. Bush Library Website: https://www.bush41.org/research.

Marlin Fitzwater's personal papers available in Special Collections, Hale Library, Kansas State University, Manhattan, Kansas.